# Strategies for Work
# with Involuntary Clients

# Strategies for Work with Involuntary Clients

Ronald H. Rooney

Columbia University Press
New York

Columbia University Press
New York    Chichester, West Sussex
Copyright © 1992 Columbia University Press
All rights reserved

Library of Congress Cataloging-in-Publication Data

Rooney, Ronald H., 1945–
    Strategies for work with involuntary clients / Ronald H. Rooney.
    p.   cm.
    Includes index.
    ISBN 0-231-06768-2 (cl.).—ISBN 0-231-06769-0 (pb.)
    1. Social service—United States.   I. Title.
    HV95.R59   1992
    361.3'2'0973 —dc20                                    92-7393
                                                              CIP
                        ∞

Printed in the United States of America

    c   10   9   8   7   6   5   4   3   2   1

    p   10   9   8   7   6   5   4   3

To Glenda and Chris:
Now I can take out the trash.

# Contents

viii   Contents

# Figures

# Preface

This book is about practice with involuntary clients. Involuntary clients include both those clients required to see a helping practitioner (such as juveniles on probation) and those pressured to "seek help" (such as the alcoholic threatened with desertion by his spouse if he or she does not get help). The book is also about "involuntary practitioners" who may be as reluctant to work with involuntary clients as those clients are to work with them.

When I entered graduate school, I intended to work with clients who wanted to work with me, who would be thankful for the insights I gave them, and who would pay my receptionist on the way out. The reality was that my clients then and later were often more interested in escaping the clutches of my agency and the law than in gaining an insight into their personalities.

Most of the intervention theory I was taught ignored these clients or considered them the exception to the rule of work with voluntary clients. When I became an instructor, I continued the tradition of teaching voluntary client methods to students who worked with involuntary clients. Independent-thinking students would ask, "But how does this apply to the people who don't want to see you?" and I would improvise answers adapting voluntary methods. This book is written in answer to those students and practitioners working with involuntary clients who find difficulty applying voluntary practice theories to involuntary practice. I suggest that involuntary clients are the rule in practice rather than the exception.

The book is written for students, instructors, and practitioners. While probably few students enter the helping professions hoping to work with people who don't want to work with them, many experience less than voluntary client contact through their field placement and internship experiences. Students should find the book useful in explaining and guiding involuntary practice on its own terms. Such practice often appears to be undertaken as a rite of passage to provide experience and toughness before graduating to work with voluntary clients. Students may also find parallels to their own situations as "involuntary" students: if they wish to graduate, they must take some required courses "for their own good" in addition to choices in elective courses.

The book is also intended for practice methods instructors who want to add material about involuntary contact to balance sources which only assume voluntary contact. Instructors teaching courses about social problems and practice settings that often include involuntary clients (such as child welfare, criminal justice, chemical abuse programs) should also find the book a useful practice supplement.

Finally, the book is written for the practitioners who work with involuntary clients. While the book is based in the social work profession, the content should be useful to other helping practitioners such as psychologists, psychiatrists, nurses, probation officers, and youth workers. The book addresses public-agency practitioners with legal mandates, large caseloads, feelings of being unappreciated, overworked, and underpaid, as well as private-agency practitioners who may not recognize that they are in fact working with involuntary clients.

The book is designed to help both the involuntary practitioner and the involuntary client become at least semi-voluntary. Guidelines are aimed at providing legal, ethical, and effective intervention. While involuntary clients differ from one another as much as they do from voluntary clients, involuntary clients share the fact that they did not *willingly* enter contact with the practitioner. Consequently, the book focuses most extensively on the socialization and contracting phase which involuntary clients have most in common. Guidelines for interventions after the contracting phase are more tentative, since there may be much variation according to specific problem and setting. The book will help practitioners prepare for involuntary contacts by providing them with realistic role expectations so that they can make clearer decisions about when they must act and when they should not act. The guidelines should lead to less hostile and uncooperative encounters, to more successful contracts, and less "burnout" on both sides of the involuntary transaction.

Finally, the book will review the philosophical debate about the conflict between social control and caring roles, and between rehabilitation and criminal justice goals. The issues are reviewed with an aim toward increasing awareness without proposing to resolve those issues herein. The book is designed to help practitioners now amid the ongoing debate.

Involuntary clients sometimes have fantasies that their practitioners will leave them alone, or forget about "helping" them. Practitioners also fantasize that they can make involuntary clients change if they can just find the right magic to make those clients think differently, or if they could exert enough force. This book will supply neither that magic nor that force. It will not provide the practitioner with a blueprint for making involuntary clients do what they don't want to do, continue to do it after intervention, and like it. The book will not provide a "laying on of hands" whereby the involuntary client is transformed into a "born again" voluntary client, thankful for insight and eager to modify his or her life patterns. It is not a manual for brainwashing or hypnotizing involuntary clients to bring them to their senses—or the practitioner's point of view. Nor will the guidelines eliminate the need for professional judgment in making decisions.

Guidelines are based on available evidence about interventions which can be used legally, ethically, and effectively across involuntary settings and populations. Where that evidence is limited or inconclusive, alternatives are presented to help practitioners make informed choices. The book also draws on the practice literature from different involuntary populations and helping professions and on my case experiences and those of my students. Practice guidelines are frequently illustrated with selections from transcriptions derived from training videotapes, some of which were conducted with actual clients. In all cases, pracititioners and clients provided informed consent and client identities are disguised. The book raises questions for further study and suggests ways that those questions can be tested.

The book is aimed at increasing understanding of the involuntary transaction and knowing how to act within it. As practitioners need to be able to explain to themselves and others why they carry out an intervention, part I provides a foundation with a conceptual framework for understanding the involuntary transaction and influencing client behavior and attitudes in a legal, ethical, and effective fashion. It draws widely from sources in law, ethics, intervention effectiveness across helping professions and problem areas, and social psychology. Chapters are organized around brief summaries of relevant literature and organizing principles. Case examples are used to clarify those principles. Many figures are provided to serve as a reminder of key points.

Those practitioners currently dealing with involuntary clients who are impatient with theory may choose to skip ahead to part II. Those who feel involuntary about their own practice may wish to begin with chapter 14. Part II offers practice strategies with specific guidelines for legal, ethical, and effective work with involuntary clients. Chapter 8 details socialization methods while chapter 9 describes contracting processes and chapter 10 illustrates techniques for formalizing the contract. Chapter 11 provides guidelines for middle-phase intervention and termination. Chapters 10, 11, and 12 are strongly influenced by the task-centered approach. While the task-centered approach is not the only voluntary practice model compatible with the concepts, theory, and empirical evidence reported in part I, it is well suited to such work because of the value placed on collaboration with clients, self-determination, specificity of treatment activities, and empirical base of the approach. Chapter 12 presents an adaptation to work with families and chapter 13 adapts involuntary practice to work with groups. Finally, chapter 14 describes the involuntary practitioner and the system, and presents guidelines for practitioner action to reduce burnout and provide more legal, ethical, and effective practice throughout the system.

This book would not have been possible without the continuing support of G. David Hollister, Director of the School of Social Work, and colleagues from the University of Minnesota. Assistance from a University of Minnesota Graduate School Research Grant permitted Charlene Carlotto, Lisa Thompson, Cheri Brady, Joseph Chandy, Mohammed Haj-Yahia, and Karen Webb to assist at key points in searches of the literature. In addition, members of the Writers' Group assisted in editing the many drafts of the book: Maura Sullivan, Sara Taber, Rosemary Link, Mary Ann Syers-McNary, Linda Jones, Mohammed Haj-Yahia, and Marie Welborn. Useful comments on earlier drafts were also provided by Frederick Reamer, Judith Cingolani, William Reid, and Laura Epstein. The book was also made possible by interaction with hundreds of students and workshop participants who tested the ideas presented here and in some cases developed training videotapes that were used to illustrate intervention methods. Among those who developed training tapes cited were Cheri Brady, Barbara Seivert, Betty Woodland, Betty Doherty, Hoan Nguyen, Bill Linden, Dick Leonard, Paula Childers, Jane Macy-Lewis, Jean Tews, Sara Gaskill, Nancy Taylor, and Walter Mirk.

# A Foundation for Work with Involuntary Clients

Practice with involuntary clients has been largely guided by voluntary models. Practitioners need to know when and why to act with involuntary clients as well as how. Part I will lay a foundation for legal, ethical, and effective practice with involuntary clients by providing concepts and empirical data. Chapter 1 introduces the issue of involuntary practice for helping professionals. Chapter 2 describes an involuntary client continuum and describes pressures in the involuntary transaction on practitioners and clients. Chapter 3 reviews the legal base for involuntary practice, focusing on issues of informed consent, due process, right to treatment and freedom from unnecessary treatment. Chapter 4 continues to build a base of ethical practice by reviewing self-determination and circumstances under which it can be ethically limited and includes guidance for appropriate use of paternalism. Intervention principles based on evidence of effectiveness are presented in chapter 5 and principles of behavior and attitude change are presented in chapter 6. Chapter 7 presents deviance, resistance, reactance, power relations, and self-presentation strategies as five frameworks for helping explain what occurs in involuntary transactions.

# Chapter 1.

# Introduction to
# Involuntary Practice

Robert, 16, slouches in his chair, squinting at the young probation officer behind the desk. While Robert considers how he might escape this situation without too much hassle, his probation officer thinks about how to help Robert before he does more harm to himself and others.

George, 32, waits in the well-appointed lobby of a private family service agency to be screened for a domestic violence treatment group led by a clinical psychologist. Although George "chose" to seek voluntary treatment for battering his wife as an alternative to prosecution, he hardly considers the choice to be free.

Alice, 45, is developmentally disabled and has lived alone in a poorly heated rural shack since her mother died a year ago. Alice is not really alone since she shares her home with the twenty cats she considers her friends. The cats also share her food, and Alice's neighbors have called social services asking that something be done. Perhaps an underlying issue in this request is the fact that Alice's shack is an eyesore that affects the neighbors' property values. An adult protective service worker is assigned to assess Alice's safety. Expecting an unpleasant meeting, she carefully puts the assignment on the bottom of the pile in her in basket.

Robert, George, and Alice do not willingly seek the services of a helper or agency and hence are not at this point voluntary clients.[1] This chapter introduces work with involuntary clients, such as Robert, who are *legally mandated* to see a helper, and *nonvoluntary clients,* such as George and Alice, who experience pressure that is no less real though not legally mandated. As the practitioners working with involuntary clients are often less than delighted to work with them, I will also introduce the concept of the *involuntary practitioner.* I will explore how the helping professions, with special emphasis on social work, have thought about and worked with involuntary clients. The issues raised for practitioners by such work are considered next, and I will conclude with choices practitioners can make in involuntary circumstances.

## Definition of Involuntary Status

Can a person be both involuntary and a client? If a client, according to *Webster's New Collegiate Dictionary,* is "a person who is under the protection of another, one who engages the professional advice or services of another, or a person utilizing the services of a social agency," are Robert, George, and Alice clients? None of the three willingly engages professional advice, nor do they voluntarily utilize services, though Alice might eventually come to be under protection. Involuntary clients are participants in a special kind of nonvoluntary relationship. Social psychologists Thibaut and Kelley define a nonvoluntary relationship as containing one or more of three elements (see figure 1.1). First, a relationship is nonvoluntary if a person feels forced to remain in it because of physical or legal coercion, because of the unavailability of attractive alternatives, or both. Second, the choice to remain in a nonvoluntary relationship may be made because the cost of leaving the relationship is considered too high.[2] For example, Robert might consider violating his court order, yet decide that the costs of an increased sentence are too much. Third, the person believes that he or she is disadvantaged in the current relationship because better alternatives are available.[3] For example, George may feel disadvantaged if he expects to be a quiet, passive observer marking time in a domestic violence group and finds instead that he is pressured to be active and that his own attitudes and behavior are scrutinized.

The involuntary client *feels forced to seek or pressured to accept contact with a helping professional.* Involuntary clients can be subdivided into *mandated clients* and *nonvoluntary clients,* according to the source of pressure experienced (see figure 1.2).

Mandated clients must work with a practitioner as a result of a legal

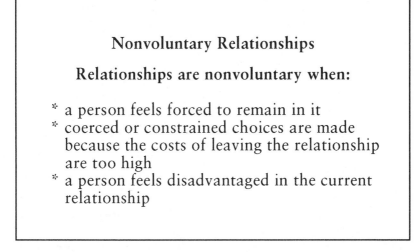

Nonvoluntary Relationships

Relationships are nonvoluntary when:

* a person feels forced to remain in it
* coerced or constrained choices are made because the costs of leaving the relationship are too high
* a person feels disadvantaged in the current relationship

*Figure 1.1*

mandate or court order. Mandated clients are often the majority of clients found in many public social service settings, human services departments, child welfare, probation and parole, and some psychiatric wards. The helping practitioners who work with them come from such professional fields as social work, psychology, psychiatry, counseling, marriage and family counseling, nursing, correctional counseling, and chemical dependency training. Many others are paraprofessionals with on-the-job training. Practitioners working in public settings with mandated clients are usually aware of the involuntary nature of their client contact since legal mandates describe practitioner responsibilities and often specify client rights.

Nonvoluntary clients have contact with helping professionals because of pressure from agencies, other people, and outside events. While clients such as Robert are legally involuntary, clients such as George and Alice are nonvoluntary. Nonvoluntary clients may also be considered the "invisible involuntary" since the pressures they face are not legal and hence are often missed by practitioners who consider them simply reluctant or resistant voluntary clients.[4] Nonvoluntary clients are harder to count because they are not defined by a legal status yet may be the majority of clients seen in public schools, hospitals, outpatient mental health settings, day treatment programs, group homes, shelters, drug

## The Involuntary Client

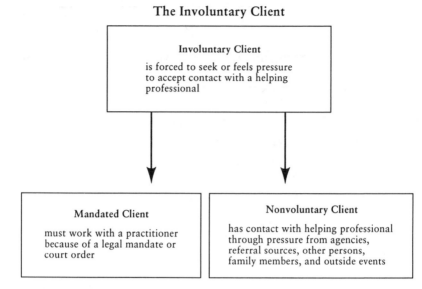

*Figure 1.2*

and alcohol treatment programs, youth services, and family service agencies.

Reluctance often occurs on both sides in the involuntary transaction. While involuntary clients are frequently plotting to escape, physically or psychologically, practitioners can also imagine more desirable working conditions than struggling with involuntary clients. Helping professionals in these circumstances may therefore be termed *involuntary practitioners*. Involuntary practitioners often understandably prefer working with voluntary clients who ask "Who am I" rather than with the involuntary client who wonders, "Who are you, why are you here, and when will you leave?"

Practitioners who work with involuntary clients come from all the helping professions. For example, psychologists and psychiatrists sometimes evaluate and provide treatment to nonvoluntary clients who do not want to be evaluated or treated. Similarly, nurses often engage in discharge planning with clients who feel that their choices are limited. Family therapists frequently work with families in which at least some members are ambivalent about participating in treatment.[5] Since social workers often work in both public and private agencies, they frequently work with mandated as well as nonvoluntary clients. Counselors placed in hospitals, schools, clinics, and prisons are also likely to work with involuntary clients.[6] In addition, the lines between public and private practice blur as many public agency practitioners also have a private clientele,[7] and private practitioners increasingly work with mandated clients as a result of purchase-of-service agreements and health maintenance organizations (HMO) contracts.

## How Have Involuntary Clients Been Viewed by the Helping Professions?

While practice literature for work with involuntary clients has developed in fields such as correctional counseling,[8] helping professions such as social work, psychology, psychiatry, and nursing have provided less practice guidance for work with involuntary clients.[9] These professions have tended to ignore involuntary clients or consider them as "prevoluntary" clients, or in a state preliminary toward becoming voluntary. Professional training usually assumes that clients are self-selected, while in fact most helpers work with many "reluctant and unmotivated clients."[10] The definition of a reluctant client, not unlike the involuntary client, is a person who does not want to be a client, who does not choose to see a counselor.[11] In fact, the term *involuntary client* is not widely used by the helping professions, and labels such as *hostile, resistant, reluctant, unmotivated, dysfunctional, hard-to-reach,* and *multi-problem* are used more frequently.[12] Terms such as *hostile, resistant,* and *unmotivated* cast a pejorative light on presumed client characteristics rather than on the nature of the contact between client and practitioner.[13] The reality of pressured involuntary contact can also be obscured when involuntary clients are paradoxically told that they are being forced to come to interviews because they *really want to but cannot admit it*—that they are "really voluntary, if only unconsciously so."[14]

Why might terms that focus on client characteristics be used more frequently than terms that focus on the circumstances of pressured contact? At least three reasons can be identified. First, greatest prestige in the helping professions has traditionally been accorded the practice of psychotherapy with voluntary clients. Second, psychotherapy theorists have tended to ignore power issues. As David Heller writes in *Power in Psychotherapeutic Practice,* "The most striking oversight in the field of psychotherapy has been the great neglect of power."[15] Third, when power issues *have* been addressed, influential theorists have questioned the use of authority. For instance, Carl Rogers wrote that "the counselor cannot maintain a counseling relationship with the client and at the same time have authority over him."[16] More recently, Anderson and

Stewart have questioned whether a family therapist can also be a person who decides whether to withdraw income or place family members in a foster home.[17] Moreover, Thomas Szasz maintains that "involuntary psychiatric interventions are not cures but coercions and I urge that psychiatrists reject such methods."[18]

Throughout the history of the profession, social workers have practiced with involuntary clients in settings such as child welfare, probation and parole, in- and outpatient mental health, and education agencies.[19] Attention to the involuntary nature of this contact, marked by times of often vigorous debate, has alternated with periods of inattention and a lack of recognition of this issue.

### Lack of Recognition

Certainly contact with involuntary clients was acknowledged before 1920. While voluntary clients were considered to make better use of social work services, voluntarism was not considered essential for social work practice.[20] By 1934, Bertha Reynolds was writing about a growing confusion in the field related to commitment to voluntary clients rather than services to the community:

This introduces something very like the psychology of private practice into a professional group which has ... been thinking ... in terms of community welfare or at least in terms of the welfare of individuals as ... seen by a professional representative of the community.... We are confused ... by the fact that the issues are not faced squarely.... One longs for a strong fresh wind to blow away all these fogs of misunderstanding and let us look about to see how things really are.[21]

The "strong fresh wind" did not blow. Casework became synonymous with voluntary contact, and little interest was shown in the study of authority.[22] Ohlin, Piven, and Pappenfort noted in 1956 that social workers in probation and parole departments were not prepared to work with unmotivated clients who "lacked treatment capacity" since social work texts made the assumption that the client selected the agency and was selected by the agency according to motivation and capacity.[23] Social workers trained to work with voluntary clients wished for warm, neutral, nonjudgmental relationships with involuntary clients, while involuntary clients saw the workers as part of a punitive, condemning system.

Rein and White suggest that ignoring the involuntary circumstances in which some client contact takes place has been pervasive in social work practice: "We mistakenly assume that clients always come voluntarily to the professional relationship in order to get help . . . [that] the help . . . is not coercive and does not get into questions of private faith, morals, or politics."[24] Rein and White further describe the beliefs that there is no conflict between individual and social needs, that power is not used, and that self-determination is always pursued as myths of the profession.[25] In fact, social workers control many important client resources and frequently act to represent the agency, the community, and others, rather than the client.[26] They delineate three solutions used by practitioners to deal with the dissonance created by the gap between the reality of power and professional myths of equality. One solution to the dilemma is to say "I am one with the client," while ignoring that other interests are also represented. A second is to maintain that "everyone really agrees" by focusing on compromise and ignoring the fact that differences of interest often remain. The third solution maintains that "I have a set of skills," which avoids consideration of differing interests between the client and the agency by focusing attention on those areas the practitioner alone can affect.[27] Rein and White suggest, however, that these so-called solutions do not eliminate the dissonance, and a malaise results from the unsuccessful efforts to implement them.

### Debate

While the writers quoted in the preceding section were asking the profession to provide *more* guidance in work with involuntary clients, others were asking whether social workers should continue to work with involuntary clients at all. Henry Miller wrote in 1968:

Social work must get out of the business of dealing with involuntary clients. . . . We are wrong whenever [we] assume that we have a right to impose unsolicited advice upon another human being and he/she is not free either to withdraw himself from the situation or act to discount the advice.[28]

Miller asserted that social workers with involuntary clients become "priests without theology. . . . God may be dead but five thousand social workers have risen up to take his place."[29] Piliavin further wondered whether a profession committed to self-determination and the interests of individual clients could continue to work in agencies whose interests often conflict with client wishes.[30]

Cowger and Atherton, on the other hand, argued that social control is the *main* function of social work. If social control is defined as those processes that support individual survival as a functional unit and include socialization, resocialization, and direct behavior control, most social workers are involved in social control.[31] Instead of denying these social control functions, Cowger and Atherton suggested that social workers should stop moralizing about the nature of humanity and start providing evidence that social services contribute significantly to society by seeking goals such as less child abuse and fewer family breakdowns.[32]

Peter Day suggested that continuing the debate about whether we are engaged in social control, or even should be, is not productive: the issue is not *whether* social workers engage in social control but rather *what* values they should support and *how* they should support them.[33] Day noted that social work not only performs social control functions for the social system but also stands for values and goals that may be a critique of that system.[34]

## Current Usage

Social work theorists have addressed the issue of involuntary practice more directly in the past ten years and efforts to develop new approaches to it are under way. While social workers use the term *involuntary client* more frequently than other helping professions do, terms such as *potential clients, candidates, resisters,* and *applicants* are still more commonly used.[35] These terms convey a sense of inevitable development: as the caterpillar becomes a butterfly, the involuntary client becomes voluntary.

This element of wishful thinking is addressed in William Reid's suggestion that *respondent* is more descriptive of persons brought "kicking and screaming" to treatment than *applicants*. He defines respondents as persons who have made no overt request for services.[36] Simons and Aigner have difficulty with the term *respondent* because of the ambiguity of the term, but also recognize the problem of describing both voluntary and involuntary people as clients. They define involuntary clients as people who do not seek the help of the social worker but rather must cooperate with the worker in order to avoid a negative sanction. A critical issue is identified when they note that "strictly speaking these individuals are targets rather than clients. The client system in such cases consists of the school, court, or general community who contends that these persons are violating the rights of others and must change."[37] According to Simons and Aigner, they are called clients rather than targets because other professions and laypeople label them this way, because historically the target was a person outside the client system, and because social workers attempt to establish collaborative relationships with involuntary clients. This definition is not entirely satisfactory because it obscures the difference of interests and viewpoints between society and the involuntary client.

The issue is now dealt with more squarely in social work. Alison Murdach defines the nonvoluntary situation as one in which a client is forced by those around him or her, such as parents, spouses, neighbors, and police, to seek assistance from social workers and other official helpers.[38] Judith Cingolani defines involuntary clients as those who must deal with a helping professional because they have behaved in ways considered annoying or troublesome to society.[39] She suggests that terms and concepts from the voluntary practice model do not fit the involuntary situation.[40] The helping perspective breaks down at the very beginning of treatment because of conflicting assumptions of involuntary clients and social workers about who "owns" the problem. Unless the issue is resolved with the client, the interaction does not make sense within a therapeutic perspective and a social conflict approach becomes more congruent. In this view, therapy is a political process in which society sanctions use of power in a context of conflict of interest.

The issues surrounding the status of involuntary clients have been neglected for too long; helping professionals must now grapple with these issues. Rather than blaming ourselves or being blamed for denying them, we should begin dealing with involuntary clients more constructively. Consider the analogy of the automatic camera.[41] When too much light threatens to overexpose the film, the aperture closes. The aperture of the helping professions, so to speak, is now opening a bit: it should cautiously take in more light. The following points summarize how this state of affairs has come about.

  1. *Voluntary psychotherapy continues to be the most prestigious form of practice in the helping professions.* The voluntary client continues to be the most taught about, written about, and most desired part of practice. For example, in social work considerable attention has been devoted to licensing, which in part promotes private practice and facilitates third-party billing. While licensing should also promote professionalism and an assurance of quality control, there is concern that it may also move social work away from service to its historical constituents, such as the poor. For example, Tom Walz describes a "middle classization of social work":

The well-developed professional services are fast becoming the province of the new middle class who . . . appreciate them and are willing to pay for them. We are increasingly becoming a nation characterized by an upside down welfarism.[42]

  2. *Practitioners have lacked theoretical concepts for understanding what occurs in involuntary transactions.* Helping professions such as

social group work and correctional counseling, which have had more experience with involuntary clients, have not influenced other helping professions as much as they might have.[43] Comparing involuntary to voluntary clients has been like comparing apples to potatoes. While both grow from the ground, they are not both fruit. Too often, we have tried to fit involuntary clients within a voluntary framework by interpreting enraged squawks as "cries for help."[44] In the stereotypic view of the voluntary intervention, the client seeks insight for better self-understanding in order to gain a happier life, yet the involuntary client rarely seeks help or desires insight.

Using available concepts is understandable, especially when appropriate alternative concepts are not available. Social work theoreticians have suggested that the stereotype of joint action to pursue insight oversimplifies the contact between helpers and clients and that social workers are in fact concerned with helping the client make a better fit with the client's situation.[45] In this broader view, the practitioner must be sensitive not only to the *client's* environment but also to the pressures in the practitioner's own work setting that affect practice.[46]

3. *Use of authority has not been fashionable*. Use of authority has been little studied, and has earned a bad reputation as coercion. Influential role models, such as Carl Rogers and Henry Miller, protest its use and few such noteworthy practitioners support it.[47]

4. *Service models centered on work with individual clients conflict with public professions that also serve the community*.[48] Professional codes of ethics espouse conflicting values for practitioners, who must simultaneously maximize client self-determination while obeying laws and following agency policies. For example, supporting a parent accused of child abuse or neglect in his/her right to self-determination may conflict with legal responsibilities to protect children from unsafe conditions. Guidance in helping practitioners choose between such conflicting values has been lacking.[49]

5. *Helping professionals often work in settings that now question whether rehabilitation is an appropriate goal*. Deemphasis on rehabilitation and increased concern with fair dispensation of punishment create concerns for helping professionals working in the criminal and juvenile justice systems. Some institutions no longer ascribe to a rehabilitation philosophy, while others work with contradictory agendas of helping and punishing, and call punishment help.[50]

## Consequences of an Undeveloped Knowledge Base

At least four consequences of the lack of a solid knowledge base for work with involuntary clients can be identified.

1. *No coherent theoretical and empirical base has been developed to guide practice with involuntary clients.* While practice approaches have been developed for particular problems and settings such as alcoholism treatment and child welfare, the practice and research literature in these areas has not influenced other forms of practice. Consequently, practitioners have to learn specific approaches for each new involuntary client or group and try to generalize from what they have been taught about voluntary clients.

2. *When dilemmas concerning conflicting values and use of authority arise, practitioners have little guidance in making difficult decisions.* Practitioners lack adequate concepts to understand involuntary transactions, and they work without knowledge of which procedures can be legally, ethically, and effectively used.

3. *Frustration over the lack of fit of involuntary clients with voluntary therapy concepts contributes to practitioners blaming the clients.* Negative responses by involuntary clients to pressured contact are often interpreted as client resistance rather than as an inherent part of an involuntary transaction.[51] When practitioners are frustrated, they may project that frustration onto involuntary clients and try to jerk them into seeing reality "correctly." They want to grab Robert by the hair and say, "Don't you see what you are doing to yourself?"

4. *Practitioners may be held responsible for influencing client changes that are infeasible, illegal, or unethical.* Practitioners are sometimes held responsible for motivating involuntary clients to change behavior or achieve outcomes that may not be feasible. For example, practitioners are sometimes evaluated by their ability to assist clients in getting jobs. They may, in fact, be held responsible despite the unavailability of jobs or appropriate training programs. In other cases, practitioners may be expected to change client attitudes and beliefs in ways that exceed the legal requirements and may in fact be violations of constitutionally guaranteed freedom of speech.[52]

## What Do Practitioners Want to Know about Work with Involuntary Clients?

The preceding consequences relate broadly to the needs of the helping professions as a whole. While perhaps mildly interested in the well-being of their profession, practitioners have more specific day-to-day concerns in improving their work with involuntary clients. Practitioners want to know how to do their jobs better, not just have informed debate (figure 1.3).

*Can I use authority legally, ethically, and effectively?* Practitioners who work with mandated clients want to know whether they can work collaboratively with mandated clients and also exercise their delegated authority. When can I intervene against a person's will, and when can I not? Are my only alternatives coercing the client with a requirement or ignoring problems when no legal mandate exists?

*Can I support self-determination in pressured situations?* Practitioners who work with the "invisible involuntary" want to be better aware of the pressures that impact their work with clients such as George and Alice. They want to know how to support self-determination while at

# What Do Practitioners Want to Know about Work with Involuntary Clients?

* Who is the client? What do I owe the person before me, the agency, society?
* Can I work collaboratively with involuntary clients and also carry out my delegated authority?
* Can I use authority legally, ethically, and effectively?
* When do I intervene against a person's will and when do I not?
* Is the only alternative coercing the client with a requirement and ignoring problems when there is no requirement?
* Can I remain sane and avoid burning out?

*Figure 1.3*

times providing help that the nonvoluntary client did not willingly seek. *Can I remain sane and avoid burning out?* Practitioners who spend most of their time working with people who don't want to work with them are aware of the strain this places on them. They know that their co-workers often do not remain with involuntary clients indefinitely. They often quit, obtain a transfer, go for further graduate training, or are promoted. Is work with involuntary clients only a rite of passage before moving on to more desirable clientele and responsibilities? Are there some practitioners who continue working with involuntary clients and, if so, what keeps them doing this work? The issues of pressure on practitioners will be addressed in chapter 14.

## Choices for Helping Practitioners

Practitioners and the helping professions have at least three choices in confronting these dilemmas.

1. *Choose to overlook the fact that many clients do not seek services.* Considering clients as involuntary implies the need for social workers to learn new concepts. New learning takes time and can unsettle old concepts. Hence, theorists, instructors, and practitioners may choose to continue considering involuntary clients as a special type of prevoluntary client.

2. *Involuntary transactions can be studied on their own terms.* Rather than transposing theories developed from a voluntary perspective to the involuntary transaction, the latter may be studied within a context that is sometimes coercive and in which choices must be made from limited alternatives. Influence and power can be acknowledged as factors in all human relationships; ignoring power can be considered in itself an abuse of power.[53]

3. *Legal, ethical, and effective practice with involuntary clients can be pursued.* While acknowledging differences of interest, practitioners can also pursue contacts that treat involuntary clients with respect. They can explore client goals as well as those set by the pressuring forces around them. While there is no compelling evidence that helping professionals have had a profound humanizing influence on institutions of social control, practitioners do not have to withdraw from all work with clients in pressured circumstances. Nor do they have to become specialists in humanitarian social control.

This book is designed to serve as a building block in establishing a legal, ethical, and effective foundation for practice with involuntary clients.

This practice must operate within the law and safeguard client rights; provide guidance to prevent a practitioner's unwarranted intrusion into the client's freedom through appropriate consideration of client self-determination and avoidance of undue paternalism; and pass tests for effectiveness in meeting goals (figure 1.4).

**Goals of Involuntary Practice**

Practice that is within legal guidelines and client protections

Ethical practice including self-determination and appropriate paternalism

Practice that meets goals effectively

*Figure 1.4*

# Chapter 2.

# The Involuntary
# Transaction

Three clients were introduced in the previous chapter as involuntary, though only Robert, the juvenile on probation, was legally required to see a helper. While helping professionals have been aware of *legally involuntary* or "captive clients" such as Robert,[1] they have been less willing to deal with the special circumstances of *nonvoluntary clients* who experience powerful nonlegal pressures from family, referral sources, and situations. Nonvoluntary clients may be considered the "invisible involuntary" since the nonlegal pressure they experience may be ignored by the helping practitioners, and hence they may lose *more* freedom than legally involuntary clients. At the same time, practitioners are also cognizant of legally mandated clients who do not appear to be moved by their status to change their actions. This chapter presents a continuum of involuntary contact that includes both legally involuntary clients such as Robert and nonvoluntary clients such as George and Alice. It will also include those legally mandated clients who are not moved to change behavior, or the "inaccessible involuntary." The continuum is defined by different sources of pressure, coercive and constraining modes of exerting that pressure, and a range of freedoms lost or threatened. In addition to individual pressure, some involuntary clients are also members of oppressed groups who already face depersonalized pressure from society as a whole resulting from that group membership.

Let us consider Martha's story. Martha, Caucasian, married, and the mother of two small children, held a part-time job and suffered from a lingering depression.

I had been depressed for about two years when I decided to seek help. When my husband and I went to see a psychiatrist for advice about what to do, he said that I needed to be hospitalized for three or four weeks where I would get the in-depth treatment and group therapy he considered most effective in treating depression. I was instantly both terrified and confused by this advice. While I knew I needed help, I didn't believe I needed to be hospitalized, since I was still able to care for my two small children and hold down a part-time job. Going into the hospital would be very complicated and embarrassing since I was afraid to tell my supervisor that I would have to be gone, and I dreaded arranging for child care. I also didn't like the idea of group therapy and talking about my problems with strangers.

When my husband and I came back to meet with the psychiatrist to further discuss plans, I told him that I would prefer to be treated on an outpatient basis. The psychiatrist then continued to explain my illness *to my husband* and why he felt I needed to be in a hospital. As I was afraid all psychiatrists would probably say the same thing, I didn't consider getting a second opinion. By the end of his explanation, we "agreed," though I was still very reluctant.

When I entered the hospital, I was more depressed than ever. On the first day, I stayed in my room most of the time, did not eat, and cried a lot. By the evening of the second day, I decided that I did not want to be treated in the hospital and I told the doctor I was leaving. He told me that he would not sign the discharge release which meant that our insurance would not pay for the hospital stay so far. As he also refused to treat me on an outpatient basis and suggested that he might pursue a civil commitment if I decided to leave the hospital, I could see no alternative to staying on the hospital's terms.

As I was now *very* depressed and withdrawn, I lost weight and contributed little to the group therapy sessions. I think that staff were informed that I was resistant, wanted to leave, and had to be watched carefully. I was told that I would have to improve a lot before I would be discharged. If I improved, however, I could go home on weekends. Since I wanted to go home, I eventually cooperated and began to feel better and returned home after four weeks.

Martha initially sought voluntary help for her depression. She describes how she became involuntary through pressure from the doctor and her husband, anticipated pressure from her supervisor, and worrying about how to arrange for child care. The continuum presented in this chapter includes *legally mandated pressures,* and *nonvoluntary pressures* of three sorts: 1) *formal pressures,* such as those from Martha's doctor; 2) *informal pressures,* such as those anticipated from her supervisor and her concern with having to find child care; and 3) *oppressed group* pressures such as the possibility that the treatment she received resulted at least in part from her status as a female. While continued hospitalization may or may not have been in Martha's best interest despite her objections, we will focus here on the fact that the transaction took place in a power imbalance in which access to desirable alternatives was limited such that Martha *became* an involuntary client.

## The Involuntary Transaction

I suggested in chapter 1 that practitioners have lacked alternative perspectives for examining involuntary transactions beyond a voluntary therapy perspective.[2] In this context, Germain and Gitterman comment:

> How a need or predicament is defined determines in large measure what will be done about it. If problems experienced by people are located within the person and defined as psychopathology, then the professional intervention is likely to be formulated in psychotherapeutic terms on a clinical model. . . . If problems are located in the interface between the person and environment . . . then the professional intervention is likely to be formulated in terms of reciprocal adaptive processes.[3]

Following Germain and Gitterman, if we lack alternatives to a therapeutic perspective, we may be inclined to perceive most involuntary client problems as pathology-based. If, however, we consider problems as occurring in the interaction between client, practitioner, agency, and society, we may be more inclined to look for solutions which may come from any of these sources.

An involuntary transaction is defined as a dynamic exchange of resources between clients, practitioners, and agencies occurring in a shifting legal and normative context and power imbalance such that the involuntary client would prefer to be elsewhere. Furthermore, members of oppressed groups are disproportionately represented among involuntary clients. The four parts of this definition will be examined separately.

1. *The involuntary transaction is a dynamic exchange of resources.* Hasenfeld describes practitioner-client interactions as an exchange of resources.

> It is commonly assumed that, since clients want help and agencies wish to provide help, they share a common goal. In fact, however, the interests of the worker and the client are determined by their respective systems. Like all living systems, the agency and the client want to maximize their own resources while minimizing the costs of attaining them. Therefore a person becomes a client in order to get needed resources and tries to do so with minimal personal costs. The agency, via the worker, engages the client in order to obtain resources controlled by him or her while minimizing organizational costs. It is this exchange of resources which makes both systems interdependent.[4]

In this context, the hospital staff wanted Martha's compliance with their plan for alleviating her depression at minimum disruption to organizational procedures. Similarly, Martha wanted help with her depression of a kind that would disrupt her life as little as possible. The transaction is dynamic because the involuntary client and practitioner can become *more* voluntary or *less* voluntary over time. While Martha began as a voluntary client seeking help for her depression, she became *less* voluntary when she felt pressure to "choose" to stay in the hospital. Finally, however, she became somewhat *more* voluntary as she found that treatment helped alleviate her depression and get her out of the hospital.

2. *The involuntary transaction occurs in a shifting legal and normative context.* Contacts between involuntary clients and practitioners are influenced by legal and professional mandates, and agency policies.[5] Legal mandates specify rights, responsibilities, and sanctions for law violations which govern practitioners and involuntary clients.[6] Legal mandates are based in cultural norms for approved and unapproved behavior and means for sanctioning unapproved behavior. Some norms are nearly universal and others vary by culture and over time within a culture. Although norms against incest and theft are very common, few other norms are so universal.[7] Laws and norms also change over time within a culture. For example, sale and consumption of alcohol was illegal in the United States from 1910 to 1930 until the repeal of the Volstead Act.[8] While drinking alcohol became legal, other behaviors have become illegal. For instance, many states now have laws requiring police to report incidents of intrafamily violence which might in the past have been considered domestic disputes and not reported.[9] Similarly, homosexuality was classified as a mental disorder with a diagnostic label until 1973. While gays and lesbians continue to face discrimination, their sexual orientation is no longer considered evidence of mental illness.[10]

In Martha's case, the psychiatrist and hospital staff were influenced by laws and professional norms to protect her from the potential danger of suicide. At the time of Martha's hospitalization in 1973, many believed that such depression could be best treated in a hospital setting. It is now more likely that Martha's desire for outpatient care for depression that is not life-threatening would be taken more seriously.[11]

3. *The involuntary transaction occurs in a power imbalance such that the involuntary client would prefer to be elsewhere.* While power differences are most obvious in legally mandated contacts, they take place in nonlegal transactions as well. Such imbalances of power between clients, practitioners, and agencies can occur in three circum-

stances: a) if the agency depends more on outside resources than on those provided by the involuntary client; b) if there is greater demand for agency services than there are supplies available; or c) the agency has a quasi-monopoly over access to services such that the client does not have ready access to alternatives; then d) the client may have little choice but to accept services on the terms they are offered.[12]

Martha was at a power disadvantage since the hospital did not depend on her consent for resources and her access to other alternatives was limited. Similarly, when George was given the "choice" of entering a program for batterers or risking prosecution, he had to select from a limited supply of programs offering such services.

4. *Members of oppressed groups are disproportionately represented among involuntary clients.* Power imbalance falls disproportionately on members of oppressed groups.[13] Oppressed groups are defined by: a) a lack of alternatives to preferences enforced by the majority society; b) prejudice against the group is depersonalized; c) bias is not private or narrow but entrenched in the larger society; and d) members of the group are visible and aware of the discrimination.[14] By this definition, many social groups such as the poor, the aged, the disabled, refugees, women, children, gays, and lesbians are often oppressed.[15] Of particular concern, however, are those people of color who can be visually identified as a member of an oppressed group (see figure 2.1).[16]

Oppressed group status is compounded when oppressed groups overlap. For instance, the term *ethclass* describes the intersection of ethnic group and social class.[17] When poverty and gender status is combined, we discover that while female-headed households represented 16 percent of American families in 1986, they represented 51 percent of those in poverty.[18] When ethnicity is added, we find that over half of the African-American and Hispanic female-headed households were in poverty in 1985 compared with only 27 percent of Caucasian female-headed families.[19] The intersection of these statuses has highlighted the increasing feminization of poverty and the growth of the so-called underclass.[20]

Membership in an oppressed group often means disproportionate access to resources and substandard living conditions. For example, when federal budget cuts were enacted in the 1980s, social programs that primarily benefited low-income clients and people of color, such as job training programs, educational loans, and Medicaid, were cut while programs benefiting the middle class, such as Medicare and Social Security, were not cut and benefits to the wealthy were increased through reduced capital gains taxes.[21] Such actions, which put certain groups to disadvantage, have been described as institutional racism.[22]

## Oppressed Groups

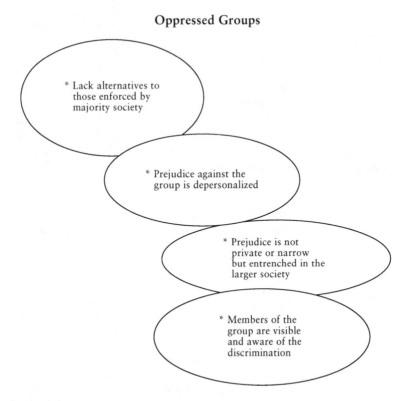

* Lack alternatives to those enforced by majority society

* Prejudice against the group is depersonalized

* Prejudice is not private or narrow but entrenched in the larger society

* Members of the group are visible and aware of the discrimination

*Figure 2.1*

Members of oppressed groups often find their own behaviors the focus of change, rather than the limited access to resources and care, with an emphasis on their "private troubles" rather than "public issues" that contribute to the perpetuation of oppression.[23] Members of oppressed groups frequently come into contact with helpers as a result of a coercive referral from systems of authority such as the courts or school.[24] This contact is often conducted in transactions with "street-level bureaucrats" who must manage chronically limited and inadequate resources for dealing with their appointed tasks. This resource limitation in turn often leads these bureaucrats to become "people processors" who focus on rationing services, and controlling and limiting clients.[25] The care received by members of oppressed groups is more likely to be institutional and custodial than private and individualized.[26] Low-income minority children are more likely to enter social-control institutions and foster care than Caucasian middle-class children.[27] In Martha's case, her status as a woman probably contributed to a more directive treatment style than would have been the case had she been male.[28] On the other hand, her status as a Caucasian middle-class married woman in all probability protected her from further power imbalance.

### Attempts by Involuntary Clients to Regain Power

How can involuntary clients attempt to regain power in an unbalanced power situation? They have five options: 1) offer resources which the practitioner or agency will accept in exchange; 2) look elsewhere for the resource; 3) coerce or pressure the practitioner to provide the resource; 4) become resigned to getting along without the resource; or 5) meet the agency or practitioner's requirements to get the resources.[29]

While most of these responses refer to an individual's options, members of oppressed groups sometimes organize to redress collectively the balance, as was the case with the National Welfare Rights Organization.[30] Even when involuntary clients decide that they have no alternative to meeting the requirements of the resource, they still have control over the *way* they decide to comply. For example, involuntary clients can reframe the situation to some personal benefit by seeing their involuntary situation as an opportunity to learn how to deal with other unequal power situations, or by working on their own goals at the same time as meeting the conditions set by the sources of the pressure (figure 2.2).[31]

Martha attempted several of these responses: 1) she tried to persuade the psychiatrist to provide her with outpatient services; 2) she resigned herself to getting along without outpatient treatment and decided to accept the hospital's terms, although unwillingly; and 3) she also seemed to personally reframe the situation by becoming very motivated to get out of the hospital and complying in order to meet this goal. She also could have sought a second opinion or chosen to leave the institution against medical advice (despite the risks). She might also have sought the services of a hospital ombudsman or contacted associations of clients with mental illness. The imbalance of power in Martha's case meets Thibaut and Kelley's criteria for nonvoluntary status since she was aware of desirable alternatives and felt deprived or blocked from getting them.[32] Other voluntary patients in the hospital may not have been aware of preferable alternatives and hence not felt deprived or involuntary.

## A Continuum of Involuntary Clients

Additional concepts are needed to aid us in identifying all involuntary clients, especially the "invisible involuntary" who face pressures practitioners often miss. While the above definition gives us a start in identifying when an involuntary transaction occurs, it does not always help us determine *how* involuntary the transaction is since some transactions are more involuntary than others.[33] Most continuums developed to date have focused on the legitimacy of sanctions or what Studt has called "the extent of responsibility for dealing with the problem assumed by the community."[34]

Figure 2.3 depicts a continuum of involuntary contacts based on legitimacy of sanction with legally mandated as the highest responsibility assumed by the community, followed by nonvoluntary pressure from

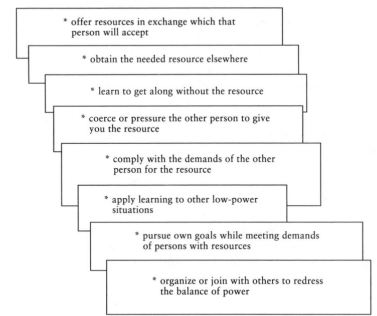

**Responses to
Power-Dependent
Situations**

If another person controls a resource
which you feel you must have, several
alternatives are available:

* offer resources in exchange which that
  person will accept

* obtain the needed resource elsewhere

* learn to get along without the resource

* coerce or pressure the other person to give
  you the resource

* comply with the demands of the other
  person for the resource

* apply learning to other low-power
  situations

* pursue own goals while meeting demands
  of persons with resources

* organize or join with others to redress
  the balance of power

*Figure 2.2*

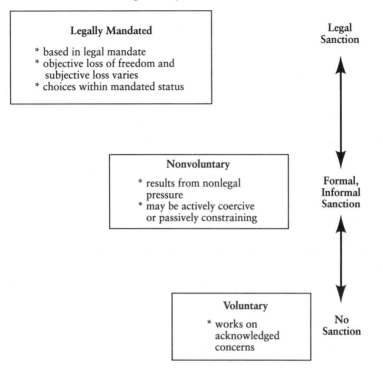

One-Dimensional View
Based on
Legitimacy of Sanction

**Legally Mandated**

* based in legal mandate
* objective loss of freedom and
  subjective loss varies
* choices within mandated status

Legal
Sanction

**Nonvoluntary**

* results from nonlegal
  pressure
* may be actively coercive
  or passively constraining

Formal,
Informal
Sanction

**Voluntary**

* works on
  acknowledged
  concerns

No
Sanction

*Figure 2.3*

formal and informal sources. Basing the continuum on a legitimacy-of-sanction dimension sensitizes us to the fact that only legally mandated clients have *legal* consequences for failure to comply with a program, and nonvoluntary clients have more legal choices. When we assume that legal sanctions mean that a person is *more* involuntary than a person who does not face legal sanctions, we may be assuming that legal mandates entail extensive loss of valued freedoms for the involuntary client. For example, clients court-ordered into a treatment program as part of a prison sentence may feel very involuntary since they are losing many valued freedoms.

Yet there are anomalies which this one-dimensional view does not explain. In other words, some legal sanctions do *not* mean the loss of valued freedoms, while some nonvoluntary pressures mean the loss of more highly valued freedoms than experienced by some legally mandated clients. For example, foster care workers have sometimes found that biological parents who opposed placement of their child out of the home become accustomed to the freedom from child care and feel little motivation to "work" to regain custody of the child.[35] Hence, a legal sanction with the loss of many freedoms may be experienced by some parents as a *relief* rather than a loss! On the other hand, clients such as George who are not legally mandated to receive services may lose many valued freedoms: he may find the cost of his "volunteering" for the domestic violence group includes attending group sessons for over a year and a commitment to change many behaviors and attitudes. Similarly, Martha sought help yet found that the "help" came in an all-or-nothing "package deal" in which she felt pressured to accept unattractive helping methods such as group therapy sessions and inpatient care. Clients such as Martha and George have often been characterized as "resistant" voluntary clients rather than involuntary clients, since definitions of involuntary have focused on the legitimacy of the sanction rather than the freedom lost.[36]

Let us consider a three-dimensional model that presents an attempt to resolve these anomalies by considering legitimacy of sanction and the loss of valued freedoms as possibly independent events. The loss of valued freedoms contains both the objective extent of lost or threatened freedoms and the perceived magnitude of that loss by the person. For example, hospital rules for visitation and participation in group therapy may be required for all patients on the ward. Whether or not such rules are felt to be a loss of valued freedom depends on whether the person feels that important freedoms are endangered that are not easily obtainable in other ways.[37] Hence, Martha experienced this as a loss of valued freedoms, while other patients who value group treatment experiences or are resigned to going along with the program might not experience such a sense of loss.

This also introduces fate control as a third dimension in describing involuntary transactions. Fate control refers to the degree to which one member of a dyad, such as the practitioner, can effect the future goals or actions of a second member, such as the involuntary client, if that client decides to leave the dyad before the practitioner is ready.[38] Fate control then represents the power to *coerce* or *constrain* actions or choices. Coercive power is the ability of the practitioner to restrain or compel a client to an act or choice by force or threat.[39] Having fate control or the power to coerce does not mean that it must or will be used.[40]

Applying this three-dimensional conception permits us to see many variations of the involuntary experience. For example, clients who experience legal mandates, high fate control, and high perceived loss of valued freedoms might be considered *highly involuntary;* for instance, many men court-ordered to participate in treatment for sexual abuse. Referring to circumstances of legal mandates, high fate control, and low perceived loss of freedom, the biological parents willing to lose custody of their children might be considered *inaccessible involuntary* since they are willing to accept the punishment and forgo the rewards controlled by the agency. A third category of clients do not experience legal mandates, yet experience high fate control and loss of valued freedoms. George and Martha are examples of the *invisible involuntary* who may have stronger negative reactions to services than those clients in the second category. Finally, a fourth category includes circumstances in which there are neither legal mandates nor appreciable fate control or loss of valued freedoms, into which many *voluntary clients* may fit.

Use of such three-dimensional modeling allows us to extend our awareness beyond legal sanctions to include fate control and loss of valued freedoms. Such a view enables us to "see" the *invisible involuntary* and *inaccessible involuntary* clients who are faced with ineffective sanctions should the client be prepared to give up the threatened freedom.

We will now examine each kind of involuntary transaction in greater detail through analysis of the source of pressure, fate control, and loss of valued freedoms. Involuntary clients include persons who are legally mandated to see a helper, and nonvoluntary clients who see a counselor through nonlegal pressure.[41] Nonvoluntary pressures can be further broken down into formal, such as agency or referral source pressures, and informal, such as from family members and situations, and oppressed group pressure brought about by mere membership in a said group. While mandated clients and nonvoluntary clients differ in the source of pressure, they may be similar in the fate control exerted (coercive or constraining) and in the extent of loss of valued freedoms. Further characteristics of each type of involuntary transaction are considered below.

## The Legally Mandated Transaction

A legally mandated transaction is one in which either the client or the practitioner has no legal alternative to contact without incurring legal punishment. Hence the sources of pressure are legitimated sanctions based in legislation and court orders.[42] Settings that frequently deal with legal mandates include criminal justice, child welfare, adult protection, mental health, and substance abuse.[43] Clients who have no legal alternative to participation in a legally mandated transaction are therefore termed *legally mandated clients.*[44]

Legally mandated clients interact with practitioners in three combinations. In the most common, a legally mandated client meets with a practitioner who works for a mandated agency. Robert, the sixteen-year-old on probation, is a legally mandated client because he has no legal alternative to participation with the probation officer. Similarly, Robert's probation officer is a legally mandated practitioner required to implement court orders. While the consequences for noncompliance differ, *both* are influenced by legal requirements. If Robert does not comply, he may return to court for a more restrictive sentence. If the probation officer does not carry out the court order, she may risk the loss of her job.

In the second combination, some legally mandated clients are served by practitioners who do not work for legally mandated agencies. With the advent of purchase-of-service agreements and health maintenance organizations, private practitioners are frequently called on for such tasks as chemical dependency or mental status evaluations and to provide treatment for legally mandated clients.

There are also circumstances in which a practitioner is required to contact a potential client with the client's status dependent on the outcome of that contact. For example, the adult protective service worker may be required to carry out an investigation about Alice's safety (see chapter 1). If the evaluation does not result in a protective order, Alice will not be legally involuntary and will be able to choose whether she wishes to have services. If, on the other hand, the investigation uncovers serious doubts about her safety, she might indeed become legally involuntary. In other circumstances, a practitioner may be required to offer services which the potential client can choose to accept or reject. For example, in some areas public social service workers are required to offer information and services to single-parent mothers of newborns. While the practitioner is required by the agency to make the offer, the mothers are not required to accept the information and services.

Finally, helping professionals in both public and private agencies are legally mandated reporters for suspected child abuse and neglect.[45] Relationships that begin on a completely voluntary basis can change should clients threaten their own lives or endanger someone else such that the practitioner is legally and ethically bound to break confidentiality.

By definition, legally mandated transactions involve fate control with either *coercive* or *constraining* pressures or both. For example, should the probation officer have discretion over deciding how often to meet with Robert, that pressure may be actively coercive. Discretion may be based, however, in a set of permissible options that might act as constraints. The presence of coercive or constraining power does not determine how it must be used. The probation officer may choose to negotiate with Robert from a set of acceptable options about the frequency of contacts.

Legally mandated transactions entail a range of loss of valued freedoms from the loss of many to the loss of few and insignificant freedoms. For example, requirements to participate in a work squad, pay restitution, and report to his probation officer for six months might be perceived by Robert as the loss of many valued freedoms. Should he find that the requirements are ultimately helpful in finding a job or meeting other personal goals, then he may come to feel more of a gain than a loss of those freedoms. The loss of freedom experienced by some legally mandated clients is minimal. As described above, such clients might be described as the inaccessible involuntary. For example, first-offender shoplifters may be required to attend a single education session. While some may find this intrusive, others may experience it as a brief inconvenience. Still others may find the session to be a helpful warning about harmful consequences of continuing such behavior.

### Nonvoluntary Transactions

Nonvoluntary transactions are characterized by nonlegal pressure from formal and informal sources.[46] Formal pressures are exerted by agencies, practitioners, and referral sources outside the home. Informal pressure is exerted by family members, friends, employers, and disturbing situations. Each of these pressure sources is explored in more detail below.

*Formal pressures* come to bear in at least five ways. First, both public and private agencies establish requirements, policies, and define overall goals appropriate for client-practitioner contact. For example, many probation offices have formulas for deciding how often probation officers will see their clients based on an assessment of risk. Second, agencies influence client and practitioner decision-making processes by limiting the range of alternative services and specifying decision rules.[47] Third, client-perceived problems are often redefined to fit within agency policies and resources.[48] For example, parents often bring their adolescents to family agencies with the request that the adolescents be "fixed." The families are usually *not* requesting family counseling, but may find that agency policy requires the participation of all family members as a condition of service. The family is, of course, legally free to seek help at another agency or to decline service. If, however, continuation with this agency is contingent on accepting their terms or if other desired alternatives are unavailable, then the decision to accept services is a constrained one.[49] Fourth, agencies also often use teams to make decisions about client contracts. While teams can act to curb the idiosyncracies of particular practitioners, they can also provide additional pressure when their plans differ from what clients wish for themselves.[50] Finally, professional referral sources are also a source of formal pressure. While a doctor's recommendation is often not a legal mandate, the practitioner and client may feel pressure to consider it. For example, we notice in Martha's case that she did not consider a second opinion as she might have in other important decisions in her life such as buying a house or a car. Similarly, practitioners who control important resources for their clients are the source of powerful advisory pressure. Strings may be attached to acquiring a resource, such as public assistance with approval contingent on "volunteering" to have a chemical dependency evaluation (figure 2.4).

*Informal pressures* are often invisible to the practitioner, since their source is neither formal nor official. The "invisible involuntary" clients experiencing such informal pressures are most evident to practitioners when they claim that they were impelled by others to seek help. For example, Ralph was one such "invisible involuntary" client. While ostensibly self-referred to an outpatient mental health clinic, he had little to say when asked why he had come. He

| Formal Pressures | Informal Pressures |
|---|---|
| 1) establish goals, policies, requirements for contact<br>2) limit services; establish decision rules<br>3) problems are redefined to fit policies and resources<br>4) teams may create goals which differ from client wishes<br>5) professionals are a source of advisory pressure | 1) pressured to seek help by other persons and situations<br>2) problems often attributed which are not acknowledged |

*Figure 2.4*

mentioned that he was having some difficulties with his wife but "nothing that we can't handle by ourselves." When the practitioner asked what he was seeking from counseling since these problems could be handled, Ralph responded that he did not really want anything. Ralph continued that he and his wife were living with his mother and *his mother* told them that they had to move out if they did not seek counseling for their arguing. Ralph's situation might have become legally involuntary had there been evidence of violence.

Responses such as Ralph's are often interpreted as denying responsibility for problems. Reid's distinction between *acknowledged* and *attributed* problems is useful here.[51] An *acknowledged* problem is one that a client admits to having. For example, Martha acknowledged a problem with depression and George might acknowledge a problem with the court system. Ralph acknowledges no problems other than perhaps needing to satisfy his mother. An *attributed* problem is one that others say that a client has.[52] Needing to accept inpatient treatment was a problem attributed to Martha and needing to learn alternative ways for dealing with situations that have led to violence was a problem attributed to George. Ralph's mother attributes marital problems to Ralph and his wife.

Informal pressures also come from the referrals of community members who attribute problems to persons whose behavior they consider inappropriate or deviant. Alice's situation is typical of many who arouse community concern. Her practitioner might agree with the referring neighbors that keeping twenty cats is not what she would consider "normal" housekeeping, yet have neither the mandated authority nor the ethical right to compel Alice to change her behavior should she be mentally competent and not violating any laws. Alice's neighbors may nevertheless be unhappy if they find that the practitioner can not force Alice to change her lifestyle and may complain to her supervisor.

Informal pressures also result from situations where the involuntary client feels powerless and impelled. For example, a patient treated in a hospital hemodialysis unit has no legal, formal, or informal pressure from another person, yet may feel impelled by a constraining *situation* if employment and other parts of life are arranged around regular times that the patient must be connected to a dialysis machine.

Fate control plays a role in the formal and informal pressures experienced by nonvoluntary clients. While legally free to choose *not* to see a helping professional, nonvoluntary clients often experience such choices as free in name only. They face *coerced* or *constrained* choices because:

1) some choices are rewarded, 2) others are punished, and 3) preferred alternatives are often not available.

1. *A coerced or constrained choice may be rewarded.* Clients may "agree" to extensive task commitments in order to obtain rewards. For example, parents wishing to adopt a child may agree to extensive life history interviewing and to attend adoption classes because the reward of adoption is so high. Clients of the federal Aid to Families with Dependent Children (AFDC) may "choose" to participate in job training programs and to pressure their children to go to school because such provisions are required for receiving assistance.[53] While they are free to discontinue their AFDC status, the choice to receive financial assistance for food and rent is constraining.

2. *Some preferred choices are punished.* Coerced and constrained choices are sometimes made because other alternatives are punishment. George may have preferred to be released with a warning. If he chose to avoid treatment, however, that choice may have meant facing prosecution and a possible prison term.

3. *A coerced or constrained choice may be made as the least detrimental alternative.*[54] Clients may also "volunteer" for a service because desired alternatives are considered too costly, are unavailable, or because some service is considered better than no service at all. Parents who feel they can no longer control their adolescents often want someone to take them off their hands. These parents often find that public social service agencies are unwilling to use scarce foster care resources if there is no evidence of severe harm. Family-centered, home-based services are often offered which are designed to maintain the family unit and avert foster care placement.[55] Hence, some families may accept such services because private placement is too costly, public placement is not available, and in-home services are considered preferable to no services.

Nonvoluntary transactions range from the loss of many valued freedoms to the loss of few or none. Those families wishing to have their teen removed from the home may find the denial of this one alternative as a major loss if they are at the end of their rope. The threat that a spouse might leave if help is not sought may involve more loss of valued freedoms than any legal mandate. The loss, however, of even a single freedom can be experienced as intrusive. For example, siblings of the "identified troubled teen" are often requested to attend family treatment sessions. If attending family sessions means missing hockey practice, the loss of one freedom may be perceived as high. Should the family be persuaded to explore the benefits of family-based service, the loss of freedom may be minimal.

## Voluntary Transactions

While this chapter focuses on involuntary transactions, voluntary transactions must also be considered since some involuntary clients become at least semi-voluntary, and because some voluntary clients become nonvoluntary or mandated. Voluntary clients work with a practitioner on concerns that those clients acknowledge without pressure from others.[56] Many voluntary clients initiate referral and remain voluntary. On the other hand, some clients start as voluntary and become nonvoluntary or mandated. In addition, some nonvoluntary clients may become voluntary and some legally mandated clients choose to work on problems voluntarily.

Keith-Lucas suggests that voluntary clients: 1) recognize a problem which they cannot resolve alone; 2) are willing to tell someone about the problem and give that person the right to advise; and 3) are willing to change in some way.[57] As ambivalence about one or more of these conditions can be expected in most situations, such "really" voluntary clients are probably the exception. Many are helped to overcome their ambivalence and become voluntary.

Self-referred voluntary clients are frequently in a more balanced power relationship with the agency and practitioner and have more viable options than involuntary clients. For example, if voluntary clients pay for services and the provider is dependent on their resources, and the supply of paying clients is limited and the paying client has ready access to other resources, the practitioner may have as much need of their services as they have of the practitioner's.[58] Dissatisfied voluntary clients can "vote with their feet" and seek another helper. Should this paying voluntary client have resources needed by the practitioner, the practitioner may modify services to fit the client's request. Such clients are most often served in private agencies, child and family services, and outpatient psychiatric clinics.

Some self-referred voluntary clients become nonvoluntary or mandated. They may find that offered services differ from what they requested. Such originally voluntary clients may "resist" the redefinition of their problems and become nonvoluntary as a result of pressure from the practitioner.[59] Other clients seek voluntary services yet receive mandated services. For example, parents who voluntarily request help in parenting from public agencies sometimes find voluntary resources to be unavailable. In some cases, those parents return later to the public agency as subjects of an involuntary investigation about a deterioration in the same problems for which they requested help. Other voluntary clients become nonvoluntary as a result of a "widening net." While help may be sought voluntarily on one problem, the practitioner may become alert to others. For example, if a client seeking help in securing employment is assessed by the practitioner as having a possible chemical dependency problem, he or she may be referred for an evaluation. In another case, a person made a voluntary application to become a foster parent for her nieces and nephews. She became a mandated client, however, when the licensing study uncovered concerns about the parenting of her own children and resulted in a child neglect investigation.

Some nonvoluntary clients become voluntary. Hence, some clients referred by others readily acknowledge the concerns expressed by the referral source and feel little pressure in agreeing to work on them. For example, some persons referred by their employers to employee assistance programs may appreciate the concern and feel it as a push in the direction of working on a problem about which they were already somewhat aware.

Finally, some legally mandated clients can become semi-voluntary around some issues if they have voluntary concerns in addition to legal requirements. For example, there are accounts of prisoners voluntarily participating in marital treatment with spouses outside the prison without any connection to their legal requirements.[60]

## Review of Mandated and Nonvoluntary Pressures

The categories presented so far may imply a relatively fixed, permanent status. In fact, pressures often change, occur in sequences, or occur simultaneously from several sources. Pressures change as intensity increases or decreases over time. As suggested above, legally mandated clients may become *more* involuntary as pressures increase. Voluntary clients may become nonvoluntary or mandated as a result of the "widening net." Pressures may also decrease; mandated services are usually time-limited and hence pressures decrease when the service period ends. Pressures originally experienced as intrusive may become less so as problems acknowledged by involuntary clients are also addressed or as the clients come to acknowledge attributed problems.

Second, pressures may be sequential and shift from one source to another over time. Martha began as voluntary and became nonvoluntary. Finally, pressures can occur simultaneously from several sources. While Robert must deal with the legal pressure of the court-ordered requirements to work with his probation officer, he may experience simultaneous pressure from other formal sources such as school officials concerned about his attendance and informal sources such as his parents and friends. His parents may be disappointed in his trouble with the law and his friends may pressure him *not* to change.

As involuntary transactions are not static and are influenced by subjective perceptions of lost freedoms, it becomes more difficult to identify involuntary clients simply by looking at legal status. There are little hard data available on voluntarism as a client characteristic.[61] Self-referral is one clue in identifying voluntary clients. Videka-Sherman reports that clients were self-referred in 18 percent of the studies of social work services in mental health she reviewed. Only 2 percent of the studies explicitly identified clients as involuntary. The remaining 80 percent are harder to classify since they were referred by agency staff, by staff in other agencies, or self-referred in coordination with staff referral (see figure 2.5).[62] This group probably contains a combination of voluntary and nonvoluntary clients.

This chapter has presented a continuum of involuntary transactions including both mandated and nonvoluntary pressures. These pressures are changeable, and often sequential or simultaneous. Practitioners should

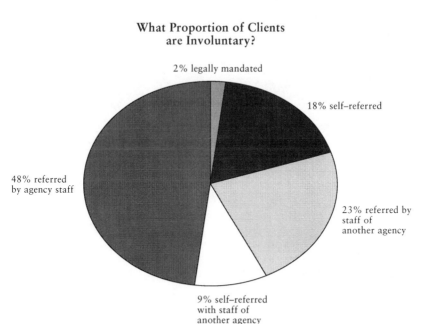

What Proportion of Clients are Involuntary?

2% legally mandated

18% self–referred

48% referred by agency staff

23% referred by staff of another agency

9% self–referred with staff of another agency

*Figure 2.5*

assess legal, other formal, and informal pressures in all cases. The identification of these pressures can then become the basis for clarifying choices and constraints. Additional tools for assessing pressures and choices follow in chapter 3, which reviews the legal basis for legal, ethical, and effective practice.

# The Legal Foundation for Work
# with Involuntary Clients

This chapter reviews the legal base for the three-pronged goal of legal, ethical, effective practice. I will focus primarily on issues affecting legally mandated clients. Among the problem areas and populations in which legal protections are most relevant are mental health, health care, chemical addictions, competency and guardianship of the elderly, work with persons with disabilities, foster care, adoption, public assistance recipients, child custody, domestic violence, delinquency, work in prison, and probation and parole. Practitioners in these settings may be called upon to act as petitioners, defendants, client advocates, expert witnesses, and mandated reporters.[1] While it is beyond the scope of this book to review legal conditions in each of these fields, major legal issues that cut across populations such as due process, confidentiality, informed consent, malpractice, and liability will be reviewed. Right to treatment, freedom from unnecessary treatment, and the principle of least restrictive alternative will also be reviewed with special emphasis on the mental health setting. Nonvoluntary clients are usually considered voluntary by the legal system and hence not accorded special protections; the special circumstance of rights of the nonvoluntary will also be reviewed. Legal issues will be reviewed while drawing on the following case study.

On October 28, 1987 a homeless woman described as "dirty, disheveled, and malodorous" was "forcibly removed" from her "home" at the 1′ by 3′ ground-level vent of a fashionable New

York restaurant as the first of 25 allegedly mentally ill "street people" to be involuntarily hospitalized at Bellevue Hospital.[2] Five earlier attempts had been made to involuntarily hospitalize Joyce Brown, but she had been immediately released each time when it was determined that she was not in immediate danger. She was involuntarily hospitalized this time because criteria used in New York City for defining risk of death or injury had been expanded from predictable harm within a day or two to danger in the foreseeable future.

At the hearing in which Ms. Brown and her attorneys successfully appealed the involuntary hospitalization, city attorneys and expert psychiatric witnesses contended that "to be seriously mentally ill and not to have it treated and deteriorate to the point of being dangerous to self or others is not a right but a cruel neglect on the part of society." Defense attorneys and their own expert witnesses contended, on the other hand, that Ms. Brown was neither psychotic nor a danger to herself. They argued that since she survived one winter on the streets, there was little reason to predict that she would be at risk of harm in the future. Her attorneys concluded: "When someone as intelligent as she decides to live on the street, she clearly has some problems. But so do many others who are not taken into custody. The program may be intended more to clean up the streets than help the seriously mentally ill." Joyce Brown maintained in her own defense that "I like the streets and am entitled to live the way I want to live. I know there are people and places I can go to if I don't choose to be on the streets . . . my rights are being violated."

## The Clash of Legal and Helping Perspectives

Joyce Brown's story provides a context for examining the legal basis for work with involuntary clients. Can a choice to remain on the streets in the cold of winter be an informed choice? Does Joyce Brown, and others like her, have the right to live as she wishes as long as she does not endanger her life or the lives of others? Some suggest that attention to legal issues can distract public attention from the need to address social problems such as the inadequacy of housing alternatives for the homeless.[3]

Her story polarized the positions of interested observers. Whereas on the one hand, many admired her hardiness and the willingness of her defense attorneys to "take on the system" to protect her civil liberties, on the other, many felt that winning this fight for civil liberties would only mean that she had earned the right to die on the streets.[4] There was agreement with Ms. Brown's sisters, who were quoted as saying that "this is not an alternative lifestyle that she has chosen. She can survive one winter, maybe two, but not a lifetime like this."[5]

Helping professionals have often been ambivalent about the expanding role of the legal system in protecting client rights.[6] They have been confronted with the task of learning many new legal procedures, which are then often obsolete by the time they appear in training texts.[7] In fact, the law plays such a large role in current practice with legally mandated clients that practitioners have been urged to "think like lawyers."[8] Lebensohn has noted that "severe mental illness . . . can be as great an impediment to full freedom as iron bars and locked doors. It is one of the great tragedies of our time that countless numbers of mentally ill remain untreated and prisoners of their mental illness all in the name of civil liberty."[9] Attorneys and mental health professionals may approach the same situations from a different perspective such that lawyers are more concerned with the sanctity of legal principles and advocacy of civil rights, while mental health professionals are more inclined to provide help regardless of issues of loss of liberty.[10] Some attorneys argue that this commitment to help often means that practitioners act as if client rights are forfeited upon entering a program.[11] Furthermore, they note that mentally ill, retarded, and juvenile clients who are institutionalized are often members of oppressed groups who have limited power to protect their own rights.

Practitioners working with involuntary clients are often caught in the middle of such controversies over community and individual rights and frequently have to deal with fluctuating standards. The pursuit of legal, ethical, and effective practice involves conscious use of practitioner influence to affect the behaviors, attitudes, and decisions of involuntary clients in some situations and conscious efforts to avoid influence in others. Public practitioners such as the helping professionals in the Joyce Brown case are often mandated to act to protect the community or defenseless persons from self-harm or harm from others. Similarly, practitioners in private settings often attempt to influence nonvoluntary clients and bring to bear agency, referral source, family, as well as their own pressures.

Helping professionals have rarely been trained in how to carry out their legal roles. Social workers, for instance, are advised in their professional code of ethics to "make every effort to foster self-determination on the part of clients," to consider their responsibilities to the client as primary, yet are also told to "adhere to commitments made to the employing agency."[12] As these directives often conflict, social workers are left with difficult choices.[13] Confusion often ensues about the nature of the responsibilities to involuntary clients, family members, the agency, and the community.

One frequently cited solution to these dilemmas is for the agency-based practitioner to be guided primarily by law and agency requirements.[14] In fact, many practitioners begin their professional work with legal inservice training or an informal, trial-and-error approach to learning the law, policies, and procedures, since these areas are often inadequately covered in their academic programs. This chapter will next explore the growth of procedural safeguards for legally mandated clients designed to curb arbitrary discretion and guarantee fundamental fairness such that constitutional rights to life, liberty, and property are not endangered without due process. The perspective presented here is in line with Reed Martin's observation that "rather than assuming there is an inherent conflict between rights and therapy, professionals must realize that appropriate therapeutic intervention includes client rights."[15]

## Principal Legal Issues in Work with Involuntary Clients

Our discussion of legal issues will begin with a brief survey of due process, informed consent, confidentiality and privileged communication, followed by liability and malpractice. This discussion will be followed by brief summaries of applications in mental and physical health, child and public welfare, criminal and juvenile justice, and children's rights.

### Due Process

Under the fifth, eighth, and fourteenth amendments of the U.S. Constitution, citizens are entitled to due process of law before they can be deprived of life, liberty, or property.[16] The fifth amendment guarantees that individuals cannot be required to testify against themselves, while the eighth amendment guarantees freedom from cruel and unusual punishment and the fourteenth amendment states that a citizen cannot be deprived of his or her civil rights without fundamental fairness. Due process safeguards include some or all of the following: the right to adequate notice of charges, an open hearing before an impartial examiner, right to counsel, the rights to cross-examine and present witnesses, right to written decisions giving reasons based on facts, and the right to appeal decisions.[17] The specific forms of notice vary and in some states there is a right to trial by jury.[18]

## Informed Consent

Informed consent refers both to a process of continually informing clients about intervention plans *and* the use of forms so that those clients can provide consent to proposed treatment with adequate knowledge of costs, benefits, and alternative procedures.[19] Informed consent is *not* satisfied by the mere completion of a written form.[20] A valid consent form is not an open-ended, blanket agreement but rather an agreement to specific procedures based on adequate information.[21]

Informed consent is relevant for conditions such as legally involuntary mental commitment, chemical dependency, use of restraints, aversive treatment, isolation, abortion, contraception, sexual disorders, and sterilization.[22] Mental patients also have the right to be informed about treatment, to refuse treatment on religious grounds, and to participate in experimental treatment or research only upon informed consent. Issues of informed consent in research with involuntary clients will be considered in chapter 5.

Valid consent must be obtained without coercion or undue influence such that a person is able to refuse or withdraw consent. However, according to Melton, "the available research raises substantial doubt as to whether most consent in health and mental health care is truly voluntary."[23] For example, Saltzman and Proch note, "Some hospitalizations which are called 'voluntary' are in fact only agreed to under the threat of commitment. Moreover, voluntary hospitalizations often turn into commitments when a voluntary patient seeks to be released."[24] There have been court rulings that institutionalized mental patients are in inherently coercive situations, when release from the institution depends on patient cooperation, such that they may be unable to provide informed consent to intrusive procedures such as psychosurgery.[25] In addition, courts have also ruled that undue force was employed when public aid clients were told that welfare benefits would be withheld unless they agreed to sterilization procedures.[26]

Circumstances do exist, however, in which informed consent is not immediately required: 1) when actions must be taken in genuine emergencies to preserve life; and 2) when a person has a mental illness or incapacitating chemical or alcohol dependency such that they are currently incapable of providing such consent.[27] The ability to provide consent cannot be determined by membership in a general class of persons such as those with severe mental illness, but must be based on a mental status examination. If mental status fluctuates, it may be possible to give or withdraw consent during lucid phases. Standards used to determine competency include the ability to comprehend relevant facts, appreciate one's circumstances, understand and manipulate information, and test reality.[28]

Research on implementation of informed consent suggests, however, that the spirit of informed consent is often violated. Consent forms are often drafted in legal terms incomprehensible to clients, or are often presented as a mere formality, alternative forms of treatment are rarely presented, and full information about negative or harmful side effects is often omitted.[29] Rather than treating informed consent as pro forma, it should be an opportunity to engage in a collaborative relationship consistent with a therapeutic philosophy of basic respect for all people.[30]

## Confidentiality and Privileged Communication

Confidentiality refers to the obligation of helping professionals not to reveal without permission records or client information obtained in the course of practice.[31] Privileged communication refers to client rights to prevent a helping practitioner from testifying against them in a court of law.[32] Some helping professions do not have privileged communication and other have it in some states but not in others. Consequently, practitioners should be prepared for possible subpoena of records.[33] Confidentiality of records such that those records or information contained in them could not be revealed without prior client consent is a goal of the helping professions. However, some professions have more legal rights in some areas than others such that some helping professions can be court-ordered to turn over records. This often leads to keeping superficial records, in order to avoid having to legally turn over information which might be damaging.

Circumstances exist in which a practitioner is required to violate privilege. For example, if a client is currently suicidal or imminently violent toward a certain person, the practitioner is obliged to breach confidentiality for that person's protection or issue a warning to the intended victim.[34] In addition, most practitioners are legally required to report possible child abuse.

Practitioners need to make clear their relationship with clients from the beginning so that clients understand the circumstances under which their confidentiality may be violated.[35] Clients often have legal access to their own records upon notice, and those records should be provided with the confidentiality of others referred to in the records protected.[36]

## Liability and Malpractice

Helping professionals have been increasingly faced with legal liability concerns and malpractice. Malpractice has been defined as professional misconduct, unreasonable lack of skill or fidelity in professional duties, evil practice, or illegal or immoral conduct.[37] Malpractice can be based on incorrect diagnosis or treatment, bad effects of treatment, poor results, failure to appropriately consult or refer, injury resulting from violation of confidentiality or a failure to warn.[38] In order to charge malpractice, it must be established that: 1) there is a legal duty to perform or refrain from performing certain acts; 2) there is a breach of duty in a failure to act or failure to refrain; 3) there is injury to property or person; and 4) there is a causal relation between that breach of duty and injury.[39]

Malpractice has a longer legal history in the medical profession in which the doctor's responsibility to the patient is clearer. For other professionals, such as social workers and family therapists, the person(s) to whom the duty is owed is often less clear. In addition, a professional standard of care must be in place by which the action can be assessed as in an accordance with or a dereliction of duty.

Additional concerns have been raised, however, about the liability of public agency employees, who are now less frequently protected by immunity from litigation.[40] For example, child protection workers can be sued for failure to report or investigate, improper selection of or failure to monitor placement, wrongful removal or detention, and failure to locate permanent placements.[41] The best protection against such suits is careful practice, following procedures which are compliant with the law, keeping good records, and access to adequate supervision.[42]

## Legal Issues in Mental Health

Let us turn now to a brief survey of legal issues in several settings in which mandated and nonvoluntary clients are encountered. Practitioners needing more specific guidance about particular settings should consult cited resources and other texts for more detailed guidance.[43]

Within mental health, discussion will focus on three issues: the least restrictive alternative principle, the right to treatment, and freedom from unnecessary treatment. At issue with Joyce Brown was involuntary civil commitment. Such commitment refers to state-imposed compulsory treatment, hospitalization, confinement, or other restriction of liberty premised on mental illness.[44] Commitment is based on evidence that a person is mentally ill, a danger to self or others, and in need of treatment. The U.S. Supreme Court decided in *O'Connor v. Donaldson* that mental illness alone without danger or need of treatment was insufficient to justify involuntary hospitalization,[45] which in turn led to the development of more restrictive criteria for determining appropriateness of involuntary hospitalization. Joyce Brown's case is pertinent here as some have suggested that the criteria have become too narrow and inappropriately restrictive through hospitalization of the mentally ill homeless.[46]

As involuntary psychiatric commitment is a major instrusion into freedom of action, due process requires the presentation of clear and convincing evidence that people are not competent to manage their own affairs and are in danger of incurring serious harm to themselves or others over a specific time period.[47] Joyce Brown's case arose when the time frame for predicting such danger was expanded from immediate risk of death or injury (within a day or two of the examination) to danger in the foreseeable future. Predicting danger over a longer period becomes more difficult, though a history of dangerous acts has been used to to predict such behavior.[48]

Attorneys and psychiatrists who advocated her hospitalization claimed that Joyce Brown was a danger to herself such that she would quickly deteriorate if returned to the street. She was described as delusional (including a delusion that she had been unfairly incarcerated), unpredictable, and withdrawn. The fact that she had neatly cut up dollar bills and burned them was cited as a ritualistic expression of her mental illness. Other evidence cited for her mental illness were that she defecated on the streets, used an assumed name, and rejected food from caregivers.[49]

Defense attorneys argued that Joyce Brown was a lucid, rational woman down on her luck and not a threat to herself or others. Defense psychiatrists found her to be in excellent health, not psychotic or seriously mentally ill. Her attorney asked the court, as he was also of the opinion that she had been unfairly incarcerated, would he too be considered delusional?

Joyce Brown testified on her own behalf with explanations for her so-called bizarre behavior. She had changed her name to keep her sisters from finding her, since they had earlier tricked her into entering a psychiatric ward. She reported a "daily income" from panhandling of $8 to $10 a day with a budget of $7. As she felt that keeping this excess money on her person at night in the street would put her at risk of robbery and violence, she admitted tearing up paper money but only when people insisted on throwing it at her and only when she had enough: "If money is thrown at me and I don't want it, of course I am going to destroy it. I have heard people say 'Take it, it will make me feel good.' But I say I don't want it. I don't need it. Is it my job to make them feel good by taking their money?" She admitted defecating in the streets since nearby restaurants would not allow her to use their facilities and railroad stations were too far away. She further admitted shouting curses and chasing city outreach workers who offered her food and clothing—including on one occasion throwing a bag lunch at them—because they had already "swooped down" and taken her to a hospital in handcuffs three times: "Every time I was taken there before, I was treated like a criminal. I didn't need their food, their conversation, I didn't need them around."

City psychiatrists had advocated her involuntary hospitalization on the grounds that she had deteriorated significantly in the weeks prior to the hospitalization. After receiving medication at admission to the hospital, she declined further medication until the hearing. City psychiatrists suggested that her rational demeanor in court might be caused by the medication she took upon admission, while defense psychiatrists suggested that the medication would not normally have such a long-lasting effect.

Judge Lippman ruled that the case had not been proven that she could not live safely on the streets, since qualified psychiatric experts for the defense and prosecution disagreed. In his ruling he stated:

She can not be held accountable for being unable to afford an apartment and her decision not to live in a city shelter where conditions are criticized might in fact prove she's quite sane. . . . I am aware that her mode of existence does not conform to conventional standards, that it is an affront to esthetic senses. It is my hope that the plight she represents will also offend the moral conscience and send it to action.

Lost, however, in the controversy over Joyce Brown's case was the judge's praise of the hospitalization program as a useful first step in the the right direction to help the homeless mentally ill, and that twenty-three other people were hospitalized without appeal, while the one other appeal was denied.

At issue here is the degree to which Joyce Brown and persons in her situation are capable of providing informed consent and the definition of criteria which constitute danger to the self. Qualified experts often disagree on predictions of danger. With standards in flux, practitioners work in an ambiguous atmosphere. Her case also demonstrates, unfortunately, how focus on legal rights and therapeutic needs can distract from attention to broader social issues such as the availability of housing and other services.[50]

1. *Least restrictive alternative.* The fourteenth amendment has been further interpreted by some federal district and state courts to include rights to the least restrictive alternative such that when two methods are available that would achieve the same result, the individual is entitled to the form that would restrict least.[51] In Joyce Brown's case, this would

mean that involuntary commitment could be ordered only when less restrictive alternatives were not available or appropriate.[52]

2. *Right to treatment.* Some courts and state statutes have moved to ensure that persons deprived of their liberty for purposes of treatment are entitled to adequate treatment that is not merely custodial.[53] In defense of a right to treatment, Judge Johnson wrote:

> To deprive a citizen of his or her liberty upon the altruistic theory that the interference is for humane and therapeutic reasons and then fail to provide adequate treatment violates the very fundamentals of due process. . . . If adequate treatment is not provided, it is equal to incarceration.[54]

Among the safeguards proposed have been rights to: a) an individual plan of treatment with a goal of better coping or return to the community rather than merely custodial care; b) that that plan is to be the least restrictive necessary to reach treatment goals; c) services that must be considered adequate by professionals and that cannot be deficient because of limited budget allocations; d) medical evaluations within 48 hours of admission to a hospital and ongoing information about the course of treatment; and e) basic rights for committed patients to privacy enjoyed by other hospitalized patients such as use of the telephone and mails.[55] In addition, many institutions are required to have human rights and ethics committees that include representation by outside professionals and attorneys.[56] These proposed guarantees to adequate treatment are not, however, recognized in all states. Questions have also been raised about the limits to court expertise in prescribing standards for treatment and their ability to implement those standards.[57]

3. *Freedom from unnecessary treatment.* The courts have also sought to protect persons involuntarily hospitalized from unnecessary treatment. In the case of extreme procedures such as use of restraints, electroconvulsive shock, and lobotomies, the least restrictive principle requires adequate justification, including informed consent from the patient or a qualified conservator. Under the rights to privacy, use of some mind-altering drugs which have harmful side effects have been opposed as prohibiting freedom of thought.[58]

The range of what is considered necessary and unnecessary treatment is under dispute. Some states now include use of neuroleptic drugs in nonemergency situations among those procedures in which patients are entitled to a legal review.[59] While supporters of this legislation consider such a review an important protection of the rights of the committed from the medication's harmful side effects of questionable benefit, opponents claim that such judicial review of medication is equivalent to practicing medicine without a license.[60] They state further that time now devoted to required medication review hearings takes valuable time away from direct patient contact and damages working relationships.

## Legal Issues with Other Health Care Populations

Ironically, since there is no constitutional right to medical care, those who are voluntarily admitted for treatment do not have the same access to a right for treatment as the involuntarily committed.[61] Informed consent alone is relied upon to protect the rights of voluntary clients. They must therefore be competent to provide voluntary, uncoerced consent that is knowledgeable about consequences and alternatives.[62] Voluntary hospitalization supposedly raises few legal questions since in theory there is no unwanted restriction of individual rights. Saltzman and Proch note, however, that "it may be difficult to determine the voluntariness of consent in certain situations which may be coercive by nature such as when someone is required to execute a consent for the release of full medical records to obtain welfare benefits."[63] Under the schema suggested in chapter 2, this could be nonvoluntary contact based on formal pressures. Even those who are determined legally incompetent can be represented by guardians who are acting under the principle of substituted judgment as they believe the patient would have wanted.[64]

Most nursing home residents are considered voluntary since they are treated in private facilities with the assumption that they are free to leave.[65] Many nursing home residents, however, are placed without a hearing or adequate representation. Once again, these legally voluntary clients may be the "invisible" nonvoluntary with decisions often constrained by pressures from doctors, family members, physical inability to leave, and lack of alternatives.[66] However, nursing home residents who are Medicare or Medicaid recipients are protected by a bill of rights that includes, among others, the rights to be informed about their health and medical condition, to participate in planning total care and treatment, to refuse treatment, to freedom from restraints except under specified conditions of care, to choose a physician, and to be free from physical or mental abuse.[67]

Hospitalization for drug abuse is also presumed to be voluntary, though this voluntarism often includes external pressure from the legal system or elsewhere. Drug abusers cannot be sentenced to participate in a particular program. They must be offered a set of viable choices that can include treatment as an alternative to imprisonment.[68] This nonvoluntary contact based on coerced choice has been questioned by some experts who suggest that the choice be expanded to include at least two alternative forms of treatment in addition to imprisonment. Concerns are raised about rights to free speech, to freedom from cruel and unusual punishment, and due process in some treatment programs. Questions as to intensive confrontation that does not permit the client to defend him or herself and punishments such as standing with nose and toes touching the wall have been raised as to their legality.[69] Melton suggests that there are indeed de facto sanctions when patients have to stay in the hospital to think about their decision while awaiting evaluation.[70]

At this writing, there is additional social pressure to expand civil commitment to drug users who have not committed other crimes.[71] While many believe that acceptance of powerlessness over drugs is an essential first step for recovery, others suggest that civil commitment for drug use will allow drug users to get needed treatment. Drug addicts do not fit current civil commitment laws unless they have committed a crime or are a danger to themselves or others.

## Legal Issues in Child and Public Welfare

Due process rights have expanded in public welfare regarding decisions to deny individual requests for assistance or termination of Aid to Families with Dependent Children (AFDC) benefits. A client in danger of such a revocation is entitled to fair notice, an oral hearing before an impartial examiner, the right to confront and cross-examine witnesses, present witnesses and evidence in support, the right to a written decision based on facts stipulating reasons, and the right to be represented by counsel.[72]

Extensions of due process in child welfare have resulted in rights to adequate preventive services, regular reviews, and orders for temporary custody that are clear and convincing.[73] Decisions about the best interest of the child have also been couched in terms of the least detrimental alternative.[74] Parents have the right to know what approach will be used, for approximately how long, what they can expect from contact, and what is expected of them, including the criteria for completion of the program. They are entitled to know the scope of confidentiality, to be involved in the development of treatment plans, the right to refuse treatment, and to be notified of the cost of that refusal.[75] In addition, Native American children are protected by the Indian Child Welfare Act from inappropriate out-of-home placement unless active efforts to prevent placement have failed.[76]

## Legal Issues in Criminal and Juvenile Justice

Prisons remain perpetually underfunded, understaffed, and overutilized. Prisoners are protected by the eighth amendment against cruel and unusual punishment and by the fourteenth amendment to due process and equal protection under the law.[77] Under the first amendment, they have the rights to use the mail and to legal services, and to adequate medical and health care.[78] Rights to adequate treatment and freedom from unnecessary treatment have also been extended to those who are incarcerated under the protection from cruel and unusual punishment.[79] Treatment is considered cruel and unusual when it is torture or grossly excessive compared to the offense, unfair, or shocking and disgusting to people of reasonable sensitivity.[80] The rights of prisoners have been curtailed by the increasingly prevalent attitude toward the need to maintain order. Hence, the Supreme Court has ruled that prisoners do not have a right to privacy in the cell: they can be searched and property recovered.[81]

Clients on probation and under parole are entitled to procedures of due process relating to revocation. They are to be given adequate notice including the grounds for revocation, they have the right to present witnesses and cross-examine adverse witnesses, they are entitled to presentations based on fact, and they have the right to counsel.[82] Probationary and paroled clients are also protected against self-incrimination, and from cruel and unusual punishment. They have the right to separate hearings for detention, adjudication, and disposition.[83]

Legal rights for delinquents, defined as minors who have violated or attempted to violate any federal, state, or local law, have greatly expanded as a result of the landmark Gault decision of the Supreme Court.[84] Due process protections already accorded adults, such as adequate notification, specific charges, rights to a hearing, a transcript of the proceedings, representation by counsel, and rights against self-incrimination, are extended to juveniles as well.[85]

## Legal Issues in Children's Rights

Some observers have suggested that children are the largest unrepresented minority group, as they cannot vote, and have no political influence or affirmative lobbying.[86] In *Parham v. J. R.*, the Supreme Court ruled that parents could admit children to mental institutions against their wishes.[87] The Court decided that children's rights could be protected between the efforts of parents, the courts, and helping professionals.[88] Children are also frequently involuntary when they enter outpatient counseling. Their very participation is often arranged between parents and counselors and their own treatment goals are often considered secondary to the goals set by parents and therapists.[89] In addition, child victims of abuse are often brought to treatment reluctantly, are sometimes not informed about the purpose of the treatment, and may not see the abuse as a problem.[90]

Some practitioners therefore argue that a potential conflict of interest exists between parental wishes and the rights of the child.[91] Children are entitled to informed consent, to refuse treatment, to treatment which is the least restrictive alternative, and to be fully informed about treatment.[92] According to Christian, Clark, and Luke, "Children have the right to be told the truth, to be treated with personal respect, to be taken seriously, to have meaningful participation in the decision making which applies to them.[93]

## Nonvoluntary Clients

This chapter has focused primarily on legal issues pertaining to legally mandated clients. As I have already noted, however, legal guidance and protection of rights for clients considered legally voluntary are much more limited.[94] Hence, legally voluntary clients such as mental patients, health care recipients, nursing home residents, and children frequently make decisions that are coerced or constrained by other persons, situations, and a lack of alternatives.

In the absence of legal guarantees, Martin urges that practitioners voluntarily extend similar protections to nonvoluntary clients as are accorded legally mandated clients. Nonvoluntary clients should have a right to privacy, to be left alone, unless their overt behavior qualifies them for inclusion in a program.[95] They should have the right to their own thoughts as a basic requirement to ensure freedom of speech.[96] They should be entitled to treatment that is the least restrictive and guaranteed quality of care.[97] Other writers have suggested checklists of legal protections for clients and practitioners in a variety of helping programs (figure 3.1).

## Assessment of Legal Impact on Work with Involuntary Clients

The legal framework is one major element toward a goal of legal, ethical, effective practice. That framework is the basis for when to intervene involuntarily, when not to intervene, and understanding the rights of clients in these circumstances. As a result of expansion of legal guidelines for legally mandated clients, practitioners, agencies, and insti-

## Questions Regarding Client Legal Rights in Treatment Programs

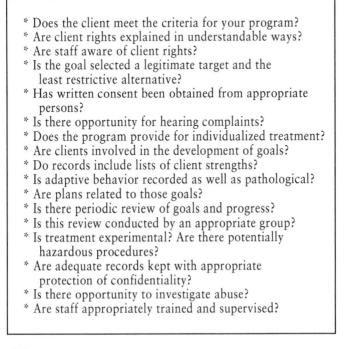

* Does the client meet the criteria for your program?
* Are client rights explained in understandable ways?
* Are staff aware of client rights?
* Is the goal selected a legitimate target and the least restrictive alternative?
* Has written consent been obtained from appropriate persons?
* Is there opportunity for hearing complaints?
* Does the program provide for individualized treatment?
* Are clients involved in the development of goals?
* Do records include lists of client strengths?
* Is adaptive behavior recorded as well as pathological?
* Are plans related to those goals?
* Is there periodic review of goals and progress?
* Is this review conducted by an appropriate group?
* Is treatment experimental? Are there potentially hazardous procedures?
* Are adequate records kept with appropriate protection of confidentiality?
* Is there opportunity to investigate abuse?
* Are staff appropriately trained and supervised?

*Figure 3.1*

tutions have become much more aware of client rights and protective statutes and are engaged in a continual updating of knowledge of changing standards. In addition, more specific criteria for decision making have been developed in key areas concerning restriction of liberty such that many harmful practices have been stopped or reduced. Finally, there is an increased reliance on oversight committees and review boards when decisions which would limit client freedom are considered.[98]

These benefits have not been achieved without cost. For example, the expansion of due process procedures has not created more resources for direct service to clients, and in fact has reduced such direct service provision because of more paperwork and court appearances.[99] Some practitioners fear that an overemphasis on the law and procedures has led to an unwillingness to take risks and a failure to advocate for fear of being sued.[100] Decisions to act have been increasingly dichotimized between either coercive action when legal grounds exist or inaction when legal grounds do not.[101] Furthermore, the focus on the rights of mandated clients has overshadowed the rights of nonvoluntary clients who often face unfair coerced choices. Finally, many helping professionals have reservations about the least restrictive principle when they consider more restrictive means to be more effective and they often question client ability to judge this effectiveness.[102]

Practitioners must work with procedural protections developed to protect the rights of legally involuntary clients.[103] It has been argued that nonvoluntary clients whose capacity to provide informed consent is often constrained by formal and informal pressures should have their rights protected, taking those pressures into account. In chapter 4 I will consider the second base, ethical practice, by focusing attention on the issue of client self-determination and determining appropriate circumstances for paternalistic action which may be contrary to a client's wishes about his or her own welfare.

# The Ethical Foundation for Work with Involuntary Clients

While law provides one foundation for legal, ethical, effective practice, it provides little guidance for practice with nonvoluntary clients who often provide consent under duress. In addition, laws and regulations cannot cover all contingencies in work with mandated clients. When are involuntary clients free to act without influence from practitioners and agencies? When should such influence be attempted? Can mandated intervention sometimes be legal but ethically questionable? Are practitioners only responsible to help involuntary clients cope better with the system or are they also responsible to advocate for changes in that system?

Social workers are guided in their *Code of Ethics* to pursue client self-determination.[1] Yet they are also bound to follow laws and carry out commitments to employing agencies. This chapter will explore guidelines for the pursuit of client self-determination and circumstances in which client interests conflict with the interests of others. Second, the concept of paternalism will be explored in circumstances in which a client's best interest is at stake rather than the protection of third parties. Finally, guidelines for practitioner comportment and behavior with involuntary clients and an integration of legal and ethical perspectives will be presented.

## Self-Determination and Autonomy

Most practitioners would agree that they are committed to the best interests of the client. Disagreement occurs when they have to decide who the client is and what best interest is.[2] Guides to such issues can come from review of the concepts of self-determination and autonomy. Self-determination means action toward one's own goals, wishes, and desires. The concept can be further divided into *positive* self-determination, which means having the knowledge, skills, and resources necessary to pursue one's own goals, and *negative* self-determination, or autonomy, which refers to free acts that are not coerced, or made under duress or undue influence.[3] For example, actions to assist Martha (see chapter 2) in her goal of receiving outpatient help for her depression would be regarded as positive self-determination, while actions to assure that her participation in the inpatient program was not coerced would be negative self-determination.

Does self-determination take precedence in all situations?[4] A critical problem occurs when the rights of one person conflict with the rights of another. Reamer suggests that we have to choose in such situations between prima facie values or ones that, other things being equal, are both acceptable.[5]

John Stuart Mill provided one guide for such choices when he argued that "the sole end for which mankind is warranted, individually or collectively, in interfering with the liberty of any of their number is self-protection, that the only purpose for which power can be rightfully exercised by any member of a civilized community against his will, is to prevent harm to others. His own good, either physical or moral, is not a sufficient warrant. Over himself, over his own body and mind, the individual is sovereign."[6]

While Mill's statement is often quoted as an extreme position on self-determination, Mill cited prevention of harm to others as a condition in which self-determination should not be supported.[7] Many agree with Mill that one person's self-determination stops where another person's begins.[8] In fact, harm to others is generally agreed upon as legitimate grounds for ethical and legal intervention in limiting self-determination. As stated by Reamer, when a client acts to endanger others, the endangered person's right to the basic preconditions to action such as health, food, and livelihood take precedence over the client's right to freedom of action.[9]

Is protection of others the only circumstance that justifies limitations to self-determination? Several writers have suggested that self-determination should be supported: 1) when the rights of others are protected;

2) when client choices are realistic, rational, reasoned, and constructive rather than unexamined impulses; 3) when those choices fit the law, agency, and society; and 4) when those choices are within the client's capacity to self-determine.[10]

I agree with McDermott who suggests that use of criteria such as these results in efforts to contain self-determination by limiting it to socially acceptable, trivial goals.[11] Commitment to self-determination does not mean that the practitioner must agree with unwise client choices. McDermott suggests that persuasive influence toward making better choices can be ethical in such circumstances.[12] Clients can also be helped to distinguish between the changeable and the unchangeable and the range of choices can be increased.[13]

## Paternalism

While there is general agreement on limitation of client self-determination in order to protect others, there is less when such interference is justified solely by the practitioner's judgment of the client's best interest apart from immediate danger to others. Paternalism refers to just such limitations on client self-determination for a person's own good rather than the good of a third party.[14] For example, Joyce Brown's self-determination was limited because of paternalistic concerns for her own safety and well-being rather than for the safety for others (see figure 4.1).

Paternalism may take three forms: 1) opposing client wishes; 2) withholding information from the client; or 3) providing deliberate misinformation thereby manipulating the client to the practitioner's viewpoint.[15] Paternalism is obvious when the client's direct wishes for his or her own good are directly contradicted. Less obvious is paternalism when information is withheld or the client is manipulated to the practitioner's viewpoint. Paternalism is frequently practiced with clients not considered entirely rational, including children and those judged mentally incompetent.[16] Martha, described in chapter 2, experienced paternalism in that her wishes were interfered with, information about alternatives was withheld from her, and she was manipulated to the viewpoint of inpatient staff.

Practitioners such as those working with Martha who practice paternalistically usually assume that they are acting for the clients' own good, that they are sufficiently qualified to judge that good, and that client welfare justifies their action. New York City psychiatrists and staff certainly justified their paternalism with Joyce Brown on just such a basis.

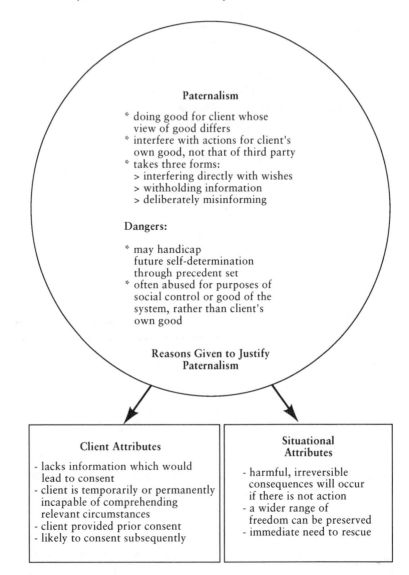

Paternalism

* doing good for client whose
  view of good differs
* interfere with actions for client's
  own good, not that of third party
* takes three forms:
  > interfering directly with wishes
  > withholding information
  > deliberately misinforming

Dangers:

* may handicap
  future self-determination
  through precedent set
* often abused for purposes of
  social control or good of the
  system, rather than client's
  own good

Reasons Given to Justify
Paternalism

Client Attributes

- lacks information which would
  lead to consent
- client is temporarily or permanently
  incapable of comprehending
  relevant circumstances
- client provided prior consent
- likely to consent subsequently

Situational
Attributes

- harmful, irreversible
  consequences will occur
  if there is not action
- a wider range of
  freedom can be preserved
- immediate need to rescue

*Figure 4.1*

Four client attributes are routinely used to justify paternalism:[17] 1)
that clients lack information that would lead them to consent to interference; 2) that clients are temporarily or permanently incapable of comprehending relevant information; 3) that clients have given prior consent

to paternalism; and 4) that such consent is likely to be given later in any event.[18] City psychiatrists probably considered Joyce Brown to be temporarily or permanently incapable of comprehending relevant information. Frederic Reamer suggests that clients may give invalid prior consent to paternalism under duress of a threat of withdrawal of service.[19] In addition, some programs such as chemical dependency may have norms to prevent impulsive decisions to leave treatment.[20]

Three situational attributes are also used to justify paternalism: 1) that harmful consequences are likely to be irreversible without interference; 2) that a wider range of freedom can be preserved by restricting it; and 3) that there is an immediate need to rescue.[21] These criteria are often interpreted so broadly that city psychiatrists might have justified paternalistic action with Joyce Brown under any of them.

This discretionary range in determining potential harm contributed to the legal movement to ensure due process. Paternalism is subject to abuse since paternalistic acts are more often motivated by the interests of the organization or society than by the client's.[22] (Attorneys defending Joyce Brown argued that she might have been hospitalized more out of a desire to remove an unsightly presence from the streets than from any real concern for her own welfare.) Second, once a decision is made to limit self-determination through paternalism, the way is often paved for further limitation.[23] Hence, the fact that Ms. Brown had been hospitalized in the past might be given as a reason for renewed paternalism.

Because of the potential for paternalistic abuse, Frederic Reamer suggests that practitioners and organizations are responsible for providing a compelling case for the need for paternalism rather than holding the client responsible for proving that paternalism is *not* needed.[24] He suggests that ethics committees can be helpful for consulting on difficult cases and for educating practitioners and administrators and developing agency guidelines.[25]

Reamer further proposes guidelines for making paternalistic decisions. He argues that temporary interference to determine whether the conditions of informed choice have been met is justified when clients threaten or actually engage in behavior, such as self-destructive actions or severely debilitating alcohol or drug use, that results in harm to themselves.[26] This interference is justified long enough to determine whether: 1) the action would be incapacitating or fatal; 2) the choice is made voluntarily, knowledgeable of consequences, circumstances, and alternatives; and 3) the proposed interference would not cause physical or economic dependency on others or endangerment.[27] Reamer admits that these guidelines fall short of a precise formula and notes that judgment is called for, concluding, "If we err in the direction of too much intrusion, we risk alienating our client and the sins of commission. If we err in the direction of leaving too much alone, we risk nothing less than neglect and the sins of omission."[28]

## Legal and Ethical Guidelines for Work with Involuntary Clients

While the legal guidelines described in chapter 3 are sometimes consistent with these ethical guidelines, they often point in different directions. Four general guidelines integrating the two perspectives for practitioner behavior with involuntary clients in which legal and ethical guidance is consistent are considered. These will be followed by more specific guidance in a matrix of legal and ethical influences when these influences indicate different directions (see figure 4.2).

### *Informed Consent and Due Process*

As each citizen is constitutionally entitled to due process before rights can be endangered, all clients are entitled to be informed about their rights and programs for which they are eligible, as well as limitations to those rights and programs.[29] In instances in which the client is not competent to provide informed consent, such consent can be sought from proxies who can act to consider the issue as the person judged

## General Legal and Ethical Guidelines

* act to facilitate informed consent and due process
* commitment to empowerment, co-planning and contracting
* commitment to honest communication: avoid manipulation and deception
* advocacy for social justice and fair treatment practices
* inform clients of rights, program eligibility
* act to increase choices
* use and conduct research to assess practice
* affirm problem-solving ability of clients
* affirm dignity, individual worth of clients

*Figure 4.2*

incompetent would have done, in line with their life goals and preferences. Practitioners should describe their own limits and obligations such that clients know about circumstances both in which they are legally entitled to confidentiality and in which practitioners might have to violate that confidentiality or act against client wishes. Pursuit of informed consent and due process with Martha would have entailed informing her of alternatives, and costs and benefits of the choices available.

### Commitment to Empowerment, Co-Planning, and Contracting

One solution to the dilemma of determining who is the client is to pursue the empowerment of involuntary clients within legal limits. Legal requirements do not preclude affirmation of the worth, dignity, and uniqueness of involuntary clients and their ability to resolve problems.[30]

Respect for individual worth and empowerment can be enhanced through the use of contracts. Contracting is a consensual agreement and acceptance of reciprocal obligations and responsibilities to perform certain tasks, and deliver goods within a time-limited period.[31] Contracts are similar to involuntary service agreements used in mandated situations that specify target problems, goals, and client expectations. Service agreements, however, are often "corrupt contracts" imposed on captive clients without negotiation. Such service agreements are less contracts and more "notices of agency intent" or "notices of consequences" analogous to the citation a motorist receives when stopped by a police officer for speeding.[32] Such a citation is not negotiated, though it may offer a coerced choice (paying a fine or appearing in court).

Contracts with mandated clients are obviously not entirely consensual as legal requirements are not negotiable. There are, however, other areas open to discretion and negotiation such that clients can participate in decisions affecting their rights and their range of choices can be broadened.[33] Contracting entails negotiation on such discretionary issues and exploring work on voluntary issues beyond mandated requirements. The practitioner can also help mandated clients be aware of areas which are not covered by their legal restrictions.[34]

As nonvoluntary clients, by definition, do not face legal limitations, contracting is a particularly appropriate way to assure that there is informed consent to proceed on agreed upon problems without duress.[35] Agency policies may specify that clients be aware of constraints involved in their decision to accept services. Specific guidelines for contracting with involuntary clients will be explored below in chapters 9 and 10.

## Commitment to Honest Communication

Professional codes of ethics proscribe exploitation of clients for the practitioner's own gain or satisfaction and practitioners are urged not to use their expertise to dominate or manipulate clients.[36] Manipulation, however, often occurs through keeping plans hidden, maintaining a mysterious distance, and not raising questions an unquestioning client should raise.[37] As Keith-Lucas notes, "Some clients are still given the illusion of free choice when in fact they have been pressured or manipulated into a formal contract that has nothing to do with their real wishes."[38] In addition, deceptive treatment methods have come to some prominence in which clients are not informed about the purpose of activities for fear that foreknowledge might doom the influence and hence deception is "for the client's own good."[39] In addition, there may be superficial agreement with client goals, masking a commitment to a hidden goal. Whittington notes a basic inconsistency between such practices and commitment to client self-determination: "Is there not an inconsistency in believing so firmly in client self-determination, on the one hand, and on the other hand having in mind treatment goals toward which we are trying to move him although he may not know what the goals are?"[40] The motto for such efforts might be: "Start where the client is in order to get him or her to where you want to go!"

Such withholding of information alleged to be for the client's good is paternalism, which should best be considered using the narrow ethical guidelines suggested above. Should voluntary clients choose to remain in a counseling relationship that utilizes deceptive methods, their continuation may be based on agreement concerning the overall goal of contact and satisfaction with progress in counseling. Mandated and nonvoluntary clients, however, suffer consequences in leaving such relationships, and should be protected from the use of deceptive methods when they have not agreed to or have been pressured to accept goals set by the practitioner.[41] Hence, practitioners working with mandated and nonvoluntary clients should avoid use of deceptive methods. Such methods constitute an unethical paternalism and do not lead to the development of a trusting working relationship because of manipulative behavior.[42]

## Advocacy for Social Justice and Fair Treatment

While the above guidelines refer to comportment with individual involuntary clients, practitioners also have ethical responsibilities to advocate for fair treatment for involuntary clients in their setting. The ethical practitioner should challenge demeaning, unfair, discriminatory practices and institutional restraints that limit client opportunities for change.[43] For example, practitioners working with Martha in the hospital could work toward the development of ethics committees that would develop guidelines and training for the use of informed consent, which embodies the spirit of client protections, rather than pro forma use of written releases. Such practices may call for efforts to reform policies from within and form alliances with outside professional groups.[44] Unfortunately, many practitioners are usually better trained in methods for influencing personal rather than structural change.[45] Many are committed to it but do not know how to effectively advocate within and from outside the agency. They have less training in advocacy than interpersonal change. If they do not engage in efforts to humanize services, they are susceptible to providing "social control with a smiling face" (see chapter 14 for further details and guidelines).

## Integrating Legal and Ethical Perspectives in a Matrix

The above four guidelines can be applied generally in involuntary transactions. In order to help the practitioner think about both legal and ethical issues simultaneously, an integrative perspective is needed that asks both legal and ethical questions and suggests possible actions based on those questions. The guiding issue in this perspective is to determine whether there are legal and ethical grounds for restricting client freedom. For such action to be legal and ethical, two sets of criteria need to be satisfied.

The legal questions are: 1) Do you have delegated legal authority to restrict freedom in this instance? 2) Does client behavior fall within the domain of that delegated authority?[46] and 3) Is the decision to take action to limit client freedom based on clear, unbiased criteria?[47]

The principal ethical question is whether there is *imminent danger to self or others.* Ethical action to limit client freedom is justified when irreversible, clear, and present danger will occur if prompt and positive action is not taken.[48] Also, when one person acts to endanger others, the endangered person's rights to health, food, and livelihood take precedence over the client's right to act freely[49] (see figure 4.3).

When the answers to these four questions are affirmative, then action to at least temporarily limit freedom can be both legal and ethical (cell 1 in figure 4.3). Cells two and three refer to unbalanced situations in which legal criteria are met while ethical criteria are not (cell 2), or situations in which ethical criteria are met while legal criteria are not (cell 3).

## Legal-Ethical Matrix

| | Ethical Criteria Met | Ethical Criteria Not Met |
|---|---|---|
| **Legal Criteria Met** | **Cell 1:** Legal, Ethical Intrusion<br><br>1) clarify rights, responsibilities, roles<br>2) distinguish non-negotiable requirements from free choices | **Cell 2:** Intrusion is Legal but Not Ethical<br><br>1) advocate for change in law or policy through internal advocacy or external organization<br>2) overt or covert resistance of policy<br>3) choose to leave agency or setting |
| **Legal Criteria Not Met** | **Cell 3:** Intrusion is Ethical, but Not Legally Based<br><br>1) practitioner must be guided by informed consent and self-determination if legal criteria or grounds for appropriate paternalism do not exist<br>2) attempt ethical persuasion<br>3) offer an incentive to influence choice<br>4) advocate that the harm be made illegal | **Cell 4:** Restrictions on Freedom are Neither Legal nor Ethical<br><br>1) act according to negative self-determination: avoid coercion of choices<br>2) consider positive self-determination in assisting to reach goals |

*Figure 4.3*

Finally, cell 4 refers to circumstances in which there are neither legal nor ethical grounds for interference. Specific guidelines for each cell are suggested in the following sections with case studies to illustrate their use.

*Cell 1: Situations in which limitations on client freedom to act are both ethical and legal.*

In order to explore legal and ethical limitation of freedom, let us consider the following situation. Police have reported to a Minnesota public child welfare agency that two children aged one and two were found home alone while the mother, Agnes Jones, 19, was found across the street in a bar.

1. *Does the practitioner have legal authority?* Following the sequence of legal and ethical questions suggested in figure 4.3, we ask first whether the child protection practitioner has authority and domain over the alleged action. Child protective service does have legal authority and domain over allegations of child abuse, neglect, and sexual abuse. Minnesota state law requires that such allegations be promptly investigated by the child protection agency and that highest priority in conducting such investigations is given to assuring a safe environment for endangered children. A second priority is a preference for giving parents an opportunity to agree to a voluntary plan to assure child safety without removing children from the home.[50] In this case, the answer is yes, the child protection practitioner does have legal authority to investigate the allegation.

2. *Does client behavior fall within the domain of that authority?* Mr. Brown, the child protection worker, consulted agency criteria for assessing danger and found that leaving small children unattended is included within the behaviors justifying investigation.

3. *Is the decision to limit client freedom based on clear, unbiased criteria?* Agency criteria for assessing risk in such conditions include the following: a) the child is exposed to dangerous surroundings, and b) infants or very young children are left alone or in the care of other children too young to protect them.[51] Criteria are less specific in determining what constitutes dangerous surroundings. Stein and Rzepnicki suggest concrete examples such as the presence of exposed wiring will assist in developing clear, objective criteria in order to decide whether to act to limit freedom, thereby making it less subject to the discretion of the investigating practitioner.[52]

Less objective criteria require more discretionary interpretation and hence may be more subject to bias. For example, the agency's own criteria in this case guided Mr. Brown to rate the situation as low-risk if the "parent is remorseful; this is a first incident; the parent seeks help and there were extenuating circumstances" and to rate the situation as high-risk if the parent is "denying responsiblity and blaming others."[53]

In the event, Agnes responded to the investigation by saying that she was out of the home for only a few minutes and was nearby, across the street. In addition, a neighbor was supposed to be checking in with the children. She raged that she should not have to spend all of her young life with babies and if she chose to go out occasionally and have a drink, that was her right. Agnes went on to say that she felt cooped up and wanted to get out to get her GED and a job so that she could get off welfare.

By the agency's parental response criteria, Agnes' children would have been considered at high risk. Such criteria emphasize parental motivation rather than considering normal situational responses to threatening situations. We will explore in chapter 7 alternative explanations for responses to threatening situations. For now, it is sufficient to consider that a negative response to the possible threat of removal of children can be a normal situational response. On the other hand, superficial cooperation may indicate use of ingratiating strategies of self-presentation to neutralize a threat in a less than sincere fashion (see self-presentation strategies in chapter 7). As a consequence of the difficulties in attributing the "real" motivation for hostile and cooperative behaviors, practitioners should place higher emphasis on more objective criteria such as the fact that the children were left alone than on parental responses which may be aggravated by the involuntary nature of the transaction.

4. *Is there imminent danger to self or others?* Leaving small children unattended would also justify ethical action to limit Agnes' freedom if such behavior endangered them. Norms vary in different cultures about child rearing and child safety practices. For example, the age at which children are considered old enough to care for others varies, the length of time they can be left unattended, and the responsibility entrusted to an older child for getting adult help in times of possible danger. It is sufficient here to note that there may be a conflict between what Agnes and her neighbors might consider unsafe practices and the definition of such by the investigating agency. When the practitioner is employed by a legally mandated agency and a legal threshold of danger to others is reached, the client's right to self-determine is temporarily superseded by the rights of others to act freely. In this case, the small children's rights to adequate supervision takes precedence over Ms. Jones' right to free action.

Can such intervention to limit freedom be done in a way that maximizes self-determination within legal limits? General guidelines toward this goal follow; more specific guidance will be provided in chapters 8 and 9.

The first task in ethical and legal intrusion is to clarify rights, responsibilities, and roles. First, the reason for contact should be explained clearly and nonjudgmentally, including the specific criteria that led to contact. Mr. Brown should then clarify what the authority invested in him requires that he and Agnes do. Third, Mr. Brown should clarify Agnes' legal rights.[54] Fourth, any requirements for behavioral change should be interpreted narrowly and should not include implied conditions or threats.[55] Finally, should those behavioral requirements entail work on goals that Agnes does not share, she is entitled to an explanation for those goals.[56]

Next, the practitioner distinguishes non-negotiable requirements from choices the client can make.[57] Mr. Brown can promote self-determination within legal limits toward the goal of achieving a semi-voluntary contract by including non-negotiable requirements, negotiable items, and voluntary concerns of the client.[58] Self-determination in mandated situations can be promoted in at least four ways: 1) reframing the client's own concerns to blend with mandated requirements; 2) emphasizing freedoms untouched by requirements;[59] 3) clarifying areas for discretion and negotiation; and 4) addressing additional client concerns voluntarily or referring them to others.[60] As some mandated clients may not wish to explore these voluntary concerns with a mandated practitioner, referral to other practitioners and the freedom *not* to work on any additional concerns should be emphasized.[61] In sum, the mandated client can be helped to a measure of self-determination by clarifying choices to: 1) not comply with non-negotiable requirements and risk consequences; 2) comply with non-negotiable requirements; and 3) work on additional concerns with the practitioner or someone else.

In Agnes Jones' case, while maintaining the children safely was a non-negotiable priority, establishing whether she could keep custody of them in her home with assistance was negotiable. Mr. Brown noted that he could see that she did care for her children and would not wish them harmed *and* that it was also true that the police report indicated that her small children were at home unsupervised and hence were by agency standards at acute risk. He asked if there had been a fire or other emergency, how might the children have been able to take care of themselves? Since keeping the children safe from harm was a goal they both shared, he suggested that they could plan together for ways to improve her child care relief including arrangements with friends and relatives, day care, and drop-in centers.

Mr. Brown also noted that indeed her drinking that evening and getting out of the house was her own business as long as it did not endanger the children. He also empathized with feeling cooped up, taking care of babies all the time, *and* that it was also true that they were entitled to be in a safe place. He could refer her to others who might help with her goals of getting a GED and a job if she wished. She could also handle these concerns alone or choose to do nothing about these goals at this point. As the non-negotiable requirement was that the children be in a safe environment, court intervention which might involve removal of the children from the home could be avoided if they could agree on a plan for safety.

*Cell 2: Situations in which limitations on client freedom are legal but not ethical.*

The above example assumes that the practitioner has the appropriate authority and that the behavior falls within the domain of that authority. A different circumstance of authority and domain would occur if during the course of a conversation between Agnes and her AFDC worker or her counselor at a mental health clinic, she mentioned that she had left the children alone briefly while she took a "stress break." While neither of these practitioners would have the authority or domain to directly intervene, both are legally mandated to report allegations of possible child abuse and neglect to child protective services.

While making such a report is legally mandated, is it always ethical to do so? Reamer suggests that if the mandated reporter considers the child to be at substantial risk, then the danger should be reported.[62] However, Heymann suggests that reporting some allegations of abuse may be harmful if the loss of control happened once rather than as a pattern, if it happened several years ago rather than currently, and depending on an assessment of what will happen to the parties and the working relationship as a result of reporting.[63] Both Reamer and Heymann describe situations in which reporting resulted in greater harm for clients than not reporting might have done and therefore suggest that there are instances in which following legal requirements to report alleged abuse or neglect would be unethical.

How does a practitioner determine when it is unethical to obey the law? Reamer suggests that while the obligation to obey laws to which one has freely consented ordinarily overrides one's rights to freely violate those laws, circumstances exist in which an individual's rights to well-being may override obedience to those laws.[64]

The point at which the practitioner determines that those individual rights override laws is the problem. In the above abuse or neglect reporting example, Reamer and Heymann seem to be suggesting that the mandated reporter may be able to intuitively assess whether behavior or conditions meet objective standards for abuse and neglect as well as or better than trained child protection workers.

Failure to make a mandated report of possible abuse or neglect is illegal. It is my opinion that practitioners should not make such determinations to violate the law unilaterally. Since clients should be appropriately informed at the beginning of contact about circumstances in which client confidentiality must be violated, they can be informed that a circumstance has occurred in which the practitioner is legally required to make a report. An appropriate ethical and legal response would be to make the mandated report and include, with client permission, any mitigating information, should it be the practitioner's opinion that current conditions do not indicate serious danger. While such reporting may well be harmful to the working relationship with the client, there is also danger when that relationship is valued more highly than risk to a vulnerable person.

Situations do, however, exist in which client rights are being violated while intervention may yet be legal. Consider the situation of Mary, 36, a person with serious and persistent mental illness, who contracted to live in a community residence. Mary was not legally committed to the facility and hence was technically voluntary as she could choose to live elsewhere. As she had limited alternatives for living arrangements, she made a constrained choice to live in the facility.

Mary was not an easy resident; she had trouble remembering when to take her medication, had to be helped with daily living skills such as keeping clean, and had been known to have sudden fears (such that she ran downstairs naked from the bath saying that she was afraid she would drown).

Of particular concern to staff was her preoccupation with talking about going back to school and getting a job. On one occasion, she had taken a bus out of state, without notifying anyone, to look for a job and then had to call staff to come get her when she discovered that she had no place to live. As staff considered her goals of getting a job and going back to school unrealistic at her current state of competence, her obsessive talking about these subjects was irritating to staff and possibly other residents.

Consequently, staff developed a "contract" which stipulated that for every morning in which Mary did *not* talk about going back to school or getting a job, she would be permitted to do whatever she wished in the afternoon and would be rewarded with a soft drink. However, on those mornings in which Mary talked about school or jobs, she would be expected to spend the afternoon in her room with no soft drink. Implicit in the contract was also the threat that Mary might be asked to leave the facility if she did not meet such contracts. In fact, Mary did *not* meet the "contract" and was discharged with a notation in her record that she acted confused and talked about jobs and school to get attention.

Nonvoluntary clients such as Mary may agree to "contracts" such as the above under duress. While it is legal for an institution to develop rules to protect residents and run an orderly facility, there is some question whether the above contract was ethical if marginally legal. While Mary's erratic behavior may have included unrealistic goals and irritated staff and other residents, and limitations to prevent imminent self-harm are legal and ethical, it is difficult to justify limiting Mary's freedom of speech in this fashion. In addition, while Mary enjoyed generating solutions to her own concerns, there is little evidence that staff tried to negotiate with her around any approximations of her goals, such as supported work or private study. In short, the "contract" appears to have been imposed on her as a captive client without negotiation and with coerced agreement under duress. Practitioners should be careful about using their position to impose personal standards or carry out unethical paternalistic acts designed to sustain the organization.[65]

Practitioners have at least three alternatives in situations in which intervention appears to be legal but unethical. First, they can advocate for changes in the law or policy either through internal advocacy or working with outside professional and client organizations. For example, a practitioner in this setting could have questioned whether this contract met appropriate standards for paternalism. She might also have referred the situation to an ethics committee or advocated that such a committee be organized to develop agency policy and clarify client rights. She might also have worked with outside professional organizations or client advocacy groups to develop or publicize existing standards. Similarly, those who consider current reporting laws too broad and require reporting in circumstances which are not considered harmful have alternatives to failure to report. They can advocate that reporting requirements be made more specific to include more serious evidence of harm.

Second, the practitioner may choose to overtly or covertly resist the law or policy. As suggested above, there may be instances in which obeying a law or policy appears to be unethical and some practitioners have chosen to violate the policy openly or covertly. For example, in a school program to assist students who were in danger of dropping out, practitioners discovered a policy that required students who missed more than six days for whatever reasons to be expelled. Some practitioners chose to violate this policy by not reporting some absences which they considered justified. Similarly, the practitioner in Mary's home might have chosen to modify the contract about talking about jobs or work, or spoken with her about those subjects privately.

There can be no firm guidelines about when the line between protection of client interest and obeying laws and policies is crossed. Practitioners are urged to attempt to deal with changing the law or policy openly. Should they choose to resist the law or policy covertly, they should do so with full knowledge of the potential consequences both for themselves, their agencies, and their clients.

Finally, practitioners can choose to leave the agency or setting. There are some instances in which the law or policy that the practitioner considers detrimental to client interest appear to be unchangeable. For example, it is now legal in some states for offenders to be tracked by electronic homing devices and some have argued that helping professionals have no place in implementing such unduly repressive measures to instill conformity.[66] Practitioners who consider practices to be unethical may choose to leave the setting and perhaps advocate more freely from the outside for changes.

*Cell 3: Situations in which limitations on client freedom may be ethical but are not legal.*

Intervention to influence client choices can be ethically appropriate in some situations in which a legal threshold to limit such choices has not been reached. In other situations, practitioners may face ethical decisions in which the law is not an issue. Case studies will be described for each of these two situations.

A neighbor contacted a county agency requesting that an investigation be made about the safety of Alice (whom we met in chapter 1). Under the state law to protect vulnerable adults, the practitioner (Ms. Jones) was mandated to visit Alice and determine whether she might be in danger. Alice, 46 and mentally retarded, had lived alone in a poorly heated rural shack since her mother died two years before. Specifically, there was concern that she might not have adequate heating in the winter and eating off the same plates as her cats might be contaminating her food.

As Alice had lived alone through two previous winters and was informed about heating resources available to her, Ms. Jones assessed that danger from this source was not imminent. Similarly, the cats had not contaminated her food and her health was good. Consequently, Ms. Jones decided there was insufficient grounds to support a petition to declare Alice incompetent. Following figure 4.3, while the practitioner did have the authority and the case fell within her domain, criteria for legal intervention were not met.

Is Ms. Jones' job complete with the determination that coercive action is not justifiable? When paternalism is not justified, Gadow suggests guidelines to assist clients in making informed choices: 1) helping clients clarify their own values and intentions; 2) asking clients what information they need in order to decide; 3) clarifying the practitioner's own position; and 4) stepping back and avoiding interference with client decisions once this process is complete.[67] The client has a right to learn from experiences and even to fail when those actions are not incapacitating.[68]

Ethical concerns are sometimes raised with nonvoluntary clients and private practitioners in which legal issues are not relevant. For example, Mr. and Mrs. Marble sought counseling with a private practitioner about marital issues.[69] Mr. Marble, however, was less voluntary than Mrs. Marble; she had threatened to leave him if he did not seek help for his alcoholism and come with her to counseling. Consequently, Mr. Marble made a coerced choice as a nonvoluntary client influenced by the informal pressure from Mrs. Marble to deal with his alcoholism in an effort to save his marriage. At first, Mr. Marble reported in counseling sessions that he had begun to attend Alcoholics Anonymous sessions and that he had stopped drinking. Quite by accident, Ms. Berg, the private practitioner, encountered a very drunk Mr. Marble in a bar. Mr. Marble pleaded with Ms. Berg not to tell Mrs. Marble about this slip since he really wanted to save the marriage. When Ms. Berg offered to help Mr. Marble tell his wife, he declined, still appealing to her to assist him in deceiving Mrs. Marble.

In the following, four guidelines are suggested to influence practitioner decisions in situations such as with Alice and the Marbles in which action seems ethically compelling but which cannot be required legally.

1.  *If the behavior is not illegal, the practitioner cannot require the client to change and should be guided by informed consent and self-determination.* If harm to self or others has not met legal criteria, then the practitioner cannot coerce the client to change. However, coercion or ignoring are not the only alternatives. The practitioner does not have to support dangerous or unethical actions which are not illegal, and noncoercive influence may be attempted.[70] A first step with Alice would be for Ms. Jones to assure her that she cannot be forced to leave her home or accept services if her situation does not meet legal criteria for acute or imminent danger.

Similarly, Ms. Berg cannot force Mr. Marble to tell his wife that he is drinking again. Ms. Berg can, however, place limits on *her own* behavior even if she cannot coerce Mr. Marble. Ms. Berg can explain that withholding information from Mrs. Marble would be a violation of her professional ethics and she would be forced to withdraw her counseling services. Mr. Marble would be faced with a coerced choice to continue the deception on his own or find a way with Ms. Berg's assistance to share the information with his wife. Ms. Berg is definitely using influence in this case, but Mr. Marble is left with a choice on how he wishes to proceed.

2. *The practitioner can act ethically to attempt persuasion.* Persuasion means helping clients consider the possible consequences of their choices and exploring alternatives in terms of their own best interest. Persuasion is not the same as coercion when the influence attempt is open, does not resort to threats, and ultimately respects the client's power to decide.[71] In reviewing those alternatives and consequences, the practitioner may share his or her own opinions about the client's self-interest.[72] The practitioner can explore voluntary concerns which the client may have and share the concerns of referring sources as a context for decision making. At the end of this exploration, the practitioner should accept the client's decisions about his or her own behavior rather than insist on the practitioner's advice. Should the client express no concern for which he or she wants help, the practitioner should leave, having assisted the client in informed consent through awareness of options and consequences.

Alice was understandably suspicious of an offer from a person who she suspected had power to take away her freedom. She said that she did not want to be put in a hospital and made to give up her home and her cats. Ms. Jones clarified that there was not sufficient danger to make her leave her home and she could choose to continue at home without services. She asked Alice what she thought might happen to her and her cats if there were insufficient heat or if she became ill from contaminated food. In order to avoid such a situation, Ms. Jones was willing to help her become safer in her home. In this regard, she mentioned SSI (Supplemental Security Income) benefits and emergency fuel assistance as resources which might help Alice provide better food and heat for herself and her cats.

As complying with Mr. Marble's deception would be unethical though not illegal, Ms. Berg attempted to persuade Mr. Marble in light of his alternatives and potential consequences, without limiting him to one action. Once those consequences and options were explored, Ms. Berg left Mr. Marble to consider his options and make his choice.

3. *The practitioner can offer an incentive to influence a client choice.* Incentives are consequences which are used to strengthen or increase a behavior.[73] Use of incentives is more intrusive than persuasion but less so than coercion. Inducement should not be used as a barter for basic

necessities but rather as an *additional* benefit which the client can choose to select or ignore.

In this regard, informing Alice about her possible rights to SSI benefits should not be used as an incentive. Ms. Jones might, however, offer to accompany her to Social Security or to have her talk with other clients who received SSI benefits without having to go into the hospital. Similarly, Ms. Berg might offer to assist Mr. Marble in explaining his return to drinking to Mrs. Marble.

4. *Finally, the practitioner can advocate that the legal threshold for harm should be expanded.*[74] If the practitioner thinks that client safety is in fact endangered despite not reaching legal thresholds for coercive intervention, the practitioner can advocate that the legal threshold be changed. For example, practitioners in mental health settings have advocated for limited hospitalizations to determine if clients are competent to make informed choices.[75]

*Cell 4: Situations in which limitations on client freedom is neither legal nor ethical.*

Situations occur in which practitioners are pressured to intervene with clients who have neither done anything illegal nor behaved dangerously to their well-being or others. For instance, while Alice's current situation was assessed as not presenting an immediate danger to her, her choice to live with twenty cats in a dirty home conflicted with community sensibilities.

In such situations, commitment to the principle of *negative self-determination* applies first. Voluntary choices which neither cause serious danger to self or others, nor physical or economic dependency, nor violate laws, should not be subject to undue influence.[76] As stated above, the practitioner may register her disagreement with a plan and help the client explore alternatives, but the client ultimately has the right to decide. Hence, Alice could be reassured that she has the right to determine where and how she will live and is not required to accept services so long as those decisions do not harm her or violate laws.

Second, *positive self-determination* should be considered. In addition to not opposing or coercing client choices, how can those choices be positively supported? Ms. Jones could offer a contract to Alice to help her maintain her independence, protect herself and her cats through the winter, or attain other goals which Alice desired. Part of self-determination is respecting that Alice has every right to decline this offer, however well intentioned and potentially supportive of Alice's interests the offer may be.

This chapter has described the ethical foundation for work with involuntary clients. While legal and ethical issues with involuntary clients deserve books of their own, practitioners have limited time to review the relevant issues thoroughly in a turbulent, demanding environment. Confronted with decisions that need to be made quickly, and reports that must be written, practitioners need flexible guidelines for making decisions. The proposed guidelines fall short of precise prescriptions but move beyond impotence in the face of dilemmas.

While these guidelines should assist practitioners in making difficult decisions and improving local conditions, they fall short of the kinds of changes needed to ameliorate prejudicial societal conditions, such as inadequate resources, which may engender deviance and hence produce involuntary clients. Entire treatment institutions have been found to violate both legal rights to adequate treatment and the most basic ethical standards of respect for human dignity. While practitioners do not have the legal power to close down such institutions, they can advocate for better conditions, greater access to resources, and more fair treatment for clients. It may feel safer for practitioners to report illegal or unethical methods in *another* institution rather than their own. While it may be harder for an employee of an institution to risk their job security to report unethical or illegal methods, work with institutional ethics committees can reduce the risk to an individual who reports such matters.

Should practitioners ignore issues of prejudice and unfair conditions in the larger society, they run the risk of providing social control with a smiling face: using otherwise ethical means to pursue unethical goals. Many practitioners resolve these conflicts by following orders and leaving concern for law and ethics to others, while others attempt to resolve the tension by "fleeing" to private practice. Consent under duress, however, is a pervasive problem which will still follow them in work with nonvoluntary clients despite the setting.

The choice to pursue legal, ethical practice means making judgments and decisions committed to both law and ethics. Pursuit of such a course does not avoid conflicts; involuntary clients have negative reactions when freedoms are limited, however ethically or legally done. Similarly, pursuit of such a legal and ethical course may conflict with agency practices which are unduly paternalistic, which include corrupt contracts or notices of consequences rather than legitimate contracts. Such pursuit may also mean advocating that legal thresholds be changed to include more people who are in clear and present danger of "dying with their rights on." While pursuing a legal and ethical course will bring conflict, it may also assure personal self-respect and integrity as no small benefit.

As effective practice augments legal and ethical practice as the third foundation, chapter 5 will hence review evidence about effectiveness in work with involuntary clients.

# Research on Effectiveness
# with Involuntary Clients

The previous four chapters provide a conceptual basis for understanding the context of work with involuntary clients and principles for legal, ethical practice. As practitioners not only want to *understand* that context but also to *intervene effectively*, this chapter provides a review of studies of effective intervention with involuntary clients. By effectiveness we mean *the power to produce a desired effect* and by efficiency we mean *doing so with little waste*. This review is presented in the form of generalizations that will be a basis for the specific practice guidelines presented later in chapters 8 through 13.

Given the relative lack of attention to involuntary clients compared to practice with voluntary clients, the generalizations presented in this chapter are necessarily preliminary. A major reason for the lack of research is necessary attention to avoidance of coerced involvement in research for legally mandated clients. The chapter will begin with a brief review of the ethical issues in research with involuntary clients. As coerced involvement in research is illegal for most legally mandated clients, and truly informed consent free from pressure is hard to get, there have been limitations on access to data for research on practice with involuntary clients. I will review the evidence that has supported the belief that "nothing works" with involuntary clients. I will then examine three summary generalizations about effectiveness with involuntary clients. Finally, generalizations about treatment adherence will be presented.

## The Ethics of Research with Involuntary Clients

A fundamental tenet of research ethics is that human subjects should be protected from harm caused by participation in research.[1] Consequently, research with human subjects is governed by the principles of informed consent described above in chapter 3. Emphasis on informed consent results from a tragic history of harm and death befalling unwilling or unknowing participants in biomedical research.[2]* Unwilling participants in biomedical research in the concentration camps under Nazi rule died as a result of the "research" conducted there. Uninformed participants infected with syphillis continued to be observed in the United States from 1932 into the 1970s, well beyond the development of antibiotics that might have aided their condition.

There are special problems in the application of informed consent principles to involuntary clients since their ability to provide informed, competent consent without force or duress cannot be assumed. Mandated clients in restricted environments such as prisoners and mental patients may be especially susceptible to small inducements such as being excused from a work assignment.[3] Similarly, nonvoluntary clients may find that the request to participate in research comes from a person with power to decide whether they can receive the treatment service at all, and hence imply a subtle persuasion. For example, if research participation is presented as part of a "package deal" to a nonvoluntary applicant who received court pressure to "seek" a domestic abuse treatment program, then the applicant may face a constrained choice to accept the package deal, look elsewhere for scarce services, or return to court. Even when acceptance into a treatment program is not connected to research participation, involuntary clients may believe that more favorable treatment will ensue if they "choose" to participate in research, or that they will receive less favorable treatment if research participation is declined.

Such concerns raise important questions about the potential costs and risks to involuntary clients as individuals because of participation in research. These risks must, however, be balanced with the potential benefits to society of expanding knowledge about effective service. For example, if research is so restricted as to discourage its use, then practice may continue with untested, possibly ineffective treatment methods.[4]

---

* MDBO

Research on effectiveness can, for instance, determine whether restriction of freedom is necessary to reach desired outcomes or is actually cruel and unusual punishment. Hence research on effectiveness may both protect clients from serving as guinea pigs for untested interventions and aid institutions and agencies in discovering effective and eliminating ineffective interventions.

Some suggest that restrictions have unduly limited research with human subjects and argue that unobtrusive research methods such as standardized tests and secondary analysis of data should not be subject to the same restrictions applied to biomedical research.[5] Similarly, Davidson and Stuart suggest a continuum of informed consent protections, ranging from no consent needed in observation studies with no potential for harm as assessed by a research review panel, to informed consent and multiple review panels for higher-risk interventions.[6] This continuum is useful in balancing benefit to society with considerations of potential risk to participants.

It is my position that research with involuntary clients must address these costs and benefits and define acceptable risk for individuals and society.[7] These questions need to be addressed in a way that both protects involuntary clients from danger and also protects society's right to discover methods that are safe, humane, and effective. Guidelines that consider both costs and benefits to involuntary clients and to society are suggested below.

1. *Informed consent must be sought from persons competent to provide it.* When competence is questionable, then consent must be sought from surrogates such as parents, guardians, and legal representatives.[8] The request for consent must include an appraisal of possible discomforts, risks, benefits, and alternate procedures.

2. *Consent must be voluntary, free from coercion or undue influence.* A review panel should assess potential for duress in securing consent in both mandated and nonvoluntary settings. Such an assessment should include:

a. Use of inducements must avoid an unwarranted effect on the decision to participate.

b. Implied influence should be avoided by making sure that the person requesting research participation does *not* have an authority relationship with the client.

c. It should be explicit that there will not be more favorable treatment for those who agree to participate in research or unfavorable for those who decline.[9]

d. Participants must be free to withdraw consent at any time.
e. Confidentiality of information shared in research must be guaranteed.
f. The research should yield results not obtainable in less obtrusive ways such that any discomfort or risk to participants must be outweighed by benefits to society.[10]
g. Deception should be avoided or minimized by debriefing participants after research participation.

Employment of these guidelines should provide involuntary clients with a fair opportunity to decide whether to participate in research or not. Since involuntary clients perceive restriction of freedom as part of the definition of involuntary status, it should be expected that many involuntary clients will exercise one of their limited freedoms by sometimes choosing *not* to participate in research. Hence, those involuntary clients who voluntarily choose to participate in research may *not* be representative of the population. As Videka-Sherman noted in her review of social work effectiveness in mental health settings, "It is also true that involuntary social services are underrepresented in this sample since human subjects review and the ethics of social research depend on clients' willingness to participate in the research. This willingness is, in all likelihood, associated with willingness to participate in treatment.[11] While generalizations from studies employing free, uncoerced research participation to other clients who choose not to participate in research may have limited applicability, knowledge about those participants would not be gained at the expense of individual rights.

## "Nothing Works" with Involuntary Clients

It has been conventional wisdom in social work, other helping professions, and fields such as corrections, treatment of alcoholism, and child maltreatment that outcomes with involuntary clients are less successful than outcomes with voluntary clients. Social work's pessimism about the effectiveness of work with involuntary clients is partly based in broader reviews of social work effectiveness. When Fischer looked at experimental studies of social work practice conducted between 1930 and 1972, he found that none of the eleven studies reviewed clearly showed positive, significantly measurable changes, and he concluded that "at present, lack of evidence of the effectiveness of professional casework is the rule rather than the exception."[12]

While Fischer's review is well known in social work, the fact that five of the eleven studies reviewed were conducted with predelinquent, probably involuntary clients is less so. None of the five studies suggested that social work services prevented delinquency.[13] For example, Meyer, Borgatta, and Jones concluded in a three-year study of intervention with predelinquent girls: "The conclusion must be stated in the negative when it is asked whether social work intervention with potential problem high school girls was . . . effective."[14]

When Katherine Wood reviewed the studies reported by Fischer, as well as eleven additional studies that included quasi-experimental designs, she also concluded that "the outcomes of these studies indicate that group work or psychotherapeutically oriented casework used alone or as the major intervention, have not been effective in preventing or ameliorating delinquency."[15] Wood went on to identify the first major clue to effectiveness: the lack of fit between client and practitioner motivation as a factor in the low outcomes of earlier research.

> None of the studies began with the adolescents' own perceptions of what their problems were and what help they needed. . . . The intervention did not grow out of a contract between helper and helped concerning problems and goals that were meaningful to the clients. Thus there could be no investment in or commitment to change on the part of the clients, that is, no "motivation." With no agreed upon problem areas for work and no contracted goals, neither clients nor workers could have been clear about what was the clients' share of the change task and what was the workers' responsibility.[16]

The negative findings about delinquency prevention in social work were similar to other findings about treatment of deliquents such that it became conventional wisdom that "nothing works." This contention was further supported by Martinson's conclusion in his 1974 review of 231 research studies completed prior to 1967. "With few and isolated exceptions, the rehabilitative efforts that have been reported so far have had no appreciable effects on recidivism."[17] Shireman and Reamer respond that Martinson's conclusion that nothing works is overdrawn since many programs with at least quasi-experimental designs have been shown to be effective.[18] For instance, there are indications that intensive supervision of probation is associated with reduced recidivism among males and females under age eighteen.[19] Further, Adams notes that the point of view that "nothing works is a meaningless piece of correctional wisdom. It offers no credible basis for planning, decision making and research in corrections."[20] Despite the fact that this conclusion may be overdrawn, it does appear that there is little reason to believe that a clear way has been found to reduce recidivism among delinquents since even for successful programs, it remains high. Shireman and Reamer echo Wood's theme about a lack of motivational fit:

Subjects have quite commonly been drawn into programs intending to produce change in their attitudes, behaviors and life styles and life situations without regard as to whether they wished to be targets of intervention. We are only now beginning to realize the frequent futility of such endeavors.[21]

## Summary Generalizations Regarding Effective Interventions with Involuntary Clients

In this section, three summary generalizations from the subsequent research evidence will be presented.[22] These include: 1) court-ordered clients can achieve as successful results as legally voluntary clients; 2) voluntary clients are rarely distinguished from nonvoluntary clients in the data collection; and 3) clues to more positive outcomes appear to be based in client-practitioner interaction including *motivational congruence*. Interventions toward motivational congruence include: a) enhancing choices and sense of personal control; b) enhancing socialization into appropriate roles; c) use of behavioral contracting; and d) facilitating treatment adherence through client commitment to goals and participation in task design and selection. Each of these generalizations will be examined in more detail.

1. *Court-ordered clients can achieve as successful outcomes as legally voluntary clients.* Recent reviews have suggested more positive outcomes with court-ordered clients. For example, Videka-Sherman found in her review of social work studies in mental health that "clients' motivation for intervention as indicated by voluntary participation was not associated with differential outcomes as indicated. . . . In fact, studies of clients with mixed or involuntary motivation yielded higher . . . effect sizes for the more severely impaired population."[23]

Brehm and Smith reach a similar conclusion in their review of involuntary outcomes in the psychology literature: "Though many therapists and counselors are firmly convinced that successful therapeutic outcomes are substantially more difficult to achieve with nonvoluntary client populations, the results of applied (and therefore, necessarily correlational) research on this issue have not provided support for this belief."[24]

Four studies cited by Brehm and Smith will be briefly reviewed here to assess their support for this conclusion. Three of the four studies explicitly refer to involuntary clients in the context of mental commitments while the fourth refers to adolescents in residential placement. In the first study, Gove and Fain found in a follow-up telephone interview study that legally committed mental patients were as favorable about treatment as those not legally committed.[25] Similarly, Spensley, Edwards, and White found no significant differences in satisfaction at follow-up between involuntary and voluntary patients, though involuntary patients tended to rate lower satisfaction than voluntary patients on variables such as "To what extent were you treated with dignity?" and "How satisfied were you with treatment?"[26] These two studies are limited by their use of self-report measures compounded by the fact that interviews were conducted by hospital personnel. Consequently, interviewers' identification with the setting may have led to inflated descriptions of satisfaction and well-being in the community.

A third study, by Goldenberg, Smith, and Townes, remedies some of these deficits by including measures of behavioral improvement. Involuntary and voluntary patients had similar ratings on the Missouri Inpatient Behavior Scale (MIBS) with considerable pre- to post-treatment improvement. The authors conclude that "response patterns in the MIBS ratings showed both groups apparently benefiting from their stays in the hospital. . . . The apparent homogeneity of patient groups suggests that classification as voluntary or involuntary patients may not be a useful distinction. . . . Clearly little evidence was found suggesting that involuntary patients' initial reluctance continued throughout treatment."[27]

A fourth study, by Bastien and Adelman, suggests that outcomes may be less predicted by legal status of the client than the process of interaction between the involuntary client and the practitioner or agency. This study was conducted with court-referred and nonlegally mandated adolescent residents of a social rehabilitation center. Their hypotheses that court-referred adolescents would perceive less choice to participate in treatment and would achieve lesser overall outcomes than those not court-referred was *not* supported. In a retrospective examination of factors that might have effected choice to participate in treatment, the authors found that court-referred residents who had preplacement visits, found the staff willing to reconsider objectives after a trial period, and were *as likely to perceive choice to participate in treatment* as those clients who in fact were not legally mandated.[28] This initial perception of choice was related to a favorable initial attitude toward treatment but only weakly related to the choice to *remain* in the program and to overall outcome. The choice to *remain in the program* was significantly associated with overall case outcome as measured by a self-rating, a counselor rating, and program graduation status.[29]

There is also a growing body of evidence in the fields of treatment for alcoholism and child abuse and neglect that court-ordered intervention can be effective. For example, many reviewers of the alcoholism treatment literature conclude that outcomes with court-mandated referrals are as successful as voluntary referrals when those court mandates are enforced and long-lasting.[30] However, these results have to take into consideration the fact that relapse is frequent even for those who enter treatment voluntarily: 90 percent of those who drink do so again at some point.[31]

Many reviewers conclude that some form of coercion is often necessary to motivate change.[32] On the other hand, the utility of coercion should not be overemphasized since longitudinal studies suggest that mandated alcohol abuse patients often cease treatment when their court orders end regardless of how favorably they may feel about the program.[33] Hence, Freedberg suggests that the effect of coercive means lessens over time.[34] While coercion may be necessary to lead to treatment, maintaining high pressure may have negative consequences in the long term.[35] Reviewers of progress with court-ordered chemical abuse treatment suggest that such coercion is worthwhile even if the results do not last beyond the court order as the participation in treatment, working on goals, and avoiding criminal behavior is beneficial at least for that time period.[36]

Similarly, Irueste-Montes and Montes found that court-mandated participants in a treatment program for child maltreatment participated at comparable levels to those who were not mandated. Parents court-ordered into treatment had similar attendance and similar significant increases in use of praise and reductions in criticism, to parents not court-ordered.[37] They cite other studies that also indicate that court-ordered leverage is helpful in inducing compliance and reducing dropout rates compared to voluntary clients.[38]

2. *Voluntary clients are rarely distinguished from nonvoluntary clients in the conduct of research.* Research on treatment effects has evolved from concerns about whether intervention is generally effective to more specific questions about what form of intervention works with what sort of client and problem under what conditions.[39] Such intervention research, however, has continued to focus little attention on client variables and even less on the importance of client voluntarism.[40] For example, *The Handbook of Psychotherapy and Behavior Change* does not include a chapter on involuntary clients, and the most similar group considered, disadvantaged clients, have received less study in the past ten years than in the previous ten.[41] Similarly, Reid and Hanrahan reported that the proportion of social work effectiveness studies based in public settings, and hence more likely to include involuntary clients, decreased from an earlier review by Fischer in 1973.[42] In 1985, Videka-Sherman noted in her review of 142 studies of social work intervention

in mental health that "a striking characteristic of studies reviewed is their lack of description of client characteristics."[43]

Even when client voluntarism is considered as a variable, comparisons are usually made between court-ordered clients and legally voluntary clients whose participation in treatment has been coerced. These "voluntary" clients may in fact be the nonvoluntary clients described in chapter 2. The first four studies reviewed above compared legally mandated mental patients and adolescents court-ordered into residential treatment with voluntary clients from the same settings. These legally voluntary clients may have in fact been nonvoluntary. Hence, comparisons between involuntary and voluntary clients in settings such as psychiatric hospitals and residential treatment might be better seen as comparisons between mandated and nonvoluntary clients who may have received services as a result of constrained or coerced choices.

There are similar comparisons between court-ordered clients and legally voluntary clients in studies of coerced intervention in alcoholism, drug treatment, and child maltreatment. For example, Flores notes in his study of the effectiveness of coercion with DWI participants that "voluntary clients" in the study were influenced by coercive, but nonlegal pressures: "unhappy spouses, worried friends, concerned doctors, and disgruntled bosses all make up a contingency that often uses subtle pressure to force individuals with different types of problems into counseling when those individuals do not agree that they have a problem."[44] Similarly, Peyrot defines "coerced voluntarism" in the treatment of drug-dependent persons that is only partly voluntary. He suggests that the influx of involuntary clients into a voluntary drug treatment system creates a status that is officially voluntary, yet always subject to recall by the social control system if clients fail to comply.[45] Finally, Irueste-Montes and Montes note that the so-called voluntary clients in their study of court-mandated service for child maltreatment were all involved with child protective services. These clients did not have legal consequences, but they were "encouraged or pressured to attend."[46]

In addition, other studies of voluntary clients may, in fact, include many nonvoluntary clients. For example, Edleson reports that men participating in a study of a domestic abuse program were voluntary while also reporting that all came in at a time of crisis, frequently involving a separation from the spouse.[47] Tolman and Bhosley, on the other hand, consider such men as partner-mandated if not court-mandated.[48] It may more accurate to consider such programs as typically involuntary, containing in some instances men mandated by courts and many nonvoluntary clients pressured by formal or partner-mandated, informal sources and situations.

A first step to a more solid empirical base with involuntary clients in the future will be to clarify client referral status. Referral through legal mandates should be noted as such. Clients who enter contact through formal or informal pressure such that the decision to seek treatment was coerced or constrained rather than self-motivated should be noted as nonvoluntary.

3. *Motivational congruence between client and practitioner is an important clue toward effective intervention with involuntary clients.* Reid and Hanrahan describe this fit between client motivation and what the practitioner attempts to provide as motivational congruence. They updated Fischer's earlier review by assessing twenty-two additional studies conducted between 1973 and 1979 and reported "grounds for optimism" based on their finding that positive outcomes were reported in eighteen of the studies reviewed.[49] They suggest that such congruence may be a factor in the more positive results found in their review of social casework effectiveness. The lack of fit between practitioner and client goals had also emerged earlier as an explanation for client dropout from casework and other forms of treatment.[50]

Videka-Sherman explores motivational congruence as a possible explanation for her findings of similar outcomes between involuntary and voluntary clients and suggests that "the interaction between practitioner and client once the client (captive or not) arrives for treatment better captures . . . motivational congruence than whether the client was voluntarily or involuntarily referred."[51]

How can such motivational congruence be attained or enhanced? A further review of the literature suggests that congruence can be enhanced by a) emphasizing choices and a sense of self-control; b) socialization to role expectations; c) behavioral contracting; and d) supporting treatment adherence by facilitating client commitment and participation in task design and selection.

a. *Enhancement of choices and sense of control.* Perceived lack of voluntarism can be reduced by emphasizing choices and a sense of control. Brehm and Smith suggest that

thus while the specific determinants of perceived choice to receive treatment are far from clear and may not parallel official status as voluntary and nonvoluntary, there is some support for the inference that once perceived, personal choice to remain in treatment has a beneficial effect on treatment effectiveness.[52]

Many laboratory analog studies suggest that subjects do better when given a choice of treatment. For example, snake-phobic subjects were more likely to approach a snake if they could select the treatment that would deal with this fear, or study behavior is increased when students can select the treatment program.[53] The clinical application of these studies has been limited, however, by their artificiality, short duration, focus on nonclinical populations, and use of self-report measures.

Mendonca and Brehm addressed some of these limitations in an experiment conducted in a clinical setting designed to test the impact of perceived choice with a more extensive intervention and using objective measures.[54] One half of the children enrolled in a weight loss program were randomly assigned to a "take control" condition in which choices were enhanced. The control group in fact received the same treatment program as the "enhanced choice" group but without being offered choices in the structure of the program. At the termination of treatment, children in the enhanced choice group had lost significantly more weight than the children in the no choice group. Mendonca and Brehm conclude that this is "the strongest evidence to date that treatment benefits can be gained by providing clients with their choice of treatment."[55]

The perception of choice of treatment in this study was in fact illusory since the experimenters provided the same treatment to both groups. Illusion of control is defined by Langer as an expectation of personal success that is inappropriately higher than objective probability would suggest.[56] Langer conducted an experiment in which subjects were led to believe that they might influence the outcomes of coin tossing through procedures such as encouragement to compete, coin tossing practice, and becoming familiar with the "site" of the contest. Subjects being manipulated by this false sense of control came to expect more control over the outcome than the objective reality suggested: an illusion of control.

Langer suggests that such a sense of control might be usefully enhanced in settings in which a sense of personal control is normally quite limited, such as nursing homes.[57] She conducted several studies with nursing home residents which found that residents who could predict when they would receive visitors had significantly increased alertness and stability over residents who received a form of treatment that emphasized staff care, and these differences were maintained and increased at follow-up.[58]

Similar findings about the importance of perceived choice have been found in studies of alcoholism treatment. Miller notes in his secondary review that people are most likely to persist in actions that they perceive as personally chosen and when they have alternatives from which to choose.[59] Such perceived freedom of choice is reported to reduce rates of drop-out.[60]

Since the research suggests that a client does not have to actually *be* in control in order to perceive control, should the practitioner stimulate an *illusion* of control while maintaining control over outcomes with involuntary clients? While some therapists do advocate encouraging such an illusion while maintaining real control over the process themselves,[61] I believe that real choices need to be separated from outcomes that the client cannot influence. For example, while mandated clients may not be able to avoid treatment, they may be able to make choices about the type of treatment they receive.[62] Miller notes that court-ordered status is not inconsistent with choices for participants in alcoholism treatment programs: "Even with a population required to seek treatment (e.g., drunk driving offenders), it is feasible to offer a choice among a variety of alternative treatments and to foster the perception of personal control over the change process."[63]

Sense of control can be enhanced with nonvoluntary clients by reminding them that they do not have to choose to be in treatment. Personal control and a sense of personal responsibility should be encouraged when such client efforts are likely to succeed.[64] Even in potentially successful situations, enhancing responsibility can, however, have negative side effects such as increased anxiety if clients are not confident of their ability to choose. In addition, should their choice fail, self-esteem can suffer. On the other hand, enhanced choices can produce fewer excuses for failure.[65] When clients cannot influence outcomes, they can be encouraged to avoid taking responsibility for the outcome, to learn how to endure it. For example, if length of stay in a treatment program cannot be influenced by client input, they are better advised to focus their attention on other goals such as reaching treatment objectives.[66] The success of enhancing choice interventions may be more limited for involuntary clients than for voluntary, however, as they may be inclined to take choices less seriously in an overall context of lack of control.[67]

b. *Socialization methods may assist in enhancing motivational congruence.* Role preparation is referred to in social work as socialization for treatment and has been found to be a powerful intervention. Videka-Sherman found such socialization methods to be the one intervention technique predicting better outcomes in all subsets of her review of social work mental health studies: "The better-informed the client is concerning what will occur during treatment and what the client should be doing for his or her part of the treatment process, the more likely the client is to derive benefit from the experience."[68] Similarly, pretherapy training to clarify expected behavior has had successful results as a solution to the problem of premature termination in psychotherapy.[69]

Socialization methods have received less study with involuntary clients but results are promising. Brekke found that men in a domestic-abuse treatment program who attended an intensive workshop at the beginning of contact were more likely to stay in treatment than men not attending the workshop.[70] Similarly, Tolman and Bhosley found those men attending an intensive workshop had higher attendance rates than nonattenders for the first five sessions, though differences were no longer significant at ten sessions. The authors suggest that such socialization methods may be important in achieving a good start but may have a diminished impact on later outcome.[71]

 c. *Behavioral contracting enhances motivational congruence.* Contracting refers to an agreement between the client and practitioner that sets forth the purpose of the interaction and processes through which the goal is to be achieved.[72] Similar to pretherapy training and socialization, contracts have been suggested as a means of preventing premature drop-out.[73] Reid and Hanrahan identified behavioral contracting as an important variable explaining the more positive results found in their review of casework effectiveness: "The technique of behavioral contracting has shown considerable potential . . . in which the practitioner secures from clients commitments to undertake specific problem-solving action.[74] Rubin echoes this conclusion in his updated review of the next five years: "A prominent commonality among the studies was the use of highly structured forms of practice that were well-explicated and specific about the problems the social workers sought to resolve, the goals they sought to accomplish and the procedures used to achieve these ends.[75]

 Nonvoluntary clients in the child welfare system were included among the studies that led to these conclusions. For example, Stein, Gambrill, and Wiltse found that those parents receiving a behavioral contracting approach were significantly more likely to have their children returned to their custody than families receiving traditional child welfare services.[76]

 Seabury suggests, however, that involuntary clients are among the most difficult groups with which to establish a contract.[77] In support of this conclusion, he refers to a public social service study comparing the responses of voluntary and mandated clients to contracting. Workers rated the usefulness of contracting with the 41 voluntary client families more highly than for the 36 mandated families: 90 percent of the voluntary families were rated as clear about case objectives, 80 percent about tasks, and 63 percent completed tasks while less than a third of the involuntary families were rated as clear about objectives or completed tasks.[78] Seabury concludes that it is more difficult to establish common agreement when the client fails to recognize a problem or doesn't look on the worker as a person who can help.[79] In addition, he suggests that the rational competence required to engage in contracting may rule out extremely disturbed, retarded, or brain-damaged clients and young children, though secondary contracts may be negotiated with family members and advocates.[80] Seabury considers contracting to be problematic but possible with involuntary clients: "It is crucial that the terms of the legal arrangement be distinguished from the stipulations of the social work contract."[81] Hence, we find a similar theme to the recommendation above related to enhanced choices that it is *critically important to separate negotiable from non-negotiable items.*[82]

d. *Treatment adherence can be facilitated through client participation in goal and task selection.* Meichenbaum and Turk suggest that the term noncompliance means failing to follow through with the practitioner's instructions. It implies that the patient or client is at fault. They recommend treatment adherence as a substitute term that implies active, voluntary collaboration, choice, and mutuality.[83] Evidence in support of their emphasis on mutuality is that follow-through on setting up appointments is as high as 75 percent when initiated by the patient.[84]

Meichenbaum and Turk suggest that nonadherence may refer to a variety of types rather than a single problem behavior: those who never adhere may be different than those who do so occasionally and also from those who adhere, but do so inappropriately.[85] Whatever the cause, nonadherence is a very frequent occurrence among the seemingly voluntary population of persons with physical illnesses. An estimated 30 to 60 percent of patients fail to take medications or discontinue them early, and 25 to 50 percent fail to follow through on referrals. In addition, relapse rates for addictions and alcoholism have been reported as ranging from 50 to 75 percent within 12 months of completing treatment.[86] Such failure to comply has even been high in conditions of severe, relatively immediate danger to the patient: only 42 percent of patients suffering from glaucoma who were told that they would go blind if they did not take eye drops three times a day took the medication. Those patients who subsequently lost sight in one eye through noncompliance then only increased their medical compliance to 58 percent![87]

Six factors have been put forward to increase treatment adherence: 1) make a specific request or instigation rather than a vague one; 2) overt commitments from clients to comply are associated with higher compliance; 3) training in performing the task; 4) positive reinforcement of the task; 5) tasks that require little discomfort or difficulty; and 6) client participation in the selection and design of tasks.[88]

Given such high rates of nonadherence on the part of voluntary patients, nonadherence with involuntary clients can be expected to be as high. In the absence of studies about facilitating treatment adherence with involuntary clients, the above factors are suggested as provisional guides to enhancing treatment adherence.

This chapter is the first of two exploring the knowledge base of effective intervention with involuntary clients. That knowledge base has been limited by lack of focus, varied quality of studies, and less than conclusive results.[89] These limitations may in part reflect appropriate protections for mandated clients from participating in research against their will. Further studies are needed that specify the level of voluntarism, the extent of choices and their implementation, the nature of the treatment and involuntary client responses to it, as well as more specific applications to problems and populations.[90]

A review of the effectiveness literature also suggests that legally mandated clients can have more successful results than had earlier been thought to be the case. However, these more positive results contain the caution that coerced intervention often produces *time-limited* benefits that do not last beyond the use of the external pressure. In addition, it was noted that comparisons between involuntary and "voluntary" clients often appear to be comparisons between mandated and nonvoluntary clients.

Further clues to effectiveness suggest that interaction between practitioner and client plays an important part in achieving these improved outcomes. Specifically, interventions designed to enhance motivational congruence between practitioner and client are promising sources for effective intervention. Motivational congruence should not, however, be construed as easily achieved with involuntary clients. Many choices are so constricted as to be negligible. In addition, as treatment adherence has been shown to be problematic with voluntary clients, there is little reason to expect it to be less so with involuntary clients. Mandated service agencies and institutions have community protection goals that impose obstacles to the pursuit of high congruence. Even when the setting affirms goals of congruence, time, resources, and practitioner discretion is needed to implement those goals. Such pressures often create a reactive stance that impedes the extra efforts required to seek congruence. In addition, public opinion often pressures agencies into punitive approaches and away from approaches seen as "coddling" wrong-doers.

With these reservations, the pursuit of motivational congruence is promising toward a goal of legal, ethical, and effective practice with involuntary clients. Such efforts deserve experimentation and study to enhance compliance while respecting involuntary client legal rights and their self-determination.

Several clues to effectiveness in the pursuit of motivational congruence have been suggested. Enhancement of perceived choice is the first such clue. Since nonvoluntary clients can legally choose to refuse treatment, notification of such freedom is recommended for work with all nonvoluntary clients. As such a choice may bring some negative consequences as well as benefits, these consequences should be explored in assisting nonvoluntary clients in making such decisions. Perceived choice can also be enhanced with mandated clients when they are encouraged to make constrained choices between acceptable options, including the choice to accept legal consequences rather than participate in treatment programs.

Manipulation of the *appearance* of choice for clients while withholding actual choices conflicts with guidelines suggested in chapter 4 regarding honest communication and restricting unethical paternalism. A more ethical choice is to make very clear the distinction between those issues that are required and non-negotiable and distinguishing them from issues in which clients have free choices or choices among constrained alternatives.

Additional clues include socialization and behavioral contracting methods that clarify such distinctions between the negotiable and the non-negotiable. Finally, guidelines for increasing treatment adherence including soliciting specific commitments and client participation in task selection were suggested.

The clues to intervention effectiveness developed in this chapter will be transformed into more specific practice guidelines in chapters 8 through 13. We move next in chapter 6 to review effectiveness in relation to more specific practitioner influence methods such as use of rewards, punishments, and persuasion.

# Influencing Behaviors
# and Attitudes

Practitioners trained to work with voluntary clients often prefer to see themselves as helping clients make informed choices, or facilitating their growth, rather than influencing their behavior and attitudes. Both voluntary and involuntary clients and practitioners engage in continual efforts to influence one another, whether such efforts are conscious or not.[1] For example, a client's verbal behavior has been shown to be conditioned through the interpretation of nonverbal cues from the therapist such as head nods.[2] Denial or unconscious use of influence is particularly problematic with involuntary clients since that influence is often evident to the involuntary client if not the practitioner.

We will review methods for influencing behaviors and attitudes which range on a continuum of intrusiveness into choices available to involuntary clients (see figure 6.1).[3] *Compliance-oriented methods* are at the high end of the intrusiveness continuum as they directly influence actions and attitudes through punishing undesirable events and rewarding desirable events. *Persuasion methods* are at the lower end of the continuum as they influence actions and attitudes through providing information rather than manipulating rewards and constraints. Both compliance-oriented and persuasion methods have important roles for involuntary clients, with relatively more frequent use of compliance methods with mandated clients and more frequent use of persuasion with nonvoluntary clients. The characteristics, advantages, disadvan-

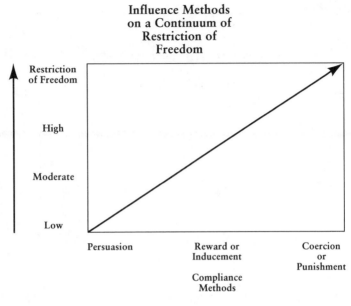

**Influence Methods on a Continuum of Restriction of Freedom**

*Figure 6.1*

tages, and guidelines for legal, ethical, and effective use of each form of influence will be presented. More attention is devoted, however, to persuasion methods, since appropriate use raises fewer ethical problems and practitioners and programs tend to be less knowledgeable about its use. Compliance-oriented methods will be introduced with the following case study.

> Gerald, 16, lived in a small residential facility for adolescents with behavior problems. As frequently occurs in such settings, the treatment program included a specific set of rules and procedures, such as rewards for approved behavior and penalties for disapproved behavior. A *token economy* system was used in which Gerald could earn points for good behavior that would accrue toward obtaining rewards.[4] For example, he could earn one point for each hour in which positive behaviors, such as paying attention in school, were demonstrated. The system also included penalties for infractions of the rules. For example, swearing, acting in a way considered rude or sarcastic by a counselor, or failure to comply with a counselor's request would result in a warning. After three such warnings, a

punishment in the form of a half-hour of work such as scrubbing windows would be administered.

If, however, the form of negative behavior included aggression toward self or others, attempts to run away, or property destruction, use of alcohol or drugs, the half-hour penalty was immediately administered. In addition, residents who were being disciplined were to "process" their punishment by discussing the reasons for the penalty with the counselor. While a punishment was being processed, residents were not to watch television, interact with peers, use the telephone, or smoke.

Gerald had been in the setting for three months and had been earning steady rewards as well as a normal amount of penalties for his behavior. On one occasion, however, Gerald returned to the group home under the influence of marijuana after a weekend visit with his parents. The counselor on duty noted his dilated pupils and the distinctive aroma of marijuana. When asked, Gerald acknowledged that he had been smoking marijuana. Returning to the group home under the influence of alcohol or other drugs was a clear rule violation. Gerald was told that the processing of the appropriate penalty would occur the next afternoon when he returned from school.

The next afternoon, Gerald did not "process" the discussion of the rule violation calmly. He was described as sarcastic by the counselors and was assessed a time-out to calm himself. Gerald was still irate after the ten-minute time-out and a half-hour restitution penalty was inflicted. Gerald refused to comply with the penalty and threatened the staff. When staff attempted to restrain Gerald, he broke free and broke a panel in a door. After he was successfully restrained and first aid applied to his cuts, two more penalties were issued. At this point, Gerald had lost 1,000 points for aggression toward self and others, had earned five hours of restitution, and further unsupervised home visits were now suspended. In addition, he was now suspended from outings with peers for six months. Staff told Gerald that he had hurt his parents by violating the rules: they could no longer have unsupervised home visits with him. Gerald became angry and had to be restrained once again.

Gerald had lost so many rewards and accrued so much punishment at this point, that there was little incentive for him to try to succeed in the program. We will explore in the following sections how a compliance-oriented system can both work effectively and ethically to limit behavior and also go wrong, as in this case, to acquire its own momentum and produce results worse than the behavior that they were designed to curb. We will also explore how a better understanding of compliance methods might have permitted a different result.

## Compliance-Oriented Methods

Compliance behavior occurs when a person accepts influence in order to escape a punishment or achieve a reward or approval.[5] Such methods are appropriately used to protect others and to modify behavior dangerous to the client. The residential program where Gerald was placed attempted to use compliance methods to reach individual and institutional goals. Many practitioners in mandated and institutional settings use compliance-oriented methods, yet may find such methods to conflict with their training as helpers.[6] In addition, such methods may be inadvertently used by practitioners and agencies not trained in appropriate use. For example, a severely depressed resident of an inpatient psychiatric unit was urged by staff to describe her feelings about childhood incidents in which she had been physically abused. The resident became very anxious about this pressure to remember and made a suicide attempt after staff continued to press her to "talk about her pain." Hence, while the ventilation was intended to be therapeutic, the pressure was experienced as punishing.

While compliance-oriented methods are ethically neutral and are sometimes used with clients who have little input into goals and methods, use of contracts that specify negotiable and non-negotiable items is preferred.[7] Such approaches have been used with many involuntary populations, including clients with severe and persistent mental illness, men with battering problems, and problems such as child abuse and neglect, alcoholism, and delinquency.[8]

Compliance-oriented approaches make important assumptions that can be helpful in involuntary situations. By considering behavior as learned, attention can be focused on changing contingencies, observing models, and rewarding alternative behaviors rather than dwelling on unchangable past events.[9] In addition, cognitive behavioral approaches have been used with problems such as wife battering by identifying chains of thoughts and behavior and learning alternative cognitive and behavioral responses; there have been impressive results in reducing the incidence of violent behavior.[10] While it is beyond the scope of this book to examine compliance-oriented approaches in detail or to include all the involuntary populations with which they have been used, key concepts for use with involuntary clients will be reviewed.

### Punishment

*Punishment* or constraint is the most intrusive compliance method. It refers to methods intended to stop or reduce an unwanted behavior through administration of adverse consequences or withholding positive consequences.[11] There are five major types of punishment. *Positive punishment* refers to the use of an aversive consequence when an unwanted stimulus occurs. For example, alcoholic clients have taken emetics to curb drinking. In the above example, when Gerald became violent, staff attempts to restrain him were positive punishment. It should be noted here that the term "positive" should not be construed to mean that this form of punishment is appropriate; it only identifies a particular form of punishment. Hence, Gerald's restraint may have been inappropriate yet would be defined as positive punishment. *Response cost* refers to withholding reinforcements when an unwanted behavior occurs. Hence, suspending Gerald's outings with other residents and unsupervised home visits was a form of response cost.[12] *Negative reinforcement* uses an aversive consequence to stop an unwanted behavior, then follows with a positive reinforcement as soon as the client emits a positive behavior. Hence, negative reinforcement is a coerced choice since some responses are rewarded. If Gerald could have immediately begun to acquire positive points toward regaining privileges following response cost, negative reinforcement would have been used more appropriately.

*Overcorrection* methods can be used to teach alternative behavior incompatible with the unwanted behavior. For example, restitution can be used to both provide an appropriate punishment and also reinforce prosocial behavior. Restitution is used in some victim-offender reconciliation programs that involve meetings between property offenders and their victims in which the form of restitution for damage done is negotiated between the two parties. Such methods may meet some of the real purposes of punishment by putting the offender in touch with the harm he or she caused.[13] Since the drug violation occurred while Gerald was under his parents' supervision, a meeting with Gerald and his parents might have more directly addressed the causes of the rule violation and assisted in the construction of an appropriate response. If Gerald and his parents had been consulted in the choice and design of appropriate penalties, their belief in the appropriateness of the penalty might be greater.[14] Finally, *time-out* can be used as an extinction method by

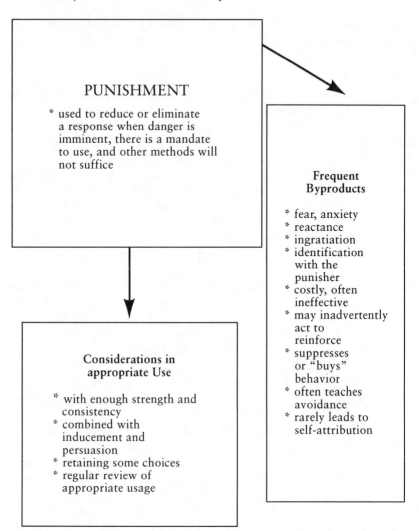

## PUNISHMENT

* used to reduce or eliminate
  a response when danger is
  imminent, there is a mandate
  to use, and other methods will
  not suffice

**Frequent
Byproducts**

* fear, anxiety
* reactance
* ingratiation
* identification
  with the
  punisher
* costly, often
  ineffective
* may inadvertently
  act to
  reinforce
* suppresses
  or "buys"
  behavior
* often teaches
  avoidance
* rarely leads to
  self-attribution

**Considerations in
appropriate Use**

* with enough strength and
  consistency
* combined with
  inducement and
  persuasion
* retaining some choices
* regular review of
  appropriate usage

*Figure 6.2*

withholding reinforcement in a nonpunitive environment, and applying it without scolding. When Gerald was sent to his room for ten minutes, this was considered time-out. Each of these five punishment methods can be used legally, ethically, and effectively in certain situations (see figure 6.2).

*Legal use of punishment.* As described in chapter 4, use of coercion is legal when the practitioner has a mandated responsibility, client behavior falls within the domain of that mandate, and criteria for employment of punishment are clear and appropriately followed. Appropriate oversight boards must develop and periodically review use of intrusive procedures such as restraints.[15] In this case, the circumstances of the use of restraint with Gerald should have been reviewed by an oversight board to determine whether in fact there was immediate danger to Gerald or others.

*Ethical use of punishment.* Use of punishment is ethical when harmful behavior or behavior at high risk of injury to the person or others occurs, when less intrusive methods are ineffective such that few alternatives can be reinforced or reinforcers removed, and when there is a panel to regularly review appropriate use of the method.[16] There is question here whether there was risk of any immediate injury to Gerald or whether less intrusive methods such as consultation with Gerald and his parents about restitution could have been attempted. As noted in chapter 4, punishment and other paternalistic behavior often arises to meet the needs of the institution rather than based on more limited, situation-specific penalties.

In addition, nonvoluntary clients in residential institutions have fewer legal protections from inappropriate use of punishment than do legally mandated clients.[17] We saw, for example, in chapter 4 how Mary, a client with serious and persistent mental illness living in a commmunity facility, was restricted to her room for talking about getting a job, despite a lack of evidence that such behavior was in fact harmful to her or others. Practitioners should act to protect client rights when compliance-oriented methods are used to regulate social deviance in matters that are neither dangerous to others nor illegal. Such methods are in particular danger of overuse with members of oppressed groups and others labeled deviant, such as those who have come to be institutionalized.[18]

*Effective use of punishment.* The effective use of punishment assumes that the practitioner has access to aversives powerful enough to stop the behavior, that the punishment is administered quickly and consistently, and that the practitioner is prepared for the drawbacks that frequently accompany its use.[19] As seen in chapter 5, the threat of punishment may be useful to induce some involuntary clients, such as those who drive while intoxicated, to enter treatment.[20] However, evidence on its effectiveness in maintaining clients in treatment or maintaining changes after treatment is less positive.[21]

Punishment works most effectively when it is used to stop or reduce a harmful behavior in the short run. Hence, the penalties that Gerald received might have had an effect in immediate reduction of use of marijuana. Punishment tends, however, to *suppress* the harmful behavior rather than eliminate it and usually does not change attitudes.[22] Since aversives work best when they are powerful and consistent, the lack of power or consistency too often results in the client learning how to *avoid* getting caught for a similar offense, rather than questioning the offense. This undesired consequence of learning avoidance rather than new attitudes may help explain why some domestic violence treatment programs report that participants are more likely to succeed in reducing physical violence while psychological violence such as shouting and otherwise intimidating the spouse may *increase*.[23] Hence, if participation in the treatment program was perceived as punishing, the results would suggest that participants may be learning how to avoid further coerced participation in such programs without modifying basic attitudes toward domination of partners. Similarly, if punishment is not combined with other forms of influence with Gerald, the most important thing he may have learned from this incident is to stop smoking marijuana *earlier* in the day before returning to the facility, to avoid detection, rather than change his beliefs about use of the drug.

Additional problems occur when aversives are neither powerful nor consistent. When this occurs, clients may learn to avoid punishment by lying, deceiving, or acting in an ingratiating fashion. Further, client beliefs in punishment as a solution to interpersonal problems may be inadvertently reinforced, that "might makes right," and lead to a displacement of aggression onto others outside the situation. Use of punishment is also frequently associated with increased fear, hostility, and feelings of powerlessness and helplessness. Furthermore, punishment does not necessarily reduce attraction to prohibited behavior but may, in fact, cause it to be more valued. Finally, if the reason for punishment is not clear, it may inadvertently punish other positive, desirable behaviors.[24] In this case, Gerald's desire to smoke marijuana *again* when unsupervised may have increased and his general collaboration in the positively oriented token economy system may have decreased.

Effective use of punishment requires control of sufficient aversive resources. These resources may need to be used indefinitely if alternative behavior does not become reinforcing or client attitudes change such that clients choose to continue the alternate behavior. Further, when a relationship begins on the basis of punishment, it is difficult to change to a relationship based on reward or persuasion as the practitioner and agency may be only associated with punishment.

However, access to sufficient coercive resources contains its own dangers. Availability of coercive resources encourages their use to exercise control and exert retribution.[25] Continued use of punishment can contribute to alienation and distancing from clients, including labeling and blaming those clients for negative responses to its use. There is little doubt that in the circumstance described, staff response focused primarily on Gerald's negative response to sanctions rather than questioning the appropriateness of their use.

Finally, punishment may continue to be used despite evidence that it is not stopping, and may in fact be reinforcing, behavior. Despite ineffective use, practitioners and agencies may be inclined to use "more of the same" punishment strategies as a relief of tension for the punisher. Hence, punishment once used may be continued habitually without reexamination of its appropriateness or effectiveness.[26] For example, I once worked with an elementary school client who was sent to the principal's office daily for classroom misbehavior. As she found the principal's accepting attitude and attention reinforcing, she misbehaved daily and was "punished" by going to the rewarding environment of the principal's office. In Gerald's case, we saw punishment escalate to produce a worse outcome than the infraction. A review should have been conducted when a clearly undesirable result had occurred from following procedures. In Gerald's case, the immediate escalating administration of punishment with little alternative for returning to the generally positive behavior that had characterized his stay prior to the infraction should have been reviewed.

## Inducement

Inducement is a second compliance-oriented method that occurs when a person is influenced by the hope of receiving a reward.[27] Inducement is used to increase a behavior through providing rewards contingent on performance of that desired behavior (see figure 6.3).[28] Use of inducements will be discussed below based on consideration of the following case study.

Nathan Brown had a serious and persistent mental illness. In order to receive public assistance, Nathan had to demonstrate reasonable efforts to gain employment. While Nathan was faithful in making the required number of job applications, he was never selected for a job interview. One reason for this failure was the fact that Nathan did not take regular baths, wash his clothes, or shave. His

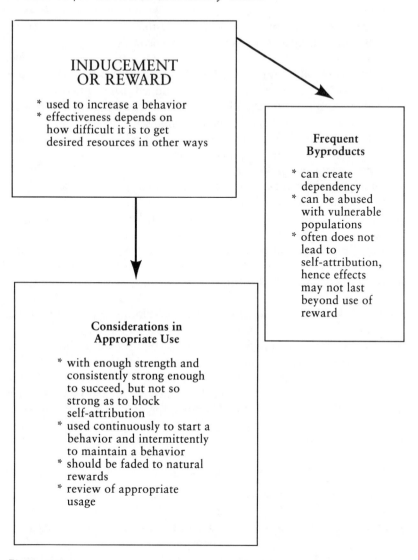

**INDUCEMENT
OR REWARD**

* used to increase a behavior
* effectiveness depends on
  how difficult it is to get
  desired resources in other ways

**Frequent
Byproducts**

* can create
  dependency
* can be abused
  with vulnerable
  populations
* often does not
  lead to
  self-attribution,
  hence effects
  may not last
  beyond use of
  reward

**Considerations in
Appropriate Use**

* with enough strength and
  consistently strong enough
  to succeed, but not so
  strong as to block
  self-attribution
* used continuously to start a
  behavior and intermittently
  to maintain a behavior
* should be faded to natural
  rewards
* review of appropriate
  usage

*Figure 6.3*

public assistance worker proposed that for a one-month period he
be offered the option of working on hygiene instead of making job
applications.

Nathan acknowledged the hygiene problem and wanted to get a
job, but had not succeeded on his own in improving his hygiene.

He agreed to a plan that called for a gradually increasing number of shaves, showers, and clothes washings prior to job interviews. He understood that at the end of this trial period he would be expected to try and maintain the new cleanliness habits into a renewed job search.

Nathan's hygiene tasks were now successful and the resumed job search began to result in some actual job interviews. In addition, Nathan reported that friends had begun to compliment him on his cleanliness.

Inducement can be less intrusive than coercion by providing a *choice* to begin a behavior influenced by available rewards rather than stimulated by avoidance of punishment. Hence, in Nathan's case, carrying out hygiene tasks was reinforced by the reward of public assistance and the temporary suspension of job search expectations.

However, such choices are typically constrained by limited access to alternative resources. A decision to not try the behavior desired by the persons controlling the resources often means choosing to get along without the desired resource. In this case, Nathan had a constrained choice of continuing to carry out job interviews or participating in the alternative hygiene program, or choosing not to apply for assistance. In the sections that follow, guidelines for the legal, ethical, and effective use of inducement will be explored.

*Legal issues in use of inducement.* Institutional programs such as the one in which Gerald was placed have long used token economies in which residents can earn tokens or points toward larger rewards though performing desired behavior.[29] Courts have ruled, however, that some penal programs have started at such a low baseline level that the program was in fact punishing rather than rewarding. Specifically, programs that used sleeping quarters conditions and adequate food as rewards were found to constitute cruel and unusual punishment.[30] Hence the legal guideline here is that *inducements are not to be used to negotiate or bargain for basic rights and necessities. Inducements should be an additional resource such that a person could choose not to accept the resource.*[31]

Rewards are often used in nonvoluntary conditions with fewer checks and balances. The same legal guidelines for mandated clients should apply for the protection of nonvoluntary clients in institutional and other settings. Nathan could at least choose to continue to receive public assistance by rejecting the hygiene option and proceeding with job search requirements.

*Ethical issues in use of inducement.* While superficially inducement poses fewer ethical problems in work with involuntary clients than punishment, ethical problems also arise. As suggested in chapter 4, inducement can be used appropriately to support alternatives when behavior harmful to the self or others is occurring. Too often, however, inducements are used to exploit vulnerable clients and reinforce dependency. For example, for rewards to be effective, clients must not have ready alternative access to them. Consequently, rewards are most effective with vulnerable clients who have limited resources.

Such limited alternative access can lead to misuse and abuse of the power to dispense the resource. We considered Mary's situation in chapter 4 in which she could earn soft drinks if she avoided discussion of her career plans. Had Mary ready access to money or soft drinks, this inducement might have been ineffective. In Nathan's case, we see that his limited access to other sources of income made him vulnerable to income inducements.

Does control of such resources lead to abuse with vulnerable clients? It has been suggested with behaviorally disordered schoolchildren that docility is the implicit goal.[32] Agency or practitioner control, or a monopoly of scarce resources means that compliant behavior may be elicited through discriminating or even indiscriminate use of such resources. It should also be considered that clients who are subject to a unilateral monopoly of scarce resources may attempt to restore the balance by "cheating," gaining access to the resource in other ways, and making coalitions with others in the same situations.[33] In this case, Mary's wish to consider career plans was neither a threat to her well-being nor others, so use of rewards to stop her discussion of such plans would be an inappropriate use of the power to reward. Extracting more change than is necessary to meet agreed upon treatment goals violates professional values.[34] Hence the ethical guideline in use of inducements is that their use *should empower the person and reduce dependency*. Too often, however, continued dependency on the practitioner and rewards from the program occur.[35]

*Effectiveness issues with inducement.* Inducement can be effectively used to begin a behavior. For that behavior to be maintained, however, inducement should be phased out and replaced by natural reinforcers and combined with other influence methods such as persuasion. *Continuous reinforcement* means providing an inducement *each* time a desired event occurs and is the best way to support a new behavior. That inducement must be strong enough to reinforce the behavior and applied consistently. Continuous reinforcement is often begun by rewarding successive approximations of the desired behavior. For example, starting with requests for a small number of hygiene activities from Nathan that gradually increase follows this principle.

Inducement is similar to punishment in that it is more successful at initiating a behavior than maintaining it after rewards have been discontinued. Behavior is best maintained by *intermittent reinforcement schedules* in which artificial rewards are decreased and natural rewards are substituted.[36] Behaviors are most likely to be maintained if the person attributes to themselves the reasons for continuing the reward.[37] This can be done by pointing out naturally occurring rewards.

Should rewards be *too* strong, attitudes toward the changed behavior are unlikely to change since the person is likely to perceive their compliance as forced by the promise of gaining a reward. Personal responsibility for the change is unlikely as the person may perceive that their behavior was "bought." For example, while Nathan was aware that his original compliance with the new plan was "bought" with the promise of continued assistance for this behavior, the behavior was maintained by natural reinforcers when he reported that others were complimenting him on his change. The practitioner in this case had begun with an approximation of a continuous reinforcement schedule, and lessened that reinforcement as natural reinforcers began to have an effect. While programs should work toward reduced use of inducement, frequently such programs are not well programmed to phase out rewards.

If Nathan should now say to himself and others that he was carrying out a different hygiene program because it helped him get job interviews and other people complimented him about the change, then the change would be self-attributed and would be more likely to be maintained than if he said that he persisted in the new behavior because his financial assistance was dependent on it. Following the principle of supporting self-attributed change, practitioners should use small inducements where possible, and practitioner support, praise, and encouragement for behavioral changes should not be overemphasized such that personal responsiblity for changes can be supported.[38]

We have seen that punishment strategies can be used effectively in combination with inducement in negative reinforcement. In Nathan's case, the choice to accept neither a job search nor the option of completing hygiene tasks would have resulted in denial of assistance.

When the use of inducement is contemplated, the following questions are suggested:

1. Does the situation involve such danger to self or others that a form of punishment would work more quickly and safely?

2. Is inducement used to exploit clients who are in a vulnerable state? Has it been applied in a "package deal" to reinforce attitudes, behaviors, and beliefs that are neither illegal nor dangerous? More positively, is inducement applied to limited behaviors that are clearly supportive of treatment goals agreed upon in a contract?

3. Is inducement used toward empowerment and reduced dependence?

## Persuasion

Persuasion methods are used to influence behavior and attitudes by providing additional information or reasons for making particular choices.[39] Persuasion methods can often be less intrusive and more helpful in promoting self-attributed change than compliance-oriented methods. In the sections that follow, principles for attempting persuasion and legal, ethical, and effectiveness implications of persuasion with involuntary clients will be explored.

These principles will be explored by the case study of Wilmer Jones. Wilmer had a serious and persistent mental illness that had earlier resulted in involuntary hospitalization but that now allowed him to live in the community when he took anti-psychotic medication. There was a continual struggle with his community care practitioner, Ann, however, about taking the medication. She was concerned that failure to take the medication would result in a return to the hospital. Wilmer resisted persuasion attempts, saying that the medication gave him a dry mouth, grogginess, fuzzy perception, and that it deprived him of religious experiences. Ann first referred Wilmer to a physician for a possible change of medication and dosage. However, Wilmer continued to dislike and distrust medications. Several persuasion principles were useful in working with Wilmer.

Three central assumptions about attitude change serve as a basis for most persuasion strategies (see figure 6.4). *Clients may be more inclined to change a behavior or attitude if it is shown to be inconsistent with a deeply held belief.* Several theories of attitude change share the assumption that consistency among attitudes, beliefs, and behaviors is satisfying and that inconsistency is unsatisfying.[40] Awareness of such an inconsistency is defined as *cognitive dissonance* that often leads to efforts to reduce that unsatisfying dissonance by changing attitudes, beliefs, or

## Persuasion Assumptions

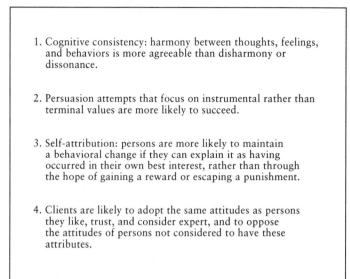

1. Cognitive consistency: harmony between thoughts, feelings, and behaviors is more agreeable than disharmony or dissonance.

2. Persuasion attempts that focus on instrumental rather than terminal values are more likely to succeed.

3. Self-attribution: persons are more likely to maintain a behavioral change if they can explain it as having occurred in their own best interest, rather than through the hope of gaining a reward or escaping a punishment.

4. Clients are likely to adopt the same attitudes as persons they like, trust, and consider expert, and to oppose the attitudes of persons not considered to have these attributes.

*Figure 6.4*

behaviors.[41] Hence, efforts to modify attitudes will be more likely to succeed if they connect with a belief already deeply felt by the person. For example, Ann determined, in talking with Wilmer, that he greatly valued living independently in the community. Taking anti-psychotic medication that had many unpleasant side effects was by no means highly valued. Some cognitive dissonance was then stimulated by exploring whether avoiding his medication was likely to result in his desired goal of living independently in the community.

*Attitudes are more likely to change around instrumental values than around terminal values.* Terminal values are desirable states of existence worth attaining. For example, having a comfortable life, a sense of accomplishment, and true friendship would be terminal values for many persons. Instrumental values relate to what the person considers to be desirable ways of acting and behaving. Hence, to be honest is an instrumental value for many people. Instrumental values are often pursued as a means to reach terminal values as terminal values are more likely to be central to the person than instrumental values. The more central the value, the more difficult it is to change.[42] Consequently, practitioners are advised to focus less attention on modifying central values than on assisting clients in bringing their values and behaviors in line with clients' own views.[43]

Ann discovered that Wilmer's driver's license had been suspended when he was hospitalized and not renewed upon his release. She recognized that Wilmer was more likely to take the medication as an instrumental value or behavior toward his central values of staying out of the hospital, living independently, and being able to drive a car than valuing the medication for itself. Consequently, she and Wilmer revised his service agreement to describe agreed upon goals of "staying out of the hospital" and "working to regain my driver's license." In this revised contract, taking a different dosage of the medication in an effort to reduce side effects became an instrumental *task* toward reaching goals that were highly valued by Wilmer. As Ann did not have the power to restore his license, she committed herself to advocating on his behalf based on his past record of safety and evidence of regular medication. Her recommendation would be included when he would apply for a reinstated license. This agreement resulted in greatly increased regularity in taking the medication and a successful effort to regain his driver's license for use in restricted circumstances.

Finally, *clients are inclined to adopt the same attitudes as people they like, consider expert, and trust, and oppose attitudes of persons not considered to possess these attributes.*[44] Research on cognitive balance theories suggests that people are inclined to adopt the same attitude as people they consider credible, likable, expert, with their best interests at heart.[45] Conversely, they are unlikely to adopt the attitudes of persons they dislike or find lacking in these attributes.[46] In Wilmer's case, Ann had a strong reputation in the community as a supporter and advocate for persons with serious and persistent mental illness, one who treated them with respect as people rather than as targets who were not consuming the right medications. These attributes undoubtedly made her efforts more persuasive with Wilmer than might have been the case had the same arguments been made by persons he did not consider credible or as having his best interest in mind.

*Legal issues in use of persuasion.* Informed consent was described in chapter 3 as a guiding legal principle in work with involuntary clients. Since informed consent requires that the client have access to information that would permit an informed choice, appropriate use of persuasion methods can assist in providing knowledge of available alternatives and their potential costs and benefits.

*Ethics of persuasion.* When should persuasion methods be used with involuntary clients? Simons and Aigner suggest they are inappropriate while goals are being negotiated with voluntary clients.[47] However, such methods are recommended to help mandated clients who have violated the rights of others to accept services. Methods such as acknowledging reluctance, conveying empathy, citing instances of success of involuntary contact, or identifying undesirable consequences of continuing present behavior, can all be ethical influences toward accepting mandated contact.[48] Efforts to persuade Agnes Jones, the parent introduced in chapter 4 accused of child neglect for leaving her small children unattended, could be ethically supported based on potential harm to her children and her mandated status.

As nonvoluntary clients fall between the extremes of voluntary and mandated contact, they are entitled to make decisions about accepting service based on information about the costs and benefits of service. Such choices are frequently constrained by the decisions of others and institutional policies. Helping nonvoluntary clients assess these real-life punishing and rewarding contingencies in making their constrained choices can be an ethical influence as long as those influences are not in fact controlled by the practitioner.[49] Hence, much of Ann's efforts to influence Wilmer toward the regular taking of his medication came from assisting him in examining the costs and benefits of the medication in light of his own perceived goals.

Ethical persuasion is therefore very much like the conditions required for true informed consent: all alternatives should be explored, not just those favored by the practitioner, and the advantages and disadvantages of each should be accurately reviewed. Unethical persuasion entails neglecting alternatives not favored by the practitioner or using inaccurate "straw man" arguments about those alternatives.[50] Recent events in national life and the entertainment media graphically portray the predominance of unethical persuasion in our culture. Following the principle of associating an opponent with characteristics disliked by voters, a presidential candidate was implicitly associated with cross-racial sexual violence in a series of television ads about furlough policies from prison.[51] Similarly, a recent motion picture featured Dudley Moore as an advertising man hospitalized for the "crazy" behavior of describing a product accurately rather than attractively.

Practitioners are often pressured to exert unethical persuasion. Raynor defines *compulsory persuasion* as beliefs that practitioners have "a set of methods and techniques that can persuade, seduce or compel people into conformity with authoritarian views of how they should behave.".[52] Practitioners are urged by many to trick or manipulate clients into accepting terms for their own good without sharing full information about costs and benefits. Such methods may create an illusion of choice more apparent than real since the choice was based on incomplete or inaccurate information.

Persuasion can be also be used unethically around issues that are neither illegal nor harmful but violate the sensibilities of the practitioner or community. Hence, an important issue in ethical persuasion is drawing the line between behaviors that the practitioner can ethically attempt to influence and those that he or she should not. For example, the fact that Alice, the client introduced in chapter 1, lives with twenty cats is not a legal issue as long as laws are not violated, nor an ethical issue unless her health or the health of others is seriously endangered. She might experience pressure from her neighbors, but it could be emphasized to her that she can choose to do something about that pressure or not. She can choose to do something about the number of cats when she is given access to accurate information about alternatives and consequences. She might be told that the number of cats was not illegal at this point. Similarly, she could be informed that if there was a danger that they could become a serious health hazard, another investigation might ensue. Such influence would be ethical. The practitioner may be tempted by neighbor and/or supervisor pressure to prey on Ann's fears by using unethical persuasion with exaggerated, inaccurate threats of harmful consequences.

In the face of such evidence of the preeminence of unethical persuasion, a call for ethical persuasion may appear naive. It is consistent with commitments to honest communication, and is likely to be associated with greater effectiveness over time should the practitioner come to be considered likable, trustworthy, and expert.

*Effective use of persuasion.* Eight practice guidelines can be derived from the three central assumptions about attitude change.

1. *A practitioner attempting persuasive influence should try to be perceived as believable, likable, and expert as it is ethical and genuine to be.*[53] We noted that practitioners such as Ann working with Wilmer could become more persuasive over time as she came to be seen as trustworthy, likable, expert, and with his best interests at heart. When practitioners lack these attributes, they may attempt to ally with others seen by clients as possessing these attributes. For example, offers of assistance from practitioners who are not Native American are often rejected by Native American clients.[54] Work in collaboration with respected tribal members may be more effective than proceeding alone.

Such efforts to use persuasion may be more difficult with mandated clients since practitioners with coercive power may find that their suggestions are often interpreted as implicit requirements. The presence of coercive power often means that practitioners are not trusted or considered to have the involuntary client's best interest at heart. However, ignoring or denying the fact of coercive power may create an inaccurate and unethcial illusion of free client choice. Hence, efforts to be likable should not extend to creating illusions about client control over consequences that are in fact decided by others.

Mandated practitioners often find that their opinions are at least initially likely to be disregarded and that high-pressure tactics often boomerang into creating oppositional attitudes.[55] Confrontation in early contact is more likely to succeed if it is restricted to non-negotiable items, legal mandates, and serious dangers to health and security.[56] Non-negotiable issues can be introduced using language clarifying lack of choice: "This is what we are required to do." Negotiable items and available choices can be introduced with language such as "It's your choice," "It's up to you," "Think about what you want to do."[57] Such language is less likely to turn into exaggerated opposition.

2. *Efforts should be made to clarify central values now held by the client rather than immediately attempt to change them.* As influence toward modifying instrumental behaviors are more likely to succeed than efforts toward modifying central values, practitioners should first attempt to identify those central values.[58] We noted that Ann was able to identify that staying out of the hospital, living independently in the community, and regaining his driver's license were highly valued by Wilmer.

3. *A practitioner might call the client's attention to a value strongly held by the person that is violated by their behavior or attitude.* Dissonance may be stimulated if a central value is identified that is violated by the client's behavior.[59] For example, when Wilmer complained of the side effects of the medication, Ann empathized with these uncomfortable experiences and asked him to describe other consequences in the past when he stopped taking his medication. Wilmer remembered that not taking his medication resulted in an involuntary hospitalization. Ann then asked whether Wilmer wished to risk another hospitalization.

4. *Involuntary clients can be helped throuch inductive questioning to see unanticipated or self-defeating consequences and to consider other alternatives in meeting their own goals.* Decisions are often made because alternatives and unanticipated or negative consequences of actions have not been considered. Inductive questioning can be used to explore such alternatives and unanticipated negative consequences.[60] One such

method of inductive questioning is called the Socratic method. In this method, a belief or assumption considered irrational can be challenged by asking a series of questions that explore exceptions to that irrational belief.[61] It is also used to help clients clarify obstacles to goals and plans. The client is first asked to describe the goal he or she seeks,[62] and then to look at possible unanticipated consequences in questions such as "What do you think might block your plan?"[63] Similarly, clients may be asked if they might have considered other ways of reaching their goals. The Socratic method is unlikely to cause much negative response when the practitioner's own suggestions are added *after* the client's own views have been heard. As the Socratic method can help clients be aware of the consequences of their choices, it can also increase the self-attribution of those choices.

For example, when Ann discovered that Wilmer did not have his driver's license and wished to regain it, she engaged in a series of inductive and Socratic questions such as: "What might prevent you from regaining your driver's license?" When he was informed that he would need a doctor's recommendation that he could drive safely before the suspension would be lifted, Ann asked, "What do you think will influence the doctor's recommendation?" When Wilmer suggested that his safe driving history prior to hospitalization would be one such factor, Ann agreed. She then asked, "What about how you act now is likely to make a difference in your safety as a driver?" While Wilmer continued to note the negative side effects of medication, he did think that taking the medication might contribute to his safety as a driver and that it might influence the recommendation.

As noted in this example, the practitioner may add other consequences and alternatives to the client's list. These consequences may include informing the client of potential punishing or rewarding consequences such as rehospitalization and alternatives such as requirements for lifting the driving suspension. Information about alternatives and consequences make it possible to make constrained choices. Information about potentially punishing consequences is not itself punishment when the punishing contingencies are not manipulated by the practitioner, and the choice, however constrained, is left to the client.

5. *The practitioner may create or reduce dissonance by attributing a different reason than the one the client gave for his or her behavior.* The practitioner can enhance dissonance by reframing the reason the client gave for his or her behavior. For example, men who have battered their spouses often say that the behavior occurred when they were out of control. Dissonance can be stimulated through questions such as "When you struck your wife, you finally stopped striking her. Why did you

stop? It seems that you were in control because you ultimately stopped yourself."[64] Hence, the possibility that some control was exercised challenges the belief that the behavior was out of control.

On the other hand, dissonance might be decreased by attributing a positive reason for behavior. When Agnes left her small children alone while she went across the street for a break, the practitioner might have said: "You thought you were leaving your children in a safe situation with a neighbor to look in on them. You have said that you would not do anything to risk their safety. You say that you were taking a break when you hadn't had any child care relief." This method can be combined with Socratic questioning to then explore unanticipated consequences: "If a fire had broken out, how would the children have been protected?" This discussion might then lead to a discussion of positive alternatives such that the children are safe and that Agnes might also get some child care relief. As a second report might result in protective service removal of the children, informing her of these punishing consequences would also help inform her decisions.

6. *The client might be persuaded to act in voluntary compliance.* Forced compliance experiments indicate that when a person can explain a change in their behavior as having been "bought" by the promise of reward or the threat of punishment, self-attribution and attitude change rarely occur.[65] Hence, if a parent is induced into attending parenting classes by the provision of coupons for free day care, this may result in increased attendance without changing attitudes about parenting as the parent may attribute their attendance to the provision of the reward. For the parenting methods taught in the class to generalize, it is important that the client come to self-attribute the reason for the attendance: "I am attending the class because I think the methods are helpful."

It follows that changing a behavior *without* the promise of reward or threat of punishment is more likely to promote self-attribution and attitude change than forced compliance. Behavior that contradicts current beliefs can be attempted on an experimental basis in a protected environment. Research on the "foot-in-the-door" method suggests that if a person accedes to a small request, they are more likely to comply with a second request.[66] If the results of the experiment are successful, the validity of the belief is challenged and dissonance may be stimulated.[67] Changed attitudes are yet more likely to occur if practice requires considerable effort and, if possible, negative consequences of carrying out the behavior are emphasized.[68]

For example, Alice, the client with a mental handicap who lived at home with twenty cats, believed that if she applied for Social Security benefits, SSI officials might attempt to hospitalize her. The practitioner agreed with her goal of keeping her independence and suggested that she would be willing to accompany Alice to the Social Security office with the assurance that the practitioner would make sure that the purpose of the meeting was only to gain information. This small task was a form of the "foot-in-the-door" method of securing agreement to try a new behavior in a small, experimental fashion without making a long-range commitment. By going on this visit with the practitioner, Alice could check out her beliefs in a safe way. While the offer to accompany her might be seen as a small inducement, it falls short of heavy-handed efforts to force her compliance.

7. *Clients are more likely to be persuaded if they hear two or more sides of an issue: the arguments in favor and against the available choices.*[69] Clients who are undecided or have an opposing viewpoint are more likely to be persuaded by a *two-sided argument* than persuasion that emphasizes only the view held by the practitioner. Steps in the two-sided argument include: a) empathizing with and showing understanding of the viewpoint or preference of the client first; b) acknowledging the limitations of one's own position; and c) considering the benefits and costs of these and other viewpoints. Presenting the client's viewpoint first with the favored viewpoint last is likely to be seen as more objective by those who hold an opposing viewpoint.[70] Use of the two-sided argument can inoculate the client against counterarguments that might be given by other influential persons in the environment.[71]

Two-sided arguments might be used with the parents who wish to have their adolescent removed from the home and find that the county social service is unable to do so. In many cases, they are offered in-home services with a one-sided argument about the benefits of such services. These arguments often fail because they do not address the problem with which the family is concerned: maintaining the family unit and safeguarding scarce substitute care resources is *not* the family goal.

Two-sided arguments that connect to the *problem* that led the family to make the request for placement are more likely to succeed. Using the two-sided argument, the practitioner might first acknowledge and empathize with the parents' frustration with the adolescent, as well as with family services as many families have long histories of unsuccessful work with prior public and private providers. The practitioners might then describe their services as *one option* that parents might select in dealing with the problems that led to the request for placement. Advantages of that service, such as offering services in the home, at the convenience of the parents, on problems of concern to the family might be presented as part of a two-sided argument. Potential disadvantages such as the fact that the service is not what they requested, or that some problems that they have experienced might not be resolved in the short-term nature of the service would also be explored. In addition, benefits and costs of other solutions might be explored such as dealing with the problem on their own and seeking private services. Such a two-sided argument should help families make an informed choice mindful of the constraints of their situation (this example is explored in more detail in chapter 12).

8. *Role reversal can be a powerful method for gaining insight into the feelings of another and can change attitudes.* Clients who have harmed others often have limited empathy for the feelings of those they have harmed or deny the harm. Empathy for others can be enhanced by exercises in which they take the role of the other.[72] For example, domestic violence groups for men often use role plays in which the client plays the role of the battered person.[73] Similarly, family members locked in disputes may sometimes be helped to greater awareness of the other's viewpoint by role playing the person with whom they cannot agree. Finally, students caught in value conflicts with one another over beliefs about the rights of groups such as gays, the poor, and racial minorities, may be helped to understand the others' viewpoint by being asked to represent it. Such methods do not end conflict, but do permit more informed, insightful dialogue. While attitudes may not change, persuasive skills may increase based on greater insight into and empathy for the position of the other.

Persuasion is most appropriate in work with nonvoluntary clients since it is a less intrusive method of influence with fewer ethical and legal concerns. Persuasion can also contribute to maintenance of changes by facilitating self-attribution.[74] Practitioners and agencies disillusioned with the lack of staying power of forced compliance might explore the combination of persuasion with other compliance methods in promoting longer-lasting change. Finally, persuasion does not use up scarce resources and can increase over time as the practitioner becomes a more credible source of influence.[75]

Persuasion cannot be the only or primary mode of influence with mandated clients, though it can play an important complementary role in enhancing attitude change and maintaining behavioral change. The effectiveness of persuasion also depends on client ability to manipulate and process information in order to make a decision informed by knowledge of potential costs and benefits.[76] Hence, clients who have limited ability to process information may be less influenced by persuasive methods. Finally, persuasion often becomes a particularly devious form of covert manipulation by providing a false illusion of choice when information about alternatives is hidden.[77]

Compliance methods, including coercion and inducement, and persuasion methods have been presented along a continuum of intrusiveness into involuntary client choice ranging from coercion at the high end, inducement in the middle, and ethical persuasion at the low end. Since compliance methods often have short-term success in promoting behavioral change, their disadvantages in maintaining behavior or changing attitudes are often ignored. Rather than exploring less intrusive methods, agencies and practitioners often use "more of the same" compliance strategies by increasing their strength if they fail to reach their goals.[78] Marguerite Warren notes, however, that the ethical appropriateness of coercive methods lies in their ability to effectively achieve socially acceptable goals. If those methods are not successful, then their use over less intrusive means cannot be justified.[79] William Miller suggests, in the case of work with chemically dependent persons, that "it seems sensible to begin with less intrusive strategies for motivating change and then move to the use of more dramatic intervention and external contingencies if those fail."[80]

I disagree with Miller that the use of more coercive means should be applied sequentially after less intrusive means. Use of coercive methods should be based on the presence of legal responsibilities and behavior that meet criteria for its use, not simply discretion of the practitioner. When law violations and/or danger to self or others are involved, the practitioner may be ethically required to use coercive means. While inducement is a less intrusive method, circumstances in which it is not used to empower the client but rather to maintain dependence with powerless clients from oppressed groups were also discussed. Hence, efforts to use inducement in ways that empower rather than weaken clients must be emphasized. Finally, the chapter has emphasized use of ethical persuasion as the primary form of influence with nonvoluntary clients and as an important supporting form of influence to enhance the possibility of self-attribution for mandated clients. The possibilities for use of unethical, coercive persuasion are many, however, as practitioners are pressured or tempted to withhold information about choices and create "straw man" arguments for less preferable choices. The practitioner should use legal, ethical, and effective forms of both compliance and persuasion methods as situations arise, appropriate to each, and frequently simultaneous use of several forms of influence is appropriate.

# Chapter 7.

# Assessing Initial Contacts in Involuntary Transactions

Review of the legal, ethical, and effective framework with involuntary clients provides a basis for planning work with them. However, use of these principles takes place in flesh-and-blood encounters that are often difficult ones in which the practitioner feels attacked and/or irritated. Principles of intervention may be far from the practitioner's mind as he or she focuses on the immediate task of conducting an initial assessment. This chapter introduces deviance, resistance, reactance, and power relations as four perspectives or alternative lenses to aid in "seeing" this interaction. The four perspectives are assessed according to how well they fit a transactional view, their empirical and theoretical bases, how parsimoniously they explain observable facts, and how well they contribute to proactive responses by the practitioner. Three case studies will be presented as an aid in exploring these concepts.

## Assessment with Involuntary Clients

Assessments are working explanations of persons, problems, and situations, and their dynamic interaction. They are developed in order to aid the client and practitioner in formulating a plan of action.[1] Assessment is used here rather than the more familiar term "diagnosis," which has the medical connotation of identifying a disease by its symptoms.[2] As clinical diagnoses are often useful in guiding medication and must be provided in many settings for reimbursement purposes, they can be a useful *part* of a broader assessment.[3] Focus on the clinical diagnosis, however, can overemphasize pathology and client passivity, and underestimate strengths and growth potential.[4] In addition, there is often limited agreement in affixing diagnoses and their connection with treatment plans is similarly tenuous.[5] Finally, there is danger that the clinical diagnosis can take on a life of its own and become a symbol for the whole person as if it were that person's only important characteristic.[6]

Since assessments should aid the client and practitioner in formulating a plan of action, they must focus on key issues and their *use* rather than gathering facts for their own good.[7] Guides for assessment often emphasize the synthesis of objective and subjective facts from a variety of sources such as background sheets, verbal reports, direct observation of nonverbal behavior and interaction, collateral information, use of psychological testing, and the personal experience of the practitioner.[8] Such guides further recommend focus on the person, his or her coping capacity, strengths, role transitions, needs and resources, aspirations and opportunities, problem sequences of antecedents, behaviors, consequences, and also an analysis of impinging systems, which can be peer or work environments that contribute to difficulties.[9]

While guides have been developed for the assessment process with voluntary clients, no such guides have been available for involuntary clients.[10] Involuntary assessment differs in at least four major ways from voluntary assessment. First, in legally mandated transactions, the practitioner is required to assess the client's situation according to legal mandates and agency guidelines, whether or not the involuntary client sees this assessment as useful. Results of that assessment may include actions against the client's wishes. Second, there are often conflicting expectations about who has a problem and who wants help; the nonvoluntary client experiences formal and/or informal pressure since assessments are often done at the request of a third party to inform a plan *for* the nonvoluntary client. Such assessments frequently start off on the wrong foot with confused and conflicting expectations on both sides.[11] Influenced by these conflicting expectations, involuntary assessment often takes place in the "heat of battle" with high client and practitioner tension. This high emotion can create further problems since practitioners are often urged to note their subjective responses to client behavior as part of assessment.[12] Responses of involuntary clients at a point of conflicting expectations, perceived limitations on freedom from coercion or constraint, and high emotion may not be representative of their behavior in other settings and might best be seen as a sample of client behavior under pressure.[13] Finally, elaborate assessments may be of little value if the nonvoluntary client decides not to remain in counseling. Similarly, required assessments with mandated clients may have little lasting value if plans are made *for* them without their commitment to implement the recommendations.[14]

This chapter will present four additional perspectives to aid in assessment with involuntary clients. We will begin with a case study as the basis for examining the first perspective, social deviance.

> Mrs. Smith brought Johnny to a medical clinic two weeks previously with a hairline fracture of his right femur. When she canceled her appointment at the clinic this morning saying that "Johnny is being such a brat," Dr. Browder considered her comment a red flag. She then remembered that Mrs. Smith seemed nervous when she brought Johnny in previously and that the x-ray technician reported that she had asked if the x-rays would show *how* the leg was broken. Dr. Browder then called social services to report possible child abuse and requested that Mrs. Smith not be informed who initiated the referral. Upon receiving the referral, Jean Burgess, a child protective service worker, initiated an investigation. The interaction between Mrs. Smith and the practitioner that follows is an example of a legally involuntary transaction in which the practitioner is required to make an investigation and the status of the involuntary client depends on its outcome. The protective service worker is required to evaluate current or potential harm and the parents' actions to prevent such harm.[15]
>
> Jean Burgess approached the door of the Smith trailer home, noted some flowers planted outside, in need of water, saw a small child's clothes hanging on a clothesline. She knocked at the door and identified herself.

PRACTITIONER: "Mrs. Smith, my name is Jean Burgess and I am a child protective service worker. May I come in?"

Mrs. Smith stood to the side of the door, hands at her sides, and Johnny hobbled up in his flexible cast. His clothes were clean, his face needed washing, but otherwise he appeared healthy. He put his arm around his mother's leg.

MRS. SMITH: "Well, I guess so, I have nothing to hide."
PRACTITIONER: "Mrs. Smith, I am here because . . ."
MRS. SMITH: "I know why you are here. It was Mrs. Jones who called you, wasn't it?"
PRACTITIONER: "I am sorry that I can't tell you who made the

referral. Can I tell you what our agency does when we receive a referral."

MRS. SMITH: "I know what you people do. You take kids away from people. Well, you just go and take Mrs. Jones kids: she's the one deserves it. She doesn't watch them and they're always in trouble. I know it was her that called. She's always causing trouble."

PRACTITIONER: "I understand your wanting to know who called *and* I can't tell you who made the referral because that would be against the law. I am here to talk to you about Johnny's health and safety. A referral has been made and I am required to investigate the referral and find out the facts."

MRS. SMITH: "You're not gonna take my kid."

PRACTITIONER: "I hope that doesn't happen either. Children are sometimes placed in foster care if they have been hurt or are in danger. I can see that you are concerned about Johnny's safety and so are we. Now, Mrs. Smith, can you tell me what happened just before Johnny broke his leg? Can you remember what went on, say, fifteen, twenty minutes before Johnny broke his leg? What was that day like?"

MRS. SMITH: "Oh God! I will never forget that day. My husband is a long-haul truck driver. He hadn't been home for almost three weeks and Johnny and I had been alone together all that time. He was supposed to come home that day but about noon, he called to say he was in Florida and then got dispatched to New York with a load of oranges. Just before he called, I had put Johnny in the high chair with a bowl of alphabet soup, a glass of kool-ade and some crackers on the tray. As I hung up the phone, I heard a crash from the kitchen. I found a total mess and John turned around trying to slide out of the chair. Well, I had had it! I tore the tray off, grabbed John by the leg and jerked him out of the chair. I remember yelling and cussing and spanking John on his bottom until my hand hurt. Then, when I took him to the doctor and his leg was broken, I just knew that they knew what I had done. Please don't take him away from me."

PRACTITIONER: "What I would like to do, Mrs. Smith, is have Johnny checked again at a medical clinic. You could take Johnny either to your family doctor or to the hospital emergency room so that he can be examined to make sure that he is healing ok. Let's talk again after the examination to see if there are any other things we might need to do."

MRS. SMITH: "I don't have a car. Could you drive us to the hospital, please?"

In the course of this discussion, Ms. Burgess noted that Johnny appeared to be adequately dressed, there was sufficient food, that her account of what occurred was plausible. She also noted that Mrs. Smith did not always separate Johnny's needs from her own. The presence of high stress and little child care relief may have contributed to her striking her son. She requested the medical examination to be sure that Mrs. Smith was doing what was possible to aid in the healing. A recommendation about services, including possible removal from the home would be made after the examination.

## Deviance as a Perspective

Deviance is commonly considered to be behavior that requires social agencies to take action.[16] Mrs. Smith's role in the harm of her child might be considered deviance in this sense as the child welfare agency is required to investigate allegations of child abuse. Her desire to know the identity of the reporter might be considered by many as further evidence of deviance.

Involuntary clients are frequently also labeled deviant. For example, Cingolani describes involuntary clients as "persons who must deal with a helping professional because they have behaved in ways annoying or troublesome to society,"[17] and deviants have been described as persons who "come to the agency coerced by state, community or family." These sources of pressure cover the range of mandated and nonvoluntary pressures described in chapter 2.[18] Deviance has been a major concern of the social work profession since at least 1929 when the proceedings of the influential Milford Conference stated that "social work characteristically deals with human beings whose capacity to organize their social capacities is impaired by one or more deviations from the accepted standards of normal social life."[19]

This view of deviance as behavior requiring the attention of social agencies is one of several definitions of deviance. This view has been described as an *individual pathology* definition because of its focus on abnormal behavior of individuals that should be corrected by social control agents and therapists.[20] The causes of deviance in this view are typically sought in the personal history of the deviant with relatively little attention to the social causes or the practitioner's role in detecting and labeling deviant status (see figure 7.1).[21]

The individual pathology view may be prevalent in social control and helping agencies assigned to work with persons labeled deviant.[22] An individual focus is compatible with the therapy training of counselors

## Theories of Deviance

| | |
|---|---|
| Individual Pathology Model | * focus on abnormal behavior of individuals to be corrected by therapy and rehabilitation <br> * tends to ignore structural, social reaction and labeling effects |
| Structural Model | * focus on restricted access to resources needed to achieve goals <br> * tends to ignore choice and rule breaking by more powerful persons |
| Social Labeling Model | * focus on social response contingencies in creating deviant role through labeling <br> * tends to ignore role of choice and blames the social labelers |

*Figure 7.1*

and the individual focus of service delivery efforts by many agencies. Following this view, it might be useful to explore Mrs. Smith's own developmental history with child discipline, which may influence current child care practices.

While the individual pathology view is compatible with the services offered by many practitioners and agencies, it also has major blind spots. According to Kirk, persons holding an individual pathology view of deviance are likely to approach clients "as if they suffer from a defective self, which leads them to come voluntarily to the agency; as if the contact with the agency and the contact with the [practitioner] is always benign and as if the relationship exists in a social vaccuum."[23] Hence, the individual pathology view may lead to errors in ignoring nonvoluntary pressures, including very real dangers to the freedom of the persons labeled deviant, and, finally, may overemphasize individual causes of deviance while underemphasizing social causes.[24]

There are several alternative perspectives on deviance that can supplement the strengths and correct for some of the blind spots in the individual pathology view. The *structural* model of deviance suggests that while goals of wealth, power, and status may be common across a society, access to opportunities and resources needed to reach those goals is often impeded for lower socioeconomic segments of the society.[25] Deviants may be seen in this view as frustrated in their attempts to use legitimate means to reach social goals and therefore are driven rather than attracted to illegitimate means.[26]

The structural model sensitizes us to the role of access to resources and opportunities as a factor in creating circumstances that lead to deviance. Following this view, we might hypothesize that more involuntary and deviant clients are *created* in times of economic hardship and lack of resources, should access to societal goals by legitimate means be blocked. For example, there are reports that one response to auto plant closings in Detroit was to increase the number of child protective service workers, on the assumption that greater stress would lead to more child abuse. The structural approach suggests society-wide prevention efforts to distribute resources and opportunities such that the conditions leading to deviance are reduced.

The structural view has its own blind spots because of inattention to individual choice and action. Not all individuals in similarly deprived conditions use deviant means. Nor does the structural view explain white collar criminals such as inside-information stock traders who would appear to have high access to societal rewards.[27]

The *social labeling* perspective is particularly relevant for analysis of the involuntary transaction. In this perspective, no behavior is considered inherently deviant. Society is seen as *creating* deviance by setting rules that define it. These definitions have considerable cultural variation in the behavior defined as abnormal with, for example, subcultural differences in beliefs about the appropriateness of physical violence in child discipline.[28] Consequently, from the social labeling perspective, a deviant is one to whom the label has been successfully applied and deviant behavior is behavior people so label.[29] The response of society may interact with the response of the person labeled deviant to create and maintain a deviant role.[30]

The social labeling perspective shares a blind spot with the structural view in ignoring the choice to participate in the act labeled deviant.[31] It is not necessary to take the position that social reaction *causes* a person to take on a deviant role to recognize that the practitioner and the agency can play an interactive role in contributing to a deviant identity. Roger Nooe suggests that the individual pathology, and structural and social labeling views can be combined such that the blind spots of each can be reduced and proactive practice guidelines that foucs on actions in

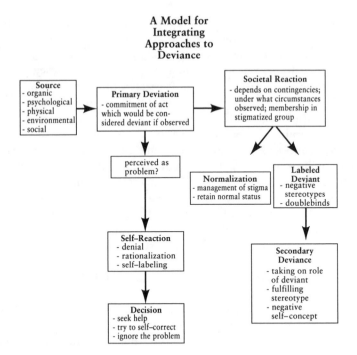

Figure 7.2

the practitioner's control can result.[32] The discussion below draws heavily on Nooe's analysis to present that integration and practice guidelines.

A key concept in the social labeling perspective is *primary deviance* that is defined as acting to violate social norms without being observed by others and hence not labeled as deviant by them. The particular cause of the original deviant act is not specified and can be influenced by organic, psychological, and environmental causes.[33] Persons committing the violation may be aware that their behavior is somewhat different from others, may or may not see the behavior as a problem, and may decide to seek help. At the stage of primary deviance, persons generally do not take on a deviant role or label themselves as deviant (see figure 7.2).[34]

For an example of primary deviance, we return to Mrs. Smith. Using undue force with a child violates social norms and can be child abuse if beating causes physical damage.[35] Mrs. Smith appears to have been alert to possible labeling as a child abuser in her concern over what the x-rays would show. The event may have occurred for many reasons, including her own developmental history, and environmental factors may have played a part given that the incident occurred at a time of high stress and little child care relief, factors that have been associated with the incidence of child abuse.[36]

Social labeling theory next focuses on *social reaction* to the primary deviant behavior, suggesting that rules for identifying deviant behavior are inconsistently applied with many intervening factors influencing labeling. For example, when, where, and by whom the deviant behavior was identified becomes important. Age, race, sex, social distance, power, and social status are among the factors influencing who will be identified as deviant and who will not.[37] Evidence for the mitigating factor of these variables includes the fact that low-income minority clients are frequently overrepresented in foster care and in juvenile institutions.[38]

In this case, the possible abuse was identified by a medical doctor, a person with high status in our society, in public circumstances in which the doctor is required by legal and professional mandates to report possible abuse. We might note that Mrs. Smith's comment that she was not bringing Johnny in for another checkup because he "was being such a brat" signaled the referral to protective service rather than her prior visit to the hospital. While the x-ray technician might have commented to the doctor at the time of that examination about her concern for what the x-rays might show, he did not.

Next, the social labeling perspective suggests that persons labeled deviant often respond to protect their identity, to avoid isolation and stigma. Included among the responses to deviant labeling are rationalizing, minimizing, or denying harm, overgeneralizing, dissembling, blaming others, discrediting the alleged victim, arbitrary interpretations, selective abstractions, and magnification.[39] These defensive response patterns have been identified as occurring with those labeled as deviant ranging from teen-aged delinquents to participants in the Watergate coverup.[40] The defensive, alienated responses are often interpreted as further evidence of pathology and deviance rather than as a response partially generated by the labeling process. For example, Mrs. Smith's immediate attempts to find out who made the referral and to derogate her neighbor's parenting might be seen as evidence of denial of harm but could also be interpreted as a predictable response to implied labeling as a child abuser.

Defensive reactions by the person labeled deviant can then interact with the social response to create a vicious cycle that can reinforce the primary deviance and become *secondary deviance:* when a person labeled deviant responds to that labeling by acting to take on a deviant role.[41]

The transition to secondary deviance is not inevitable. It may be influenced by the role of human service practitioners and agencies who act to normalize and defuse labeling or to reinforce a stabilized deviant role. Practitioners may reinforce secondary deviance by discrediting the client's own explanations for the incidents, by excluding them from treatment planning, by focusing on weaknesses, and by viewing their alienation in the labeling process as further evidence of deviance. Clients may also be rewarded with praise, privileges, and early release for confessing, and taking on a sick role while protesting such a label may be seen as further evidence of resistance and sickness.

How can practitioners and agencies assess individuals while reducing their contribution to labeling and secondary deviance? Agencies can act through alternative programs developed for diverting many first-time juvenile offenders from formal court processing.[42] Practitioners can be sensitive to the *specific* contingencies surrounding the incident and avoid stereotypic labels. Jean Burgess explored here the events of the day in which the incident occurred, its consequences, and spotted the high stress and the lack of child care relief.[43] The practitioner can also recognize client responsibility for making choices and include the client in intervention planning. In this case, while making clear that an examination would be required, the practitioner included Mrs. Smith in making plans about how the examination would be done. The practitioner can act to normalize by exploring strengths as well as pathology as here Jean Burgess did not consider Mrs. Smith's questions about the identity of the reporter to necessarily reflect a lack of concern. Finally, the practitioner can act preventively to alleviate conditions that led to the primary deviance.[44] In this case, child care relief, parent hot line numbers, and child care counseling might be among the resources explored should the recommendation be for Johnny to remain in the home.

## Resistance

Martin, 19, applied to become a resident of a supportive living community for homeless men and women. He had just been released from a hospital suffering from pneumonia and had been living on the streets prior to his hospital admission. Since Martin had been a resident twice before and had been expelled for fighting with other residents, his application was discussed heatedly at a staff meeting. Staff hesitated about readmitting him, describing Martin as hostile and resistant, a person who might abuse resources that others could use more productively. Staff finally recommended to the intake interviewer that Martin be admitted *if* he agreed to the following conditions: 1) no overnights away from the community for two months; 2) attendance to a GED class on time every day; 3) full participation in the program structure of the center; and 4) obtaining a mental health and chemical dependency assessment.

When the conditions were presented, Martin sat staring into space without speaking for several minutes, and then said: "I agree to all of it . . . but I don't like the no overnights. . . . But I have no choice if I want to move back here, do I?" The interviewer agreed with Martin's assessment but urged him to think about his decision for a day. Martin declined to wait, saying he would agree to the conditions. As Martin's alternative was living on the streets, he could be said to have made a coerced choice influenced by formal agency pressure to abide by the community rules.

In the weeks that followed, Martin followed the rules to the letter . . . but not the spirit. While he took no overnights, Martin stayed awake all night many nights *and* persuaded other residents to keep him company! After sleepless nights, he slept through GED classes that he attended every day and on time. Martin would also become ill or forget to arrange to get bus passes for his assessment appointments. Meanwhile, he continued to press for permission for overnights, saying he was "obeying the rules."

Many would consider Mrs. Smith and Martin as not only engaging in deviant behavior but also demonstrating resistance. Evidence for this assessment might be Mrs. Smith's preoccupation with identifying the source of her report and apparent minimization of harm and Martin's varied, ingenious efforts to undercut the rules. In fact, while deviant labeling and involuntary status overlap, resistance and involuntary status are often considered synonymous.[45] This is understandable since the behaviors and attitudes often grouped under the resistant label are familiar in the responses of involuntary clients: provocation, intellectualization, projection, verbosity, seduction, withdrawal, passive compliance, martyrdom, flight from the scene, refusal to answer, lateness for appointments, and changing the subject.[46]

What do these varied behaviors and attitudes have in common? They may be considered resistance if we define resistance as "client behavior that the therapist labels as anti-therapeutic or that opposes what the therapist wants to do."[47] This definition can be considered from the perspective of deviant labeling. Resistance is a label assigned by practitioners to clients who have not acted to the practitioner's satisfaction. It is not typically applied by practitioners to their own or agency behavior, nor is it typically used by clients to express their dissatisfaction with practitioner or agency actions. As the labeling is pejorative, it may have consequences for subsequent secondary deviance through reinforcing a resistant role.

This current usage of resistance differs greatly from the original meaning of the term in psychoanalytic theory. Resistance originally referred to the analytic patient's unconscious use of defenses when subjects threatening to the ego were uncovered.[48] This original definition considered resistance to be normal and expectable, unlike the current view emphasizing abnormal behavior. Second, resistance was considered to be unconscious, hence not under the client's control, while current use includes conscious opposition to plans. Third, the original use implied that the practitioner's responsibility for control or reduction, while current uses emphasize client responsibility and blame. Finally, the original use assumed application to voluntary analytic patients who, at least consciously, agreed to the goals and methods of treatment while current use routinely applies to involuntary clients.[49] In this regard, Patricia Ewalt notes that since the involuntary client neither seeks treatment nor agrees to the means by which it is conducted, the opposition is a conscious refusal to participate, "[usage of the term resistance] . . . is not proper when they have in no way agreed to the goals." Lazarus and Fay suggest, "There is a difference between the resistant patient and the nonpatient."[50]

What are the consequences of current usage of the term? On the one hand, describing a client as resistant provides a shorthand way of describing difficult, uncomfortable behavior in a way that often enlists support from colleagues. On the other hand, resistant labeling as one form of expressing practitioner discomfort becomes part of the client assessment and may form a stigmatizing label that will have repercussions far beyond the instance in which it is first applied. Ewalt again notes that "the term has become a general, non-specific way to blame the client for opposing the workers plans and locating the cause of the disturbance within the client rather than in the transaction with the agency or the worker."[51] Having labeled the client as resistant,[52] practitioners often feel discouraged and may project this helplessness onto the client.[53] Instead of leading to positive steps, this use of the term absolves practitioners and their settings from responsibility for reducing the tension in the transaction and contributes to a self-fulfilling prophecy of failure.[54] By locating the tension in the client, the question "resistant to what?"to guide intervention plans is not answered (see figure 7.3).[55]

There are several alternatives to the use of resistance as a form of deviant labeling. First, the term could be dropped from parlance as an

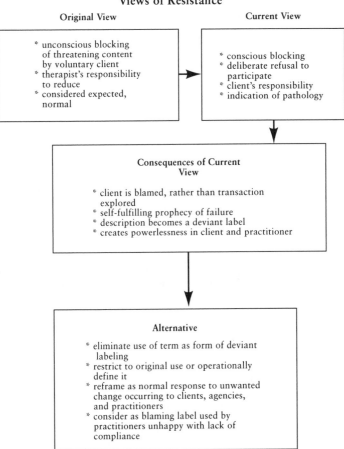

*Figure 7.3*

"undefined term, lacking criteria, connoting blaming."[56] As the term has come to mean so many things and the consequences for that broad usage are generally negative, we might vow to never use the term again. This possibility of banning word usage among practitioners is limited, however, and such elimination might lead to "term substitution" to find another way to express practitioner exasperation for lack of compliance.

Second, the term could be reserved for use in its original sense by psychoanalysts describing a phenomenon occurring in their particular form of influence. The advantage of such a move would be to reduce the pejorative connotations and not misapply to circumstances beyond the original meaning. This solution carries some of the problems of the first, however, as there is little way to monitor inappropriate usage.

Third, the term could be specified and studied more objectively and operationally defined with focus on specific behaviors and influences rather than blame. For example, Ruppel and Kaul have studied opposition to practitioner requests as influenced by the perceived legitimacy of the influence effort. They found that more opposition was generated by practitioners who were perceived to be using illegitimate influence.[57]

Fourth, the term could be reframed and used in a transactional, normalizing context. Carel Germain suggests that there may be hope for resistance as a concept if it is applied to the *whole* transaction rather than to the internal processes of the client alone. She suggests that resistance should be considered a *natural* reaction to unwanted change that occurs to clients, practitioners, and their agencies.[58] Following this perspective, sources of unwanted change would be explored including the very real possibility that the involuntary client response stems at least in part from pressures brought by the practitioner or agency. Practitioners would be alerted to recognize their discomfort with involuntary client opposition without labeling it as the client's internal problem. Practitioners might then not only consider client hesitation as normal but might acknowledge their own hesitance to see a potentially hostile client as exhibiting normal resistance.

This expanded usage of the term could also be applied to agencies and other parties to the transaction. Agency resistance can be identified when agencies set up unneccessary client hurdles and when they hesitate to change service hours to make them more convenient to clients.[59] Resistance might be applied to Dr. Browder's delay of the child abuse referral for two weeks and her wish to avoid Mrs. Smith's discovery of the source of the referral. Similarly, the homeless community staff's refusal to negotiate with Martin on any points might be considered agency resistance.

Reframing resistance is unlikely to occur on a widespread basis unless there is a shift in focus from explaining behavior as primarily internally motivated to examining its transactional aspects. Should a reframing approach not be adopted, we return to a social labeling definition of resistance as applied to client responses when practitioners are dissatisfied with less than full compliance. Application of that label has consequences, however, for reinforcing a secondary deviant role as "resistant client."

## Reactance Theory

The experienced practitioner knows that by whatever name it is called, opposition from involuntary clients frequently occurs and that opposition is uncomfortable for the practitioner.[60] While one might admire the ingenuity of Martin's efforts to bend the rules, one might also wish to wring his neck. Concepts are needed that describe responses to involuntary situations under the pressure of coerced and constrained choices. These concepts need to acknowledge practitioner discomfort while moving beyond blaming the client to suggest positive resolutions to expectable tension. Reactance theory provides an empirically based description of the behavior of persons in pressured situations that can serve as one major source.

I often introduce reactance theory in classes and workshops with the following exercise. Think about a situation in which you have been forced to do something against your will. Now, write down your thoughts, feelings, and actions in that situation as you remember them.

What do practitioners and students report? The most frequent thoughts about the coerced situations are: "Why me?" "I don't deserve this." "How can I get out of this?" "What are my rights?" "Can I appeal to a higher authority?" "This isn't fair." The feelings most frequently reported are: "I felt powerless . . . angry . . . frustrated . . . vengeful . . . confused . . . self-doubting." The most frequent actions reported are: "I did what was required *but* I sabotaged the requirement." "I complied verbally, but didn't follow throuugh." "I did just enough to get by." "I delayed, procrastinated." "I went along passively, without sharing my true feelings." "I complained bitterly." "I talked to others and tried to get them to rebel." "I went along and tried to make the best of it." "I did what I wanted within their boundaries." "I took out my anger on someone outside the situation." "I refused to do it and took the consequences."

After this exercise, practitioners and students are often struck with how much negative thinking, feeling, and half-hearted compliance, and how little "positive experience with authority"is reported. They also note how similar their responses are to involuntary clients. I do not consider their responses to be unusual because reactance theory has led me to consider that responses to pressured situations may be more normal, predictable, and nonpathological than is often thought.

Reactance theory assumes that we each have behaviors that we are free to exercise.[61] Should some of these free behaviors be threatened or eliminated, the theory suggests that a person will experience *reactance*. Reactance is often expressed as one or more of five different direct or

## Reactance Theory

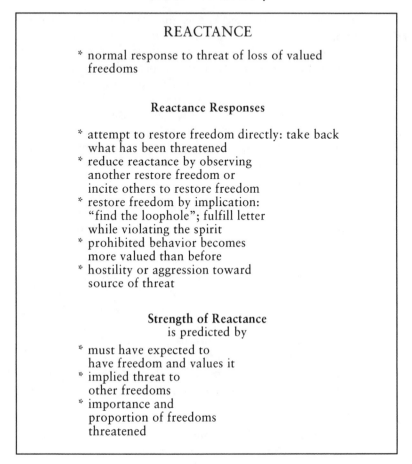

### REACTANCE

* normal response to threat of loss of valued
  freedoms

#### Reactance Responses

* attempt to restore freedom directly: take back
  what has been threatened
* reduce reactance by observing
  another restore freedom or
  incite others to restore freedom
* restore freedom by implication:
  "find the loophole"; fulfill letter
  while violating the spirit
* prohibited behavior becomes
  more valued than before
* hostility or aggression toward
  source of threat

#### Strength of Reactance
is predicted by

* must have expected to
  have freedom and values it
* implied threat to
  other freedoms
* importance and
  proportion of freedoms
  threatened

*Figure 7.4*

indirect response patterns designed to regain those freedoms (see figure 7.4).[62]

1. Direct efforts are those in which the person attempts to recapture the freedom directly in spite of the consequences. We see this effort to restore freedom directly in Mrs. Smith's challenge to the practitioner— "You're not going to take my kid"—and Martin's brief attempt to negotiate about overnight privileges.

2. As many freedoms cannot be restored directly, efforts may be

*indirect.* For example, a person may try to restore freedom *by implication* through violation of another of the same class of behavior: "finding a loophole"or breaking a norm without technically violating the rules.[63] Martin appeared to be a master at this "loophole"strategy. While he followed rules about overnights to the letter, he undercut the spirit and purpose of the rules by staying up all night and sleeping in class. This loophole pattern was also frequently reflected in practitioner responses such as:"I did what was required *but* I sabotaged the requirement." When practitioners use this strategy, they may consider it clever. When clients use it, practitioners may consider it less clever and label it passive aggressive.

3. Another form of indirect restoration occurs when reactance is reduced by observing another person attempt to restore their freedom or attempt to incite others to perform forbidden behaviors. Martin may have reduced his reactance by convincing fellow residents to bend the unwritten rules about getting adequate rest; their reactance may have been reduced by watching Martin's antics.

4. If a person is blocked from expressing their reactance either directly or indirectly such that they have to "sit"on their reactance, their desire for the forbidden behavior increases.[64] Readers who have given up an addictive habit such as smoking can attest to a rise in the attraction of the prohibited behavior. Martin's preoccupation with overnights may be explained by this pattern. The preoccupation ended when he was given permission to take them: yet he rarely used the privilege after it was earned!

5. Reactance may also be expressed in the form of hostility or aggression toward the source of the threat, even when it is unlikely to restore freedom.[65] The practitioner response that "I complained bitterly"and Mrs. Smith's initial hostility in the investigation might fit this pattern. Reactance research suggests that adolescents may be more likely to use this than their elders.[66]

The five reactance patterns are familiar and sound like many of the behaviors grouped under the pejorative definition of resistance. Reactance theory, however, is similar to the reframed definition of resistance in describing responses to unwanted change in a normalizing fashion.[67] It goes beyond the reframed view of resistance to provide a base of theory and empirical study that helps predict when reactance will occur and how it might be reduced.

Whether reactance is likely to occur and to what extent can be predicted by five factors. First, a person must have expected that they had the freedom to begin with and felt competent to exercise that freedom. Reactance occurs in relation to threats to free behavior. For example, Martha from the previous chapter experienced reactance because she felt free originally to decide what form of help might be best for her. Other patients who did not experience the decision to enter the hospital as a free behavior may not have experienced reactance.

Second, repeated efforts to restore freedom that do not succeed may lead to learned helplessness. That is, a person may learn not to try in response to uncontrollable outcomes.[68] Consequently, it may be the case that other patients experienced reactance at one time but failed efforts to regain freedom may have led to diminished efforts to exercise that freedom.

Third, reactance occurs in relation to the importance or unique value of threatened behaviors to fulfill needs.[69] If valued freedoms can be maintained with means still available, then the threatened freedom may not have unique value. So, for the parent who no longer wishes to regain custody of a child, the threat of losing that custody may stimulate little reactance. On the other hand, the danger of losing her child had high reactance potential for Mrs. Smith.

Fourth, reactance will be high if a person loses even a few freedoms should those freedoms be one of few that the person has left. Reactance occurs in relation to the *proportion* of freedoms threatened or eliminated. If the number of choices is small, removing any one will cause considerable reactance.[70] Martin's strong response to the withdrawal of freedom to have overnights might be explained by overnights being one of few valued freedoms left to him. Group home staff have mentioned that withdrawal of telephone privileges is perceived as a very severe penalty by group home residents. This may be explainable in terms of the limited number of free behaviors available.

Fifth, reactance is higher if there is an implied threat to other freedoms beyond ones immediately threatened.[71] For example, overnights may symbolize a continuation of a private social life for Martin, a connection with friends. And threat to the overnights may stimulate reactance more because of the implied threat to other freedoms than for the loss itself.

These factors then help predict whether reactance might occur and how strong it will be. Can reactance then be predicted primarily through situational variables? What about individual differences? Martin appeared to experience every kind of reactance. Could some persons experience more reactance than others? While reactance theory comes from a social psychology tradition that does not emphasize individual differences, there are indications that some individuals are more likely to experience reactance than others. For example, Dowd has developed a

therapeutic reactance scale that measures reactance as a relatively enduring characteristic across situations.[72] One study indicates that clients
scoring high on the reactance scale missed more appointments.[73] Other
studies indicate that persons with high internal locus of control and high
self-esteem are more likely to experience reactance especially under circumstances in which important freedoms are threatened.[74] While both
males and females have exhibited reactance, there are differences in the
particular threats considered important and those freedoms that males
and females feel competent to exercise.[75] Little research has been done
on reactance in groups, but there are indications that being a member of
a group may reduce the expression of reactance.[76]

Reactance theory has many practice implications including strategies
designed to reduce it and others to increase it or take advantage of the
fact that it is high. Sharon Brehm describes many ways that reactance
can be reduced. First, a client can be aided in directly restoring their own
freedom.[77] This can be done by avoiding giving directives to the client,
contracting to restore freedom, and clarifying available choices. When
the intake worker at the homeless community center suggested that
Martin think it over before deciding whether to enter the program, this
might have reduced reactance.

Second, attributing behavior to the situation rather than the person
reduces reactance. We see this in Jean Burgess' avoidance of labeling and
awareness of situational contingencies in the harm of Johnny. Third,
emphasizing the freedoms still retained should avoid reactance. When
Jean Burgess suggests that Mrs. Smith return to her family doctor, she
may be maintaining a current behavior. Fourth, avoiding dependency
implications and avoiding linkage to other behaviors reduces reactance.
Consequently, reactance is reduced when behaviors to be changed are
highly specific rather than broad. For example, a directive to Robert
(from the chapter one) that he needs to "find a new peer group"is a
global requirement that might be predicted to cause high reactance since
it means the loss of much freedom. If this requirement were modified to
"stay away from James and John," while free to maintain friendships
with others, reactance might be reduced. Hence the implied threat to
other freedoms is reduced by separating requirements from what remains free. The staff may have reduced Martin's reactance by contracting with him to restore his freedom to take overnights and emphasizing
the choices he could make within constraints, i.e., by emphasizing specific rather than global changes such as "attending and participating in
class daily" rather than "earning your GED."

Fifth, reactance can also be reduced by minimizing the strength of
persuasion efforts.[78] Providing more than one alternative should be

considered since one-sided persuasion tends to increase reactance. The protective service worker provided two alternatives when she said, "I would like to have you bring John either to your family doctor or to the hospital emergency room so that he can be examined to make sure that he is healing ok." Similarly, clients may be more willing to try new behaviors if the practitioner does not overemphasize them. Greater pressure may be counterproductive and produce a boomerang effect (see figure 7.5).

Strategies are also available to *increase* reactance, or to take advantage of the fact that reactance is high. Reactance can be increased by heightening the importance of the free behavior and implying or stating threats to future freedoms.[79] For example, had Mrs. Smith been unaware of or not taken seriously the danger of possible removal of her child, expressly describing that danger might have served to increase reactance. When reactance is high, it has been suggested that a defiance-based paradox might be a given. If reactance is high such that opposition to directives is expected, prescribing *the opposite* of what is desired may result in the desired behavior.[80] Results of prescribing defiance-based paradoxes have been mixed with some studies indicating success and others showing no more effectiveness than nonparadoxical methods.[81] Use of paradox may also create problems in developing a trusting relationship.[82]

### Assessment of the Value of Reactance Theory

Reactance theory has been seen to have many implications for the study of involuntary transactions. There are, however, several problems with the application of reactance theory to work with involuntary clients. First, the research base of the theory emphasizes laboratory experiments with a high degree of experimental control over internal validity, but relatively far removed from field conditions. Since most reactance experiments have been conducted in brief encounters with nonclinical populations, there are questions about how well these findings will generalize to severe losses of freedom such as loss of a child and long-lasting relationships with clients.[83] Sharon Brehm suggests, however, that "the more people who pose threats to a person's freedom and the more situations in which such threats occur, the more generalized and diffuse a person's anger may be."[84] Other problems include the fact that while reactance should also apply to practitioners who feel their freedom threatened, there are no studies of this[85] and little is known about the effects of reactance in groups. Finally, as reactance theory is ethically

# Methods for Reducing Reactance

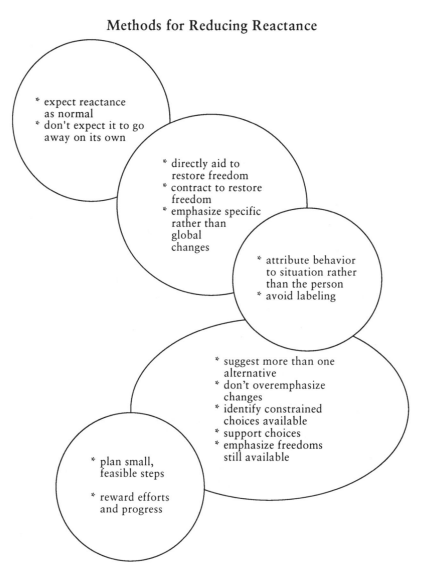

* expect reactance
  as normal
* don't expect it to go
  away on its own

* directly aid to
  restore freedom
* contract to restore
  freedom
* emphasize specific
  rather than
  global
  changes

* attribute behavior
  to situation rather
  than the person
* avoid labeling

* suggest more than one
  alternative
* don't overemphasize
  changes
* identify constrained
  choices available
* support choices
* emphasize freedoms
  still available

* plan small,
  feasible steps

* reward efforts
  and progress

*Figure 7.5*

neutral, it does not provide guidance about when increasing reactance could be ethically appropriate.

Bearing in mind these reservations, reactance theory still has a major contribution to make to understanding work with involuntary clients from a transactional perspective. It makes a very good fit with the three-dimensional version of involuntary client status proposed in chapter 2. It suggests that pressures generating reactance can be personal or in response to direct coercion (like coerced choice), impersonal or constraining barriers that make engaging in a behavior more difficult or impossible (like constrained choice), or even self-imposed.[86] Reactance theory helps unlock the puzzle of how some persons can lose many freedoms yet not seem very involuntary, while others may lose what appears to be insignificant freedom and yet experience a great deal of reactance. As Sharon Brehm notes: "Thus what may look to the observer like a mild threat directed at what appears to be an insignificant freedom on other grounds, such as importance or proportion of freedoms threatened, may to the person appear to be a threat of considerable magnitude, especially when other freedoms are implicated."[87]

## Power Relations

Deviant labeling, resistance, and reactance have been explored primarily here as ways to explain how involuntary clients respond to pressured situations. This emphasis on the recipient of influence and how practitioners influence change in desired ways rather than on the behavior of practitioners has been characteristic of much intervention theory and research.[88]

As effective, ethical use of power and influence is central to work with involuntary clients, use of power by practitioners and clients are important areas for study. If power is defined as one person's net ability to reward another over time, the involuntary transaction can be seen as an unbalanced power situation in which the practitioner has power over the client on some issues for some period of time.[89] In this context, we will review information on practitioner use of power and strategic self-presentation.

### Practitioner Use of Power

David Kipnis has studied how powerholders use influence and how changes occur to the powerholders themselves as a result of using that influence. In one early management simulation experiment, students were instructed to use their influence to get better production from a simulated work force. One set of managers was randomly assigned to a condition in which they had power to give pay raises, deduct pay, transfer or fire workers, as well as to use persuasion and the legitimate power of their position. A second set was given only the legitimate power of their position and the power to persuade. Those managers with the wider range of influence methods made more influence attempts than the managers with the restricted range. Managers with the wider range also used more coercive methods more frequently than persuasion and, after the experiment, emphasized the need for skills in manipulating power. They attributed workers' efforts to their own use of power rather than the workers' self-motivation, were inclined to keep social distance from them, and viewed the workers as less worthy than the managers with the restricted range, who stressed keeping workers motivated.[90]

According to Kipnis, the managers with more power may have wished to justify to themselves their efforts to control by keeping social distance, viewing the less powerful as less worthy, and deserving of their fate. He also notes that use of more coercive methods may in turn stimulate reactance and greater social distance.[91]

This management simulation represents an early study of use of power and cannot be easily generalized to practice situations in which practitioners have considerable real power and exercise it over time. A more recent study by Cooke and Kipnis has moved to the actual influence efforts of therapists.[92] Eleven psychotherapists, six female and five male, provided audiotapes of hour-long sessions with one female and one male client each. Sessions were coded according to strength of influence attempt and its goal. For example, "Do you feel like talking about this" would be rated as a relatively weak attempt while "I want you to tell me what you are thinking now" would be rated relatively strong. Goals of influence were coded with categories such as instruction, explanation, focusing, verbal reinforcement, information seeking, information providing, and support. The study found that the therapists did have consistent styles of influence across clients, with some therapists consistently more directive than others. Second, all therapists used less directive influence methods earlier in sessions than the more directive methods. Gender of the therapist and client was a consistent factor in the use of influence: "Male therapists made more attempts to influence their clients and interrupted their clients more often than did female therapists . . . and . . . more active forms of influence [by both male and female therapists] were directed toward female clients than male clients."[93] Specifically, female clients were more likely to be given advice while male clients were more likely to be provided with explanations and less direct guidance.[94]

Kipnis' studies can best be considered at this point as suggesting fruitful areas for future study and replication rather than as definitive. The findings about the consequences of using more powerful influence methods, including increased social distance from the recipient and the impact of gender on influence attempts, are provocative and deserve further study.

## Strategic Self-Presentation

Before moving to strategic self-presentation, we will consider a third case study. Irv and Joan were originally voluntary clients in the sense that there was no external pressure for them to get a divorce. As a precondition for granting the divorce, they were court-ordered to participate in mediation about visitation and custody for their two children, ages 4 and 5. Should mediation fail, the court would appoint a professional to make a custody recommendation. Both Irv and Joan were hesitant about court-ordered mediation and had even more reservations when they were assigned to a mediator who was a social work student in a field placement. While both wanted the divorce, the court-ordered mediation and assignment to the student mediator came as a less desirable part of a "package deal." Irv and Joan can be considered to have chosen participation in mediation as a constrained choice from a formal pressure source.

Joan, as the primary care provider, was concerned about the children's safety when they were with Irv since he had unsuccessfully completed alcoholism inpatient treatment twice, did not want to return for more treatment, and did not see drinking as a problem affecting custody. Meanwhile, Irv insisted on joint legal custody with primary physical custody remaining with Joan. Joan said that she would only consider joint custody if Irv would agree *to not drink* before or during visits.

The student mediator's supervisor felt that Irv's alcoholism would prevent him from keeping his promise not to drink. Hence, she recommended to the student that no mediation be attempted until Irv agreed to complete chemical dependency treatment once again. The student mediator, however, wanted to explore mediation with stipulated conditions about drinking and later wrote: "The more I was told to discontinue working with this couple, the more attractive the other alternatives became." The student mediator persisted in the negotiation of an agreement in which Irv would lose joint legal custody if he violated the agreement about drinking before or during visits and attorneys for both parents supported this recommendation.

The student mediator wrote later that during the sessions "Irv seemed to readily accept what I said, agree with my advice, observations and interpretations. If he didn't agree, he avoided the issue or changed the subject. Perhaps this influenced my desire to work with them."

Irv's behavior may strike us as less than candid. Just as the student mediator and other practitioners may try to create a particular impression such as empathy, competence, and fairness, involuntary clients may present selected parts of themselves in order to achieve particular goals. *Strategic self-presentation* refers to efforts to manage the impressions others have of us in order to better reach our goals.[95] Self-presentation efforts are most likely when the stakes are high, as in this case in which visitation of children and a possible return to chemical dependency treatment are the goals. Irv might have chosen to tell his wife and student mediator that he has no problems with alcohol, that they should mind their own business, that he is entitled to visitation. While this response might have been candid, it might also have prevented Irv from reaching his goal of regular visitation. Irv's quick agreement with the mediator's advice, on the other hand, influenced the mediator's willingness to work with the couple.

Six self-presentation strategies will be described including ingratiation, intimidation, facework, supplication, self-promotion, and exemplification, with the first four as particularly characteristic of involuntary situations (see figure 7.6). Irv may be using *ingratiation,* which refers to attempts to make oneself more attractive in order to influence a person in power to act favorably.[96] Ingratiation usually takes the form of flattery, public agreement with the opinions of the other despite possibly conflicting private views, overemphasizing one's own positive traits and deemphasizing the negative.[97] Ingratiation efforts are covert, since their discovery might interfere with the goal of a better impression.

Efforts to ingratiate are more likely to occur when one is in a dependent position and the stakes are high, when there are no onlookers who might spot the insincerity of the effort, and when the actors feel the circumstances of their dependency are unfair.[98] In this case, Irv's efforts might have been spotted as ingratiating by Joan. She may have chosen not to expose the ingratiation because she shared the goal of receiving mediation. There are also indications that ingratiation may be rewarded if a person in power is *simultaneously* being threatened by others in a similar lower power position.[99] For instance, other more compliant,

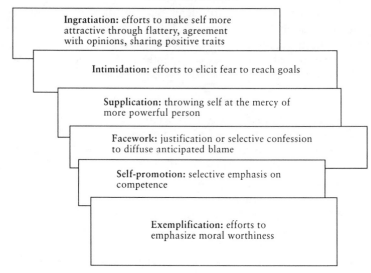

*Figure 7.6*

ingratiating residents of the homeless community might have indirectly benefited from the contrast to Martin's challenging behavior.

The student mediator noted after the case that "it took me awhile to figure out that I was not that good at my job but that he was just good at letting me think I was. Perhaps, without realizing it, his behavior influenced my decision to work with these clients and not follow the conventional treatment of chemical dependency in mediation." Are there some persons who are more susceptible to ingratiation than others? Higher-power persons who believe in cooperation, understanding, and cohesion with the lower-power person and have high self-esteem, may be *more* susceptible to ingratiation than others without these views and with lower self-esteem.[100]

Not all clients or practitioners in involuntary situations ingratiate. *Intimidation* is often used to influence the target person by creating a fearful impression.[101] Threats may be direct, or messages may be given such as "I can't tolerate stress" or "I am not responsible for what I do if I get angry." Intimidation is often used in involuntary situations when the intimidator has resources to which the target does not have access, when the target cannot easily retaliate, and when the intimidator is willing to forgo good will.[102] Consequently, intimidation may be attractive to the practitioner. There are many practice situations, however, in which involuntary clients appear to use intimidation when they do not have resources and the practitioner can retaliate. Such strategies may be overlearned and inappropriately generalized from other situations in which they were successful.

A third strategy is *supplication,* in which clients point out their own negative characteristics, advertise their dependency and inability to cope, and throw themselves at the mercy of the higher-power person in an effort to acquire sympathy and support. Supplication is most likely to be used in crises, when the higher-power person controls key rewards and can use that power arbitrarily.[103] Supplication may be costly to the self-esteem of the person using it and may not succeed with persons who do not recognize a responsibility to help the defenseless.

A fourth strategy common in involuntary situations is *facework* in which a lower-power person, anticipating blame from a higher-power person, may deny the charge, justify his or her actions, or selectively confess to particular problems in order to diffuse the impact of anticipated negative feedback.[104]

Two additional strategies not necessarily associated with involuntary situations are self-promotion and exemplification. *Self-promotion* is similar to ingratiation in emphasizing one's best qualities with the focus, however, on creating an impression of competence rather than liking. Self-promotion may be more likely in situations in which there are conflicting claims about competence.[105] Finally, *exemplification* strategies refer to efforts to convey an impression of integrity and moral worthiness.[106] Friedlander and Schwartz suggest that practitioners may be inclined to self-promote with clients in order to create an impression of competence and to use exemplification to point out one's best qualities.

Impression management theorists suggest that these strategies may be used selectively, simultaneously, or not at all. They may not be used when a person is very involved with the task at hand and when the person is particularly motivated to be candid. Strategies are stimulated by desires to increase power. Two or more strategies may be used simultaneously such as ingratiation, self-promotion, and supplication. Use of particular strategies may be influenced by personality variables and may be fairly consistent across situations.

Studies of self-presentation have similar limitations to those reviewed under reactance theory in their typical use with nonclinical populations and single contact experiments. Consequently, generalization to the interaction of practitioners and involuntary clients over longer periods of time can only be tentative. Again, not enough is known about the contribution of the situation and personal characteristics to their use. Finally, focus in the literature has concentrated on use of self-presentation by clients rather than practitioners.[107] While the strategies ring true with the responses of many involuntary clients, there is once again the danger of creating new labels for "the ingratiator" and "the intimidator." Self-presentation strategies can offer normalizing explanations for irritating behavior that has often been labeled as a personality deficit rather than a situational response. Clarifying the realities of power, including how to regain lost power, may go a long way toward reducing their use.[108] The concepts can also be applied to practitioners as well as clients. For example, students needing a client for a class project have reported using ingratiation and presumably other strategies applicable to practitioners in an effort to increase their power.

This chapter has explored the assessment of initial interactions between involuntary clients and practitioners, suggesting that involuntary client behavior in first contacts may be a sample of behavior under high stress or response to authority. Consequently, efforts to generalize from those responses to behavior outside the assessment situation are of questionable value.[109] Explanations of such initial session behavior that focus on internal causes have been overemphasized, while explanations focusing on transactional perspectives have been underemphasized.[110]

Four such transactional perspectives have been presented in an effort to augment and correct for some of the blinders of the individual pathology focus. Social labeling theory has provided insights into the process of identifying persons who will be labeled deviant and the role that practitioner and agency responses may have in rewarding and maintaining that deviance. Describing involuntary clients as resistant is a frequent source of deviant labeling that might be reduced by reframing resistance to refer to normal responses to unwanted pressures to change that may occur to clients, practitioners, and agencies. Reactance theory concepts have been presented as rich sources of hypotheses in predicting when these oppositional responses may occur and specific strategies to reduce reactance have been described. Influence and self-presentation strategies used by practitioners and clients have been explored for insights into behavior involving differences of power.

These perspectives have suggested proactive guidelines for increasing sensitivity to a transactional perspective.

1. Practitioners can be aware of their own settings and their own use of power as factors influencing the involuntary transaction.

2. Practitioners can be more aware of client responses in the involuntary transaction as explainable in part by the circumstances of the

transaction and not necessarily as pathology or labeled as resistance. Normalizing explanations for client oppositional behavior can be used including responses to deviant labeling, reactance responses, and efforts to manage impressions.

3. Practitioners can reduce deviant labeling by sticking to the facts and the objective consequences of behavior.

4. Practitioners can reduce reactance and efforts to manage impressions by clarifying the requirements of the situation, specifying the limits to that power, specifying changes needed to regain freedom, emphasizing choices, and pointing out remaining free behaviors.

# Practice Strategies for Work
# with Involuntary Clients

While part I has provided a conceptual basis and principles for legal, ethical, and effective work with involuntary clients, part II transforms these principles into concrete guidelines for practice through frequent use of transcripts of interactions between involuntary clients and practitioners. Chapters 8 through 11 present guidelines for mandated and nonvoluntary contact with individual clients. Chapter 8 presents strategies for socialization and chapter 9 presents negotiation and contracting strategies. Chapter 10 then presents ways to formalize contracts and develop initial action plans and chapter 11 presents guidelines for middle-phase work and termination. Involuntary contacts that begin in family or group settings are presented in chapters 12 and 13. Finally, we return to the involuntary practitioner and the practice setting in chapter 14.

# Chapter 8

# Socialization Strategies for Individual Involuntary Clients

Dora, 29, had a serious and persistent mental illness. While she had always lived with her parents, she now wished to leave home and move to a public housing project. The housing staff was requiring, however, that Dora either complete an independent skills program or live in a group home for three months before they would agree to let her live in their project. At her next meeting with the county social service case manager, the following transpired:

PRACTITIONER: Last month when we met with public housing, Dora, they suggested that before they could admit you, you would either have to live in a group home for three months . . .

DORA: No, I don't want to live in a group home.

PRACTITIONER: That was definitely an option you didn't want. The other option was to have somebody from the skills program work with you in your parents' house on independent living skills as a way of proving to them that you could make it in their apartment program. It's about time for me to make that referral since that is the plan that you agreed on. I'd like your okay to do that.

DORA: I know I agreed to work with skills, but after thinking about it these last few weeks, I don't want to work with them. I don't want people. . . . I'm dealing daily with my parents, that's two people and then to have six or eight other people telling me what to do, telling me how to clean, doing stupid little things that are an insult to my intelligence. I don't need people telling me how to clean.

PRACTITIONER: Right, but Dora you know the fact is you made that decision to apply for public housing and to agree to the skill program. And now you're changing that?

DORA: Well, I agreed to move into an apartment, I didn't agree to have all these people telling me what to do, breathing down my neck, making me do all these little daily things that I am capable of doing on my own.

PRACTITIONER: Yeah, I know. I know, Dora, that you want your own apartment. Right? But I think you are kind of making it harder on yourself to get that.

DORA: Harder on myself! (with anger)

PRACTITIONER: At this point, yes.

DORA: These people are making it hard on me. They are the ones making all the rules that I have to live by. No one else has to live by these damn rules. Why should I?

PRACTITIONER: Well, Dora, okay . . . rules are a way of life. I mean if you want something, you have to jump through some hoops to get there. That is just the way life is.

DORA: I'm not going to jump through hoops. I don't need them. I can just stay here in my parents' house, I don't need you. They are trying to tell me what to do and now you are doing it. Just get out of my house and leave me alone.

While Dora and the practitioner originally agreed on the goal of moving to public housing, they have become entangled in a struggle about how to meet her goal, with the practitioner feeling the pressure to accede to the demands of the agency and Dora rejecting that pressure. Motivational congruence between client and practitioner on goals and methods of practice was presented in chapter 5 as an important clue for legal, ethical, and effective practice. Much contact between involuntary clients such as Dora and her practitioner lacks congruence, however, as practitioners pressure involuntary clients to accept responsibility for their actions, to accede to the wishes of others, to work on the "right problems" for the "right reasons." On the other hand, involuntary clients often appear equally determined not to acknowledge these "right" problems attributed to them by others.[1] Conflict between practitioner and client perspectives often leads to efforts to manipulate one another: to "hook" the involuntary client and to avoid being hooked. The resulting deadlock often results in limited compliance with mandates, little self-attributed change, escalating frustration, and charges and counter-charges.

Socialization or role preparation for practitioner and client can begin to extricate the practitioner and involuntary client from this deadlock by separating the fixed and non-negotiable from alternatives in meeting requirements and identifying rights and free choices. Completion of socialization steps can increase voluntary aspects of contact and decrease coerced aspects while working for the lasting change that is likely to occur if change is self-attributed (see chapter 5). Such self-attribution of change can be pursued with both mandated and nonvoluntary clients.

Self-attribution with mandated clients occurs in a context in which compliance strategies of coercion and inducement are also employed around non-negotiable requirements. Hence, mandated practitioners must partly play an enforcer role.[2] Compliance with mandates and motivational congruence can be enhanced if the mandated practitioner also plays negotiator and compromiser roles.[3] Persuasion, negotiation, and bargaining skills can be useful tools for practitioners to assist mandated clients in making constrained choices.

Nonvoluntary clients such as Dora can be helped to make informed decisions to become voluntary clients, or at least semi-voluntary, or not to become clients at all. Should the nonvoluntary client choose to accept services and become at least semi-voluntary, the enforcer role should be limited to non-negotiable requirements of the setting. Greater emphasis should be placed on playing the negotiator and compromiser as well as sometimes acting as an advocate or coach.[4] Hence, negotiating, bargaining, and persuasion should be used more frequently with nonvoluntary clients than compliance strategies.

This chapter will present 1) preparation for initial contact, 2) initiating contact, and 3) socialization steps to prepare the way for negotiation and contracting strategies that follow in chapter 9.

## Preparation for Initial Contact

Practitioners can prepare for initial contact with involuntary clients by completing eight preparatory steps: 1) review available case information; 2) identify non-negotiable legal requirements (if any); 3) identify non-negotiable agency and institutional policies (if any); 4) identify rights, 5) identify free choices, 6) identify negotiable options, 7) examine practitioner attitudes that may interfere with service, and 8) make arrangements for initial contact. The extent to which each of these steps is completed depends on time available and caseload size, competing re-

Preparation for Involuntary
Interview

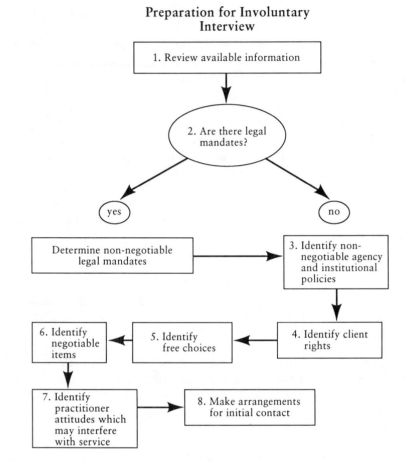

*Figure  8.1*

sponsibilities, and amount of information available prior to initial contact. The sequence of these preparation tasks is depicted in figure 8.1.

1. *Review available case information.* Available case information should
be screened for specific information to determine what brings this person
in at this time. The practitioner should focus more on the *specific behaviors and events* reported that led to contact than on pejorative labels.
For example, a supervisor might find written in Dora's case record
following the above session that Dora was "resistant, hostile, and unre-
sponsive." Such labels often come as part of a diagnosis focusing on

client pathology without consideration of the degree to which they are based on behaviors *that may be normal responses to involuntary situations.*

Without a description of what occurred, the accuracy of such labels cannot be assessed. We know, however, that Dora requested help in getting into an apartment. She did not request the group home living or skills program that came as a "package deal" from the housing agency. Her anger might be seen as normal given her view that she did not need to demonstrate readiness for such living arrangements. Practitioners frequently encounter such client labels in records without an account of the interaction that may have in part produced the label.

2. *Identify non-negotiable legal requirements (if any).* In reviewing case information, the practitioner should separate *what must be done legally* from what might be *desirable* but is not required. If legal requirements do not pertain, as in Dora's case, then the practitioner should proceed directly to step 3. What must be done legally frequently becomes confused with what the practitioner or referral source privately feels should be done. Failure to make this distinction may inadvertently sabotage the socialization and contracting process by using compliance methods on issues that are based neither on law nor policy and may affect subsequent evaluations of effectiveness. Restricting requirements to a limited number of specific behaviors should also reduce client reactance.[5]

Consequently, mandated practitioners need to identify the federal, state, and local legal parameters that limit and guide their work with involuntary clients. Practitioners employed in fields such as child welfare or probation must thoroughly understand those non-negotiable requirements that govern their behavior and determine the extent to which client behavior can be legally required to change.[6] For example, a mandated client might be court-ordered to participate in a restitution program and the practitioner would be required to link the client to such a program.

When non-negotiable requirements exist, they should be made explicit so that areas for freedom of choice and maintenance of current behaviors can then be identified and clearly understood by the client.[7] As suggested in chapter 4, the mandated practitioner needs to find out: What legal requirements apply here? What do those requirements indicate that the practitioner must do? What must the mandated client do? What recourse does the mandated client or the practitioner have in modifying the requirement? What are the consequences of noncompliance with the requirement for the practitioner and client?

3. *Identify non-negotiable agency and institutional policies (if any).*

Practitioners working in agency settings are also influenced by policies that guide service delivery. For example, job descriptions for case managers may describe how frequently contact with clients must take place and priorities in carrying out their roles. Private agencies often have policies that include "package deals." For example, the housing agency may require that if Dora "chooses" to apply for their housing, she must satisfy requirements such as an assessment that she be capable of living there safely. Similar guidelines to those developed for legal requirements then apply for non-negotiable agency or institutional policies: What non-negotiable agency or institutional policies apply here? What do those policies specify that the practitioner do? What do those policies specify that the involuntary client do? What recourse does the involuntary client or the practitioner have in modifying those policies? What are the consequences for noncompliance with the policies for the practitioner and client?

Preparation for work with involuntary clients in mandated and institutional settings too often does not progress beyond these three steps. In order to enhance motivational congruence, empower clients, and achieve greater success it is equally important to identify rights, free choices, and negotiable options.

4. *Identify rights.* Too often identifying rights is interpreted as handing involuntary clients a copy of legal rights without a dialogue about rights and options needed to pursue genuine informed consent (see chapter 3). Since the choice *not* to accept an offer of service is available for nonvoluntary clients, this most basic right should be clarified. For example, the practitioner could have prepared for the session with Dora by reminding herself that Dora could *choose* whether to pursue living in the housing project or not. Further, the practitioner should prepare to help the nonvoluntary client make an informed decision based on accurate information about the advantages and disadvantages of continuing that contact on a voluntary basis. Presenting two sides to the decision about whether to participate and emphasizing choices should reduce reactance.[8] Hence, the practitioner could think about advantages and disadvantages for Dora of choosing to work with the housing authority, and explore other available options as well.

The practitioner should remember here that mandated clients can also choose to accept legal consequences if they refuse services. The practitioner should also prepare to inform both mandated and nonvoluntary clients about their rights to confidentiality including any limitations to those rights, as well as available recourse to requirements or alternative services for which they may qualify.

For outside referrals, the practitioner should examine what the referral source is requesting in terms of rights the client has to accept or reject the recommended service. Nonvoluntary clients can often choose to work on a problem different than that attributed by the referral source.[9] The practitioner might explore, however, the consequences for the client of making such a choice.

5. *Identify free choices.* It was suggested in chapter 7 that reactance may be decreased by clarifying behaviors that are not effected by requirements. For example, mandated clients can choose their attitude to the situation: whether to comply at all, to comply passively, or to make the best of the situation by working on some of their own concerns as well. Nonvoluntary clients can choose not to accept the service, or to accept it and work on their own concerns. Hence, Dora can choose to remain at home, to accept the housing authorities terms, to explore negotiation with the authority, or pursue another housing alternative.

6. *Identify negotiable options.* Reactance should also be reduced if options or constrained choices are available in the implementation of policies and requirements.[10] The practitioner should be aware of discretion available in the interpretation of mandates and policies. For example, the practitioner might have explored whether there were alternative ways that Dora might be assessed for skills in living in the housing program without completing the skills program or living in a group home. Could she take a competence examination and, if she passed, be waived out of the program?

7. *Examine practitioner attitudes that may interfere with service.* Practitioners often come to shorthand predictions about what may occur with a client based on rapid assessment of available case information and comparisons with past experience of other clients with similar case information. While predicting the future is normal and unavoidable, prejudging has serious consequences. Such prejudging may occur when involuntary clients are accused of offenses such as child abuse or battering that are not only illegal but often personally offensive to practitioners. Practitioners' own personal history with the harm of such behaviors may cause them to prejudge if they do not strive to be aware of their own values about the alleged behavior that led to contact.

Avoiding prejudgment is important in order to make a legitimate offer of service that is not sabotaged from the outset. For example, practitioners in child welfare settings are often required to demonstrate "reasonable efforts" to help families stay together and avoid out-of-home placement.[11] Skepticism about the ultimate success of such efforts may be legitimate based on practitioner experience with similar cases. Failure to monitor this skepticism would be analogous to an instructor examining student transcripts and assigning a grade *before* the class begins. It is not in the best interest of either involuntary clients or agencies to "determine the grade" before the contact begins. On the other hand, should the agency later need to move to permanently remove children, their documentation of genuine reasonable efforts will assist in their defense of those efforts.

While some referral information may trigger negative prejudgments from practitioners, positive prejudging can also occur. Practitioners might tend to discount illegal behavior that they think should not be illegal. For example, some practitioners have experimented with marijuana and other illegal drugs and may have come to personal opinions that such drugs are not harmful and should be legalized. That personal opinion might result in discounting the consequences for involuntary clients who might be misled in thinking that laws will not be enforced.

8.) *Make arrangements for initial contact.* Involuntary clients, like voluntary clients, often pick up cues about what to expect from contact through the choices made available in arranging the time, locale, and physical arrangements of that contact. Timing choices may not be available in investigations of imminent danger or harm in which the practitioner may be required to make an unannounced contact. In such circumstances, potential protection needs may carry as an unavoidable byproduct a predictable sense of invasion of privacy and high levels of reactance. In most other practitioner-initiated contacts, however, the practitioner can call ahead or write to schedule an interview at the client's convenience.

The locale of that contact and the physical arrangement of the meeting place may also be modifiable. In many cases, the client may choose to meet in the office, in their home, or in a neutral location of their choice. Should the initial contact with the practitioner take place in an office, the practitioner can be aware of what nonverbal messages office interviews may suggest. For example, moving through a series of locked doors to an office may convey accurately that confinement is an issue here. A sterile environment without pictures and other amenities may convey threat. Seating arrangements can be made to create an expectation of collaboration by sitting to the side of a desk or arranging comfortable chairs or couches. Having toys and games available for children can communicate a sensitivity to them and their parents. Some practitioners adorn their walls with attractive pictures or posters with positive motivational statements.

On the other hand, practitioners may be unable to modify the physical arrangements of initial contact. Setting decor may be a low priority for the agency or institution, personal decorations may be prohibited, chairs may be uncomfortable or unmovable. Rather than dwell on unchangeable physical arrangements, the practitioner is better advised to be aware of what those arrangements may communicate and to modify what they can.

## Initiating Contact

Practitioners are often encouraged to initiate contact with voluntary clients by tuning in to what brings those clients in for contact.[12] Outside pressures, including those represented by the practitioner, are frequently the reasons that contact is established with the involuntary client. The guidelines that follow differ according to whether the client was 1) self-referred, 2) referred, or 3) mandated (see figure 8.2).

1. *Self-referred clients.* Contact with self-referred clients begins with: a) exploring their reason for seeking help, b) exploring any pressures effecting that self-referral, c) explaining non-negotiable policies, d) exploring negotiable options, e) clarifying rights, and f) clarifying free choices. Since many who ostensibly self-refer actually seek help as a result of pressure from others, practitioners should take seriously such self-referred clients' viewpoint that other things, people, and events brought them in. For example, when Ralph (introduced in chapter 2) met with a counselor from a mental health center for an intake interview, he said that he had no problems. The only reason he had come was that his mother threatened to make him move out of her house if he didn't stop the arguments with his wife. The counselor might consider that Ralph's own behavior probably played a part in stimulating the circumstances that led to contact, and indeed that Ralph's mother might be signaling the possibility of domestic violence in this case. It is also true that, from Ralph's viewpoint, he is responding to his mother's pressure. Rather than dismiss such an expression as a refusal to accept personal responsibility for "the problem," it is recommended that the practitioner accept that Ralph is expressing factually the problem as he sees it.

Should this initial assessment reveal external pressures that are not legal mandated, the practitioner can attempt to reduce reactance immediately and enhance voluntarism by acknowledging those pressures, helping the client assess the potential consequences of dealing with or ignoring those pressures, clarifying rights, including the choice *not to participate.* The practitioner can proceed to explore the advantages and disadvantages of continuing that contact voluntarily.

For example, Keith ostensibly made a voluntary contact to admit himself into an alcoholism treatment center. The following section

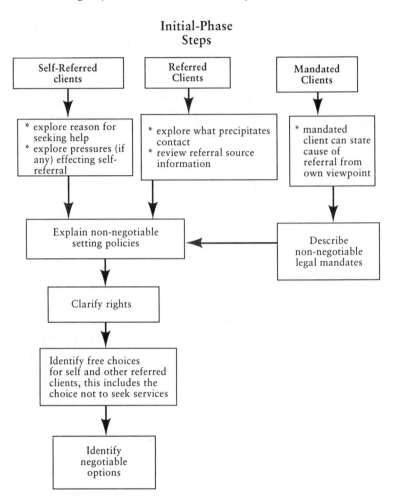

Figure 8.2

of dialogue comes from his initial contact with Dick, his alcoholism treatment case manager.[13] Dick begins by exploring the reason for coming in to treatment from Keith's viewpoint, to suggest ways that Keith can reframe the decision to increase self-attribution, and explore his feelings about the pressured contact.

DICK: Keith, I believe this is your second treatment? What brings you in for treatment at this time?

KEITH: Yep. This is the second treatment. Ah, the family life just started blowing up again. Of course, using alcohol got blamed for everything, so I got kicked out of the house, and after about a week and a half of living in different places, I decided that I might as well come into treatment to see if I missed something the first time.

DICK: So it was really your decision to come in?

KEITH: Well, it was my decision to come in, but I was caught between a rock and a hard place, either come to treatment or lose my family.

DICK: Oh, I see. So it's pretty much the family says, do this or no family. I see. How do you feel about that?

KEITH: I feel that I'm taking the brunt of everything again. I feel like if I do this, everything else is going to be okay, and I don't think that's right.

Keith has produced a good operational definition of a coerced choice: being between a rock and a hard place! Dick could now move to explicitly acknowledge Keith's view of the cause of contact and clarify the choice he is making. For example, Dick could say:

DICK: So, Keith, it sounds as if you feel pressured by your wife and family to come in for more alcoholism treatment and that pressure doesn't feel good. Are you aware that you could choose not to stay? I want to clarify that because it is important for people to make up their own minds about the program. Would it help if we were to explore the reasons why you might decide to stay here and make this work for you or to decide not to stay?

Dick should then go on to discuss the rights of patients and the non-negotiable policies and rules of the center, including policies for initiating discharge.

2. *Referred clients.* Referred clients may be amenable to such referral or may feel pressured by it. The practitioner should: a) explore what brings the referred client into contact from their viewpoint, b) review referral source information, c) review advantages and disadvantages of doing what the referral source suggests, d) identify rights, and e) clarify options. The referred client is entitled to an explanation of the circumstances that have led to contact from the viewpoint of the referral source. This explanation should be objective, nonjudgmental and concrete. As the referral may contain confidential information or diagnostic labels that may stimulate reactance, the information should be paraphrased to avoid either violation of confidentiality or inappropriate labeling. The practitioner might explore these issues with statements such as:

1. "I would like to know from your viewpoint what brought you here."
2. "I also have some information from the referral source. Would you like to hear it?"
3. "In the rest of our session we need to explore the choices you might make (develop agenda for session). The biggest one is whether you want to decide to become a client here ot not."
4. "Would it help if we looked at the pluses and minuses of the decision to become a client here?" (Review advantages and disadvantages for deciding to become a client.)
5. "If you decide to become a client here:
   a. there are some agency policies that you should know about (describe non-negotiable policies);
   b. you have certain rights (explain rights); and
   c. we also have have several choices in what we do and how we go about it (describe available options)."

For example, Mrs. Simmons was referred to Walter, a county mental health counselor by her child welfare worker. Mrs. Simmons, accused of child abuse a year earlier, had agreed to a consent decree that stipulated that she would meet regularly with her child welfare worker around child management issues in exchange for the agency *not* taking her to court. Mrs. Simmons was not now attending those sessions and the working relationship between Mrs. Simmons and the child welfare worker was distant. Mrs. Simmons was in a nonvoluntary relationship with the child welfare worker because of the consent decree; her contact with Walter was not directly part of that agreement. Therefore, she could choose whether or not to become a client of the mental health center. The initial interaction between Walter and Mrs. Simmons is reproduced below.[14] Walter begins with a description of the circumstances of the referral. His description is followed by a very negative response from Mrs. Simmons about that referral. This response might have been more muted had Walter first asked Mrs. Simmons to talk about her own understanding of the reasons for the referral.

WALTER: I'm meeting with you because the social worker involved with you and your son Jamie has indicated that there is a consent decree that says you have to meet with the social worker and follow through on recommendations. Apparently there's some problem in terms of you keeping appointments, and I wanted to see if there was something I could do in terms of helping you look at what gets in the way, and see if we could plan some way around them.

MRS. SIMMONS: Yeah. You can get him off my case. He doesn't listen to me. It's got to be his way or no way at all. I'm sorry, but I think I know my little boy a little bit better than that, and I know my own mind.

WALTER: Well, what appears to have led to this consent decree is a petition that was brought by the social worker before the court, and the petition indicates that there's been a lot of problems in school with Jamie hitting other kids, kicking other kids, apparently throwing a piece of wood and hitting a kid in the eye. One time he was banging his head on the wall. Another time he was choking himself with some sort of a necklace, and I guess I'd like to know how you see these problems.

Walter clarified that he wanted to hear her side of the story and reported objectively and nonjudgmentally the intake information received. He also requested her viewpoint. He might also have empathized here with Mrs. Simmons' anger about working with the social worker. This might also be the time to introduce her rights and choices, such as the following.

WALTER: I think it might help if we talked a little about your choices here. While you have to continue working with the social service agency because of your consent decree, you and I can decide whether we want to work together. If you decide to work with me, we can work on the things you are concerned about. We can also decide whether to take the social worker's concerns into account. You might also pursue getting reassigned to another social worker. We also need to look at what might happen if you decide not to become a client here and return to working with the social worker.

3. *Mandated Clients.* Mandated clients are entitled to a) state the cause of contact from their viewpoint, b) a description of legal, non-negotiable requirements, c) a review of negotiable options, alternatives, and consequences, d) an explanation of rights, and e) a review of free choices.[15] Since reactance can be expected to be high, available choices should be clarified from the beginning. Statements that the practitoner might make during this section of the interview might include:

1. "I would like to know from your viewpoint what brought you here."
2. "Let me share with you what I know about our contact:

  a. you and I need to meet because . . . (objective description of cause of contact);
  b. what you and I have to do is (factual description of non-negotiable requirements)."
3. "In the rest of our session we need to explore the choices you might make (develop agenda for session):
  a. you are entitled to (explain rights);
  b. you are free to (explain free choices and alternatives, and consequences);
  c. we also have some choices in what we do and how we go about it (describe available options)."

The following dialogue takes place at the beginning of contact between Paul and Bill, his probation officer. Paul was preparing to enter an adult correctional facility, so the number of non-negotiable requirements was high. Bill begins by respecting Paul's right to decide how he should be addressed and explaining why he needs to take notes. Bill then explains his own agenda for the session. He should also ask Paul for other things he would like to see covered in the session. Since Paul may be less likely to express high reactance if he describes the requirements himself rather than has them read to him, Bill asks Paul for his view of what he is required to do. Bill then continues to describe additional referral information that he has about non-negotiable requirements and explains the specifics of confidentiality.

BILL: Mr. Anderson, my name is Bill Linden, and I'm a probation officer. I've been asked by the court to supervise your probation. First of all, let me start off by asking what do you prefer to be called?
PAUL: Call me Paul.
BILL: Okay, Paul. Basically what we need to do today is to begin to gather some information to help me in supervising your probation as well as to get an understanding as to what the conditions are. As we talk today, I'm going to be taking some notes, so I can keep the particulars of your case separate from anyone else's. Do you have any problems with that?
PAUL: Go ahead.
BILL: Can you tell me what your understanding was of the sentence you received from the court?
PAUL: From what I understand from what my lawyer says, I'm going to have to go to the workhouse here on Monday, and I could have done a lot worse. But anyway, I've got to go to the workhouse, and

I'm not quite sure what I have to do around that. They said something about four or five months, but I might be getting out early if I keep a clean act.

BILL: Let me then let you know the information I received from the court just prior to our meeting. Now my understanding is that you were initially charged with two felony counts. Count one was burglary, and count two was receiving and concealing stolen goods. In return for you pleading guilty to burglary, the state dismissed count two, the receiving of stolen goods. The court sentenced you to 23 months in prison with a stay of execution and five years of probation. Does that sound familiar to you?

PAUL: Yeah, that was it.

BILL: Now what that basically means is you're going to be on probation for five years. And as long as you follow the conditions of probation, you won't have to do the 23 months of prison.

PAUL: What do they mean by probation? Do I have to show up and talk to somebody like you every month?

BILL: There are a number of conditions of probation, one of which is that you have to maintain contact with me and keep me informed as to where you're living and working.

PAUL: Do you come over and visit?

BILL: Sometimes. I do try and work the supervision around your work schedule, so that probation doesn't interfere with your working. I want to also let you know, Paul, that the information which you give me is confidential. The only ones that can have access to that will be individuals with written permission from you, except for other people in the correctional community. Other courts can get it, other probation officers can get it. But anyone outside of the criminal justice system cannot have access to this information without your expressed approval or by court order.

While Bill reviews confidentiality rights here, he should go on to explore alternatives and free choices that Paul has. Paul could appeal the sentence, or decide how he was going to do the time including exploring how he could work on his own concerns. These options are explored with Paul in chapter 9.

## Socialization Guidelines

Socialization, or preparation for assuming roles by practitioner and client, follows the steps in initiating contact. It was suggested in chapter 5 that socialization is another key clue in pursuing legal, ethical, effective practice with involuntary clients since clarity of expectations and roles is associated with better outcomes.[16] While one goal in mandated settings is to increase compliance with legal requirements,[17] socialization efforts should also reduce reactance and respect self-determination in areas other than non-negotiable legal and agency requirements. The practitioner should carry out socialization by doing the following: 1) conduct any required assessment, 2) assess response to pressured contact, 3) express empathy for pressures experienced, 4) note values expressed, 5) employ selective confrontation around non-negotiable items, and 6) reaffirm choices and negotiable options (see figure 8.3).

1. *Conduct any required assessment.* Assessment with voluntary clients typically involves exploration of strengths, weaknesses, goals, desires, and awareness of the systems of which the client is part.[18] Such voluntary assessments often assume that the process is in pursuit of a mutual plan.

While mandated assessments may ideally end in a mutual plan, they must be conducted whether or not the involuntary client wants to participate. For example, when the practitioner is mandated to assess danger, the assessment itself may be a non-negotiable aspect of contact. In some cases, investigative protocols have been developed that aid the practitioner in assessing danger in a relatively objective manner.[19] In many others, specific protocols are unavailable and practitioners must craft their own.

Too often extensive assessments are developed for meeting an involuntary client's needs that far outstretch both legal requirements and the client's own perceived wishes. Hence, such assessments often provide a source of disappointment and frustration when the client is unwilling to pursue more than a required minimum. The general issues in conducting involuntary assessments are to determine: What information is the practitioner required to collect in order to make decisions or recommendations? What information might be useful for making required recommendations or decisions but is left to the discretion of the practitioner? What information is irrelevant to explicit or implicit requirements for assessment that might, however, be collected should the involuntary client give consent to pursue an issue voluntarily?

Assessment is an ongoing process that only begins at intake. The practitioner working with involuntary clients must be aware that initial assessment takes place in a context of pressured contact. Consequently, observations about client behavior might best be seen as a sample of how that client behaves under pressured circumstances.

2. *Assess response to pressured contact.* If the exploration of the

Socialization
Phase Steps

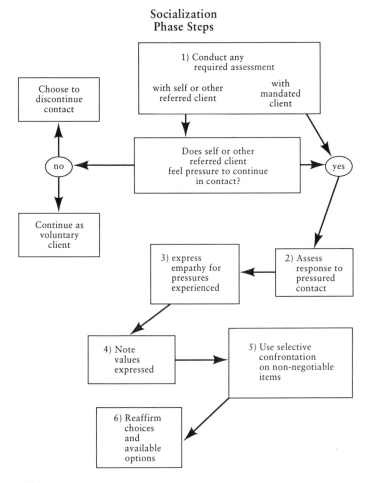

*Figure 8.3*

cause of contact reveals outside pressures or mandates, no matter how tactfully or objectively such pressures are explored, many involuntary clients will respond negatively. As described in chapter 7, a negative response is predictable in situations involving a threat to valued freedoms. Among the predictable responses are anger at imposed services or pressures from others, denial of wrong or harm, considering self as victim, blaming others as unworthy and deserving of harm, hostility toward the practitioner, passive indifference, and deception.[20] These responses have often been interpreted by practitioners as evidence of internal dysfunction, guilt, or deviance rather than considering the possibility that they are normal responses to a situation stimulating reactance.[21]

The practitioner can avoid premature labeling of such responses as evidence of pathology or resistance and consider that they may indicate reactance responses or the use of self-presentation strategies such as intimidation, supplication, selective confession, or ingratiation to defend against labeling (see chapter 7). Even if negative responses are normal and predictable, they are usually uncomfortable for the practitioner. Such responses can often, however, be reduced by expressing empathy for pressures experienced.

3. *Express empathy for pressures experienced.* Such negative responses can be so strong that the involuntary client cannot "hear" what is being said or participate fully in the session unless those feelings are given attention. While the practitioner may privately suspect that some of the involuntary client's difficulties have been brought on by his or her own actions and hence not feel much empathy for the client's responses, the practitioner can be selectively empathic about the involuntary client's feelings of being forced or pressured into contact against his or her will. It can be helpful to recall one's own reactions in coerced situations so as to better understand and empathize with the involuntary client's reactance. For example, a practitioner might say: "I'll bet it's hard coming in here when you didn't choose to be here. There are probably other things you'd rather be doing and other places you'd rather be."[22]

4. *Note values expressed.* Involuntary clients often reveal their values and strengths in their response to pressured contact. The practitioner can note those values as ones to be aware of as positive motivations for later contracting and possible use in selective confrontation about how they may be jeapordized by client behaviors.

After Bill completed the summary of the many non-negotiable requirements involved in Paul's entry into the correctional system, Paul became angry about the many losses of freedom he was soon to encounter and denied responsibility for his actions. Bill responded to the reactance at this point, avoiding a power struggle, saving selective confrontation for later in the interview. He became aware through Paul's responses that he wanted to have money to pay rent, maybe a job, and freedom to have a good time.

BILL: Paul, you appear to be kind of angry at this point.
PAUL: Well, I don't know, it wasn't that much stuff. What the hell, they had plenty more stuff. I mean they had about five televisions and

stereos. Hey, I needed the stuff, I needed some money. I've had three jobs in the last two years, and they all went to hell. I needed to get some money, I've got rent to pay and stuff. I want to go to a bar and have a good time just like everybody else, I'm entitled to it.

BILL: What I'm hearing you say, Paul, is that you are pissed off because you needed some money and don't feel you deserved the type of sentence that you got.

PAUL: Yeah. It wasn't that much. What the hell.

BILL: And I think most people would be mad in your situation about entering prison. But then I'd also ask you to take into account that you've got some choices to make and I hope you won't let your anger interfere with that. It is okay for you to be angry.

When Paul denies responsibility for the crime, denies harm to the victims and suggests that they could spare the stolen goods he needed, it is as if there is a cartoon caption over his head saying, "denial of responsibility." While many practitioners would confront Paul's refusal to accept responsibility at this point, Bill selectively empathized with the pressure experienced while not agreeing that the victims of the crime are to blame. The presence of denial does not suggest that confrontation will be effective at this point, since Bill is not yet likely to be a persuasive source of influence (see discussion of persuasion in chapter 6).

5. *Employ selective confrontation around non-negotiable items.* Many involuntary clients question the validity and interpretation of facts presented to them about the cause of contact or the fairness of requirements as Paul did. An escalation spiral of charges, defenses, and countercharges frequently ensues. We saw such a spiral occur in the beginning of the chapter in the interaction between Dora and her case worker. Such escalation often contributes to a negative assessment by the practitioner. Practitioners often wish that involuntary clients would admit responsibility for their behavior or accede to the demands of others. It seems unlikely that many involuntary clients will have the communication skills to de-escalate and move from a content to a process level by saying, "Hold on. It seems that we are in an escalation spiral here. I am angry and so are you and we are not listening to each other. Let's back up and start over." Hence, responsibility for such de-escalation rests with the practitioner.

How can mandated clients be faced with non-negotiable aspects of contact in a respectful, nonjudgmental fashion? Confrontation refers to techniques used to help a client discover blind spots, discrepancies, and inconsistencies between thoughts, feelings, attitudes, behaviors, and their consequences that perpetuate client difficulties.[23] Confrontation can also be seen as a persuasion method designed to affect attitudes, beliefs, and behavior. Many practitioners are unsure about when to confront or how to do so in ways that remain respectful and demonstrate caring. Confrontation is most appropriate when a) a law or policy has been violated or a violation is imminent, b) when danger or harm has occurred or is imminent, or c) when a client's own goals are threatened by their behavior. Hence confrontation occurs most frequently with mandated clients who have violated laws. Confrontation with nonvoluntary clients is less frequent and occurs around conditions of danger, harm, or obstacles to their own expressed goals. Confrontation is rarely appropriate if beliefs or actions are neither illegal, violations of policy, dangerous, or related to the client's goals.

Confrontation techniques range on a continuum of intrusiveness into personal choice from low intrusiveness to high.[24] At the low end of intrusiveness, the practitioner can choose to *not confront*. Following the criteria for appropriateness of use of confrontation described above, such a decision is appropriate if behavior is neither illegal, harmful, or a threat to the client's goals. Following these guidelines, practitioners can choose to confront about some issues and avoid confrontation around others (see figure 8.4).

The first level of appropriate confrontation is the use of *self-assessment techniques* to facilitate self-examination. Circumstances often exist in which behavior or attitudes may be interfering with client goals or legal mandates, or in which danger is possible but not imminent. In such circumstances, the completion of a written assessment of past behavior and attitudes relevant to the reason for contact can provide a relatively unobtrusive form of self-confrontation.[25] Such a method promotes self-evaluation to facilitate change as a model for self-confrontation.[26] Some involuntary clients may be stimulated to recognize dissonance between behaviors, attitudes, and goals without arousing much reactance. Self-assessment techniques may be most appropriate early in contact, prior to the development of an effective working relationship. The technique should not be used with the expectation that many clients will have an "ah ha!" experience in which they quickly become aware of dissonant behavior on their own. If the technique is expected rather to "plant a seed," little is lost in its use as it is relatively unobtrusive and hence provides little risk to the development of an effective working relationship. Such self-assessments should be phrased in objective, nonjudgmental terms.

Means of stimulating self-confrontation can be used much more frequently than is usually the case, with minimal risks. While such techniques may be insufficient for heavily defended clients, its use can pro-

## A Confrontation Continuum

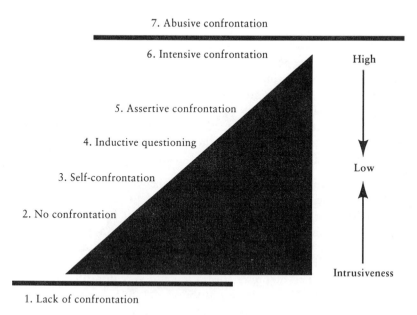

7. Abusive confrontation

6. Intensive confrontation    High

5. Assertive confrontation

4. Inductive questioning

3. Self-confrontation    Low

2. No confrontation

Intrusiveness

1. Lack of confrontation

Levels 2 or 6 can be appropriate uses
of confrontation. Levels 1 and 7 are
inappropriate.

*Figure 8.4*

vide information to guide higher levels of confrontation. If behavior includes law violations and imminent danger, self-assessment may be skipped or quickly followed with the next level, inductive questioning.

At a second level, practitioners can raise inductive questions that draw involuntary client attention to a potential discrepancy or inconsistency between behaviors, attitudes, beliefs, goals, and consequences. Discrepancies between verbal and nonverbal expression or actions can also be explored in a questioning, tentative fashion rather than as statements of fact or interpretation.[27] Inductive questioning is relatively unobtrusive and can hence be used effectively early in a relationship to plant a seed promoting self-confrontation without arousing much reactance. It may be used selectively around items in the self-assessment in which danger is probable or consequences are more serious. Inductive questioning can also be overused and many clients will not respond to the tentative linkages suggested. When behavior involves law violations or imminent harm, the practitioner must often progress to the next level: assertive confrontation.

It is often appropriate to use inductive questioning with nonvoluntary clients to explore ways that behaviors may conflict with client goals (see chapter 6). In the following section of the interview between Walter and Mrs. Simmons, he continues to gather information from her perspective about the previous allegations of child abuse and to provide selective confrontation. After exploring further what had occurred with Mrs. Simmons, the school, and Jamie, Walter moves to empathically confront and use an inductive question:

WALTER: Do you think sometimes Jamie's behaviors in the school are some of his own doing?

MRS. SIMMONS: I know he's not an angel. But he's not as bad as what they're making him out to be, either. He's just a typical, normal little boy, that yes, every once in a while, he does get into trouble. But not all of it is his fault.

WALTER: It's got to be pretty frustrating and very difficult for you to have this problem with Jamie and the school. I've seen you a couple of times with Jamie. And from what you're telling me now, and what I've seen in the past, I know you really love your son. And sometimes, as much as you love your son, it's got to be pretty difficult to deal with some of his behaviors.

A sequence of inductive questions can also be used to "plant seeds," to build dissonance or discomfort over a lack of fit between behaviors, attitudes, and goals or values. Bill had noted earlier that Paul did not believe he had a problem with alcohol and that he appeared frustrated over losing three jobs in the past year. After the series of inductive questions, Bill suggests that chemical abuse may be a problem that has gotten in the way of working. He also attempts a role reversal by suggesting that Paul see things from the employer's viewpoint (see chapter 6). When Paul mentions that he was fired at his last job for being late, Bill asks:

BILL: Why was it that they said you were late?

PAUL: I had a hangover.

BILL: You had a hangover. Had you been out drinking pretty heavily the night before?

PAUL: Sunday night. Had to go to work the next day, thought what the hell.

BILL: Has that happened before?

PAUL: Sure.

BILL: How many times?

PAUL: Go out with all the gang. Lots of times.

BILL: Lots of times?

PAUL: Sure. Go out with the guys.

BILL: Have you had other employers say to you that you're not working up to par, that they feel like maybe you're drinking?

PAUL: No. They just say maybe I could do a better job next time. I think I do a pretty good job.

BILL: So they say that you could do a better job. You feel you're doing okay?

PAUL: I'm doing fine. I don't understand. Maybe I'm in the wrong field. But I like doing what I'm doing.

BILL: So you like auto body, you'd like to stay in that field?

PAUL: Sure.

BILL: Interesting enough, right there, you've presented some ideas where I can begin to see how the presentencing investigator did see the possibility of a chemical abuse problem. If you are working—now just think about this—and you're going out and getting drunk and that drinking affects your ability to work. What would you think if you were an employer paying someone eight bucks an hour and they couldn't do the job?

Near the end of the interview, Bill again asks Paul to put himself in someone else's shoes.

BILL: I want to give you something to think about, and then during our next meeting, I want us to be able to talk about it. You are telling me that you want to stay out of trouble in the future. Let's say that you're staying out of trouble, and you do purchase a stereo and let's say, someone comes in and steals the stereo. I want you to then think about how you would react, and what you would like to have happen to the individual that took your stereo. All I'm asking is that you think about that. I don't want an answer now, I want you to think about it. Okay? And also think about how that's in line with your goal of wanting to stay out of trouble in the future.

*Assertive confrontation* refers to making specific statements in declarative form about discrepancies in thoughts, feelings, behaviors, and consequences rather than posing them as questions. Assertive confrontations should: 1) include statements about proposed linkages between dissonant attitudes, behaviors, and goals based on *specific* instances; 2) separate free behaviors from requirements and constrained choices; 3) be conveyed in an atmosphere of warmth, caring, and trust in which concern rather than blame is communicated; 4) be presented tactfully but clearly enough that the client gets the point; 5) be well timed and focused on key issues; and 6) be followed with empathy.

Hepworth and Larsen suggest a format for assertive confrontation as follows:

I'm concerned because you (want/believe/are striving to) _____

_____ (describe desired outcome) but your _____

_____ (describe discrepant action, behavior, or inaction) is likely to

produce _____ (describe probable negative consequence).[28]

Assertive confrontations are frequently employed with mandated clients around law violations, non-negotiable aspects of contact, and dangerous behavior and are also appropriate when client-expressed goals are jeopardized by behavior. When danger is high, lower-level confrontation steps are often skipped. Otherwise, assertive confrontation might follow unsuccessful attempts at inductive questioning. If, however, the behavior or attitude is neither a law violation nor a danger to self or others, nor a conflict with the involuntary client's expressed goals, it is questionable whether assertive confronation should be used.

Confrontations are most likely to be successful when they come from a respected source who identifies specific problematic behaviors and consequences.[29] As noted above in the interaction between Bill and Paul, the practitioner is at first unlikely to be a respected source. Consequently, confrontation is unlikely to be effective at the beginning of contact and hence should be used sparingly, concentrating on non-negotiable items.

The practitioner can sometimes empathize with the client's feelings about contact and then add the confrontation, using a linguistic sequence substituting *and* for *but*. This linguistic sequence affirms the validity of both the empathic statement and the confrontation rather than stating them in terms that suggest that they contradict one another.[30] For example, "I hear your frustration that your child does not obey the way you feel he should *and* striking your child with a belt, raising welts is not a legal way to get him to obey you."

Child protective service investigations frequently require confrontation around non-negotiables. In the following interview segment, Betty, a child protection worker, is meeting with Diane, the single parent mother of two small children. Diane reported that she left her children in the care of a babysitter for an evening. Police, however, found the three- and five-year-old children playing unattended in a park at 3:00 A.M. across a busy street from the housing development in which they lived. Diane had completed an outpatient alcohol treatment program. This was now the third report of behavior assessed as neglectful since the treatment was completed. Additional reports indicated that Diane was not following the aftercare program and was again drinking.

Betty has to present the facts that led to the contact, explore Diane's explanation, and empathize with her response, while remaining firm about the agency's non-negotiable demands. She also identifies some common concerns, such as the children's welfare, and begins to explore options to meet requirements. Diane began by saying that she was not responsible for what happened to the children since she left a babysitter in charge.

BETTY: It does sound, Diane, as if you thought you were leaving your children in safe care. You are concerned about their welfare as we are. *And* one of the things that the law expects parents to do is make good decisions in picking babysitters. So if kids were found alone wandering in a park late at night, the laws say that parents are responsible for that. And so that's why the police took them in.

DIANE: I'll never use her again. I'll never use her again.

BETTY: That would be a wise decision on your part. I think, Diane, if this were the first time that we had this kind of situation together, that would be the direction we would want to go. We would try to help you make better arrangements for babysitting. However, we need to look at the fact that this is the third time this year that the kids have been on a police hold.

DIANE: This wasn't my fault. This was not my fault. Maybe other times it was, but this was not my fault. You're just making a big deal out of this.

BETTY: Are you saying, Diane, that you feel blamed, that this time feels different to you since you had made what you thought were good plans for the children?

DIANE: Yes, I had a babysitter. It was her responsibility.

BETTY: While you feel this time was different, it is the third report we have received. So, we don't feel that it's safe for the kids to come home right now. There is another reason why we think that the children might be safer in foster care right now. We have also had a community report, Diane, that you have been seen drinking while with the children.

DIANE: It's not anyone's business if I drink! I already completed a treatment program. Who called in? I have enemies. You can't trust everyone who calls in.

BETTY: You are right that drinking is your own business, as long as your children are not in danger. You are also right that we can't always trust callers. It does seem as if drinking is playing a part in your child care at this point. For this reason, I am going to recommend that if you want to regain custody of the children, that you complete another alcoholism assessment and any treatment they recommend. That may involve an inpatient treatment and a halfway house program. It may also be a return to an aftercare program. The assessment might also show that you don't need any kind of treatment now.

DIANE: I already did that once. I already did that.

BETTY: I know that you did. You successfully completed the program. But the problem is that your aftercare doesn't seem to be working.

DIANE: I think this is all a big exaggeration. The only thing that happened here is that the babysitter left, and that's not my fault.

BETTY: I understand that you feel that this is an overreaction, Diane. You do have some choices about what happens from here. One is that you can decide to work with us and to come to an agreement on a contract about completing an assessment, and the other is that you can decide to go to juvenile court and talk to the judge.

DIANE: I'm not going to court. I'm not going to court. You took my sister to court, and she doesn't have her kids anymore. I'm not going to court.

BETTY: So given those two options, you'd rather work with us than go to court.

DIANE: I don't have any choice. 'Cause I'm not going to court.

BETTY: Okay, it doesn't feel like much of a choice. You would prefer that we forget the whole thing. If you do choose to work with us rather than go to court, we expect you to complete the assessment and we will support the recommendations they make. I have a list of places that could provide an assessment for you. You can pick from this list or suggest another place that we might use.

6. *Reaffirm choices and negotiable options.* Remaining empathic while being firm around non-negotiable requirements requires skill and pa-

tience. Betty presents options that Diane accurately perceives as coerced choices since the agency is unwilling to negotiate around an alcoholism assessment. Further negotiable options with Diane will be explored in chapter 9.

This chapter on preparation for initial contact and socialization skills is the first of four designed to translate the legal, ethical, and effectiveness principles developed in part I into concrete guidelines for practice with individual involuntary clients. These steps have included identification of non-negotiable requirements, negotiable issues, free choices, and rights. Additional steps have included anticipation of negative responses to pressured contact and selective confrontation about non-negotiable requirements.

The guidelines have been differentiated for mandated and nonvoluntary clients. Practitioners working with mandated clients are advised to present constrained choices, including the choice to accept legal alternatives to the services of the helping practitioner, and selective confrontation around non-negotiable requirements. Practitioners working with nonvoluntary clients are encouraged to emphasize the choice to participate in contact, including weighing the benefits and costs of such contact. Confrontation is suggested as most appropriate with nonvoluntary clients around potential consequences of decisions and inconsistency between client behaviors and their expressed goals.

The heavy emphasis on socialization is based on the observation that most work with involuntary clients appears to continue with non-negotiated involuntary service plans. Such practice often includes a cycle of low compliance with mandates, increased use of coercive measures, and the lack of maintenance of gains beyond the use of those measures. Completion of these steps is designed to enhance motivational congruence including higher levels of voluntarism, increase self-attribution, and decrease reactance, deviant labeling and use of self-presentation strategies (see part I). The capacity to carry out these guidelines is influenced by the time, resources, and discretionary powers practitioners have available to negotiate with clients.

Additional adaptations will be necessary for working with clients from specific populations and with specific issues. For example, adaptations have not been suggested here for work with members of specific subcultural groups and people of color. Some writers have suggested the need for particular cultural sensitivity on the part of practitioners to beliefs and values that the client may bring that are different from those of the practitioner or the majority culture.[31] On the other hand, John Longres has suggested that many behaviors that have been identified as cultural responses to helping may in part be responses to imbalanced power relationships.[32] For example, the widely accepted generalization that African-American and Native American clients are less likely to maintain eye contact with practitoners may be influenced both by culture and power imbalance. Hence, he suggests that members of the majority culture who are called in to meet with an authority figure are as inclined to drop their eyes as are persons from cultures in which lack of eye contact may be considered a sign of deference or respect. Additional study and research will be needed to make appropriate adaptations for work with clients with specific problems and from different cultural backgrounds.

Preparation for initial contact and socialization then prepares the way for negotiation and contracting skills to be developed in chapters 9 and 10.

# Negotiation and Contracting with Involuntary Clients

Socialization steps presented in chapter 8 lead in this chapter to negotiation and contracting steps designed to enhance motivation congruence and increase voluntarism through exploring available choices. The chapter begins with an exploration of the distinction between the "good" relationship and the negotiated relationship. Four negotiating and contracting options with mandated and nonvoluntary clients are then presented, followed by a discussion of obstacles to negotiation and contracting.

## The "Good Relationship" and the Negotiated Relationship

Most treatment approaches suggest that the development of a relationship is essential to productive change. Unfortunately, for the practitioner working with involuntary clients, the model for such relationships has been the voluntary relationship. Cingolani suggests that practitioners have been taught to value therapeutic relationships as the model for "good" practitioner-client relationships.[1] Such "good" relationships assume contact with clients who are willing to be engaged in a collaborative, contractual service and that practitioners can help by attending to client concerns in a warm, empathic, and genuine fashion. Clients who oppose such collaboration are often labeled resistive. Consequently, practitioners working with involuntary clients often find that their relationships are not "good."

Palmer suggests that these voluntary treatment assumptions ignore power and authority issues that exist in all practitioner-client relationships, whether mandated or not.[2] In addition to employing expert authority, which is invested in practitioners by client confidence in their ability, practitioners also employ legitimate power through the authority of their position, role, and agency. Finally, reward and coercive powers are also inherent in most practice relationships.[3]

Power relations can be explored more directly by considering the negotiated relationship. The negotiated relationship acknowledges use of authority. For example, practitioners working with mandated clients use reward, coercion, and legitimate powers to act as *enforcers* to induce compliance. They can also act as *negotiators* who represent the agency in bargaining with the client, as *mediators* in the interaction between the client and society, as *advocates* who identify with client interests and, as *coaches* who collaborate with clients to enhance their capacity for dealing with the environment.[4]

In order to play the negotiator and mediator, Murdach suggests that practitioners must discover the bargainable, find areas of agreement, engage in critical bargaining, exchange counterproposals, and present the results of the negotiation in a public document.[5]

As noted above, one assumption of the "good relationship" is collaborative, contractual service. Seabury defines contracting as a negotiation process resulting in a mutual agreement that specifies client and practitioner roles, goals and target problems, client rights, methods to be used, time limits, tasks agreed upon, and criteria for deciding whether goals are reached.[6] If, according to Seabury, mutual agreement on *all* goals, roles, and methods is an integral part of contracting, then contracts are rarely feasible for mandated and nonvoluntary clients.[7] In fact, Seabury questions whether contracts are possible with "captured" clients who do not acknowledge problems nor see the agency or practitioner as a source of help.[8] He describes contracts with captured clients as "corrupt" when clients have no interest in contact, little power to affect their own goals, and no items are negotiable (see chapter 5).[9] In addition, involuntary clients cannot easily withdraw from the contract and often suffer *consequences* for failure to comply with its terms. Finally, mandated clients often find such contracts to include *unbalanced accountability* as the contract is often used more to hold them accountable to the practitioner and agency than vice versa.

Such corrupt contracts were introduced in chapter 5 as *involuntary service plans* or *notices of agency intent* that include notification of non-

Voluntary Contracts,
Semi-Voluntary Contracts,
and Involuntary Case Plans

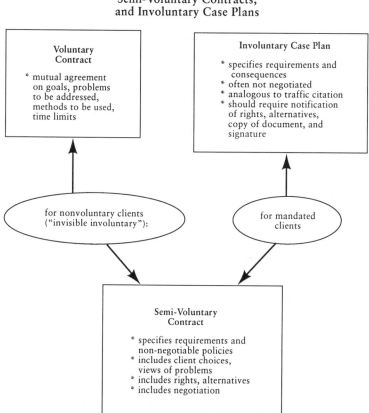

Figure 9.1

negotiable requirements, specification of rights, and consequences for failure to meet requirements. While lacking the key ingredient for voluntary contracts of *mutual* negotiation of goals, methods, and time limits, such involuntary service plans are necessary in many circumstances in which there are legal mandates and collaboration does not occur (see figure 9.1).

Such involuntary service plans have distinct limitations. Some agencies do not require that such plans be signed, or that clients see or have copies of them. When plans are developed with minimal or no client contact, they might better be described as *notices of agency intent* that detail what the agency and practitioner wish to happen and consequences to the mandated clients for failure to follow these plans. As discussed in chapters 4 and 5, such notices are analogous to traffic citations that inform the motorist of charges, evidence, legal rights, and constrained choices such as making a court appearance or paying a fine. While situations exist in which such involuntary case plans and notices of intent may be unavoidable, such plans cannot be expected to contribute to motivational congruence or the self-attribution that would permit results to last longer than would the threat of punishment (see chapter 5).

Are there alternatives to the voluntary contract, as described by Seabury, and the involuntary service plan? The *semi-voluntary contract* acknowledges outside pressures and mandates by specifying non-negotiable requirements and policies, consequences for failure to meet them, and specifies client freedoms and rights. It also includes negotiable options and client-perceived problems. Murdach and Cingolani suggest that such semi-voluntary agreements are possible with involuntary clients when a social conflict perspective is adopted.[10] In such a perspective, conflict is defined as normal and the practitioner focuses on constructive ways to manage the conflict.[11] Pursuit of semi-voluntary contracts assumes that contracting is an *intervention process as well as a piece of paper* that goes beyond fulfilling external accountability requirements and "getting the goods" on mandated clients to become a powerful service method designed to enhance compliance, motivational congruence, and self-attribution.

Many mandated clients are able to work with practitioners on semi-voluntary contracts when constrained choices are explored. Four strategies for exploring such choices are introduced briefly and then explained in detail below. Mandated clients can choose not to comply with legal mandates and non-negotiable requirements and accept legal penalties through an informed consent strategy. They can also choose to comply with legal mandates and non-negotiable requirements. The practitioner can help mandated clients find their own reasons for complying with mandates through a reframing or agreeable mandate strategy. Mandated clients and practitoners can also come to agreement through provision of an inducement in addition to working on non-negotiable requirements through a quid pro quo strategy. Finally, practitioners can acknowledge motivation to avoid punishing consequences by accepting compliance in order to get rid of the mandate.

Nonvoluntary clients can often move from semi-voluntary to voluntary contracts through strategies parallel to those for mandated clients in which they explore constrained chocies. The practitioner can first use the informed consent strategy to inform them of their freedom from legal requirements to accept or reject services based on an analysis of the costs and benefits of that service. Nonvoluntary clients can also choose to accept services for their own reasons regardless of outside pressure. They may choose to blend their own concerns with those of the outside pressure through the reframing or agreeable mandate strategy. Nonvoluntary clients can choose to accept services in order to receive an incentive through the quid pro quo strategy. Finally, they can choose to accept services in order to "get rid of the outside pressure." Though voluntary contracts remain preferable with nonvoluntary clients, semi-voluntary contracts may be beneficial for many. For example, when the nonvoluntary client enters a program or institution with a host of requirements and policies as a "package deal" (i.e., accept these requirements and policies or "choose" to refuse services), such a semi-voluntary contract may more accurately reflect the nature of the constrained choice the nonvoluntary client makes than a voluntary contract.

## Steps in Negotiation and Contracting

Steps in the negotiation and contracting phase are: 1) explore client's view of existing problems, 2) explore reframing for an agreeable mandate strategy, 3) explore a quid pro quo option, 4) explore a "get rid of the mandate or outside pressure" option, or 5) explore an informed consent option.[12] These strategies may be used in a different order and varying combinations. Variations for work with mandated and nonvoluntary clients will be presented.

1. *Explore client's view of existing problems.* Many involuntary clients present their own views of problems during the socialization phase. Such client views are often missed because they are not the "right" motivations, hence labeled as lack of motivation, refusal to take responsibility, denial, or defensive behavior. The practitioner should listen carefully for expressions of client beliefs, values, and motivations during this phase without labeling them as expressions of *no* motivation, but rather understand them as expressions of *current* motivations, values, attitudes, and beliefs.

For example, when Mrs. Torres, a single-parent mother with a full-time job, was in danger of having her child removed from an extremely cluttered home that was a serious fire hazard, she protested that she had already begun efforts to renovate her home. Jean, the child protective service worker, notes that Mrs. Torres has made efforts and compliments her. She will later suggest that

Mrs. Torres' efforts may fit in part with the external pressure to make her home a safer place.

MRS. TORRES: These are my things, you know. I'm going to get around to it sometime. In fact, when we moved in, I got some stuff cleaned up right away. But I've really been busy. It's okay, it's good enough, it's better. We've got room here to get through now. And I do have a few more things to do.

JEAN: I know that these are your things. I can also see that you really have made some efforts. What have you worked on so far?

MRS. TORRES: Well, before we moved in we painted the cupboards in the kitchen. Can you see it out there?

JEAN: Yes, they look great. That room really shows that you have been making some efforts.

Rather than labeling Mrs. Torres' efforts as merely minimizing danger, Jean supports the efforts she has made. As Mrs. Torres may feel overwhelmed with the responsibilities of working at a full-time job, managing a house, and parenting a teenager, Jean should also have empathized with the feelings of being overwhelmed. She will also explore the provision of a homemaker to assist Mrs. Torres in her efforts.

Initial attitudes, beliefs, and concerns of mandated clients often include motivations that may be blended with mandates to enhance compliance. For example, Beth was an adolescent who had traveled widely through the child welfare system with stops in residential care, chemical dependency treatment, group care, foster care, and her own home. She had just worn out her welcome in a relative placement with her Aunt Barb. Nancy, her child welfare worker, was operating under a requirement that Beth needed to be living in a stable, permanent placement. While Nancy was exploring the circumstances of Beth's latest move from her Aunt Barb's, Beth said, "I don't want people telling me how to run my life. I don't want it no more. If it ain't my boy friend, it's Barb; if it ain't Barb, it's you; and if it ain't you, it's my parents. All of you guys are running my life and all you guys got me is nowhere."[13]

Rather than labeling Beth's expression as a refusal to accept responsibility for her own part in problems, Nancy might note Beth's implied motivation by suggesting, "It sounds like you have had it with other people making decisions for you."

If involuntary clients have not already expressed problems or concerns in the socialization phase, they are now asked for their views of problems that exist or situations that could be improved. The involuntary client can reply by describing a problem, stating that no problems exist, or make no reply. These responses can further be examined for fit with outside pressures or mandates. Such concerns may be similar to the mandate or outside pressure, unrelated to the mandate or outside pressure, directed at avoiding the mandate or outside pressure, or no response to pressures is expressed. Four contracting strategies will be described below to address these contingencies.

2. *Explore reframing for agreeable mandate strategy.* The practitioner can explore expressed concerns, values, or motivations for fit with outside pressures or mandates. The agreeable mandate is similar to reframing strategies in which practitioners are trained to join clients and families rather than insist that they work on the "right problems for the right reasons." Much of the social work practice literature suggests that the practitioner "join" the resistant client.[14] Similarly in family therapy, Anderson and Stewart suggest that "there are no resistant families, only resistant therapists."[15]

a. *Variations for mandated clients.* Practitioners working with mandated clients seek to blend mandated concerns with client motivations such that mandated clients may choose to work on those required concerns for their own reasons. Use of this strategy does not mean that the practitioner joins or "hooks" the client without being clear about his or her own motivation. Mandated clients must be informed that mandated, non-negotiable concerns will be included. Three variations can be explored with mandated clients that blend client concerns with mandated concerns.

Mandated referrals often state or imply deviant labeling and an assumption of responsibility that involuntary clients are unwilling to accept. Mandated clients may, however, discover their own reasons for complying with the mandate. For example, when Jean was working with Mrs. Torres on the child protection issue related to a fire hazard, she found that though Mrs. Torres did not consider the state of her home adequate grounds for removal of her child, she acknowledged that she did not have enough help from her daughter in keeping the house clean. She wanted to have the house cleaned for the holidays, she wanted a safe environment for her child, and she wanted the child welfare agency to stop snooping on her. Mrs. Torres agreed to a contract when the practitioner pointed out that she had already begun making some efforts on her own to clean up, that she might be assisted with a homemaker, that could get the agency out of her hair, and that she could also avoid a possible placement.

When mandated clients are faced with coerced choices about requirements, they can often choose the way they respond to those requirements. As contact often begins in crisis, the Chinese definition of crisis as a "dangerous opportunity" might be shared. For example, if involuntary clients note that the problem had been building up for awhile but they had not acted to change it, the practitioner might say:

You have been wrestling with these issues for a long time. You may have thought about getting some help with these issues on your own and now something has happened that forced you to be here. You can make some choices in this situation about how you want to use your time and what you want to get out of this. You might choose to take your chances in court. You might choose to go along and ride it out, doing what you are required to do. You might also choose to use this opportunity to take a look at some of the concerns you have already been aware of.

Similarly, mandated clients might be asked to recall if there was ever a time in their past that something good came out of doing something they did not want to do. When had they made the most out of a bad situation? When had they made "lemonade out of lemons"? Could this be a time to make lemonade again?

Following this strategy, Bill, the probation officer introduced in chapter 8, helps Paul explore possible problems he might choose to work on.[16]

BILL: I want to find out if there are some things you would like to get out of probation, some things that you and I could work on together.

PAUL: Not to get in this situation again.

BILL: Okay, you don't want to be in this kind of situation again in which you are having to serve time for a crime.

PAUL: It doesn't work.

BILL: Okay. Is there anything else you and I can work on together that you would like to get out of probation? Not what the court is saying, but what you would like to get out of probation?

Some mandated clients perceive a concern similar to the mandated reason for referral without accepting responsibility for causing the problem. For example, many parents accused of child abuse think that their children are difficult to control.[17] The practitioner could provisionally accept their view of the problem while stipulating that illegal forms of child discipline would not be used and legal, effective alternatives substituted.[18]

Sometimes the mandated concern and the client-expressed problem can be reframed into a new statement that includes both by grouping them at a higher level of abstraction. For example, Beth, the adolescent who thought that "too many people are trying to run her life" was faced with a mandate that she live in an approved placement. Her concern and the mandated problem were blended in a reframed agreeable mandate: Beth thinks that too many people are trying to run her life. She wants to explore independent living. Such a reframing affirms the validity of the client's own concern without blaming or attaching a deviant label to it, while remaining firm about non-negotiable requirements.

b. *Variations for nonvoluntary clients.* Nonvoluntary clients can choose to avoid the outside pressure altogether, to work on their own concerns without regard for that pressure, or to work on a reframed view that includes both the outside pressure and their own concerns.

For example, Mr. Porter was an elderly patient hospitalized with a broken hip who wished to return to his home upon discharge. He was, however, locked in a struggle with medical staff about discharge plans. He did not accept the plans developed by hospital personnel and found ways to circumvent those plans he had not participated in developing. While medical staff were reluctant for Mr. Porter to return to an unsafe environment and recommended nursing home care, Mr. Porter resented intrusions into his independence.[19] In working with Mr. Porter, his hospital social worker presented several options. First, he could choose to avoid the outside pressure altogether. As there was no legal mandate at this point, the medical social worker reaffirmed that he could legally choose to return home against medical advice. She proceeded to present a two-sided argument to assist him in making that decision. Should he choose to return home without assistance, he would be taking chances that he might be reinjured and need to return to the hospital. The social worker also reminded Mr. Porter that he had expressed a wish to return home safely and not to return to the hospital. Hence, he could choose to work on his own concerns without regard to the outside pressure. The social worker then explored the possibility that his concern with returning home safely and not returning to the hospital could include the hospital staff's concerns about his safety. When his own goal of returning home safely was reaffirmed, Mr. Porter became more willing to consider staff advice about how to make that return. The staff meetings that had been structured to convince or pressure Mr. Porter to accept staff views were then restructured. When staff agreed to take the role as consultants to assist him in planning for a safe return and he was able to attend staffings, Mr. Porter and staff negotiated an agreement that included safety provisions he found acceptable such as assistance in repair of a broken bannister and arrangements for a visiting nurse.

The previous strategies assume that many involuntary clients do not wish to work on "the right problems for the right reasons" in the sense of acknowledging the problems attributed by others. This is of course not always true as some involuntary clients genuinely seek help despite the outside pressure or mandate, and accept responsibility for both the problem and the resolution of it. Some involuntary clients readily acknowledge attributed problems, saying things such as: "I know that I need to get in touch with my inability to control my impulses"; "I need to accept my disability"; "I need to get in touch with my codependency issues" "I need to pay attention in class"; "I need to keep a job"; "I need to stay sober and accept my responsibilities." Such rapid acceptance, including all the right words and motivations, may indicate internalization, ownership of responsibility for the problem, insight, and confession.

If, however, the admission sounds too good to be true, it may be. Such admissions may be an ingratiating self-presentation strategy designed to reduce pressure through rapid, selective confession (see chapter 7).[20] Such expressions may reflect the possibility that the involuntary client is "bilingual" and speaks the jargon of the helping professions. However, rather than labeling such expressions as manipulative or passive aggressive behavior, the practitioner might consider less than full candor understandable and in fact reinforced in many settings. For example, involuntary clients experienced in residential, correctional, chemical dependency, or educational systems (among others) may have been rewarded for confessing or owning problems as seen by the staff that indicate that they are "getting in touch with their issues." There is no immediate way of knowing whether such admissions are genuine or, in fact, "too good to be true." Practitioners may accept such admissions at face value while suggesting that many in similar situations have mixed feelings about being pressured into contact.

The agreeable mandate option is the most positive of the four strategies to be presented and should be frequently explored. If agreement is reached, it should lead to greater compliance of mandated clients, empowerment through making at least constrained choices, self-attribution and longer-lasting change.[21] The option requires both practitioner time and skill in reframing. Time is, however, often very limited at initial contact and a crisis state may preclude extended negotiation. In addition, the practitioner may think that agreeable mandates effectively link concerns but the involuntary client does not see or accept the linkage.

Should the practitioner and involuntary client settle on an "agreeable mandate," they can then proceed to elaborate upon a semi-voluntary or voluntary contract. If the problems cannot be readily reframed, the involuntary client's expressed concerns do not fit the mandated or outside pressures, or the practitioner wishes to explore additional sources of motivation, the practitioner then proceeds to consider the other strategies presented below.

3. *Explore the quid pro quo option.* Often no or weak intrinsic motivation for dealing with the mandated concern is found through the agreeable mandate option. In such cases, exploring use of inducements can strengthen compliance with mandates. In a quid pro quo version, the practitioner offers to supply an incentive to a mandated client to make compliance with the requirement more attractive. The practitioner can supply an incentive to nonvoluntary clients *in exchange* for their choice to work on a problem attributed by others. If no acceptable deal is made, the practitioner can continue to explore the strategies that follow.

a. *Variations for mandated clients.* Since practitioners cannot barter on non-negotiable requirements with mandated clients, this option can be used to support mandated compliance by working on an additional voluntary concern, providing incentives, or supporting choices in the *form* of compliance with the mandate.[22]

i. *Work on an additional voluntary concern.* When a problem is expressed that is unrelated to the mandated concern, practitioners can sometimes make a deal to assist with that concern *in addition* to work on the mandated problem. For example, Jean, the protective service worker, became aware that Mrs. Torres thought that her daughter was not helping her enough around the house and generally did not follow her rules. While these problems were not directly related to the mandated concern with safety, Jean offered to help Mrs. Torres work with her daughter around house rules and her role in helping make the home a safer place. In addition, Mrs. Torres expressed many times her concern that her valuable things not be discarded in an effort to make the home safe by the standards of others. Jean agreed to help her protect her valuable things as long as they were not a safety hazard.

ii. *Provide an incentive.* The practitioner can offer to provide an incentive to enhance compliance. For example, in a diversion program for prostitutes, a practitioner agreed to advocate for a reduction in loitering tickets contingent on the prostitutes' willingness to participate in treatment programs.

iii. *Support choice within the bounds of compliance.* Practitioners can support the selection of options in the way that requirements are implemented. For example, when Mr. James became aware that he was going to be involuntarily hospitalized, he became extremely agitated and struggled with mental health staff. A mental health aide then clarified for him that the permission for involuntary hospitalization had been gotten and Mr. James could not immediately change that. He could choose, however, how he would go to the ward, and he could be helped to initiate a legal appeal after he got to the ward. If he continued struggling, he would be forcibly restrained and taken to the unit. If he was able to become calmer, he would be able to walk up to the unit accompanied by mental health aides but without restraints. Mr. James calmed himself and chose to walk up to the ward, accompanied by the aides.

b. *Variations for nonvoluntary clients.* Use of incentives with nonvoluntary clients must not involve rights, entitlements, and basic necessities, but rather entail *additional benefits* that the practitioner or agency is not required to provide. Its success depends, however, on the ease with which the nonvoluntary client can acquire similar incentives in other ways. Hence, the quid pro quo option is subject to abuse with vulnerable clients from oppressed groups. For example, a Native American woman from Minnesota left her child with relatives out of state. When she did not return at the agreed upon time, the relatives contacted social services and requested that the child be placed. When the woman returned, she discovered that her child was in a white foster home. She was assessed as having a drinking problem and the agency did not agree to release her child to foster care in Minnesota or return the child to her until she completed a chemical dependency treatment program and got a job. These requirements were illegal as Native American children are entitled to placement in Native American homes as a first option, without condition.[23] Similarly, transfer of the child to Minnesota was a right, not a privilege. In this case, establishing conditions for placement of the child in a Native American home and in Minnesota was illegal and an unethical abuse of a vulnerable client from an oppressed group. Capacity to parent the child might be appropriately assessed by social services in Minnesota in a way that did not violate these legal and ethical rights.

i. *Work on an additional voluntary concern in exchange for compliance with external pressure.* Wilmer, the client of a community support program formerly hospitalized for psychotic behavior, was introduced in chapter 6. His community support worker attempted to persuade Wilmer to take his psychotropic medication in order to avoid rehospitalization. Wilmer found the side effects unpleasant and considered mention of rehospitalization a threat to force him to take the medication. While the benefits of taking the medication appeared obvious to the practitioner to support Wilmer's continued life in the community, Wilmer certainly saw no intrinsic value in taking them. He was, however, concerned that his driving license had been revoked when he was hospitalized and not restored upon return to the community. The practitioner suggested that Wilmer would be more likely to regain his driver's license if he complied with the medication and in fact offered to advocate on his behalf, should he comply with the medication. She agreed to advocate with the understanding that a review board would make a decision and a positive decision could not be guaranteed. In addition, she offered on a noncontingent basis to have his medication reviewed for appropriateness, since this was a right and not an additional benefit. Wilmer had his dosage changed and agreed to take the medication toward the goal of regaining his license. Hence, taking the medication was resumed not for any intrinsic appreciation of its benefits but as an instrumental means toward regaining his license.

ii. *Provision of an inducement.* Alice, the client described in chapter 1 who lived in a home with many cats and just above the threshold of legal danger, agreed to explore her eligibility for social security benefits if the practitioner would accompany her and arrange transportation to the office. In this case, since assistance with client transportation was not a client right, it might be provided as a legitimate inducement.

There are four concerns with the quid pro quo option. As suggested in chapter 6, it is unethical to barter basic rights, entitlements, and necessities for compliance with mandated or externally pressured goals. Inducements must be an additional benefit beyond normal entitlements. As practitioners and agencies are sometimes tempted to cross this legal and ethical line, the strategy is subject to abuse with vulnerable involuntary clients from oppressed groups who have limited alternative access to desired resources.

Second, this option may "buy" behavioral compliance without changing attitudes or promoting self-attributed change. Some practitioners and settings may reject behavioral compliance without prior attitude change as "working on the right problems for the *wrong* reasons," insisting on acceptance of mandated or externally pressured changes for the right reasons. While such acknowledgment of attributed problems might be desirable, insistence on attitude change as a precondition for behavioral change is rarely successful. This option makes it more likely that behavior will change and attitude change may follow. However, compliance should not be expected to be maintained indefinitely unless that compliance becomes intrinsically rewarding or rewarded in the

environment. To support self-attribution and longer-lasting maintenance, the inducements should be small and phased into natural reinforcers (see chapter 6).[24]

Use of this option also presumes that the practitioner has access to
valued resources, is empowered with discretion to make deals, and has
the time required to negotiate. Many agencies have policies that discourage making special arrangements on the grounds that they are unfair to
other clients not offered such options. Hence, much of the legal reform
in work with public agencies has focused on removing discretion and
establishing uniform procedures. Even when negotiation is permitted,
practitioners often lack access to incentives and have limited time for
exploring them. With these reservations, the examples above suggest
that with imagination and sensitivity, practitioners can be aware of
issues that can act as ethical incentives for clients.

Finally, practitioners must learn how to negotiate. As negotiation
requires the practitioner to engage in an exchange of proposals and
counterproposals, practitioners have to learn how to continue negotiation without personalizing the problem even when an unacceptable
counterproposal has been presented. For example, when Jean offered to
advocate for the placement of a housekeeper to assist Mrs. Torres in
cleaning up her home, Mrs. Torres responded that she wouldn't mind
having a homemaker if she was under her control. Jean then clarifies the
conditions under which a homemaker might be provided.

MRS. TORRES: You know, I wouldn't mind having a homemaker if I
could tell her what to do. Now, I don't want you guys to be running
my house. I mean this homemaker, I'd be in charge of her, I could tell
her what to do, you guys wouldn't tell her to come and take all this
stuff out?

JEAN: Well, that's a good question about who would be in charge. I
am here to make sure that you and Julie are safe. So the homemaker
would be working for the agency as part of our plan to help you get
the house into a safe condition and not directly working for you. You
could work with her in identifying the valuable things you want to
keep and the things that you just consider junk.

4. *Explore the "get rid of the mandate or outside pressure" option.*
Many involuntary clients express no concern or acknowledge only the
pressure to see the practitioner as a concern: "Other than being here
with you, I've got no problems." Such responses are often interpreted as
denial, resistance, or failure to accept responsibility rather than accepted
as an indication that the involuntary client does not acknowledge at-

tributed problems. The practitioner can take the initiative by suggesting that facing a mandated situation or pressure from others may be a problem that the involuntary client might wish eliminated.[25] In this "get rid of the mandate or outside pressure" option, the involuntary client may agree to contact in order to avoid or eliminate pressure rather than by acknowledging the validity of the outside pressure or mandate or through actions to receive an incentive. Hence, this option relies on punishment avoidance motivation, rather than the inducement and self-attribution motivations characteristic of the first two options (see chapter 6).

If the involuntary client accepts this option, the practitioner can proceed to formalize a semi-voluntary contract with the client. Should no agreement be reached, the practitioner can proceed to an informed consent strategy.

a. *Variations for mandated clients.* Mandated clients often respond to mandated pressure as if to punishment, whether or not that pressure is designed in part to help or rehabilitate the client. Rather than continuing to argue about the merits of work on the mandated problem, acknowledging a motivation of punishment avoidance or elimination can be a useful step toward some motivational congruence. For example, some involuntary clients find the option to end the contact early more acceptable than contracting around a problem they consider invalid. Since many adolescent clients on court-ordered supervision consider requirements for regular contact with a practitioner aversive, the practitioner can capitalize on this motivation by negotiating frequency and number of contacts based on compliance with a set of required tasks.[26] This option can sometimes be used at a point in which more positive motivations have not been found. For example, after the home investigation revealed that Mrs. Torres would need to clean and remove boxes if Julie were to be safe, she did not respond placidly to this news.

MRS. TORRES: I don't know why you people are making such a big deal. The people down the street are yelling and fighting and I hear them screaming and playing music; and here I got a few too many boxes and you people come in here and tell me how to run my life. This is my house and these are my things, you shouldn't be able to tell me I have to get rid of them. Why don't you investigate those people, who are about three houses down, they've got trash out in their backyard and they are always yelling and screaming in the middle of the night. And here you are picking on somebody like me. I'm working, taking care of my kids, you guys make me sick.

JEAN: I can see that you are very angry because of my comments about the boxes in the other room.

MRS. TORRES: Well, of course I'm angry. You come in here, you high and mighty, you think you're so good. Why wouldn't I be angry, did you ever have anybody tell you about your house, that they don't like it?

JEAN: No, that has not happened to me, but I'm sure that I would be angry too.

MRS. TORRES: Well, I am. I am.

JEAN: I can hear that you are angry. If we had gotten a report on your neighbors, someone would have to conduct an investigation.

MRS. TORRES: Well, I ought to report them and get you off my back. I'm working hard.

JEAN: You want me out, huh?

MRS. TORRES: Yes.

JEAN: Well, again, I'm here because we need to make sure Julie is safe. And the way to do that is to help get the house into a safe condition. If you want me out, as soon as Julie is safe and the house is safe, I'm out.

This option may also be used simultaneously with other more positive contracting strategies. After the above exchange, a semi-voluntary contract was agreed upon with Mrs. Torres including: 1) she wanted her home clean for the holidays and to retain custody of Julie (agreeable mandate); 2) she would receive the assistance of a homemaker for a time limited period; 3) Jean would work with Mrs. Torres and Julie to help them work together in cleaning up ("let's make a deal"); and 4) Mrs. Torres wanted to "get you people out of my hair" (get rid of mandate).

b. *Variations with nonvoluntary clients.* While nonvoluntary clients can choose to avoid working with the practitioner, they may also choose to work on ridding themselves of the outside pressure without acknowledging its legitimacy. For example, many schoolchildren are referred to counselors and social workers for a variety of attributed problems such as inattention, truancy, and inadequate study skills. While they frequently do not acknowledge these teacher-attributed problems, they often acknowledge other problems: "Other students provoke me, get me in trouble with the teacher"; "The teacher picks on me." Hence, if the problem is framed according to an acknowledged problem such as "to get the teacher off my back," a semi-voluntary contract may be reached.[27] For example, Walter summed up the situation with Mrs. Simmons, who was in a nonvoluntary relationship with the county worker over care of her child.

WALTER: From what you're telling me, you are pretty concerned about what's going on at the school. The school has concerns and you have your own concerns. You think that something needs to change between Jamie, the school, and yourself.

MRS. SIMMONS: Yeah, something definitely needs to change there.

WALTER: If we can can get things changed at school, so that the other kids and teachers aren't picking on Jamie, and so that his behavior improves there, that will satisfy the court. If we start making some progress, the court would probably dismiss that consent decree early. You'll get them off your back. It will also get the school off your back. It also sounds as if Jamie's behavior at home could also be the focus of some attention. It can't be a lot of fun to go to work in a high stress job, then come home and have the teacher calling you and saying, "This or that happened today, and I want you to do something about it." And then for you to tell Jamie you want him to do something, and he tells you, "No." It's got to be frustrating. And I think that maybe we can look at that too, if you'd like.

Since this option focuses on removing a threat of punishment, it entails less positive motivation than the first two. As noted in chapter 6, negative reinforcement strategies may enhance compliance without leading to self-attribution. Consequently, this option runs the risk of buying compliance only for the length of the contract and, like the "let's make a deal" or quid pro quo strategy, may be seen as working on "the right problems for the wrong reasons" by some referral sources and agencies. It does, however, connect with client motivation to restore freedom and hence may reduce reactance and enhance compliance. In addition, practitioners with access to coercive power may be tempted to overuse it (see chapter 7). For example, practitioners working with mandated clients may frequently find punishment avoidance motivation immediately available and may be tempted to begin with it. In order to support motivational congruence and self-attribution, it should be attempted *after* or in conjuction with the more positive strategies described above.

5. *Explore informed consent option.* Should none of the above achieve a level of motivational congruence, the practitioner can pursue a final *informed consent* option. Mandated clients can be reminded of their right to accept the consequences for failing to work on legal requirements or choose to comply with the minimum acceptable level to satisfy the requirement. Nonvoluntary clients can be reminded repeatedly through the contracting sequence that they can choose not to accept services. The decision not to accept services should, however, be informed by potential consequences of that choice.

a. *Variations for mandated clients.* Some mandated clients experience such a negative reaction to forced contact that even agreeing to "get rid of the mandate" is not acceptable since it symbolizes some compliance in a disagreeable process. Hence, some mandated clients may choose to accept a legal penalty or the threat that a penalty will be imposed, or choose to comply with the bare minimum.

Those choices and their consequences can be clarified including the potentially self-defeating consequences of deciding not to contract. By refusing contracting options, the mandated client places most decision making in the practitioner's hands. For example, after having several contracting possibilities rejected by a teenaged client referred for delinquency, one practitioner proceeded to write her assessment in the client's presence. When the client asked what she was doing, the practitioner explained that since he had not chosen to participate in contracting, she was proceeding to carry out her job requirements and develop a plan without his input.

Some mandated clients reconsider when the consequences of failure to reach agreeement are clarified and earlier options can be reexamined in search of a semi-voluntary contract. If the mandated client does not reconsider contracting, the practitioner can empathize with pressures felt, and proceed to reaffirm the non-negotiable requirements of contact. The practitioner's role will essentially be one of enforcer at this point in contact, though more voluntary contracting may be possible later. For example, had Jean and Mrs. Torres been unable to come to an agreement, their interaction might have been as follows:

JEAN: Mrs. Torres, I want to make sure you're clear that my job is to make sure that Julie is safe.

MRS. TORRES: Julie is safe and will be fine.

JEAN: As we have discussed, we don't agree on that. If the house isn't at a level that will pass a safety inspection then I will be forced to recommend that Julie move to an out-of-home placement.

MRS. TORRES: Well, I don't think you can do that. Julie will never move, she's fine here. Julie and I are real close, she's not going to leave.

JEAN: I am sure that we both want Julie to be safe. It is my job to help you make sure that she is safe.

MRS. TORRES: You guys make me so sick, saying "We'll remove her from the home." Ha, there's people down the street that beat their kids, and I've never laid a hand on my daughter. And you say she's not safe.

JEAN: I agree with you that you have done what you could to parent

Julie and have not physically abused her in any way. I do also say that in the current situation, she is not safe. We have talked about ways that I can try to help you with the cleaning up, if you decide that you want to do that. I also want to make sure that you understand the consequences of the house not being at safety standard levels.

MRS. TORRES: You say it's because I've got a few extra boxes here, that you can take my daughter away from me.

JEAN: Yes, I do say that the extra boxes are adding up to a fire and health hazard for Julie and yourself. I would like you to take some time to think this over, about your choices, and make up your mind. I would like to leave my card in case you change your mind. If you decide not to change your mind, then I will be contacting you with a court date to consider out-of-home placement.

MRS. TORRES: I don't know. This makes me sick . . . I just hate it when you guys come in and try to tell me what to do.

JEAN: Yes, I know that you do hate it when other people come in and put pressure on you when you are trying to do what you can. You want to have us out of your life and to continue raising Julie as best you can. This has been a rough time for you. Why don't you take some time to think things over and then you can decide if you'd like to call me?

MRS. TORRES: Well, I don't know. I don't think I ever want to see you again, but you can leave your number here if you want to.

JEAN: Yes, I am sure you want me out of here as soon as possible and I would like to be out of your life too. I will leave my card.

Jean has attempted to empathize with Mrs. Torres while being clear about non-negotiable requirements and options. Failure to reconsider may indicate high reactance and, if so, that assessment is based on attempting several strategies to reduce reactance rather than based on a premature conclusion at the beginning of contact.

Some writers have suggested that high reactance in the form of opposition to all practitioner initiatives may call for use of a *defiance-based paradoxical strategy*. For example, if lack of compliance with practitioner initiatives can be predicted, then the practitioner might prescribe the *opposite* of what is desired.[28] Caution in use of defiance-based paradoxes is recommended with mandated clients. While evidence suggests that paradoxes can sometimes be effective in achieving compliance with practitioner goals, that achievement often occurs without self-attribution of gains.[29] The short-term compliance gains may also jeopardize the potential for influence later in the relationship since persuasive influence may be more likely to occur if involuntary clients come to see the practitioner as trustworthy (see chapter 6).

b. *Variations for nonvoluntary clients.* As the decision to accept or reject services is the legal and ethical right of nonvoluntary clients, any form of heavy-handed pressure is inappropriate. Hence, outreach efforts to potentially "at risk" clients such as teenaged single parents of newborns should provide information that can assist in making informed choices. For example, the practitioner might plant a seed with inductive questions about possible future difficulties experienced by others in similar situations and give the client information about resources they can seek should they come to have concerns in the future.

This chapter has presented contracting strategies designed to enhance compliance with mandates and non-negotiable requirements and also to facilitate motivational congruence, self-determination, and achievement of client-defined goals. Use of the contracting options should empower the practitioner and involuntary client toward more frequent semi-voluntary or voluntary contracting solutions. Practitioners skilled in these strategies should be able to reduce client reactance in the initial phase of contact, increase compliance with mandated goals and non-negotiable policies, and achieve more frequent motivational congruence. While these hypotheses are based on theory and research reviewed earlier in the book, they will require further testing with specific target problems and client populations before thay can be accepted as effective (see chapter 14).

In addition, many obstacles to use of these strategies can be anticipated in advance. Obstacles coming from involuntary clients, practitioners, and agencies can be anticipated when there is lack of resources, competence, or skills, or adverse beliefs. Suggestions for dealing with these obstacles are also presented.

## Lack of Resources, Competence, and Skills

Lack of adequate resources, competence, and skills can impede negotiation and contracting. Many involuntary clients lack competence, skill, or experience in contracting. Since contracting is largely a cognitive process, some clients lack the capacity to negotiate complex contracts. Further, practitioners sometimes consider that since some clients make impulsive decisions or ones based on factors the practitioners consider irrelevant, they cannot effectively participate in contracting. We noted above how Wilmer's decision to take antipsychotic medication was not based on an acceptance of its value for its own sake. Whether or not the client's decision making process is one that the practitioner considers acceptable, clients continue to make decisions. Use of the options in simple, concrete form should produce greater motivational congruence and success than if such congruence is not pursued.

Lack of resources, competence, and skills can also occur with practitioners and agencies. Social services frequently struggle with limited resources, often resulting in large caseloads and limited attention to individual clients. Consequently, practitioners can sometimes barely carry out the minimum mandated requirements while keeping up their paperwork. They may have little time to work on problems other than mandated or required concerns. Such overload can lead to standardized rather than individualized case plans, crisis-driven work and "going through the motions" (see chapter 14).

In addition, practitioners may not be permitted discretion to make deals such that they have little leverage over the packaging and form of requirements. Court orders and agency non-negotiable policies are sometimes written such that discretion in interpretation is unclear, or discretion is actively discouraged. Mandated goals may be required by funding bodies and ways of individualizing those goals not encouraged. For example, the frequency of contacts between a probation officer and client may be dictated by results of an assessment instrument rather than negotiated with the mandated client. Consequently, involuntary clients may desire a resource that the practitioner cannot provide and hence an acceptable exchange may not be attainable. Even when resources and discretion are available, effective use of the options requires practice and increasing skill in reframing and bargaining through separating the non-negotiable from the negotiable.

Use of the contracting options will not resolve resource deficits or increase discretion, and additional strategies are needed to influence such system needs (see chapter 14). In the short run, the practitioner might be advised to attempt using the options as time permits. As experience and competence in use of the strategies increases, it should be possible to use them on a larger proportion of the caseload.[30]

In addition, involuntary contacts often occur in a state of crisis such that involuntary clients fight with all their energies to preserve the status quo. Providing help with the perceived crisis is often an essential first step. For example, the home builders' model for family intervention recommends that immediate focus on assisting families with basic necessities is essential before moving on to effective contracting.[31] Practitioners and agencies also have crises. For many key involuntary positions such as child protection work, turnover is high and new practitioners enter work with limited training. Sudden additions to an already pressured caseload may put the practitioner in a crisis state, whether or not the client is actually in crisis. Finally, agency resource limitations can create a crisis mentality in the agency. The strategies presented here are proactive and can, in the long run, reduce some kinds of client and practitioner crises by ensuring that there is motivational congruence with at least some clients.

Since even semi-voluntary contracts involve an exchange of goods and services acceptable to all parties, sometimes an acceptable exchange is not reached. As involuntary clients may decide that requirements are unfair, unreasonable, or impossible to attain, they may decide to improve their situation outside of negotiation.[32] When coerced choices entail "godfather's choices" between unacceptable alternatives such as accepting services or being prosecuted, many involuntary clients will not consider these as choices. Since perceived intrusiveness of a threat to freedom varies such that what is considered overwhelming by one person may be acceptable to another, agreements may be reached with some and not others. Practitioners should advocate for fair, nondiscriminatory options. Should they not succeed in modifying unfair options, then high client reactance, apathy, and powerlessness may be expected as a consequence of overwhelming unfair requirements.

## Adverse Beliefs

The contracting process may also be inhibited by adverse beliefs on the part of clients, practitioners, and agencies, including the need to *work on the right problems for the right reasons,* beliefs that contracts and case plans are paperwork formalities rather than inherently valuable intervention processes, that the other party to the negotiation cannot be trusted, that goals conflict, and that oppose negotiation.

Practitioners working with involuntary clients are often influenced by approaches that insist on early ownership of responsibility for harm caused and for the success of change efforts. While self-attributed change is desirable, insistence on early ownership of responsibility may produce counterproductive stalemate and prevent later influence. Consequences of such beliefs in required early ownership of responsibility may be a continued struggle to outsmart involuntary clients and ultimate reliance on power to reward and punish. Practitioners operating under such beliefs in the necessity of the right reason for the right problem may have to accept as inevitable that they will continue to pull teeth and to work harder than the involuntary client who may appear oblivious to problems or needs to change. Failure to produce coerced change may reinforce pessimism and contribute to beliefs that congruence is not possible, that clients are not changeable, and lead to further client labeling.

The options presented here suggest that while complete congruence is frequently impossible, some congruence is often better than none. Use of the strategies does not mean practitioner acceptance of responsibility for outcome but rather acceptance of responsibility for *facilitating congruence*. It may be easier for a practitioner to reach such a position if the agency has also come to terms with what can and cannot be changed (see chapter 14). To use a baseball analogy, use of the strategies should increase the practitioner's batting average: skills in facilitating congruence does not mean that the practitioner will have a hit each time at the plate, but should connect more frequently. Averaging 3.5 hits in 10 opportunities is often enough to win batting titles and may be a desirable goal for practitioners working with involuntary clients.

In addition, contracts and case plans are often considered paperwork formalities by both involuntary clients and practitioners.[33] Practitioners may approach them as non-negotiable paperwork requirements completed to satisfy the needs of invisible state or agency auditors and visible supervisors. There may be few positive consequences for writing them effectively and negative consequences for lateness, checking the wrong box, or inconsistent use of the form. Practitioners may also have found that such paper transactions bear little resemblance to a reality in which involuntary clients sometimes provide superficial agreement, provide signatures without intending compliance, or may not even *see* the case plan. Similarly, involuntary clients may have experienced such "agreements" in the past as a railroaded formality. Use of semi-voluntary contracts will hence require some belief in the value of the process by practitioners. Involuntary clients without prior experience in other systems may be more optimistic about their value.

While contracts should build trust, there are many reasons why practitioners suspect lack of candor from involuntary clients and involuntary clients have similar suspicions of the practitioner. As the practitioner is not the agent of the mandated client, those clients have reason to be careful in deciding what information they will share. Their own perceived problems may have appeared petty and were punished in the past as a lack of accepting responsibility for "the problem." As suggested above, early confessions may have been rewarded in the past, whether or not they were sincere. Such experienced involuntary clients may have found that you may not have to comply completely as long as you say the right words.

Similarly, involuntary clients have reasons to be suspicious of practitioner candor. Practitioners and agencies often *do* have hidden agendas. Mandated practitioners are not in place primarily to serve involuntary clients. Practitioners may practice manipulative, hooking strategies in which the axiom "start where the client is" is an instrumental technique used "to get them to where you them want to go." Hence, strategies of superficial agreement on one set of goals while in fact pursuing a hidden agenda to get at the "root problem" is common practice.[34] Some writers have suggested that complete candor may impede effectiveness as the client system may oppose any overt change effort.[35] Similarly, service decisions are not always made on the merits of the case but according to agency policy and resources. For example, while reducing out-of-home placement costs has played at least a part in the current movement toward home-based services, this reason is not always shared with families.[36]

In addition, agencies may not expect or wish for the contract to succeed. If they assess high probabilities of failure, they may be unwilling to take chances and in fact be prepared to go through the motions of making reasonable efforts. While greater candor on all sides might make for a better world, it would be more realistic at this point to accept lack of complete candor as expectable in involuntary transactions. Accepting such lack of candor without labeling it as a client characteristic then prepares for contracting that may empower both practitioners and clients by building dual accountability. Greater candor may be facilitated by modeling it: talking about power, its requirements and limits may increase trust.[37] Such candor entails clarity about non-negotiables, consequences, and also practitioner hopes for changes beyond those required. While complete candor is probably impossible for either side of the transaction, the amount of energy devoted to hidden agendas should be reduced since modeling candor may facilitate greater effectiveness (see chapter 6).

Lack of trust is also related to conflicting goals, both shared and unshared. Involuntary clients may agree to goals that they are ambivalent about reaching. For example, clients wishing to receive public assistance often find that a requirement for such assistance to be a record of regular job seeking. If they are living in a depressed economic area in which the possibilities for employment are limited, feelings of hopelessness about getting a job and procrastination with completing job applications might be expected.

Similarly, agencies have multiple, conflicting goals in which they must simultaneously placate different constituencies such as taxpayers, supervisory boards, state oversight agencies, advocacy groups, and professional associations. Responsibilities to involuntary clients may play a small role in such considerations. In such circumstances, agencies may have given the message to the practitioner openly or covertly to make the involuntary client change "by hook or crook," "bring them in dead or alive," in which collaborative methods may be preferred but other means are approved if deemed necessary. The organization may believe that intervention can be used deterministically to change behavior and attitudes regardless of client wishes.[38]

Such pressures often lead to involuntary service plans that include a large number of non-negotiable requirements designed to comply with the wishes of outside parties. Such service plans might be termed "cover your posterior" or "kitchen sink" contracts designed to demonstrate to outside constituencies that all bases have been covered, though there may not be enough hours in the day to touch all those bases. While such arrangements may appear to outside parties as thorough case plans, under the premise that the more treatment the better, they may in fact be doomed to fail. They may be used to demonstrate lack of client competence when in fact their purpose may be to demonstrate that an effort has been made, though in fact the effort may be primarily cosmetic.

Difficult issues are raised when such contracts are developed to protect involuntary clients and their vulnerable dependents. Compromises with the safety of others must not be made. Nor, however, should contracts that have no reasonable chance of succeeding be standard practice. In foster care, the consequences for developing overwhelming requirements and not providing supportive services left the public with expensive out-of-home care costs and often returning children home without adequate services. These conflicts of interests are real. Rather than deny conflicts of interest, expressing them openly should enhance the negotiation process.[39]

Clients, practitioners, and agencies may be also be opposed to the negotiation process. Alienated involuntary clients may see practitioners with name tags as signals identifying them as members of occupation forces. Negotiation may be perceived as trickery to get them to do what they don't want to do. Negotiation may also be perceived as a sign of weakness that can be overcome with intimidating self-presentation (see chapter 7).

Practitioners and agencies may also distrust negotiation. For example, it is sometimes believed that delinquent youth need a corrective experience with authority in which it is important to present a firm, fair set of requirements that cannot be undermined and overwhelmed. From this viewpoint, delinquent youth need and subconsciously want a structure that will hold them accountable. Consequently, negotiation might be seen as presenting a weak role model of authority, of coddling when firmness is required. Such beliefs imply that negotiation might give away critical power and authority, and model susceptibility to intimidation and manipulation. Constructive models of authority do not, however, require rigidity on all issues. Firmness on non-negotiable requirements and flexibility on negotiable items may be an alternative model of authority. Skills are then required in separating the non-negotiable from the negotiable.

Agencies and practitioners will need to explore the extent to which the obstacles described above occur in their practice. If such practice can be facilitated in its setting, the practitioner can proceed to develop a formal contract. Consequently, we proceed in chapter 10 to present guidelines for developing a formal contract and initiating mutually developed task plans for implementing that contract.

# Formalizing the Contract and Initial Task Development with Involuntary Clients

If application of the guidelines discussed in the preceding chapters results in a preliminary semi-voluntary or voluntary contract, a variety of specific intervention models can be selected according to setting and type of problem. For example, particular chemical dependency treatment models or alternatives to aggression approaches might be selected for work with chemically dependent clients and men who have problems with violence.[1]

Rather than present problem-specific approaches, this chapter will present adaptations of one model, task-centered casework, that can be useful across many involuntary problems and populations. The foundation constructed in part I of this book is empirically based, drawing on theory eclectically and assuming a multisystems approach. Further, that foundation strongly emphasizes motivational congruence and careful limits on paternalistic prescriptions about client problems. Each of these features is a component of the task-centered approach, as will be described below. Other task-centered features, such as time limits, are adapted only in part, since much work with involuntary clients is not short-term. While the task-centered approach is not the only general model to serve as the basis for adaptations, it is hoped that those developed here will be useful on their own and might also serve as a model for how other approaches might be adapted.

Based in the task-centered approach, techniques for *formalizing the contract* and *developing initial tasks* in semi-voluntary contracts and involuntary service plans will be presented. Voluntary contracts will not be reviewed in detail since considerable guidance is available for working with voluntary clients. Four adaptations of the task-centered approach to work with involuntary clients are presented in *specifying target problems, establishing clear goals, developing general tasks,* and *establishing time limits.* The chapter continues with guidelines for developing *initial client tasks, initial practitioner tasks, anticipation of obstacles, providing a rationale for task completion, necessary incentives, guided practice,* and *summarization of task plans.*

## Introduction to the Task-Centered Approach

The task-centered model is a time-limited, empirically based approach to intervention that focuses on the reduction of specific, agreed-upon target problems through the planning and implementation of client and practitioner tasks to be carried out in the environment.[2] The model was developed by Reid and Epstein at the School of Social Service Admimin-stration of the University of Chicago in the early 1970s, based on research on time-limited treatment conducted by Reid and Shyne. That study indicated that the recipients of planned short-term service (PSTS) gained as much from treatment as clients receiving continued service (CS). Further, most gains tended to occur early in treatment with diminishing gains thereafter and maintenance of gains was similar for both PSTS and CS clients. Additionally, whatever the planned length, most treatment turned out to be brief. Finally, there were fewer drop-outs from time-limited service, and client satisfaction was as high with PSTS as with CS.[3] Reid and Shyne's findings have been supported by subsequent reviews that continue to report relatively brief duration of contact, benefits early in contact, and results equivalent to open-ended or long-term contact.[4] The task-centered approach has been tested in work with the aging, family agencies, foster care, public schools, corrections, and mental health.[5] While the field studies testing the model vary in quality and rigor, they consistently report that clients appear to be helped with their primary target problems, especially when those problems are specific and relatively limited in scope.[6]

The task-centered model is based on two explicit values: 1) the client's expressed, considered wish is given precedence over other problems as defined by the practitioner, the agency, or significant others;[7] and 2) knowledge developed from empirical research is valued more highly than knowledge based primarily in theory or practice experience.[8] Within the parameters of these two values, the task-centered practitioner may eclectically select explanatory theories to fit specific target problems. The three key concepts in the approach are target problems, tasks and time-limits. Target problems are specific problems in living perceived by the client, expressly agreed upon with the practitioner, and limited in scope such that they can be feasibly alleviated in a time-limited period.[9] As introduced in chapter 2, this approach distinguishes between problems *attributed* to the client by others and problems that the client *acknowledges,* with emphasis on the latter.[10] Such focus on acknowledged target problems minimizes deadlocks, is congruent with client interests, facilitates independence and right of choice, and maintains as much client control over fate as possible.[11] Since involuntary clients are regularly faced with attributed problems, it is important to know that use of the task-centered approach does not prevent the practitioner from exploring attributed problems and needs as well as acknowledged problems and wants. According to Epstein:

The reality of much practice makes the separation of voluntary engagement and social control often impossible: it is often not possible to fuse treatment and social control. Therefore it is advisable to deal with them separately, even though both are present. This means confronting ourselves and our clients with the opportunities and requirements of both social treatment and social control and using the authority we have been given by legislation and collaboration (as with courts and police). However, we have no right to impose our views by using our authority over vulnerable clients who may see the world differently.[12]

Hence, the task-centered practitioner may work simultaneously on mandated and voluntary problems, and indeed mandated problems cannot be ignored when the consequences may be severe losses to client interest and well-being.[13] Normally, mandated problems are agreed to on the condition that the client's own target problems are accepted by the practitioner.[14] The approach distinguishes between attributed problems that are legally mandated and those that are not. If an attributed problem is not legally mandated and the client's view appears incomplete, the task-centered practitioner may raise other problems or ways of looking at problems and attempt to make a persuasive case for those additional views.[15] However, the client is free to reject the practitioner's suggestions *unless* the problem happens to be legally mandated. Exceptions to use of the approach occur when the client is currently incompetent, incapable, homicidal, or suicidal. In such cases the practitioner may have to act to prevent clear and present harm.[16]

The task-centered approach also distinguishes between *wants,* the lack of something desired by the client, and *needs,* something that others suggest that the client should have.[17] For example, Paul, the mandated client introduced in chapter 8 as preparing to enter a correctional facility, said that he *wanted* to stay out of trouble with the law and to get out of prison with as little hassle as possible. Others, however, saw a *need* for Paul to have a chemical dependency evaluation. Task-centered work focuses wherever possible on wants as well as needs.

Clients are aided in reducing target problems through the development of tasks that are activities planned in the session by the practitioner and client, to be implemented by the client or practitioner outside of the session. Tasks are further specified into general tasks that are broad plans of action and operational tasks that are the specific plans that a client might undertake between one session and the next. For example, making job applications might be a general task and developing a first draft of a resume before the next session might be an operational task.

The normal time limit for the approach is six to twelve sessions and clients can usually be helped to reduce two or three target problems within this time period. Since some clients have continuing longer-term contact with practitioners, the model includes provisions for recontracting, moving to a monitoring status, or linking to other forms of treatment.[18]

The task-centered practitioner attempts to set change into motion in target problems through a self-understanding, verbal, reflective strategy.[19] Such work is enhanced by practitioners who convey acceptance, respect, and understanding to clients. Hence, task-centered practitioners try to actualize warmth, empathy, and genuineness within a problem focus.[20]

## Adaptations of the Task-Centered Approach to Work with Involuntary Clients

The task-centered approach has been studied in a variety of mandated and and nonvoluntary settings including child welfare, aging, probation, juvenile detention, chemical dependency, and public schools.[21] While certain aspects of the approach fit well with involuntary work, other aspects fit less well (see figure 10.1).

Several advantages of the task-centered approach for work with involuntary clients have been described in the literature. Foremost among these is *goal focus*. For example, Goldberg notes that the model's requirement for clear, specific goals helps practitioners focus on feasible action and reduces preoccupation with unattainable goals.[22] This goal clarity can help specify vague surveillance duties that otherwise often take the form of aimless visiting, "purposeless probation," and "hover-

## Advantages and Disadvantages of Task-Centered Approach in Working with Involuntary Clients

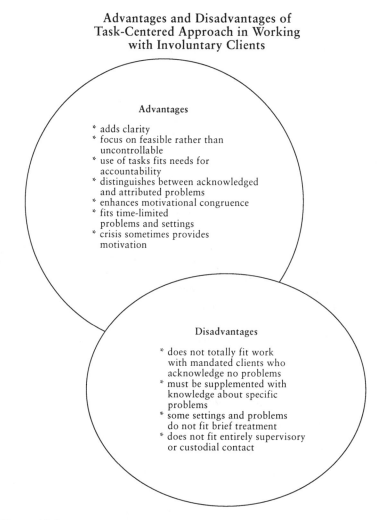

**Advantages**

* adds clarity
* focus on feasible rather than uncontrollable
* use of tasks fits needs for accountability
* distinguishes between acknowledged and attributed problems
* enhances motivational congruence
* fits time-limited problems and settings
* crisis sometimes provides motivation

**Disadvantages**

* does not totally fit work with mandated clients who acknowledge no problems
* must be supplemented with knowledge about specific problems
* some settings and problems do not fit brief treatment
* does not fit entirely supervisory or custodial contact

*Figure 10.1*

ing" over clients.[23] Work on limited goals is often also possible while at the same time progress on other problems may be less so.[24] Finally, goal specificity matches social service trends emphasizing accountability and objective measures of service delivery.[25]

The task-centered approach also assists in pursuit of *motivational congruence*. Emphasis on client-acknowledged problems moves away from preoccupation with totally imposed treatment plans by enhancing client collaboration and respect, clarifying expectations and rights, and distinguishing between mandated and voluntary problems.[26]

Third, *planned brevity* and *focus on client tasks* fits many involuntary settings that feature brief contact or require action to determine recommendations for termininating contact. Finally, the *crisis state* in which initial involuntary contact often takes place can provide at least temporary motivation to work on attributed problems through redefinition to include agreed-upon target problems. Such contracting around the crisis can then provide direction and hope for restoring equalibrium.[27]

The task-centered approach fits less well with the needs for practice with involuntary clients in other areas. Since the task-centered approach is a model of voluntary, or at least semi-voluntary, contact, it does not readily apply to work with mandated clients who do not acknowledge any problems or agree to work on tasks.[28] In addition, time limits do not readily lend themselves to prolonged contact in settings such as residential treatment.[29] Also, while studies conducted in public services have indicated that one-third to one-half of public social service clients could be served within the task-centered approach,[30] other circumstances remain in which contact is primarily supervisory, custodial or supportive. Agency purposes can also be so problem-focused that the scope of additional target problems that clients might wish to address is limited. For example, chemical dependency counselors may be instructed to address chemical use problems and make outside referrals for additional client-defined problems. In addition, clients sometimes express target problems that conflict with the protection of the interests of others.[31] Finally, the task-centered model is primarily a structure for providing service that must be augmented by information on particular problems and supporting theories.[32]

Several adaptations to the approach have been developed to facilitate work in involuntary settings. First, in settings that have a particular problem focus, task-centered work can be facilitated by *limiting the permissible scope of target problems.*[33] For example, Rzepnicki reports work in foster care with biological parents wishing to regain custody of their children that is limited to eliminating barriers to achieving permanency.[34] Second, the powerful role played by referral sources and mandated agencies with involuntary clients has resulted in guidelines to *maintain close involvement with referral sources,* informing them regularly of progress and agreements.[35] Third, in long-term treatment settings such as community care of clients with serious and persistent mental illness, *continuation contracts* have been used in which a series of task-centered contracts may be completed with the same client.[36] These sequences may occur one after the other or with breaks in which

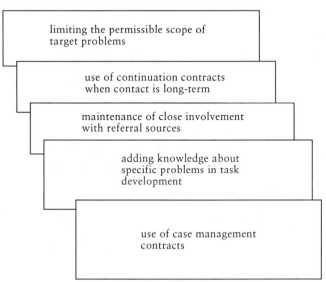

Adaptations of
Task-Centered
Approach to
Involuntary
Settings

limiting the permissible scope of
target problems

use of continuation contracts
when contact is long-term

maintenance of close involvement
with referral sources

adding knowledge about
specific problems in task
development

use of case management
contracts

*Figure 10.2*

monitoring or non-task-centered contact continues. Fourth, *case management contracts* are sometimes developed that include tasks that link clients to other forms of treatment such as drug treatment.[37] Finally, *specific information about particular target problems can be consulted in the development of tasks.* For example, task-centered work in foster care includes a focus on tasks to facilitate parental visitation that is informed by foster care research (see figure 10.2).[38]

## Formalizing the Involuntary Contract

Additional guidelines for formalizing the involuntary contract adapting the task-centered approach are now presented. These guidelines include specifying target problem conditions to be changed, establishing clear goals, developing general tasks, and establishing time limits (see figure 10.3).

*Specifying target problem conditions to be changed.* Intervention plans

## Task–Centered Contract

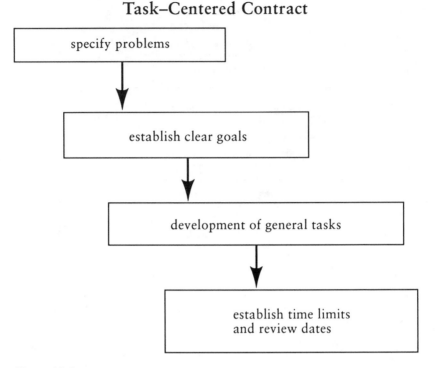

*Figure 10.3*

can be more focused if the specific conditions of the problems to be rectified are identified. Target problem conditions include those that occur with some frequency and those that are either present or absent. For example, the number of job applications completed, a condition that can be measured with some frequency while securing court permission for independent living, is a present/absent condition. In some cases, assessment tools are available that can be used to measure the extent of a problem.[39] In other cases, practitioners may need to develop their own indicators of the problem conditions.

When conditions are identified, a baseline measure can then be taken of the current extent of the problem to develop a standard of progress toward resolution. For example, a client might have made 3 job applications in the past week as the baseline for a condition of job seeking efforts. Similarly, the baseline for securing court permission for independent living might be that no such permission has been given.

Too often involuntary practice has included the unilateral establishment of target problem conditions by the practitioner rather
than the mutual development of indicators. In the following section, Nancy and Beth, introduced in chapters 8 and 9, attempt to
identify conditions around the target problem of "too many people
are running my life," based on Beth's reports that her foster parent,
her parents, her boyfriend, and Nancy herself too often told her
what to do. Hence, how often people tell her what to do would be
one target problem condition. They also previously identified exploration of independent living as a possible solution to this problem. An additional mandated problem was that "Beth does not
now live in an approved placement that meets legal standards for
permanency." This mandated problem led to a present/absent condition of approved placement.

   In the following segment, Beth and Nancy identify that having a
job or being self-supporting and having parental permission would
all be conditions required for securing permission for independent
living as one form of approved placement. Notice how Nancy
elicits these conditions in part from Beth, rather than lists them
herself. This technique should have a byproduct of reducing reactance as adolescents frequently seem to trust their own explanations more than those of practitioners.[40]

NANCY: What do you think the requirements for getting independent
   living would be?
BETH: Finding a place, getting a job.
NANCY: So finding a place to live and getting a job would be required.
BETH: Yeah, household stuff.
NANCY: You mean like furniture?
BETH: Furniture, dishes.
NANCY: Do you know what the court would expect of you? Do you
   know what the law is as far as going back to the judge and saying, "I
   want independent living"?
BETH: I have to have a job.
NANCY: Yes, you have to have a job or a way that you can demonstrate
   that you're going to be financially independent of your parents. Right?
BETH: Right.

Less verbal or cognitively impaired clients may need more assistance in specifying problems and conditions. For example, Mike
was an adult with a developmental disability who currently lived

in an adult group home. As case management services were not mandated for Mike, he could choose whether to work with a case manager or not. Jane, a case manager for a county agency, met with him to explore whether he might wish to use her services. If he were pressured to work with Jane or work on problems that he did acknowledge, Mike would have become nonvoluntary. By focusing on Mike's concerns, Jane's contact with Mike quickly moved toward voluntary contact. Notice how Jane helps Mike be specific about problems in the group home.[41]

JANE: So, you have told me that things aren't going so well at Bertha's group home. Why don't you tell me a little bit more about what is not going so good?
MIKE: Everything's just going rotten.
JANE: Tell me some of the things that aren't going so well.
MIKE: Bertha ain't the best.
JANE: So you're not real happy with her right now?
MIKE: Nope.
JANE: What kinds of things is she doing?
MIKE: Everything.
JANE: Like?
MIKE: Hmmm.
JANE: What kinds of things is she doing that you're not real happy with?
MIKE: Only giving us five cigarettes a day.
JANE: Okay. So your cigarettes are getting limited.
MIKE: Right.

> Jane is beginning to explore the target problem that "Mike is not happy living in his group home." Among the specific conditions identified are limited access to the number of cigarettes Mike can smoke a day. Later, curfew times and amount of spending money are also identified as conditions.

*Establishing clear goals.* Development of concrete, realistic, measurable goals assist in monitoring progress such that all parties can determine whether the conditions of the contract are met.[42] Goals may be addressed to reducing or increasing the frequency of target problem conditions. For example, Beth might want to decrease the number of times other people tell her what to do. For a present/absent condition such as a recommendation for independent living, then receiving a positive recommendation might be the goal. Goals may also include movement to a new situation in which the target problems are less likely to occur. For example, Jane and Mike developed a goal of living in a situation in which Mike felt more freedom.

Practitioners sometimes have reservations about developing specific goals or agreeing to goals that they consider unwise. For example, some practitioners hesitate to develop specific goals for fear that they will be locked in to goals that later either prove to be unworkable or too rigid if new circumstances arise. While new law violations may indeed influence recommendations about the conclusion of service, notifying mandated clients that this could occur is preferable to operating without goals. Vague goals often lead to vague efforts. More specific goals can empower the involuntry client by narrowing the scope of efforts.

In addition, involuntary clients sometimes express goals that the practitioner considers infeasible or in other ways inappropriate. For example, when contacted by her parents, whose parental rights had been terminated, expressing a wish for their adolescent daughter Cheryl to return home, Cheryl told her foster care worker that she wanted to return to her biological parents and would undermine any foster placements or adoption planning. Simply rejecting or dismissing the goal on the grounds that it appears unfeasible or unwise may have little to do with Cheryl's commitment to the goal.

A wiser course might have been to ask Cheryl to list all the reasons why she would want to return home to her biological parents. Next, the practitioner might ask her to list any reservations she had about this idea and any obstacles to such a plan. The practitioner might add suggestions to both lists. Such efforts do not guarantee that the involuntary client's wish for an apparently infeasible goal will change. They do, however, respect the involuntary client's right to express desires. Efforts can then be undertaken to explore their feasibility. When working as a foster care social worker, I once asked a twelve-year-old who was unlikely to ever return home to her biological parents where she would want to live. She indicated that she would be happy living with an aunt out of state. I dismissed her wish as fanciful only to find that a year and a half later she had indeed gone to the out-of-state aunt when other options failed.

In Beth's case, Nancy had reservations about the feasibility of her goal to achieve independent living. Rather than dismiss the goal, she was straightforward in helping Beth see the factors that would influence such a recommendation.

*Development of general tasks.* While goals refer to the outcome sought, general tasks are the means to be used to reach those goals. It is important to distinguish between goals and general tasks for two reasons: 1) general tasks are sometimes completed while goals are not reached; and 2) goals are sometimes reached without completing general tasks. For example, a man participating in a domestic violence program might carry out tasks to complete anger logs, attend sessions regularly, and practice relaxation. Despite completion of these tasks, he might also continue to be violent and the recommendation to the court is more likely to be influenced by the *outcome* of the efforts rather than completion of tasks. On the other hand, clients sometimes reach goals by alternative means than those originally planned. For example, the Native American client introduced in the previous chapter who wished to regain custody of her child in foster care achieved success with controlling her alcoholism problem through work with a Native American religious group rather than through participation in a white aftercare program.

In Beth's case, her goal was to gain a positive recommendation for independent living and her general tasks included exploring housing possibilities, employment, schooling, and soliciting parental permission. Additional general tasks could have included acting in assertive ways that decrease the situations in which others were in a position to tell her what to do. Mike's goal of living in a situation with more freedom can be pursued by simultaneous exploration of ways conditions could be rectified in the current group home and exploring other living arrangements. Hence, arranging visits to alternative living situations was included, as well as discussions with Bertha about the current living situation.

*Establishing clear time limits.* Much contact with both voluntary and involuntary clients occurs at times of crisis that frequently have a natural time limit of approximately six weeks.[43] In addition, studies continue to show that whatever the planned length, service frequently lasts ten sessions or less.[44] Finally, establishment of time limits takes advantage of a goal gradient effect in which client and practitioner activities appear to increase near the end of a time-limited period.[45]

Involuntary contact is sometimes necessarily long-term, as in the case of continuing case management relationships with clients with disabilities and serious and persistent mental illness, and in work with clients in institutional settings. Such long-term contact can lead to lack of focus and burn-out on both sides of the desk. Both practitioners and clients can be helped to retain focus by cutting large problems and goals into smaller segments. Progess can then be evaluated at the completion of these break points and decisions made about continuing on the same goals, changing goals, changing forms of service, and terminating contact. For example, when I worked with a single parent client who was attempting to regain custody of her eight children placed in foster care, achievement of this goal was not feasible within a short term. It was, however, feasible to establish an initial, renewable contract with the goal of securing unsupervised visitation with the children by the end of the first twelve-week contract. When that goal was achieved, the contract was renewed with a goal of regaining custody of one child in the next twelve weeks. Several additional time-limited contracts were negotiated over the subsequent one and a half years.[46]

## The Task Implementation Sequence (TIS)

Developing a clear, specific strategy follows the formalizing of the contract around both mandated and agreed-upon target problems and goals. The task implementation sequence (TIS) was designed to guide practitioners in the development of a sequence of tasks to reduce the intensity of target problems.[47] Steps in the sequence to be reviewed and adapted here include: development of initial client tasks, initial practitioner tasks, anticipation of obstacles, provision of a rationale, appropriate incentives, rehearsal, and task summarization (see figure 10.4).

*Development of initial client tasks.* Task-centered research indicates that client *expression of verbal commitment* to carry out a task is a stronger predicter of task completion than the source of the task, whether it was the client's or the practitioner's idea.[48] However, it might be expected in the pressured circumstance of involuntary contact that reactance would be reduced if the involuntary client's task ideas are considered first. Five factors should be considered in the development of initial client tasks: a) determine which target problems the involuntary client would like to begin with; b) find out how the client has attempted to resolve this problem in the past; c) explore the involuntary client's ideas about what tasks might be attempted; d) practitioner suggestions for client tasks; and e) development of required tasks for mandated clients.

a. *Determine which target problems the involuntary client would like to begin with.* In general, those target problems that are approached first should be those that would make the most difference if resolved and those that are most feasible to reduce. However, nonvoluntary clients have no legal constraints blocking their choice in the order of target problems they begin to work on. Mandated clients can often make constrained choices in selecting the order of work on problems. While mandated clients frequently have a list of non-negotiable tasks that they must complete if they are to avoid legal consequences, it is frequently impossible to undertake all of those requirements simultaneously and mandated problems often have no required sequence. In such cases, involuntary clients may recommend an order of problems to address

# Task
# Implementation
# Sequence (TIS)

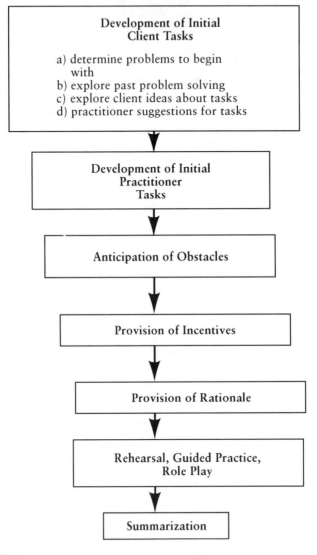

**Development of Initial
Client Tasks**

a) determine problems to begin
   with
b) explore past problem solving
c) explore client ideas about tasks
d) practitioner suggestions for tasks

**Development of Initial
Practitioner
Tasks**

**Anticipation of Obstacles**

**Provision of Incentives**

**Provision of Rationale**

**Rehearsal, Guided Practice,
Role Play**

**Summarization**

*Figure 10.4*

first. While some practitioners have suggested that given choice, involuntary clients will "start with the easy ones and avoid the hard ones," developing a momentum through successful completion of tasks can make it possible to complete more difficult tasks later. Unfortunately, there is often a negative generalization when the involuntary client is overwhelmed with competing requirements in the beginning. If there are compelling reasons why some problems should be undertaken before others, joint or sequential selection might occur in which the involuntary client might pick the first problem out of a required list and the practitioner might pick the second, and so on.

In the following section, Jane (introduced earlier in this chapter) describes briefly what task-centered work would entail and helps Mike decide which problem he would like to begin work on.

JANE: You've told me that you're pretty unhappy about your living situation and where you're working right now. So it sounds like there's the possibility for us to do some work together on these problems.

MIKE: I agree.

JANE: We can work together around these two and try to figure out together how we could make them feel a little bit better for you. We can figure out what you can do, what I can do, and kind of piece by piece see if we can get this feeling better for you.

MIKE: Good.

JANE: What's the one that's making you most uncomfortable, what's the thing that you want to work on first?

MIKE: Moving.

JANE: Moving. You want a new place to live.

MIKE: Right.

Notice that Mike is already tipping his hand about his solution to the problem of being unhappy in his living situation: he wants to move. Jane notes this and will return to it, while exploring other solutions to his current unhappiness in his living situation as well.

b. *Find out how the involuntary client has tried to resolve this problem in the past.* The practitioner can then move to review prior problem solving efforts. Such review sometimes uncovers good problem solving skills that may have been impeded by a crisis. In other cases, the review may indicate that the problem is a new one that the involuntary client has little experience in resolving. After exploring possibilities for adapting to the current living situation and finding little promise in them, Jane begins to explore Mike's knowledge of alternative living arrangements.

JANE: Let me go back and make sure that I'm remembering everything correctly. When you moved up here, part of the reason that we said that you wanted to live here was that there weren't too many choices about where to live in the town where your folks were, and you wanted to be closer to work. And that's why you ended up at this particular group home. Right?

MIKE: Right, I agree.

JANE: So that's how you got here. Now it seems like we need to talk about what some of the other options might be about where to live. Have you thought about where else you might want to live?

MIKE: Not right offhand, no.

JANE: Do you know anybody else that's left the group home?

MIKE: No, I don't.

JANE: I was wondering, because if you knew somebody that left, we could talk about where they moved to. Do you know some of the other folks that you work with out at the plant, where do they live? What kind of places do they live in?

Jane continues to pursue Mike's knowledge of alternatives before moving to add her own knowledge of potential resources. In other cases, review of past efforts may uncover unsuccessful prior efforts. Such exploration may provide information about a lack of problem solving skills or a misunderstanding of an otherwise effective method. For example, a client once told me that she had tried time-out to discipline her child but it didn't work because after she would lock him up in his room for several hours, he would demolish his room! As I was preparing to suggest time-out as a method that she might try, I began to see how she might have misunderstood the specific, time-limited nature of the time-out procedure.

c. *Explore the involuntary client's ideas about what tasks might be attempted.* Practitioners should attempt to help clients develop initial tasks that are clear, specific, and likely to succeed. Successful completion of such initial tasks should help create a positive momentum that can contribute to completion of more complex tasks later.[49]

After reviewing prior problem solving efforts, the practitioner can initiate brainstorming about possible tasks to attempt. As reactance may be activated by starting with the practitioner's own ideas, the involuntary client's ideas about which tasks to attempt should be explored first. Involuntary clients frequently have good ideas about how to proceed or present ideas that can be made workable with a little revision. The practitioner should encourage any promising ideas and even those ideas that appear less promising give clues about the client's general problem solving ability. In the following section, Nancy begins work to explore Beth's ideas about possible tasks to attempt toward achieving independent living and also clarifies what kind of job she wants to seek.

NANCY: On the problem of job seeking, what do you think would be a reasonable way to start between now and next week?

BETH: Go out looking for a job. And then there is the newspaper.

NANCY: Going out and making applications and getting a newspaper are good ideas. How else have you heard about jobs in the past? You've worked at at a restaurant. How did you find that job?

BETH: Through friends.

NANCY: So you could talk to some friends about jobs that they might know of that would be available. Do you have any restrictions on the kind of jobs you want to get?

BETH: I don't want to work in no nut house like Randy's Restaurant.

NANCY: So you don't want to work in a place where there are a lot of difficult people to deal with?

BETH: Yes, a lot of drunks.

This exploration of possible client tasks should enhance involuntary client feelings of empowerment. By listening to Beth and supporting any promising ideas, Nancy is helping Beth figure out what she is willing to try. Sometimes practitioners have additional ideas that might revise client suggestions or expand their options.

d. *Practitioner suggestions for client tasks.* Practitioners often have useful ideas for client tasks based on empirical research, experience, and practice wisdom. Involuntary clients often reject these suggestions if they are pressured into the "best" solution rather than given suggestions as part of a brainstorming process. The practitioner should become expert at *helping* involuntary clients solve problems rather than necessarily be an expert in solving all problems. On the other hand, neither should the practitioner agree to work on problems blindly without consulting available sources. Practitioners should become familiar with evidence to support particular empirically supported task strategies. For example, practitioners working with depressed involuntary clients should explore empirically supported methods such as cognitive behavioral strategies developed by Aaron Beck.[50] In addition, practitioners can draw from their own practice experience with similar problems, and that of their peers, supervisors, and consultants.

As initial tasks should be clear, specific, and likely to succeed, practitioners can also use their expertise in fine-tuning client suggestions to make them more feasible. In the following section, Nancy suggests revisions to make Beth's job-seeking efforts more specific and feasible.

NANCY: What do you think about getting a couple of newspapers for a week. Does your aunt get a newspaper?

BETH: No.

NANCY: So you would have to go out and buy one. You might look through a newspaper at least every two to three days and circle the ads that look interesting to you. How does that sound?

BETH: Okay.

NANCY: So you have the money you would need to get a paper for a week or so?

BETH: Yeah, that's no problem.

NANCY: We could find a newspaper around here and circle some today if you want.

BETH: No, that's okay, I can do it at home.

NANCY: You might then also talk to some friends that might know something about job openings. I would suggest that you write down all the possibilities that you come up with and bring them in for us to look at. You could go ahead and apply for some if you want to, but it would be enough to get us started to have a list of possible jobs. How does that sound?

BETH: Okay.

e. *Development of disagreeable tasks.* Mandated clients always have required tasks to complete and nonvoluntary clients often encounter disagreeable tasks as part of a "package deal" of agreeing to be served even within a contract that includes some of their own concerns. If a mandated client does not object to completing a required task, then no special provisions beyond the above suggestions for client and practitioner tasks are needed. The broader problem, then, is assisting both mandated and nonvoluntary clients in completing tasks that they might consider disagreeable. The following six guidelines are designed to both facilitate treatment adherence and facilitate empowerment through offering at least constrained choices. It should be noted, however, that required or disagreeable tasks should be kept to the minimum and should not stretch beyond the guidelines for limiting self-determination and exercising paternalism described in chapter 4 (see figure 10.5).

i. *Consequences of a choice not to complete the required task can be explored.* Even when choices are so constrained that failure to complete

## Completion of Disagreeable Tasks

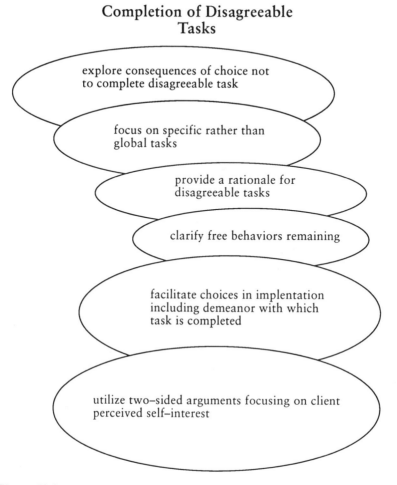

explore consequences of choice not to complete disagreeable task

focus on specific rather than global tasks

provide a rationale for disagreeable tasks

clarify free behaviors remaining

facilitate choices in implentation including demeanor with which task is completed

utilize two–sided arguments focusing on client perceived self–interest

*Figure 10.5*

the disagreeable task is likely to lead to punishing consequences, the mandated client can choose *not* to complete the task and accept those punishing consequences. For example, Mrs. Carter had eight children removed from her home because of child neglect and a drinking problem. Mrs. Carter continued to maintain that her drinking was of no concern to the court and balked at following through with a chemical dependency evaluation and treatment program. Rather than continue in a stalemated position, the practitioner informed her that she could choose *not* to have the evaluation or treatment. She should know, however, that in the next hearing, the judge would be informed of progress with the required evaluation. She could choose to hope that her task completion in other areas would favorably impress the judge without work on the perceived alcohol problem. Mrs. Carter chose for the time being to run the risk of a negative response in choosing not to follow the court order completely. Later in contact, she came to recognize a need for further alcohol treatment on her own and entry into treatment was facilitated.[51]

Nonvoluntary clients also often face disagreeable tasks that, while not legally mandated, exert an unwelcome pressure. For example, some clients find that agencies have policies requiring *all* family members to participate in treatment. If the family is unwilling or unable to comply with this requirement and if the agency policy is not negotiable, family members can be referred to other settings who do not have such policies.

ii. *Focus on specific rather than global tasks.* Reactance is likely to be high if the involuntary client perceives there to be a global assault on valued freedoms. Reactance may be reduced by focusing on specific rather than global tasks. For example, Mrs. Torres (introduced in chapter 8) was angry about what she considered to be overwhelming and unjust pressures to clean her house. Her opposition was somewhat reduced by focusing on specific tasks to remove fire hazards such as garbage with a goal of eliminating five boxes a week, establishing clear walkways, and obtaining a separate bed for her daughter. Small, specific tasks were developed such as agreeing to sort ten boxes and getting rid of the contents of five by the following week.

iii. *Provide a rationale for disagreeable tasks.* Involuntary clients are entitled to an explanation for *why* the task is required. It was explained to Mrs. Torres that minimum standards existed for determining fire hazards and client safety. Involuntary clients may continue to disagree with the rationale, but they are entitled to an explanation.

iv. *Clarify free choices remaining.* Required tasks can be distinguished from other areas remaining in the free control of the involuntary client.[52] For example, Mrs. Torres felt that the agency was pressuring her to get rid of valuable things she had inherited from her mother. The practitioner clarified that valued items from her mother were her own business and not the business of the child welfare agency. The agency was only concerned about safety hazards and would support her in keeping her valued inheritance if it did not continue to be a safety hazard. Indeed, the practitioner could assist her in seeking inexpensive storage facilities as a way of protecting her valuable things.

v. *Choices in implementation can be facilitated including the demeanor with which the disagreeable task is completed.* Involuntary clients can have choices in the manner in which they implement disagreeable tasks. As described earlier in this chapter, practitioners can often negotiate the order of required tasks including which ones to begin with. For example, Mrs. Torres chose to begin by sorting her boxes and deciding what was garbage and thrown away, what could be given away or sold, and what could be kept. The practitioner assisted in securing a homemaker to facilitate this process. Obtaining another bed was postponed until these tasks were completed. Mrs. Torres was free to choose what materials would be kept, discarded, given away, or sold as long as five boxes full of garbage was discarded.

Practitioners sometimes contribute to their own and involuntary client frustration by not only expecting that the disagreeable task be completed but that the involuntary client also appear to *enjoy it*. By separating the behavior from the attitude displayed in completing the task, the practitioner can restore some freedom while recognizing that behaviors often change prior to attitudes (see chapter 6). This practitioner attitude implies some tolerance for involuntary client complaints about not liking the task. The practitioner can empathize with the feeling of not liking to be pressured to do required tasks, while remaining firm about the consequences of failure to comply. For example, Mrs. Torres continued to complain about not liking the house-cleaning tasks while also continuing to complete them. She would often complete them with a new twist, such as selling some clothes, that had not been discussed but was her right and did not violate the agreement to discard a certain amount of items.

The practitioner can also solicit involuntary client input in fine-tuning required tasks. For example, alcoholism treatment programs sometimes require that clients read about alcoholism. There are often ways, however, that such required tasks can be tailored with client input. For example, Dick, the residential treatment counselor introduced in chapter 8, was able to negotiate with Keith about the amount of reading and the time frame for completing the required task of reading in the "big book."[53]

DICK: I'm sure you are familiar with the "big book," the Alcoholics Anonymouse book, from your first treatment. Keith, I'd like to know, do you like to read?

KEITH: I hate it.

DICK: You hate to read. A lot of people do. I'm not a very good reader myself, and I can relate to that. The first five chapters in the big book are kind of a synopsis of what the whole program is about, where it started, why it was developed, what they wanted to do. There is a lot of reading in it; it is a big book. I wonder if 20–25 pages would be too much to read in a week? Do you think you could handle that?

KEITH: I think I can handle that.

DICK: Well, why not, instead of concentrating on all the first five chapters, concentrate on just chapter number five? I think it's only about 25 pages. Do you think you might have that done in a week?

KEITH: Sure, I'll do that.

vi. *Two-sided arguments emphasizing client perceived self-interest can be utilized.* Practitioners may feel called upon to represent the community and others potentially harmed by the involuntary client's behavior. Persuasion efforts, however, are unlikely to be successful when they focus on values *not* held by the client that the practitioner thinks the involuntary client *should* have (see chapter 6). The practitioner should avoid nagging, browbeating, or attempting to elicit guilt around values that the client does not hold. Focus on the values that the involuntary client openly expresses should be more productive. Hence, Jean emphasized Mrs. Torres' own expressed motivation to have the house clean for the holidays and the agency people out of her life. The consequences of choosing not to carry out the required task can be reviewed. Potential costs and advantages of choosing to complete the required task can also be reviewed with the involuntary client left to make the decision.

Sometimes practitioners are unable to find values and motivations to support required changes for mandated clients. In such circumstances, practitioners can recognize problems in proceeding without motivational congruence by limiting their own expectations for progress beyond the impact of available compliance methods.

### Development of Initial Practitioner Tasks

Explicit practitioner tasks can enhance a sense of partnership in resolving problems.[54] Practitioner tasks should facilitate client efforts without doing things for involuntary clients that they can do for themselves. Hence, practitioner tasks are actions that the involuntary client cannot complete, would take too long for them to complete to be of value in addressing target problems, or those that are of no long-term value for the involuntary client to learn. The number of practitioner tasks depends also on available practitioner time and norms of the agency or setting. For example, practitioners often act to influence the social system to facilitate client action through arranging referrals and acquiring information.[55] If the involuntary client is unlikely to need such information or initiate such referrals on their own in the future, then the practitioner might offer to do it. The number of practitioner tasks may also decrease over time with increased client capacity.

There are also many intermediate steps between tasks that are either undertaken solely by involuntary clients or solely by practitioners that can be negotiated. Could the involuntary client complete the task with additional resources? Would skill practice or rehearsal help? Would it help if the practitioner or someone else did the task jointly with the involuntary client or accompany them (see figure 10.6)?

For example, one of Beth's requirements for achieving independent living was to secure parental permission. In the following section, Beth and Nancy negotiate a joint client-practitioner task of contacting Beth's parents

NANCY: How do you think we should let your mother and dad know about your plans?

BETH: That's left up to you, I don't want to talk to them.

NANCY: You don't want to talk to them alone. How would you feel about me accompanying you to talk to them?

BETH: That would be okay. I'd like to find out before I go through all the hassle of doing it and then they don't want to give me permission.

NANCY: Okay, so my task between now and then is to get in touch with your mom and dad to set up a joint session.

Nancy might have explained her reasons for preferring to share the task rather than do it for Beth. If Nancy can assist Beth this time, she may be able to negotiate other things on her own next time rather than be dependent on Nancy.

*Anticipating obstacles.* Task plans can be fine-tuned by anticipating obstacles to their successful completion. The questions suggested above for looking at possible joint client-practitioner tasks can also be adapted to tailor any client or practitioner task: What might get in the way of task completion? Does the client have adequate resources to carry out the task? Does the client have adequate skills to complete the task? The practitioner can begin by asking the involuntary client to think of things that might get in the way of completing the task and then to add their own ideas to the client list. Practitioners may find that they are more likely to identify obstacles to tasks suggested by clients than to tasks that were the practitioner's own idea. It would be wise for practitioners to ask involuntary clients for possible obstacles to practitioner-originated tasks as well as to those suggested by clients. If this review uncovers potential obstacles, then task plans can be revised to avoid them. For

## Considerations in Completing Practitioner Tasks

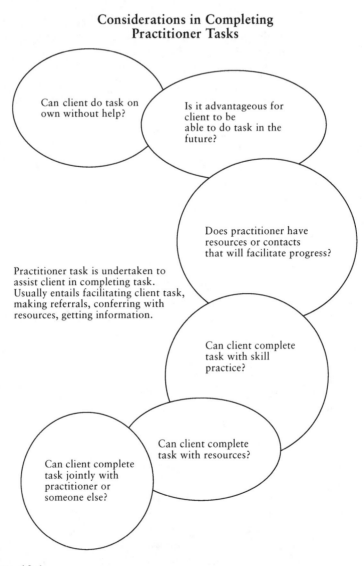

*Figure 10.6*

example, in the following section, Jane explores potential obstacles with Mike about a move from his current group home to Dexter, thirty miles away.

JANE: What do you think might get in the way of moving to Dexter?

MIKE: Maybe my buddies who I used to drink with.

JANE: So, the fellows you used to drink with live in Dexter. How might you handle their asking you to drink with them?

MIKE: Refuse them.

JANE: You sound pretty definite about that. Have you been able to see them without drinking with them in the past?

MIKE: Yes.

JANE: So, you have been able to do that already. We might have to keep checking on that one since I know that you have told me that you don't want to go back to drinking.

MIKE: I agree.

JANE: I can think of a couple of other things that might get in the way. I wonder if the transportation back up here to work every day would be hard for you since you would have that extra half-hour ride each day.

MIKE: I agree.

JANE: Let me just sum up where we are with thinking about a possible move. On the plus side, we've got the fact that you know more people in Dexter and you're closer to your folks, which is important. On the down side you might have to worry about some of your old buddies trying to get you back to drinking.

MIKE: Right, I agree.

Jane and Mike have identified being around Mike's buddies who continue to drink and the ride to and from work as obstacles. Additional tasks might then follow to prepare Mike for telling his buddies that he does not want to drink with them. He might also experiment with the bus ride a few times to see if he could handle that.

Practitioners' tasks can also result from obstacle analysis. For example, John lived in a community residence for homeless persons. One condition of this residence was that he be actively engaged in efforts to seek employment and eventually other housing. His job seeking efforts had been partly impeded by limited access to the community phone in the residence. In the following section, John and Cheri, his case manager, explore ways to facilitate his job seeking tasks.[56]

JOHN: I made some applications but they haven't been calling me back yet. I wonder if I will even get a message with that phone out there in the Center.

CHERI: It is a busy phone. We've talked about getting another line here at the center. We have talked about your taking the initiative to call them back to check on your application. If you were going to make those phone calls this week, can you think of anything that might prevent you from completing the calls?

JOHN: Well, the noise out there. It gets pretty rowdy out there, sometimes. But other than that, no.

CHERI: Well, I was wondering about that. Depending on what time of day that you called them, I'd be willing to let you use my office phone here if that would be helpful.

JOHN: Sure, it would.

CHERI: I know that you also said that you were not quite sure of what to say to them on the phone, not wanting to sound too "needy." We could talk over what you want to say to them and maybe practice it a little before you call.

JOHN: I don't feel comfortable making the calls out there, that's for sure.

CHERI: What about if we practice here and then you could make the call here with me present or by youself, however you want to do it.

JOHN: It would be okay to practice. I would rather make the calls then by myself, though.

CHERI: Okay. Let's try that.

Cheri and John have explored two options to making the call alone on the community phone. John has expressed preferences for how he would like to make the calls and Cheri has offered support in practicing the skills needed to make the call and feel more comfortable doing it. She might also move ahead to advocate more strongly for increased access for other residents to a more private phone.

*Provision of rationale.* Self-attributed change may be enhanced if the involuntary client has a clear idea of the specific reasons for how carrying out the task would be a step toward reducing the target problem and reaching the goal. As with exploring task ideas and identifying potential obstacles, practitioners can empower clients and support self-attibution by asking the involuntary client for the connection between the task and the agreed upon problem before supplying their own ideas. If involuntary clients cannot think of reasons to complete the task, then they may be unlikely to complete it or do so only under pressure to comply. Similarly, if involuntary clients originate the task idea, they may be more likely to understand the rationale for the task than if the task idea came from the practitioner. As with anticipation of obstacles, practitioners frequently forget to explore the rationale for ideas they originated since that rationale is usually obvious to the practitioner if not the involuntary client.[57] This may be particularly true when the task is a required one for mandated clients or part of a "package deal" for nonvoluntary clients. In the following section, Dick reviews Keith's required task for completing a self-inventory of prior drinking behavior and bringing the answers into the treatment group.

DICK: When you fill out the answers to the questions about your past history in the book, you will have something to share in common with the other men in the group. We find that men can often learn from each other's past experiences through this kind of sharing in the group.

KEITH: Okay. But some of those questions go way back to where you can't even remember.

DICK: That's true, they do go back quite a ways. How about going through the book and answering those questions that are really important to you, that promote feelings, and answer those questions first? Then come and talk to me about it, and we'll see how far you want to go. Because in two weeks, I'd like you to tell the group some of the highlights of your life. Would you be willing to do that?

KEITH: You have to tell them *all* the highlights?

DICK: That sounds like you think it could be embarrassing to share some parts of your past with people you don't know very well.

KEITH: Yeah, I don't know these people.

DICK: You can make that decision as to what you want to tell them. By the time you do this, maybe the group will become more familiar with you and you will be better able to decide what you want to tell them. Okay?

KEITH: Okay.

While Dick has provided the program's rationale for completing the self-history for sharing in the group, Keith raises reservations about sharing potentially embarassing information with people he doesn't know. Dick has attempted to empathize with that concern and clarified the choices Keith has in deciding what to share.

*Provision of incentives.* Some situations require the involuntary client to carry out initial tasks that may be anxiety-provoking or have some punishing elements. In such circumstances, providing a concrete or symbolic incentive can be helpful in stimulating new behavior that is not at this point inherently reinforcing.[58] However, as described in chapter 6, in order to support self-attribution, concrete rewards should be only large enough to succeed and should be phased out soon to be replaced by symbolic rewards.[59]

In the following section, Hoan, a social worker in an outpatient mental health center, is working with Jim, a depressed nonvoluntary client, who has targeted the problem of "not being motivated to do anything." It is interesting to note that while Jim had a clinical diagnosis of depression, he does not acknowledge this attributed problem but focuses on the more specific acknowledged problem of lack of motivation. They have together identified washing his clothes, which had been piling up for weeks, as a desirable task in beginning to alleviate his lack of motivation. Earlier in the session, they decided to break up this large, depressing task into a series of steps including getting enough tokens for the washers and dryers, sorting the clothes on one day, and taking down a first load on the next day. In the following section, they review possible obstacles to this task and explore possible incentives to enhance completing a difficult task.[60]

H O A N : Okay. So I will write down here that you plan to wash your clothes by Sunday. Can you think of any other things that might get in the way of your washing these clothes?

J I M : I hate washing clothes. It is one of the things I hate most.

H O A N : So your head tells you, I hate to wash clothes. Is there something that can help you get over that, something you can tell yourself that might help you feel better about doing it?

J I M : Not that I know of. Not right off hand.

H O A N : You mentioned earlier that you want some clean clothes in order to go back to school.

J I M : That whole issue is separate. I don't see it as part of the same issue.

H O A N : Okay, thinking about how you could use the clean clothes isn't a helpful idea for you. Would it help if I give you a call maybe on Friday to see how things go with the first step of separating the clothes?

J I M : Yeah, that would be all right.

H O A N : I also wonder if there is something special you can do for yourself when you try this hard first step.

J I M : You mean like a reward or something?

H O A N : Yes, what would be something you could do to reward yourself for separating the clothes?

J I M : Maybe I could go out to a movie or something.

*Rehearsal.* Some tasks are of such complexity that breaking them down and rehearsing parts can assist in task completion.[61] For example, Nancy could have practiced looking through the want ads and making a list of job possibilities with Beth during the session. In addition, interactional tasks can be practiced in role plays. The practitioner can model how to complete the task, assist the client in practicing, assess together the strengths and weaknesses of that modeling, and then rehearse the desired behavior again.[62] For example, it was suggested above that Cheri and John might have rehearsed the phone call to a potential employer. As adults are sometimes more hesitant than children in carrying out role plays,[63] a modified form of role play can be employed in which the task is walked through with questions such as "What do you plan to say? What do you think he/she will say back to you?"

*Task summarization.* Practitioners frequently end a session by reading a list of client tasks and asking the client for affirmation that the list is accurate. Practitioners often interpret "uh-huh" responses as indications of understanding and commitment. Such practitioner recitations may only indicate that the practitioner understands what the task agreements are. In some instances, task summaries may be enhanced by use of a written task-sheet with copies for both the client and practitioner.[64] Such a sheet can be completed by either the client or practitioner, listing who will do what by what date. Using such a task list, the practitioner might begin to sumarize by saying, "These are the tasks I have agreed to complete. What are the ones you are planning to do?" If involuntary clients can then recount tasks, compliance may be enhanced. If, on the other hand, the involuntary client leaves a task off the list, it may indicate reservations about completing the task. The practitioner may then add to and amend the summary provided by the client, exploring any reservations.[65] For example, Cheri reviews tasks with John at the end of their session.

CHERI: So to review, I said that I would make my phone available for you to call potential employers and possible references before our next meeting. What were the things that you're going to work on before we meet on Friday?
JOHN: I'm going to call Browntank tomorrow morning. And then I'll put out a couple more job applications. I don't know if I'll have to call for references until I talk to them.

This chapter has provided specific guidelines for formalizing the involuntary contract and developing initial task plans based in the task-centered approach. As a general rather than problem-specific model with an eclectic theory base, the task-centered approach has several elements that are compatible with involuntary client work. Use of the adaptations suggested should enhance motivational congruence and promote self-attribution (see chapters 5 and 6). The adaptations should reduce reactance by breaking down large problems, which often make both involuntary client and practitioner feel helpless, into smaller components. The specificity of task development also enhances clear recordkeeping and assists in developing mutual accountability. Adaptations have also been suggested for working with time-limited subcontracts when involuntary client contact is not brief.

The task-centered approach is not a panacea for the problems of work with involuntary clients. It provides no magical answers in working with those mandated clients with whom there is no motivational congruence. Choices in the form of implementation and timing of required tasks have been suggested. Such techniques may assist some involuntary clients in coming to greater motivational congruence over time. Otherwise, as stated earlier, involuntary work supported primarily by fear of punishment and promise of reward often achieves results that last only as long as those compliance methods are available. There is little substitute for motivational congruence in achieving self-attributed change.

While chapters 8 and 9 presented techniques for enhancing motivational congruence that might be built upon with adaptations of other voluntary models besides the task-centered approach, adaptations for specific populations and settings are needed. It is hoped that the task-centered adaptation presented here can serve as a model for other such adaptations. However carefully developed, initial tasks often fail. When this occurs, practitioners need to have ways to support positive momentum and not reinforce an expectation of failure in which the involuntary client feels "this is just another example of how I mess things up and cannot complete what I try to do." I will next present the middle phase of involuntary client work, including how to review progress, support successes and efforts, and look objectively at what gets in the way of task completion. A special form of mid-phase obstacle identification, mid-phase confrontation, will also be presented. The chapter also considers adaptations of guidelines for case management roles and provides termination guidelines.

# Chapter 11

# Middle-Phase Intervention and Termination with Involuntary Clients

This chapter builds on the guidelines for the initial phase described in chapters 8 through 10 to present guidelines for middle-phase intervention and termination. The greater attention devoted to the initial phase than those that follow it is based on the assumption that reaching some motivational congruence is a key to successful work that lasts longer than the threat of punishment and the promise of reward.

The chapter begins with a review of middle-phase intervention principles adapted from the interpersonal influence literature described in chapter 6. As many practitioners working with involuntary clients do so as case managers, adaptations of the approach for that role follows.

Guidelines for middle-phase intervention follow that continue the adaptations of the task-centered approach begun in the previous chapter. These guidelines include progress review, task review, assessment of obstacles, dealing with crises, and task plan revision. Special attention is devoted to confrontation since confrontation is more likely to be successful in the middle phase of work than earlier. The chapter concludes with consideration of issues in termination with involuntary clients.

## Middle-Phase Change Principles

Chapter 6 described the use of influence methods including punishment, reward, and persuasion to enhance treatment adherence, self-attribution, and empowerment. It was noted that while reward and punishment methods can be used to support the development of a new behavior or reduce an undesirable behavior, continued use of such methods is unlikely to produce the self-attribution needed to support the maintenance of behavioral change.[1] Consequently, middle-phase work should include reduced reliance on compliance-oriented methods and increased use of methods that enhance self-atribution such as facilitating expression of verbal or written commitment by involuntary clients to task completion,[2] facilitating choices in task selection and enhancing freely chosen behavior,[3] and increased attention to natural rather than artificial rewards.[4]

As behavioral change often precedes attitude change,[5] the socialization and contracting guidelines presented in chapters 8 and 9 emphasized behavioral changes more than attitudinal changes. Attitudinal change may, however, be more subject to influence in the middle phase if the practitioner has come to be considered a persuasive source of influence.[6] Hence, selective practitioner confrontations may become more effective in the middle phase than was typically the case in initial contact.[7] Attitudes and beliefs may be further influenced in the middle phase through trying out new behaviors on an experimental basis through the "foot-in-door" method in which the involuntary client may agree to try out a new behavior on an experimental basis.[8] Should those new behaviors succeed, they may become naturally reinforcing and also challenge prior beliefs that they would be unsuccessful. Further references will be made to these principles as they apply to practice guidelines later in the chapter (see figure 11.1).

## Case Management

Many practitioners who work with involuntary clients do so as case managers. The case manager assesses need, links clients to needed resources, has responsibility for service coordination, monitors progress, and advocates to ensure that the client receives appropriate services in a timely fashion (see figure 11.2).[9]

Case management is typically provided to clients with multiple attributed problems such as those with serious and persistent mental illness and those with disabilities.[10] General goals of case management often include reduction of inappropriate utilization of services, increased continuity of care, and empowering clients through access to service.[11] Individual case goals often relate to attaining adequate levels of client functioning in areas such as independent living and vocational skills.

Definitions of case management functions vary, which contributes to

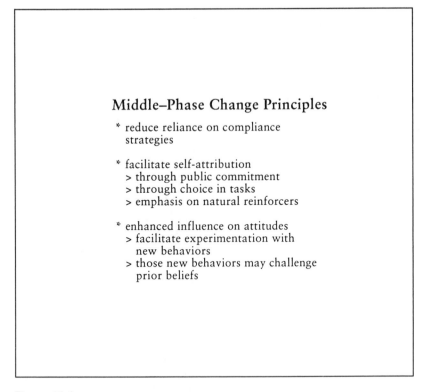

**Middle–Phase Change Principles**

* reduce reliance on compliance strategies

* facilitate self-attribution
  > through public commitment
  > through choice in tasks
  > emphasis on natural reinforcers

* enhanced influence on attitudes
  > facilitate experimentation with new behaviors
  > those new behaviors may challenge prior beliefs

*Figure 11.1*

confusion in implementation. Job descriptions have tended to focus on organizational arrangements defining what agency is responsible for arranging what service with relatively little emphasis on practice techniques. For example, there is little agreement on how much of the role is administrative and how much relates to client/worker interaction.[12] There are further variations in the autonomy and responsibility accorded the case manager and the complexity of the tasks to be assumed by him or her.[13] Is the case manager primarily responsible for coordinating care provided by others or providing direct service?[14] Lamb argues that the case manager must provide a primary therapeutic relationship lest case management become impersonal and bureaucratic.[15] Often, however, case managers are expressly not to "do counseling" with their clients but rather to link them with others who will provide such resources. In other circumstances, case managers may be permitted to counsel or intervene as problem solvers yet find that large caseloads and heavy

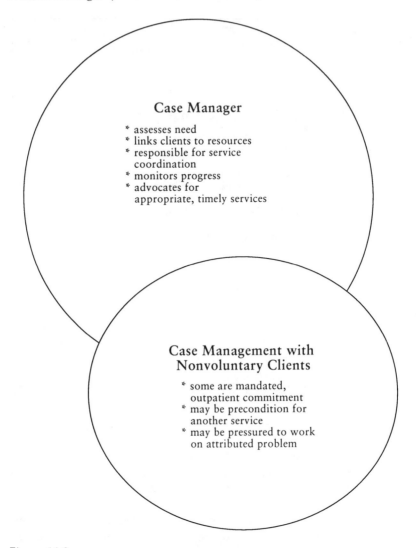

*Figure 11.2*

paperwork requirements often limit them to coordinating paper more than actual services.

Further, case management with clients such as those with severe and persistent mental illness has been considered difficult, unglamorous, and unrewarding. The emphasis on psychotherapy in community mental health centers has often meant that case managers have lower status and prestige than psychotherapists and consequently many case managers appear to be indifferent to intervening in the social system as it is lower-status work than seeking insight with psychotherapy clients.[16] Rose and Block, however, suggest that case managers can play important roles in advocacy and empowerment with these client groups.[17]

Case managers can work with involuntary clients in at least three ways. First, some clients may be mandated to work with a case manager in the community as part of an involuntary out-patient commitment.[18] Second, many clients have no legal mandate but may experience non-voluntary pressure to work with a case manager as a precondition for receiving another service. For example, a client with serious and persistent mental illness such as Dora (introduced in chapter 8) may find ongoing contact with a case manager to be a precondition to independent living. Finally, some clients may be willing to work with a case manager but feel constrained when such work focuses on attributed needs rather than client wants.

Case managers working with involuntary clients can act to empower them by advocating for their choices using the guidelines provided for negotiating and contracting found in chapters 8 through 10. For example, when Mike (introduced in chapter 10) first became Jane's client when he moved into the community after living in a residential institution, he came with recommendations from that institution that he "needed" to work on his impulsive expression of anger. Jane considered his expression of anger not to be a legal mandate but rather a possible obstacle that might interfere with his achievement of his own perceived goals. She chose to focus on what Mike was angry about, such as unhappiness with his living arrangement, rather than his expression of anger as a primary focus. Within this focus on an acknowledged target problem, Mike became voluntary. The processes of task development described in chapter 10 may, however, focus more on linkages with other resources rather than on tasks to be completed directly with the case manager.

*Linking clients with resources.* Frequently involuntary clients identify problems that would involve utilizing other services. Research on the linkage process suggests that often fewer than half of clients referred for services are actually linked with the designated resource.[19] The resource linkage process varies according to the source of the suggestion and the strength of the pressure. The involuntary client can perceive the need for the resource first, the need can be identified by the practitioner or a referral source, or the resource may be required as part of a legal mandate.

The practitioner should attempt to help the client make an informed choice about pursuing the linkage by sharing available knowledge about the quality of services.[20] If the client perceives the need, the process includes a straightforward assessment of whether an adequate resource might be available from within the agency. If that resource is available internally, then the linkage might be made directly. For example, in some family preservation service programs, problems are identified with a lack of recreational opportunities for children. Some family preservation programs have funds available to pay for children's participation in recreational programs. If the agency does not have the resource or cannot directly facilitate its use, then external resources can similarly be assessed. For example, Jane provided Mike with information about the living possibilities available and facilitated visits in which he could make his own assessment.

Should an appropriate resource be identified, a sequence of steps can be followed to facilitate the linkage. Simple directions in providing a name and address are sufficient for clients who are motivated to receive the service and capable of following those directions.[21] Providing the name of a contact person makes the linkage easier in circumstances that might involve a complicated intake process. Similarly, providing the client with a letter of introduction that describes the problem and what the client would like to have done can facilitate the linkage. The practitioner can also help by making a phone call to the desired resource. Finally, facilitating in-person contact can occur by accompanying the client or arranging for a friend, relative, or case aide to accompany the client to the resource. These more complex means of facilitating linkage are useful with clients who cannot follow complex directions or have some ambivalence about pursuing the resource.

If the practitioner or another referral source initiates the suggestion for a resource that is recommended but not legally required, then a possible source of nonvoluntary pressure has been initiated. In this case, persuasion methods, including two-sided arguments, assessment of potential benefits and costs of pursuing the resource, or choosing not to pursue it can be used. Since the source of pressure is nonvoluntary, the client's right *not* to pursue the resource should be emphasized. For example, Jane encouraged Mike to enter an independent living skills group that might help him prepare for living outside the group home. She emphasized that he could choose *not* to join this group; however, acquisition of those skills might make a move to new housing easier.

Should the resource linkage be mandated, a similar sequence to nonvoluntary pressure can be followed with the added emphasis on legal consequences should the resource not be pursued. Even in such mandated situations, the involuntary client can choose not to pursue the resource and accept the consequences, as did Mrs. Carter (introduced in chapter 10) when she chose not to get a chemicial dependency evaluation while aware of the fact that chemical use would be reported to the court.

Should the client agree to pursue the resource, connections can be "cemented" through one of four methods. The client can: 1) report back to the practitioner after contact; or 2) the practitioner can contact the client after the connection; 3) the practitioner can also schedule sessions preceding and following the contact; or 4) referral visits can be interspersed with the practitioner's own sessions with the involuntary client.[22]

## Guidelines for the Middle Phase

The task development process described in chapter 10 often kindles hope in the involuntary client and practitioner that progress can be made. These hopes are often dashed in progress review sessions in which the best laid plans have gone awry. Successful completion of *all* tasks should be considered the exception, however, rather than the rule. *Task failure* should not be interpreted as *person failure*. Focus on failure contributes to disillusionment, blaming, and reinforcement of helpless, powerless feelings. Hence, building positive momentum and avoiding blaming is a critical goal in the middle phase. The guidelines that follow can be employed by both case managers and practitioners who have more frequent and intensive client contact.

The following guidelines are designed to build positive momentum through: 1) reviewing progress on target problems and mandated problems, 2) reviewing task progress, 3) identifying obstacles to progress, 4) dealing with crises, 5) employing appropriate middle-phase confrontation, and 6) revising and summarizing task plans (see figure 11.3).

1. *Reviewing target problem progress.* Task-centered work focuses on reduction or elimination of agreed-upon problems. Legally mandated clients are also engaged in reviews of progress on mandated problems, whether agreed upon or not. Review sessions should begin with a review of how these mandated, semi-voluntary or voluntary target problems appear to be changing or not changing according to the conditions of the problem identified in the contracting stage. It is useful to separate review of the problem conditions from the completion of tasks since problems sometimes change without task completion and, conversely, tasks may be completed without improvement noted in the problem conditions. For example, Beth reported that no one was now telling her what to do (a condition of her target problem) since her aunt kicked her

## Guidelines for Middle Phase

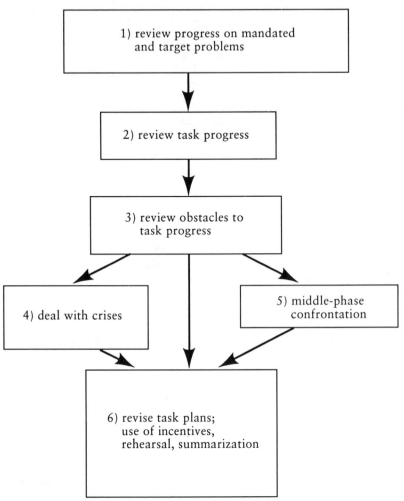

*Figure 11.3*

out of the house! This was obviously not a task, but did temporarily reduce that pressure. On the other hand, tasks may be completed without change in conditions. In the example below, John has completed some of the tasks related to pursuing a job without any change in actually getting a job. The involuntary client's assessment of change in conditions can be probed for specifics and practitioners should then add their own assessment of changes.

In the following section, Cheri has a mid-phase review meeting with John, the nonvoluntary resident of a homeless program introduced in chapter 10. John has missed two appointments with Cheri and does not appear eager to talk about his job-seeking efforts. He talks more about his experiences near the Minneapolis Metrodome during the World Series. Such apparently irrelevant discussion often occurs when clients are either having difficulties with their tasks or are not really sure they wish to work on the target problem. Cheri reviews that the last appointments were not kept in a matter-of-fact way without blaming. She supports his initial efforts while also noting John's reservations about talking about job seeking. She empathizes with his discouragement.

CHERI: Hi, John, I'm glad that we could finally get together. It's been a while. It's been three weeks since we've met.

JOHN: Has it been that long?

CHERI: Yes, it has. Originally we decided to meet at least once a week. How's it going?

JOHN: Well, it's going okay. I've got a lot of time on my hands. It's been kind of fun spending some time down at the Dome with all the excitement down there. It's been a lot of fun.

CHERI: Well, I'm glad to hear that you're having some positive things happen in your free time.

JOHN: I've got a lot of that.

CHERI: Let's just back up a minute, because I know that after we first met and went over what you were going to do about finding a job, we scheduled another appointment, and then you said you couldn't come because you had another job interview. We both thought that that made sense to miss that meeting, because getting a job is the main thing that we're working on together. I didn't hear from you after that, we rescheduled and you didn't come, and I'm wondering what happened.

JOHN: Well, I had the job interview and it went okay. And then he told me he was going to give me a call on Wednesday, and that's the reason that I didn't come in, and I hung out in the lobby out here waiting for him to call and waiting for him to call. And I just said the heck with it. And he didn't call, so I just split. I went down to Frank's and had a beer.

CHERI: I see. So you made an application and were waiting for a call. And you felt discouraged because you didn't get the call. I can understand that it is hard to just be waiting. I'm glad you made the call and am sorry it hasn't worked out yet. It will probably take a lot of applications, as you know, before we are successful with this. Maybe today we can work on ways to be more active in contacting the places where you have made applications. In the future, I would also appreciate it if you would let me know in advance if you can't come to one of our scheduled meeting.

2. *Reviewing task progress.* The practitioner can now review task efforts, including both involuntary client efforts and practitioner tasks. It sometimes occurs as above, that clients immediately report on task completion as part of the target problem review step. As tasks are often not fully completed despite diligent efforts, task efforts can be praised. Praise should not, however, be overemphasized, as too much praise may undercut self-attribution of changes.[23] That is, involuntary clients might come to feel that they are completing tasks to please the practitioner rather than doing them because they will produce some personal benefit. Since task review often leads directly to review of obstacles in completing tasks, an example combining the two steps is provided below.

3. *Review obstacles in completing tasks.* When tasks are initially developed, anticipating that some tasks probably will not have been completed successfully is one way of avoiding preoccupation with failure. In addition, after praising task efforts, obstacles that blocked success on some tasks can be explored. Such obstacle exploration should focus on *what* got in the way rather than *who*. Examining a variety of possible causes for task failure can prevent the practitioner from prematurely concluding that tasks were not completed because of a lack of involuntary client motivation. Lack of incentive or rationale for a task is indeed a possible explanation for task failure, but several other possibilities should also be examined (see figure 11.4).

The most basic question in obstacle analysis and identification is to find out whether obstacles have blocked the specific tasks or whether the problem is one that motivates the involuntary client, or both. If obstacles have blocked a specific task while the client remains committed to working on the target problem, the following include many of the possibilities that might explain that blocked effort: a) lack of client skill, b) lack of client capacity to complete the task, c) lack of practitioner skill in task development, d) the task was not adequately specified, e) inadequate resources, f) occurrence of an emergency or crisis, g) inadequate

# Obstacle Analysis

Was obstacle
related to the
specific task?

* lack of client skill
* lack of client capacity
  to complete task
* lack of practitioner
  skill
* inadequate specification
  of task
* occurrence of emergency
  or crisis
* task lacks rationale
* lack of reinforcement
* debilitating anxiety
  or fear
* adverse beliefs
* environmental obstacles
* lack of support
* lack of power

Was obstacle
related to the
target problem?

* problem is attributed rather
  than acknowledged
* client is not aware of consequences
  of failure to work on mandated
  problem
* client has conflicted wants
* client has little hope that problem
  can be reduced

*Figure 11.4*

rationale for the task, h) lack of reinforcement, i) debilitating fear or anxiety, and j) adverse beliefs.[24]

If the problem does not motivate the involuntary client, the practitioner can examine whether: a) the involuntary client might have been pressured to acknowledge a problem attributed by others; b) the involuntary client is unaware of consequences of failure to work on a mandated problem; c) the involuntary client has conflicted wants such that work on this problem might jeopardize other benefits; or d) the involuntary client has little hope that the problem can be resolved.

If obstacles have arisen that block a specific task, the practitioner can proceed to revise tasks mindful of those blockages. If the problem is not motivational, the practitioner can attempt to reframe the problem or examine incentives and consequences in the case of mandated problems.

In the following section, Cheri reviews and praises task effort with John and probes for obstacles. She discovers both obstacles related to the specific task and the whole target problem.

CHERI: What else did you agree to do?

JOHN: Well, I agreed to look for job ads in the newspapers. But that's real hard.

CHERI: How have you been going about that?

JOHN: I go through the newspapers. It's not hard to do. But it's like you sit down and read the newspapers, and I just feel this same kind of feeling when I'm waiting for the phone. I just want to crumple the thing up and throw it away.

Several obstacle possibilities emerge here. The task of looking in the newspapers might have been inadequately specified and he may lack skills in reviewing the ads. Most pertinent are his mention of feeling discouraged that suggests that the task is not rewarding and that he has doubts about whether it will be successful.

JOHN: But there was an ad in there that I responded to . . .

CHERI: Oh, you did?

JOHN: Down at Brown Tank. Yeah.

CHERI: Great.

JOHN: I filled out an application and mailed it into them. I mailed it into 'em, and there I wait. So I haven't heard from them. It would be a good job. I'd like to have it.

CHERI: I'm glad to hear that you made an application. I also hear that just waiting and wondering is something you are frustrated about.

JOHN: This is not a pleasant place to be here. I don't want to be here, but here I am.

CHERI: You really have been active before this in efforts to find a job and you've done a great job in the things that you agreed to do. And I can also tell that you're feeling frustrated and overwhelmed about the situation and not real optimistic. I think it's important to keep working at it and to keep doing the small things because that's how you do get a job. I think that's great that you sent in that application to Brown Tank. So now you're waiting for them to call you?

JOHN: Yeah. They didn't want people coming up there, so you had to mail in the application. So I mailed in the application, and there's nothing else I can do except wait for them to call me or not call me.

CHERI: What is it that you would like to know about Brown Tank right now, as far as where you stand with them?

Obstacle analysis now appears to be centering on lack of resources as John has not heard from Brown Tank. Cheri has praised John's efforts and empathized with his frustration. His lack of hope may be realistic if he lacks skills or jobs are unavailable. Specific job readiness skills might be explored here. We will return to this exploration with John below in the sections on appropriate middle-phase confrontation and task revision.

4. *Dealing with crises.* Crises within the task-centered context are large-scale obstacles that block all task efforts. They are also defined as stress problems touched off by disruptions such as substantial change in the environment, loss of physical functioning, accident, or other losses.[25] Involuntary clients are often members of oppressed groups with low incomes, inadequate housing, and limited health care such that environmental crises frequently occur. Rather than prematurely concluding that involuntary clients are crisis-ridden and disorganized, serious exploration of the nature of those crises is in order. Task-centered research in foster care indicated that clients experienced an average of three or more crises in twelve-session contracts yet were still able to have at least partial success in fulfilling the contract.[26]

Consequently, practitioner response to crises is important in not losing hope for further progress. Several possibilities can be explored when crises occur: a) Can the crisis be handled through focusing problem-solving efforts in one session? 2) If the crisis is unlikely to be quickly resolved, should target problems be revised to include it or should it become a new target problem? 3) If the crisis can be resolved within the session, can task work continue simultaneously on targeted problems? 4) When crises are generated by client decisions, the practitioner can clarify consequences of those decisions without blaming.

In the following section, Nancy, introduced in chapter 10, discovers that a crisis has occurred. She helps Beth assess the extent and consequences of the crisis, revise the target problem, and make plans for next steps. Nancy clarifies the new circumstances without judging or blaming Beth. Instead, she describes consequences that have resulted from choices Beth has made.

NANCY: It seems that a lot of changes have happened since the last time I saw you; why don't you fill me in?

BETH: Well, Barb called the cops four times since you've been on vacation. The fourth time she had me and Jimmy removed from her premises by the cops and she wanted me to be taken up to juvenile hall and the cops said they couldn't do it. And they let me go on my own until you got back. Just that I had to contact your supervisor.

NANCY: Which you did, I know that.

BETH: And here I am.

NANCY: So you're out of Barb's and you feel that there is probably no chance that you'll be able to go back there?

BETH: I heard that she wanted me to come back but I don't want to go back.

NANCY: So, you want to change your plan, which was to stay at your aunt's until the hearing in June. The problem you wanted to work on of getting along with your aunt until you could get out on your own and support yourself on your own isn't appropriate anymore?

BETH: Right.

NANCY: So we will need to retarget and think about the problem you have now in your living situation. You don't have a job yet and I know that that has been something that has been very difficult for you to find a job. The other change is that you'll have to go to court earlier since you are not now living in an approved placement. I will have to notify the judge that you have moved out of Barb's and he will have to approve or disapprove of the new arrangements.

5. *Appropriate middle-phase confrontation.* Within the task-centered framework, confrontation can be considered a special form of obstacle identification undertaken by the practitioner. A continuum of confrontation was introduced in chapter 8, ranging from no confrontation through assertive confrontation. Assertive confrontations should be more successful in the middle phase if the practitioner has come to be trusted as a person who has the involuntary client's interest at heart, is expert, and likable (see chapter 6). Even when assertive confrontations are carried out following the guidelines for use of descriptive, non-blaming

statements described in chapter 8, such confrontations are still frequently interpreted as a put-down, verbal assault, or inappropriate criticism. As assertive confrontation is more intrusive than inductive questioning, higher levels of reactance can be expected to be generated by its
usage including possible boomerang effects in which behaviors and attitudes solidify rather than change. It often provokes anger, helplessness,
anxiety, fears, or remorse.

In the following section, Cheri combines use of inductive questions
and assertive confrontation in her responses to John's concerns
about the program and his frustration with it. Notice that she
empathizes with his feelings of frustration, does not confront them,
focusing confrontation rather on the requirements of the program
and obstacles to John's own goals.

JOHN: Well, yeah, you know. And it's not my fault. I'm not like these
guys that sit out in the lounge. They are half loaded, they get in the
bag, and they're gone. I was a good worker up there in the mines. I
was a good worker. It's just—I just get so frustrated, because I'm
down here. I went to the school, get laid off, I go to the school, they
tell me, take the school. You can be a welder, you can do okay. Go
down to the cities, make some money. So I take the school. I do all
the things that I'm supposed to do, but it just doesn't work out. I get
pretty pissed off about what's going on. 'Cause they tell you to do
this, and you do it. They tell you to do that, you do that. And then
you shake your head, and I'm supposed to go out, and this lady's
going to help me here. I'm still stuck here. What am I supposed to do.
I don't want to be here. This isn't my idea of a picnic, here.

CHERI: I can see that you would rather be someplace else. You're
feeling like I'm here telling you what you need to do, too. Nothing
seems to be helping.

JOHN: Well, it seems to me that I'm supposed to be here.

CHERI: You mean here, in my office?

JOHN: I mean like, what happens if I don't come here?

CHERI: Well, that was one of the first things about your participating
in this housing program that we talked about, when we first met.
There were a couple of things, for you to be here, to live here and eat
here, that you needed to agree to do, which you did do. Do you
remember what those were?

JOHN: I agreed when I came here that I would do some of the handi-
work around here in exchange for room and board. That I'd take care
of myself. Well, mostly that I would do the odd jobs around here,
some of the small maintenance things.

CHERI: You've done a great job, by the way. You've been the first one that's been able to fix that window. That's great.

JOHN: Well, thanks. And the other part is that I agreed that I'd come in here and see you. And that I would be active in my job search.

CHERI: Right.

JOHN: Which I did—I've been out there doing my stuff.

CHERI: Yes, you have been. One of my main roles here is to work with the people that are participating in this program to help them find employment and to be kind of a support person and to help get the ball rolling. It is important that you see me regularly.

JOHN: I hear that.

CHERI: I know that you don't really like being here, and I don't want you to have to be here either. I want you to have a full-time job so you can be on your own.

In the next section, Nancy carries out a series of assertive confrontations with Beth about not carrying through with plans to contact an alternative school. She makes the confrontations with specific facts followed by expressions of empathy.

NANCY: So you wanted to contact the high school to see if you could enroll this quarter and get one more credit and have that for when you want to take your GED test and want to get a high school diploma, right?

BETH: Right.

NANCY: What about GED studying, are you thinking about doing that now or are you thinking about doing that in the future sometime?

BETH: I could do it now.

NANCY: What do you know about where you could study for your GED?

BETH: I could try to enroll in Fresh Start. I could take my GED but then I couldn't take the credit that I need. All I get is my GED and not my diploma.

NANCY: Beth, when we started four sessions ago, you were talking about Fresh Start at that point and you didn't contact Fresh Start, and we talked about it at the second session and you said you had forgot and that you had been real busy, so you said you would contact them again, and you didn't contact them the second week. Is there something about Fresh Start that is holding you back?

BETH: Right now I want to get that one credit because then I can get that diploma instead of just a plain old GED. And if I go to Fresh Start, I can't get it because they don't give credits at Fresh Start.

NANCY: Are there any other things about Fresh Start that turn you off?

BETH: The work, I don't really, I don't think I could get into building houses, or apartment houses.

NANCY: The construction work doesn't appeal to you.

BETH: Not really.

NANCY: Did you say that to them when you were interviewing there? That it wasn't work you thought you could really get into.

BETH: No, I didn't say much of anything when I went there.

NANCY: Oh. Why didn't you say anything to them about that?

BETH: 'Cause I wasn't really sure.

NANCY: You were under some pressure to come up with a plan too, I know, at that time for the court.

BETH: Yeah, I was.

NANCY: It just seemed to me when you kept putting off contacting them that there must be something going on then. It just didn't fit with the way you saw yourself. Or the way you wanted your life to turn out, so I think it's a good idea but I don't want you to come up with that idea just to have one more idea for me. I want the ideas to be ones that are important to you.

Consideration of confrontation so far has concentrated on use of inductive questions and assertive confrontation. In some circumstances, intensive confrontation that is longer-term and from multiple sources is appropriate. Intensive confrontations sometimes can be utilized when illegal behavior has occurred of a very serious nature or when serious harm to self or others has occurred or is imminent. If the concern is about self-harm, evidence should demonstrate that without intensive intervention harmful, irreversible consequences are likely to follow (see chapter 4). In circumstances that fail to meet these levels of harm or danger to self and others, involuntary clients should be able to choose to receive the intensive confrontation or avoid it.

For example, the intervention techniques used to persuade persons with chemical dependency problems to consider accepting treatment can be considered intensive confrontation. In such circumstances intervention is defined as presenting reality in a receivable way to a person out of touch with it.[27] Many experts consider chemically addicted behavior not to be "free" behavior under the control of the normal powers of will, but rather a driving physical and emotional need. According to this view, the driving need arouses a set of rigid defense mechanisms that are impervious to normal means of persuasion.[28]

Such interventions may take the form of a professionally guided intensive confrontation in which a group of family and friends meet for an extended period of time with the chemically dependent person to express both caring and concern. Those persons considered likely to be influential with the chemically dependent person are asked to compose letters that recall specific situations of loving and concern and specific instances of the harm caused to self and others by the chemically dependent person's behavior. Letters are edited to describe specific instances of harm without shaming or blaming. The chemically dependent person is asked to listen to the group while they read their letters before responding. After this response, specific options for dealing with the chemical dependency problem are strongly recommended.

Variations of such intervention methods have included preparation of the spouse of the alcoholic to carry out the confrontation. In Thomas' unilateral family therapy model, the spouse specifies a directive to enter treatment or decrease consumption and includes a consequence such as marital separation if the alcoholic refuses.[29] Preliminary model testing of this form of Thomas' unilateral family therapy method, including this programmed confrontation, has been supportive of the effectiveness of the technique. Thomas notes that while agreement with the programmed confrontation would be desirable in all cases, it is sometimes necessary to settle for less. In all cases, however, the spouse may be helped to consider his or her options if the intervention does not succeed and the chemically dependent person may move closer to acknowledging the problem. Sometimes alcoholics respond to the programmed confrontation by choosing to reduce consumption on their own. In this event, the practitioner attempts to gain a commitment from the chemically dependent person to enter a treatment program if reduction does not reach specific levels within a specific time limit.[30]

It is interesting to note that Thomas reports that chemically dependent persons sometimes select an alternative that would address the alcohol problem but that is *not* the specific recommendation made by the intervener and spouse. For example, some clients insist on finding their own treatment program rather than the one recommended.[31] One explanation for these responses can come from reactance theory. Presenting one option may stimulate more reactance than presenting two or more, including those generated by the chemically dependent person.[32]

Some treatment programs for persons who have committed crimes of physical violence, including sex crimes, make frequent use of intensive confrontation rather than situation-specific use. In such settings, discussions of use of intensive confrontation frequently focus on the type of person who "needs" intensive confrontation, those who are highly defended, resistant and sociopathic. Repeated use of intensive confrontation is sometimes based on beliefs that clients who commit crimes have erroneous thinking styles that maintain illegal, deviant behavior.[33] These thinking styles are considered to include pervasive self-deception, refusal to take responsibility for actions, and a manipulative orientation that is impervious to all but the most intensive confrontation. Hence, it is argued that confrontation should not necessarily be in short doses nor surrounded by messages of caring and acceptance. Rather, the dose must be large and the impact of the confrontation not dulled by acceptance of manipulative or self-deceptive behavior.

Intensive confrontation is sometimes used in ways that conflict with the guidelines for confrontation presented earlier in chapter 8. Those guidelines suggested that: 1) confrontation should meet specific circumstances of law violation, harm, or danger or choice to receive it by the involuntary client; 2) it is most effectively and ethically delivered when it includes specific examples, is conveyed with caring, respect, and support by a person respected by the involuntary client; and 3) that it is unlikely to be either ethical or effective when it emanates from the frustration of the practitioner rather than from client circumstances. If confrontation is done inappropriately, it can lead to fear, anxiety, resistance, and heightened defensiveness.[34]

Assertive and intensive confrontation can also lose their situation- and behavior-specific, caring qualities and become *abusive confrontation* in which the client is subjected to a blaming, uncaring onslaught (see chapter 8). Factors influencing inappropriate usage of confrontation can include program and client variables, situational variables, and practitioner variables.

*Program and client variables.* Confrontation is sometimes used in frequent, intense doses as the method of the program rather than as a confrontation for specific clients and circumstances. Such usage is described by those programs as necessary to influence particular kinds of clients. Such high-frequency usage of intensive confrontation can have expectable consequences in involuntary client behavior. Efforts to protect oneself from intensive confrontation may be interpreted as further evidence of resistant behavior with little attention to the degree to which intensive confrontation *contributes to* behavior that is labeled defended and resistant. In fact, intensive confrontation as a frequently used method should be expected to generate high reactance as a byproduct of its usage. Further, if intensive confrontation is not carried out with accompanying messages of support from persons considered likable and trustworthy, the influence can easily be perceived as punishing rather than persuasive.[35] If the influence method is perceived to be abusive, then it may *reinforce* the belief that might makes right by modeling intrusive behavior on the part of the practitioner. There is further concern about overgeneralizing the use of intensive confrontation methods beyond the circumstances that call for it. For example, Lieberman, Yalom, and Miles reported that frequent use of attacking methods that pressured encounter group members to change quickly led to a higher number and proportion of group casualties than in groups in which leaders employed more selective confrontation.[36] Inappropriate overuse of intensive confrontation methods might be avoided through increased use of self-assessments, inductive questions, and assertive confrontation early in contact.

*Situational variables.* When motivational congruence with involuntary clients has not been achieved, practitioners often experience frustration with involuntary client failure to complete required tasks. While the intention may be to jolt the involuntary client in the interest of his or her ultimate well-being, there is little reason to believe that an uncaring unslaught will change attitudes or provide more than a brief release of tension for the frustrated practitioner. When frustration is vented with the practitioner acting as prosecutor or critical parent, change may occur but only through fear of punishment and enhanced dependency.[37] Further, such undifferentiated use may make clients *less* voluntary by ignoring areas of possible motivational congruence, contributing to distancing from involuntary clients and labeling them resistant.[38]

*Practitioner variables.* Finally, it has been suggested that some practitioners overuse or inappropriately use confrontation when they lack other helping skills. For example, Forrest suggests that some practitioners are consistently angry, manipulative, exploitative, and pathologically confrontive.[39] Egan suggests that "the confrontation specialist is often a very destructive person, a person who is not even good in his own speciality." Practitioners lacking empathy skills may try to overcome such lack of skills with overly reactive, negative confronting styles.[40] Rather than assume that overuse of intensive confrontation is primarily a result of personality deficits of practitioners, I suggest that exposure to the continuum of confrontation skills in the context of other helping methods may be more useful in extending the practitioner's skill repertoire. The real issues are then flexibility in use of confrontation methods, the ability to determine when confrontation is appropriate, and if so, of what intensity and with what expectable consequences. Practitioners who rigidly use particular modes of confrontation might explore more flexible use of confrontation, including in some cases less frequent use so as not to diminish the effect of appropriate assertive confrontation.

Underuse of confrontation is also a problem. Practitioners trained to work with voluntary clients who value the "good relationship" (see chapter 9) may be hesitant to use confrontation for fear that it will damage the relationship. Remembering that involuntary clients who find themselves in a position of low power may be inclined to use self-presentation strategies and act with less than full candor can help in preparing for appropriate use of confrontation (see chapter 7). Such practitioners should remember that the *lack* of confrontation in circumstances of potential harm, danger, law violation, or behavior that conflicts with client goals can be as damaging as inappropriate overuse. They can then experiment with increased use of inductive questions and assertive confrontation as appropriate, respectful methods that can enhance the working relationship.

6. *Revising task plans.* The purpose of obstacle analysis and appropriate middle-phase confrontation is to improve the chances for more successful task plans. As in initial task planning, rationales for completing the tasks, possible incentives or rewards, and use of simulation or role play may be considered. Practitioner tasks may also be useful here in facilitating client action.[41] In the following section, Jean and Mrs. Torres (introduced in chapter 9) are making plans about the next steps in their work together related to making her home safer place. Notice how Jean is both specific and picks up on Mrs. Torres' ideas about how to limit the tasks. Mrs. Torres also puts her stamp on the particular ways she intends to carry out the tasks.

JEAN: Okay, how many shelves do you plan to clean?

MRS. TORRES: Well, I think those three that are right by the cupboards where I want to keep the extra groceries are probably the most important.

JEAN: Okay, that makes sense, since you will use them the most. So you plan to clean three?

MRS. TORRES: Yeah, I'll do that bunch right next to those cupboards, I'll do those, because a lot of that I think can be thrown away.

JEAN: That makes sense to do those three.

MRS. TORRES: But I'll have Julie help because some of that stuff she might want to keep. It's a lot of spare parts, and stuff.

JEAN: Yes, that would help.

MRS. TORRES: If I'm going to do the shelves first, I think that I should only try to do four boxes.

JEAN: Okay, I think that sounds good. If for some reason you get really ambitious, you know, and you really are on a roll, you can do more than what we agree on, you don't have to stick to this. It sounds as if you and Julie worked well together doing the boxes and and a lot of things got done during that time. So, if you decide to do more, you might try that.

MRS. TORRES: Besides that, then we mark on the outside of the boxes what I've got in there. We got a marker and then we marked it down. Because since we moved then I forgot what is in what box, you know.

JEAN: Yeah, that can get very confusing if you do that.

MRS. TORRES: Okay, I'll start writing down, I'm going to make a list of things, I think I'll put that on here. Yeah, because I'm going to make a list of all the different kinds of things that Julie could help me with and then she'd be able to choose.

JEAN: That works well for you when Julie has a say in what parts she helps with.

## The Termination Phase

Approaches to work with voluntary clients often consider termination with trepidation and predict that many clients at this stage will feel abandoned and regress to earlier stages. If the client has come to depend on the practitioner as a major source of support and problem-solving expertise without having enhanced his or her own skills and support systems, then such feelings of abandonment are both understandable and predictable.

Involuntary clients are less likely to experience such regrets. Since they did not seek contact, termination may be approached with relief that an unsought pressure will be removed. In fact, regrets may be a *good* sign since involuntary clients are only likely to feel them if contact had ultimately come to be valued. In fact, one family that I worked with as a result of required contact with an adolescent who was absenting from school noted as I finished my last session that the family sessions were "not so bad"!

Termination with mandated clients often involves practitioner decisions and recommendations about when to let go of contact. Such decisions can be difficult because rarely are all problems resolved. In addition, some clients continue to have frequent crises or do not have access to ongoing support.

Decisions about termination can be made more easily when specific goals were established during the contracting phase. In the absence of such specific goals, the involuntary client is maintained in a relatively powerless state without a focus for energies and reactance may be reinforced. When such criteria focus on essentials rather than the ideal, termination is more likely to be successful.

The practitioner using the task-centered approach begins to prepare for termination in the first session by focusing clearly on the schedule of sessions, by reminding the client of the number of sessions completed and the number remaining. This focus on available time makes use of the "goal gradient" effect described in chapter 10 in which client and practitioner activities can be expected to pick up in pace when the end of a time-limited contract approaches. Second, practitioners can also gradually become less active in task formulation and obstacle analysis, expressing confidence in client ability to resolve problems. Practitioners can also limit the scope of work undertaken in later sessions by narrowing or reducing goals to more feasible levels.

It is often hoped that work done in time-limited contact will generalize to situations after contact is ended. Beth was interviewed after her contact with Nancy had ended and she had been approved for independent living. Below, the interviewer explores the possibility that task-centered work on her own target problems may have also taught a problem-solving process that might generalize when Beth approaches new situations.

INTERVIEWER: You had been working with Nancy for quite a while but in February, she changed gears and worked a little differently with you, did you notice any differences?

BETH: Yes, I wasn't arguing with her as much. I felt that she was letting me take charge of my life and letting me make the decisions and not her. Which helped me a lot because I realized that it was all on my hands and nobody else and that made me sit down and think that I better get my stuff together and that helped a lot.

INTERVIEWER: Over the last couple months you've done quite a few tasks or things that you worked out with Nancy. I'm wondering if you've learned anything about not just carrying out those tasks but solving problems on your own that you've been able to take to other problems, other than the ones you talked to Nancy about?

BETH: Well to me at first when I did have Nancy, they all just seemed like a pain in the butt, but now they have become more real that they are a problem, that they can be worked out in time. That you just have to spend a little bit more time on each one of them and not try to solve them all in one day because it just doesn't work.

INTERVIEWER: So one of the things you do differently is you don't try to solve them all in one day?

BETH: Right. I take one step at a time if it takes a week for one problem, then it's a week I have to spend on it. If it takes more, then it has to take more, but some can take just one day, but others take a month to figure out. And I learned from my problems, not to make mistakes twice.

INTERVIEWER: I understand that you got a notebook of your own and you were writing down some of your own tasks for yourself.

BETH: Yeah, after me and Nancy had gone through the eight-week sessions I started writing down tasks that I thought were important to myself, that I had to do to succeed. And I still do that and I write down the daily things of what I have to do and the end of the day before I go to bed I'll check them off. What I didn't do goes on the next days list.

It appears that Beth was quite aware of making more decisions and was taking more personal responsibility for issues in her life. She has a grasp of prioritizing problems in order to reduce the feeling of being overwhelmed by them and she generates tasks for herself. Successful efforts in this time-limited contact do not mean that her life will continue without setbacks nor that she will never again have contact with social services. How can the practitioner working with involuntary clients prepare for termination in such a way that such self-attribution is encouraged? Four options can be considered in the final phase: 1) termination, 2) extension, 3) recontracting, and 4) monitoring.

*Termination.* When the end of the time limit is reached, many involuntary clients and practitioners will be ready to terminate because problems are substantially reduced or a preset limit of sessions has been reached. *Extensions* can be negotiated if substantial progress has already been made and more can be expected with a few more sessions. For example, a client who wanted to increase her job-seeking skills extended her contract for two sessions when an important job interview was scheduled for a week after the scheduled final session. The extension was planned to prepare for that interview and to review the interview and the total contract in a final session. *Recontracting* refers to the development of an additional contract on new problem areas if the client and practitioner both expressly wish to continue and there is good reason to believe that substantial progress will be made on the same or additional problems. Recontracting assumes that the agency will permit more lengthy contact. Recontracting may also be done when a large problem has been broken down into smaller time-limited sequences. Hence, the client may proceed to a second sequence if the first has been productive. It is often the case that case management contact continues after a period of more intensive contact has ended. Such *monitoring* works best when it is carried out for a specific, contracted purpose rather than waiting for something to happen or go wrong. Such monitoring can take place through brief in-person and telephone check-up sessions. Monitoring can be useful to assess the maintenance of gains after a period of more limited contact. Monitoring may also occur to support linkages made to other resources.[42]

When a decision to terminate services or shift to a different mode of contact has been made, a termination or transition session can include the following steps.

1. *Review problem reduction* on each target and mandated problem by examining change in conditions. Concrete data for assessing change can be shared. For example, Beth and Nancy reviewed Beth's work on conditions that would be reviewed in court when the recommendation for independent living would be considered. Specifically, conditions of parental permission, having a place to stay and a source of income, or participation in an educational program were reviewed. In addition, Beth's feeling that too many people were telling her what to do was also reviewed, finding that completing tasks had moved her to a more independent place in which there were fewer people in a position to tell her what to do.

2. *Review tasks completed* and obstacles encountered, focusing on successes and learning obtained from that process. Beth and Nancy reviewed her efforts to get a job and enter an educational program and the obstacles related to both.

3. *Review the general steps in problem solving* used in the case as a reminder of methods that can be used with remaining problems. For example, it can be recalled that steps included: a) identifying specific concerns or target problems, b) prioritizing mandated problems and those voluntary problems that might make the most difference, c) considering task possibilities and anticipating potential roadblocks, and d) reviewing progress and attempting to "fix" tasks that didn't work based on obstacle analysis.

4. *Consider remaining needs on targeted problems and other problems of concern* to the client. The practitioner helps the involuntary client to plan how he or she might go about maintaining changes. The practitioner should also help the involuntary client anticipate potential obstacles to this plan and to consider how those might be overcome. For example, Nancy and Beth discussed several problems that might occur after she was in indepedent living and how she might pursue help for them.

# Chapter 12

# Working with
# Involuntary Families

The chapter presents an involuntary perspective for work with families who experience pressures ranging along a continuum from little or no pressure (voluntary treatment) through nonvoluntary to mandated pressures. Issues in involuntary contact as considered in family therapy literature follow. While beyond the scope of the book to develop a fully elaborated model for involuntary family work, specific guidelines for the contracting phase are presented that adapt the family therapy technique of *reframing* and include viewing family resistance from an interactional perspective.

We begin with interaction between a practitioner representing family-centered, home-based services and Mrs. King, single parent of 16-year-old Christine. Mrs. King called a public child welfare agency requesting that Christine be removed from her home because she was not obeying house rules, skipping school, and suspected of drug use. Mrs. King and Christine were then referred for a home-based service assessment. Family-based services often require as a precondition that family members agree to work to remain together as a unit rather than separate as would be the preference for some.[1] Hence, while an offer of home-based service is welcomed by many as a better alternative than placement out of the home, some are court-ordered to receive services and others feel pressure to accept the service and would prefer other services. The following exchange occurred during an initial home visit to explore the situation and make an offer for home-based services. While the practitioner and Mrs. King talk, Christine sits staring into space, portable-radio earphones planted firmly on her head.

PRACTITIONER: I explained to you briefly about home-based services on the phone. Home-based services is a program that the county offers for families who are having difficulties similar to what you described to me. A team of workers would come into your home to meet with your family for at least an hour a week for 6 to 9 weeks. In that time, we would talk about what's going on and try and find some resolution to some of the difficulties that are going on in your home.

MRS. KING: You know, when I called Child Welfare, I thought that you were going to come and get her out of here. I just thought that you were going to come and tell me the procedure for getting her out of the house. We can't have her here.

PRACTITIONER: So, you thought that I'd be putting Christine into placement.

MRS. KING: I think, you know, that's pretty much what I said over the phone . . .I'm telling you what I need.

PRACTITIONER: I can understand that you are disappointed that we can't offer the placement out of the home you wanted. We place children and adolescents out of the home in fairly restricted circumstances. We have found in the past that if the problems aren't worked on in the home, the child often returns after placement to the same situation. So, we are now offering in-home family-based service to help you with the problems that caused you to want to get her placed out of the home.

MRS. KING: So you're telling me how I'm going to be able to solve my problem, and I'm telling you what my problem is, and I know how to solve it. And that's to get her out of the house here. I mean this stuff of having her still live here, I mean she's just causing too much trouble.

While Mrs. King made a voluntary request for service, she can hardly be described as voluntary during the above conversation. She discovers that the out-of-home placement service she requested is not available and she experiences pressure to accept home-based services as a substitute service. Further, 16-year-old Christine has not yet been addressed and hence at this point may be more an involuntary target than client.

Practitioners frequently have involuntary contact with families, including persons such as Mrs. King and Christine. They often draw on family therapy perspectives in planning what to do with such families. Such perspectives permit analysis of family communications and role structures that have been found useful far beyond their original development in voluntary family therapy. Similarly, family therapy techniques for assisting families in making behavioral changes have been attractive alternatives to methods that focus primarily on seeking cognitive or emotional insight.

Family therapy perspectives, however, require many adaptations for work in involuntary family situations. In addition, many practitioners work with families regarding issues such as discharge planning and concern with the welfare of an elderly relative, in which family therapy is neither the service offered by the practitioner's setting nor sought by clients.

## How are Families and Family Members Involuntary?

Margolin notes that it is typical for some family members to be more eager to participate in therapy than others, raising the issue of voluntary participation for the latter.[2] In fact, family contact often begins with an interview with one or more family members who are concerned about the problems of an absent family member.[3] That family member is frequently a child or adolescent and the problem is often viewed as their troublesome behavior. "Identified targets" such as Christine frequently participate minimally, occasionaly rousing to defend themselves against parental accusations.

In other situations such as alleged child abuse or neglect, the practitioner initiates contact. In such situations, the family does not seek help and may not be willing to reveal problems. For example, when a child is at risk of placement, the only problem the family sees may be keeping the child at home and family contact is considered primarily as fulfilling requirements.[4] Such families are often perceived to be dysfunctional with labels attached such as having rigid, confounded problem solving methods, being conflictual, enmeshed, prone to externalize, with serious problems of multiple or long duration, with little executive capacity, overwhelmed, crisis-oriented, with critical communication, depleted goals, unempathic, either abdicating responsibility or too focused on the child.[5]

With such negative practitioner perceptions, it may not come as a surprise that "the therapist often meets a barrage of angry feelings, particularly . . . before members are actively engaged."[6] Such families are described as fearful, angry, distrustful, viewing helping professionals as intimidating parent figures who will not seek or accept their views and who are insensitive to their needs for privacy.[7] Similarly, families are described as feeling victimized by the court, schools, and social service staff, and are often seen as resistant to change despite orders, pleas, exhortations, and the combined efforts of many agencies. The practitioner assigned to work with them often feels frustrated and exhausted.[8] The fact that such families are often headed by harried, low-income, single-parent mothers from oppressed groups is often neglected in the literature.

Family therapy has also been used with families likely to include at least one involuntary member in settings as diverse as drug and alcohol abuse, delinquency, home-based services, spouse abuse, and in prisons.[9] For example, Stanton describes the utility of work with families of chemically dependent persons.[10] The functions that drugs serve in the family can be examined, including the ways use is overlooked, treatment is sabotaged, and how significant others can influence maintenance of drug use.[11] Similarly, when family methods have been used in the treatment of alcoholism, alcoholics are said to sometimes experience less isolation, feel gratified by the spouse's participation, and feel less need to be defensive and responsible for the entire problem.[12] The spouse can play a critical role in assisting new learning.[13] Use of family methods in delinquency has had some success not only with the behavior of the delinquent family member but also in preventing delinquency of nondelinquent siblings.[14]

It is beyond the scope of this chapter to review in detail the applications made in these varied fields to less than voluntary populations. The intention at this point is to note that applications have been made and to explore in more detail the implications of involuntary status. For example, some families may not seek out family treatment but have it thrust upon or "strongly suggested" to them. As argued in chapter 2, voluntary clients may find themselves becoming "resistant" to a reframed view of the problem, but they may withdraw from such circumstances without suffering enduring negative consequences. Nonvoluntary clients, however, may suffer a negative consequence from failure to adapt to the practitioner or agency's reframing. More frequently, some family members may be voluntary if their view of the problem is addressed, while other family members may be seen more as targets of change than as clients. To further explore these possibilities, a continuum of involuntary family contact is presented.

## A Continuum of Involuntary Family Contact

An involuntary family transaction refers to contact between a helping professional and two or more family members in which at least one participant experiences external pressure to participate in that contact. This definition focuses attention on the presence of factors outside the person as influencing initial contact. These pressures range from formal and informal nonvoluntary pressures to mandated pressures. The family as a total unit may fit on a continuum of external pressure. In addition, individual family members may be scattered throughout the continuum, with some experiencing nonvoluntary pressure, some experiencing mandated pressure, and while others may be voluntary. Further, families and family members may become more or less voluntary during contact. For example, Mrs. King may have begun the request for service as a voluntary client while Christine experienced informal nonvoluntary pressure from her mother to participate in that contact. Voluntary, nonvoluntary, and mandated points on the continuum are elaborated below.

The voluntary family is one in which family members seek assistance from a helping practitioner without outside pressures from legal, formal, or informal sources. For example, a couple may seek marriage counseling without either formal pressure or informal pressure from one spouse who is more committed to seeking help than the other. If the resource sought comes without strings attached by the agency or practitioner providing the resource, or if informal pressures are not present, then the family unit may be voluntary. As Mrs. King's situation suggests, some family members may be voluntary as long as the problems they perceive are addressed and they do not experience mandated, formal, or informal pressure. The dilemma for family practitioners is that accepting the agenda of one person such as the parent often implies work with another family member as involuntary target. Hence, circumstances in which all family members are voluntary are probably the exception to the rule.

Nonvoluntary family contact occurs when at least one family member experiences a coerced or constrained choice from formal or informal pressure to participate in contact. Formal pressure may take at least five forms: 1) a desired service or resource is not available; 2) family service is presented as the only alternative to a punishing option; 3) family contact may be a precondition or *perceived to be* a precondition for receiving a desired resource; 4) the original request for individual treatment is reframed by the practitioner as a family problem; and 5) family service may be the policy of the agency. Each of these forms of formal pressure will be presented separately with examples to illustrate them.

1. *Desired service or resource is not available.* Clients such as Mrs. King who may make a voluntary request may become involuntary when that request is not accepted. If their other options are limited, they may experience a constrained choice.

2. *Family service is presented as the only alternative to a punishing option.* Some families may experience a coerced choice to seek family counseling influenced by the expectation of avoiding major punishers controlled by outside agencies. Hence, juveniles and their families are sometimes presented with the coerced option of accepting family treatment or entering a residential treatment program.

3. *Family contact is a precondition or is perceived to be a precondition for receiving a desired resource.* Such preconditions may be intentional or unintentional, explicit or implied. For example, families seeking approval to become adoptive parents often find that a thorough family assessment is an intentional explicit precondition. Similarly, couples seeking divorce may find that the services of a mediator are a required precondition for judicial approval of their divorce request.[15] Family members may encounter agency expectations that they attend counseling in support of the residential treatment of a family member. For example, Stanton and Todd report that when parents and siblings were required to attend family sessions in support of a chemically addicted family member, 94 percent of the families that attended the first meeting continued in treatment and family therapy substantially increased the number of days the patient was free from drugs.[16]

In other cases, family contact may be *perceived* as a precondition when the suggestion that it take place comes from a powerful person or agency that controls major resources. The precondition may be implicit. For example, some referral sources such as foster care workers may recommend family therapy with the implied message to the family may be: "Take six months of family therapy and we will review your plans to regain custody of your child."

That message may be unintentional. Unless free choices are clarified and the consequences for complying or not complying with the suggestion are clarified, family members may take the suggestion from a powerful person as an implied requirement. For example, Mrs. King may receive the impression that she must agree to home-based services as a necessary hurdle to show that lesser methods have not succeeded for out-of-home placement to be considered.[17]

While families experiencing a coerced or constrained choice to "seek treatment" may have little doubt about its involuntary nature, practitioners receiving the "request for service" may be less aware of the coerced or constrained nature of the request if they are unaware of the benefits and punishers controlled by the referral source. Similarly, the referring practitioner may be unaware that the family is responding to a suggestion as if it were an implied requirement.

4. *An original request for individual treatment is reframed by the practitioner as a family problem.* As noted above, family members frequently come for help with concerns about another member of the family who is not present.[18] They may voluntarily seek help to have a troublesome person "fixed." If the practitioner agrees to "fix" the identified target, the family members initiating contact remain voluntary. Practitioners with a systems view of family problems may, however, search for indicators for how the family system supports the identified target person's symptoms. If such practitioners attempt to reframe problems to the family system level, family members may experience a constrained choice to accept a "package deal" in order to receive attention on the problem that led them to seek help.[19] Reluctance of family members to accept such a reframe is explained by Anderson and Stewart:

Most families are at least skeptical about, if not overtly resistant to, the concept of family therapy. The anxiety-producing experience of beginning any kind of therapy becomes complicated by the seemingly illogical request that the entire family come in to be seen when the problem clearly resides in one member. Why should the family be seen when it is Johnny who doesn't like school or Mary who is "acting up"?[20]

Finally, there are many circumstances beyond family treatment in which a practitioner may suggest that other family members need to be consulted in order to resolve the problem presented. For example, adults sometimes seek help when they are concerned about the living conditions of their frail relatives. The practitioner may well seek to include those relatives rather than operate on them as targets.

5. *Family service may be the policy of the agency.* Some agencies may have a policy of refusing to see the family unless all family members are present or strongly suggesting family involvement. According to Margolin, family members should be informed that other agencies and therapists may not have the same preference and assistance should be offered for such a referral.[21]

In addition to formal pressures, family members often experience informal pressures from the rest of the family in addition to formal pressure or where no formal pressure from the practitioner or agency has been applied. For example, siblings may initially attend sessions because "Mom and Dad made me come" or because family therapists requested that they attend in order to see the "identified client" in the context of family interaction.

While nonvoluntary contact is probably the most frequent form of family contact, mandated family contact also occurs. For example, persons who have abused or neglected their children are sometimes court-ordered to receive family counseling.[22] The involuntary nature of such an arrangement is usually clear to the family and the family practitioner carrying out the court order. Expectations for reporting on family progress to the court are often discussed and the power issues involved are often considered openly. Consequences, however, of failure to complete treatment or change in specified ways are often unclear.

Practitioners may also initiate an involuntary investigation. According to Reid, "many of these cases involve 'mandated' problems which essentially are problems that are defined not by the family but by the community and its representatives including the practitioner. . . . The social worker needs to reveal to the family at the outset the general shape of those mandated problems."[23] In some cases, practitioners are able to work with the family and relevant community agencies in an effort to negotiate definitions of the problem acceptable to those involved.[24]

## Issues in Adapting Family Treatment Pespectives to Work with Involuntary Families

While family treatment approaches have made important contributions to work with persons in less than voluntary situations, there are difficulties in exclusive reliance on family treatment for guidance in such work. These problems include: 1) lack of fit with setting; 2) lack of attention to other systems levels; 3) goal conflict; 4) the resurrection of resistance; 5) issues in definition of practitioner role; and 6) ethical issues.

1. *Lack of fit with settings.* Many practitioners have contact with families in settings whose function is not family treatment.[25] For example, social workers often deal with practical problems such as assistance in finance and housing, dealing with illness, disability, locating and linking clients with resources, and acting as public agents around the well-being of children.[26] Practitioners may work in discharge planning, consulting in an emergency room, returning children from foster care, and mediating conflict in which problems of illness and poverty often predominate.[27] Caseloads may vary from small to hundreds.[28] Clients served in such community organizations are often "not seeking the help

offered." Yet while such work "in the trenches" may be the mission of fields such as social work, prestige is often accorded to practitioners by their distance from such work.[29]

The practice of helping professionals in such settings is shaped by factors such as their function in the organization, the kinds of problems and clients served and their level of training.[30] William Reid suggests that a framework for work with families is needed that includes both conventional forms of family treatment and other kinds of intervention, which is adaptable to work in the community, and which fits with an ecological problem-solving view in which the family is one of several systems.[31]

2. *Lack of attention to other system levels.* While family therapy has been greatly influenced by systems perspectives, there are great variations in the way those perspectives are applied. For example, some approaches suggest that families are homeostatic systems that only superficially invite change while in fact they struggle with great determination to maintain the status quo.[32] More recently, some family theorists suggest that family systems are not always static opponents of change. In this cybernetic view, families are seen as simultaneously engaged in efforts to change and also to maintain systems integrity.[33]

However, according to Pinsof, "unfortunately, in much of the family literature, system has become virtually synonymous with family."[34] Harriet Johnson further suggests that while family approaches are often presented as systems approaches, they often redefine environmentally generated emotional distress as inadequate family or interpersonal functioning.[35]

In general, however, family systems theorists treat the family as a closed system omitting from their assessment any meaningful investigations either of the biological subsystems of individual family members or the social, economic and organizational factors which may be suprasystems in which the family is enmeshed. . . . Instead, there is a tendency to focus almost exclusively on interpersonal transactions; the focus is primarily interpersonal rather than systemic.[36]

Finally, William Reid suggests that an overabsorption with family dynamics to the neglect of individual and environmental causes creates problems for social work similar to the absorption with intrapsychic processes that reflected the psychoanalytic emphasis of an earlier age.[37] More current approaches have attempted to redress this balance with greater attention to extra-family systems.

3. *Goal conflict.* Sturkie suggests that family therapy methods can be conceptualized according to the goals of treatment.[38] Goals vary from

seeking to enhance personal and interpersonal awareness to altering functioning through changing the family's organizational structure and sequences of interaction.[39] For example, in structural approaches, insight may be seen as inhibiting change.[40] Some approaches suggest that family conceptions of problems may be caught up in problem definitions that will not actually permit change. For example, they might suggest that "getting Christine out of the house" is a view of the problem that will not permit real change. Until the focus is shifted to "second order" change that gets at the way the family defines and solves problems, real change will not occur.[41] They suggest that practice with a restricted problem focus and explicit priorities may lead to "symptom chasing."[42] These second order change goals may include attempting to restructure roles in the family and adapting communication patterns, including methods of resolving conflict, assisting in the differentiation of roles, and examining patterns across generations.[43]

Working on these second order goals does not preclude agreement with families on working to achieve some resolution of the problems that they brought to treatment. Some question whether families need to be aware of these second order goals. According to Anderson and Stewart: "It is not necessary or desirable that family members agree with all of the therapist's goals for the family, particularly such general ones as 'less enmeshment.'"[44]

Tolson suggests, however, that if practitioners conclude that there are necessary preconditions to work on client-defined problems, then they must be careful to assure "that the outcome goal is indeed achieved. Furthermore, they must effectively educate and persuade their clients that work towards theoretically derived goals will produce an important end point for the client."[45] Hence, she urges that the family-perceived goals not be misplaced in an attempt to address underlying issues. Work on theoretically derived goals may be an important step toward resolving family concerns. If so, that connection should be explained to them.

A further issue arises when the goals of the setting for the provision of service conflict with the goals of the families who receive the service. For example, family-based services to families is often described as having the goal of "empowering families." Yet the funding for such services is usually at the public expense and not for reaching family goals per se but at least in part influenced by societal goals of reducing costs of unnecessary out-of-home placement. Evaluation of the effectiveness of family-based services has tended to focus on counts of unneccessary placements prevented more than on measures of family functioning.[46] Hence, empowerment may occur if family goals are agreed upon which are compatible with a larger system goal of preventing unnecessary out-of-home placement. Many clients of family-based services may be readily convinced that in-home services are a means to reaching their goals and hence not be nonvoluntary, or only temporarily so. Parents of teens, however, frequently seek out-of-home placement and may accept home-based services as a second-best alternative.

4. *The resurrection of resistance.* Conflicts between client-perceived goals and hidden second order goals held by the practitioner can resurrect resistance. Perhaps because of the interactional nature of family work and the influences of a systems perspective, family practitioners have been more likely to consider family resistance in terms of interactional phenomena and less likely to attribute resistance to individual pathology. Consequently, use of the term resistance has had less negative connotations, including less blaming and more consideration of resistance as an expected phenomenon that is the practitioner's responsibility to address.[47] For example, in the cybernetic view, the practitioner's role is to support both a need for stability and ally with efforts to change.[48]

De Shazer suggests that the concept of resistance is a byproduct of a homeostatic systems view in which resistance is seen as an individual condition opposed to change rather than a product of therapist/family interaction.[49] De Shazer reframes resistance as the family's unique way of cooperating. In this view, the family tries to resolve problems in the best way they know how. This form of cooperating is seen as a process rather than a condition.[50] The resistance concept, according to de Shazer, locks practitioners into a relationship in which, like opposing tennis players, they need to win in order to control the relationship.[51] De Shazer's reframed view puts both the practitioners and the family on the same side of the net, trying to defeat the problem.[52]

In contrast, Stewart and Anderson argue that the resistance concept does not imply a homeostatic system, nor is it only located in the family, as resistance can also occur to practitioners and the agency as well.[53] They define resistance as all those behaviors in the therapeutic system that interact to prevent the therapy system from reaching the families goals for therapy.[54] These authors include behaviors across the system as resistance including families missing appointments, practitioners not checking back when they miss appointments, and agencies not opening their doors after 5:00 P.M. or having adequate meeting space.[55]

5. *Role conflicts.* The role of the practitioner varies with the system they represent. For example, the purpose for public agency contact may be different than in child guidance and hence the practitioner may be power broker or part of the system of power.[56] Anderson and Stewart suggest that

larger systems make family therapy difficult because they place therapists in the position of both therapist and policeman . . . when the practitioner is asked to do family therapy while simultaneously playing a role in which they must hold a threat over the family's head that their income may be withdrawn or one or more family members will be placed in a foster home or institution. . . . Families are understandably hesitant to admit a potentially threatening professional into their confidence. They really would have to be crazy to welcome such an intrusion into their lives . . . conducting any kind of therapy under these conditions must seem rather like trying to slay a very large dragon with a very short sword.[57]

These role conflicts are further complicated when the practitioner's agenda differs from the family's. Practitioners frequently perceive dangers and feel more commitment to change them than do families.[58] When the practitioner takes on the role of the mastermind searching for leverage in changing a recalcitrant system, families may feel discounted.[59] If the family's view is discounted, the relationship can quickly become adversarial.[60] For example, while use of deceptive means may be effective in the short run, families may eventually conclude that the therapist views them as too inept or childlike to be dealt with in a straightforward manner.[61]

Further role conflicts occur when practitioners play multiple roles with different family members. Practitioners may be engaged in individual treatment with residents of treatment institutions at the same time as they are family therapists with other members of the family. Anderson and Stewart suggest that it may be possible to play such dual roles if the family is positively motivated for the contact, if the practitioner can mobilize adequate support systems, if caseloads ae small enough to permit frequent contact, and if the practitioners can manage to demonstrate to families that they genuinely care about what happens to family members.[62]

6. *Ethical issues.* As suggested above, much work with families starts with a request that the behavior of one family member be "fixed." If in fact that person's behavior is the target for work, then it is misleading to suggest that the focus is work on a relationship.[63] Margolin suggests that when one person such as a child is opposed to treatment, there are many advantages to including an advocate for that person and negotiating goals.[64]

Second, informed consent can be difficult with families in nonvoluntary situations. Pursuit of informed consent, including explanation of roles, possible discomforts, and risks, as well as benefits, may greatly assist the engagement process.[65] However, when the practitioner may be inclined to use methods that rely on secrecy for their success, failure to describe those methods limits true informed consent.[66] Such secrecy may be useful with voluntary families who have agreed upon the goals for treatment since they have the option of leaving if they are opposed to the methods. Additional ethical issues are raised when families are court-ordered to receive treatment on issues that differ from those that arise through the practititioner's own assessment. Manipulation of involuntary families who pay a cost for withdrawing from treatment violates the limited provisions for paternalism described in chapter 4.

## Overview of Adaptation for Work with Involuntary Families

Practitioners who work with involuntary families have at this point been able to choose from three alternatives: approaching involuntary families within a voluntary family therapy format; rejecting family treatment perspectives in involuntary settings and roles; or blending family therapy perspectives with involuntary work on a case-by-case basis.

William Reid suggests a fourth alternative that includes family treatment perspectives within a larger ecosystemic perspective in which the family is one of several systems. This alternative includes work with individual family members, work on environmental problems, and includes settings and roles in which family therapy is not the service offered.[67] In Reid's family problem solving approach, the practitioner acts to facilitate family problem solving to the extent possible, interceding only to the degree necessary to remove obstacles, identify resources, and facilitate change in the immediate context.[68] Consequently, high priority is given to reaching agreement with families on problems to be resolved. The practitioner moves to more intrusive measures only in response to obstacles encountered in achieving resolution to those agreed-upon problems.

The approach to work with involuntary families described here is generally compatible with the family problem solving approach. Guidance for specific steps in the engagement phase with involuntary families are suggested since many approaches suggest that negotiation should take place, yet fail to show how to negotiate or persuade family members to engage in contact.[69] Interventions beyond the engagement process will be described more briefly since it is assumed that the primary issue with involuntary families is achieving at least semi-voluntary status. When semi-voluntary status is achieved, a variety of voluntary approaches including the family problem solving approach may be consulted for further guidelines.

Primary assumptions underlying work with involuntary families include:

1. *A relevant systems perspective encompasses not only the practitioner and family but also those forces that impel the family into contact with the practitioner.* It is useful in most initial contacts between families and helping practitioners to assume that one or more family members have been impelled into contact at least in part by mandated, formal, and informal pressures. Such a perspective would include exploration of the pressures felt by Christine and Mrs. King in initiating contact.

2. *The practitioner and/or agency may become a source of formal pressure when attempts are made to redefine or reframe voluntary requests to focus on family issues.* It is useful to recognize that when the family-based service practitioner made an offer for service that differed from the request made by Mrs. King, formal nonvoluntary pressures were being exerted. Further, if the practitioner works on a hidden agenda to effectuate change in problems that family members have not chosen to work on, the practitioner may be creating additional pressures for families.

3. *Role conflicts can occur between family wishes and practitioner responsibilities to outside constituencies.* For example, practitioner responsibilities to make recommendations on such issues as child placement can create role conflict.[70] In the above example, family-based services are often offered as part of an agency policy of preventing unnecessary out-of-home placement. This policy can be compatible with family wishes or contrary to them.

With these assumptions as a basis, guidelines are provided for initial work with involuntary families including: 1) initiating contact, 2) pursuit of informed consent, and 3) contracting.

1. *Initiating contact.* Guidelines for initiating contact vary according to whether the family is ostensibly self-referred or referred by others. Contact with families who are not self-referred begins with step *a* while contact with self-referred families begins with step *b* (see figure 12.1).

a. *If the family is not self-referred,* family members are entitled to an account of the circumstances that have led to that contact. For example, any requirements or information from the referral source about suggested issues should be shared. Second, client options, rights, and choices in response to this referral should be clarified. Hence, family members need to be made aware of their choices and the potential consequences of such choices. Family members should also be asked about their views of the circumstances that led to contact. When contacts occur through

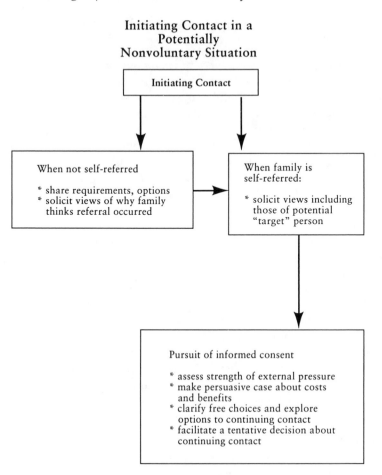

*Figure 12.1*

outreach, there is need to respect and validate the family system, identify positive aspects of behavior, recognize dilemmas faced by family members, respect cultural values, and support networks.[71] When this step is completed, the practitioner can proceed to step *b* with families who are not self-referred. For example, in the following section, a home-based service team follows up on the initial contact made at the beginning of the chapter.[72]

PRACTITIONER: I am glad that you both were willing to meet with us today. I understand that you met with Karen last week to talk about some of the concerns that you were having about how things were going here in the home. Betty and I are a home-based service team and we came here today to talk to you more about your situation and the choices that you have as you and Christine decide whether you want to continue with this. I understand that you had some reservations about whether you thought this was the best thing for you to do. You talked with Karen about having explored things on your own. You've gone to a number of other counselors, and you haven't felt as though things have lasted, so you have some reservations. I would think, Christine, you may have some reservations about how this might work for you as well.

b. *If the family is self-referred,* the practitioner might begin by soliciting the views of family members about what they see as concerns and eliciting their views about what they would like to see accomplished. Practitioners should be sensitive to suggestions of pressured contact in their presentation of concerns. If the request includes a desire that a family member be "fixed," this step includes asking that "target" person to state their view of concerns. This may also take the form of separate interviews with adolescents or children if they are unwilling or unable to share those concerns with the family.

2. *Pursuit of informed consent.* Upon hearing the circumstances that have led family members into contact, the practitioner can attempt to enhance voluntarism by pursuing informed consent. This involves several steps: a) assessing the strength of pressures and requirements; b) making a persuasive case about the benefits and costs of continuing with the practitioner; c) exploring options to continuing contact; and d) facilitating a tentative decision about whether to continue.

a. *Assessing the strength of external pressures.* If the above steps have uncovered pressures experienced by one or more family members, then the scope of those pressures can be assessed. For example, if contact is court-ordered, then the specific requirements of that order for the family and practitioner should be clarified.[73] The consequences of noncompliance with court orders should also be reviewed.[74] Similarly, any nonnegotiable agency policies should be shared. For example, in the case of family-based service, the ground rules of working within a framework of time-limited contact toward the goal of preserving the family system would be described. In the case of a family treatment program for spouse abuse, the preconditions and beliefs of that program would be shared. As the family is considered to be living in a currently or potentially dangerous situation, concurrent or completed individual or group treatment for the abusive person may be required. Similarly, the belief of the program that family violence is never justified is shared here as an agency belief.[75]

When there is informal family pressure on a reluctant individual, coerced participation by the practitioner is unethical. The practitioner can, however, strongly encourage a family member to attend at least one session to discover what contact may offer. The practitioner can also explore the reasons contributing to that person's reluctance. Finally, the practitioner should clarify the extent of involvement expected. In some cases, this may only require participation as an observer so as not to impede progress.[76]

b. *Make a persuasive case about the benefits and costs of continuing with the practitioner.* Families often feel ambivalent about service. Those families seeking residential placement for their troubled adolescents want problem relief and often see placement as the only alternative. Yet they often feel pain, guilt, and a sense of failure in pursuing this alternative. Family-based services can be presented as another option.[77]

Family members can be assisted in making an informed decision by knowing about the costs and benefits of the service that the practitioner can offer. For example, Weideman suggests that abusive partners be told that on the one hand, the abusive partner may not always get what he or she wants by participating in the program. On the other hand, if the violence continues, the relationship is likely to be lost.[78]

As suggested in chapter 6, arguments are more likely to be persuasive when they relate to values, attitudes, or goals that family members already hold. For example, in the case of family-based services, connection of the service offer to the problem expressed by the family should enhance its acceptance. Since out-of-home placement was a solution to a problem seen by Mrs. King, the practitioners can share Mrs. King's concern with the problem without agreeing with her solution. They can empathize with the family duress that led to the request for help and offer to provide help with those problems.

Other potential benefits of the service can also be explained. For example, in the case of family-based services, it can be explained that such services are provided in the home at times agreeable to the families, without financial cost, that practitioners are available on a twenty-four-hour emergency basis, and that relief is often provided in a relatively brief time period.[79]

Potential costs and drawbacks of work with the family option should also be explored. For example, non-negotiable policies of the agency or service would be reviewed here. Circumstances in which confidentiality would be violated as in mandated reporting of suspected abuse or neglect should be shared. Similarly, policies in some settings that require work with all members of a family should be explained and possible referral to settings with less restrictive policies considered.

Practitioners are advised not to oversell the family option that they represent. For example, family suspicions of the effectiveness of family-based services in resolving *all* their problems are well founded and their disappointment at not receiving immediate relief from all concerns they raise should be acknowledged. The time-limited nature of that work should also be explained. Later in the session with Mrs. King and Christine, the practitioner comments in support of realistic expectations:

PRACTITIONER: There wouldn't be tremendous changes overnight. We would be working on making some changes, such that Christine might do some things differently, and you would also do some things differently. You would notice some little changes, at first. Our experience is that over time those changes can build up, so that the situation that brought you to the point a week ago where you thought you really couldn't stay together with Christine wouldn't be there anymore. On the other hand, I don't think it's realistic to expect that all of the concerns that you and Christine have about each other are going to be cleaned up if we were going to work together ten weeks.

c. *Exploring options to continuing contact.* Alternatives to family contact should be explored. In the case of legally mandated contact, families can be advised that they may return to court to attempt a change in the order. In nonvoluntary cases, other options, including *not* working with the practitioner, should be explored. Such options might include dealing with the problems on their own and exploring other forms of help. In the initial session with Karen and Mrs. King, alternatives to home-based services were explored.

KAREN: I want to make sure that you are clear that you do *not* have to accept our service. You can look at other possibilities. While foster placement by the county is not now an option, you could choose to explore private placement. If you feel as if you might do a better job working on these issues your own, you would also be free to choose to do that. You could call parental stress lines for assistance. You might also get some respite help from a friend or relative.

d. *Facilitate a tentative decision about whether or not to continue family contact.* Schlosberg and Kagan suggest that a power struggle and adversary relationship often occurs at this point, as the practitioner increases pressure in response to family opposition. Reviewing options as above and facilitating a decision about whether to continue with contact demonstrates respect for the family process and does not proceed without their approval.[80] Sometimes family members need time to make this decision. Family commitment to explore continuation even on a trial basis should be respected and seen as at least slightly increasing voluntarism. On the other hand, the option to pursue other directions should also be respected. For example, later in the follow-up session with Mrs. King and Christine, the practitioner asks the family for direction in considering their decision.

PRACTITIONER: We are at a point now where you need to consider whether you want to continue working with us or go in another direction. We've identified some issues each of you have individually and then together. If we agreed to go ahead, then we would probably pick a specific issue to start with and see if we can get something going on that right away. I don't know if it would be worthwhile for either of us to go much further in discussing home-based services until you decide whether you want to give this a try or you want to go another direction.

3. *Explore contracting.* Should the family be willing to pursue further contact at this time, the development of a contract can be explored. In the case of emergencies, such as a lack of basic neccessities for food, shelter, safety, the practitioner would proceed to help the family acquire needed resources before pursuing more formal contracting. The contract should include any non-negotiable requirements such as provisions about confidentiality and sharing information, problems to be worked on, goals set, time limit and methods to be used.[81] Such contracting should enhance voluntarism and prevent focus on hidden agendas.[82]

a. *Non-negotiable requirements.* Provisions for confidentiality and sharing of information should be included with all families. More specific requirements related to legal issues and requirements of the service provision should also be clarified. For example, in the case of marital work in spouse abuse, the agency goal of maintaining the family when this can be done without further risk of abuse or danger would be shared.[83] Specific methods such as the development of a violence avoidance plan and anger diary required for work toward this goal would also be shared.[84] Also, in family-based service, if service is delivered under the overall premise of avoiding unnecessary out-of-home placement, that condition is shared in contracting, as well as any other legal requirements. For example,

PRACTITIONER: We need to be clear that the service together needs to take place within a goal of keeping Christine from having an unnecessary out-of-home placement. In addition, there are laws about attending school and truancy that will influence what we do.

b. *Explore agreed-upon problems.* Having set parameters of requirements and non-negotiable conditions, the practitioner can proceed to pursue semi-voluntary or voluntary status by assisting family members in identifying problems that family members now agree exist. This method is advised even in instances in which practitioners feel that *reframing,* or movement to another problem that the family has not expressed, will be useful.[85] The process should first follow original family conceptions of the problem in pursuit of problems that all family members now agree exist. Such original conceptions often locate the source and solution of the problem in the behavior of one person or a system outside the family. For example, parents tend to see the child as at blame and feel blamed by other counselors, court, or probation officers. On one level it is possible to join families on some concerns similar to the "get rid of the pressure" contracting strategy presented in chapter 8. Similarly, Kagan reports that families who had no other goals were often agreeable to getting the court out of their lives.[86]

However, when family members locate the blame in the behavior of one person, the practitioner may accept that this is their view while ensuring that all family members can state their views.[87] For example, when Mrs. King and Christine were asked for their views of problems, Mrs. King included that Christine was truant and did not obey curfew, she had a "nasty attitude," she had "bad friends," she did not take care of her younger brother or do other chores. Christine responded that her mother yelled and tried to control her too much, did not respect her friends, and did not pay her for taking care of her younger brother. Mrs. King and Christine did not readily frame issues as family problems and blamed one another for problems that existed. The practitioners might look here for problems that both Mrs. King and Christine agree now exist. For example, both mention problems with her friends and with taking care of her brother. Hence, a first attempt at stating these problems in a more useful, nonblaming way would be to ask whether they would agree that "disagreement on Christine's friends and her responsibilities in taking care of her younger brother" were concerns both shared.

Reframing is used to recast problems in an interactional form or to define the problem in a slightly different way.[88] Reframing is useful in constructing workable realities that make change possible.[89] Practitioners sometimes reframe by identifying patterns of interaction or other problems that the family has not considered. They may also attempt to cast problems in a more favorable light.[90] For example, Schlossberg and Kagan describe a case example in which parents describe their child as "horrible, terrible." The practitioner recognizes the family's efforts and suggests that they have become exhausted by working so hard.[91] On the other hand, when parents feel as if they have been inadequate parents who should know how to deal with their child, Tavantsiz suggests reframing their view to suggest that they are "good parents who need all the help they can get."[92] In the following example, the practitioner working with Mrs. King and Christine attempts to reframe issues expressed by them as a lack of trust.

PRACTITIONER: I'm wondering if trust and not knowing what to believe is an issue with both of you. You don't know when you can trust Christine, and you're feeling that your mother doesn't trust you about your friends. Is the lack of trust between you something you are concerned about?

One danger that practitioners need to be aware of in reframing by casting difficulties at a higher level of abstraction is that it may not capture what the family sees. They may reject the reframing or agree only superficially. Consequently, the practitioner should phrase the reframe tentatively to determine whether it is relevant to family members.

c. *Explore reciprocal or individual problems.* Some families do not accept such reframing and persist with noninteractional views. This is particularly frequent in instances in which adolescents have a history of law violations and blaming of the adolescent may have been reinforced by corrections systems.[93] It is sometimes possible in such instances to pursue reciprocal or quid-pro-quo exchanges. In the above instance, Mrs. King considered trust to be a lesser issue than obedience to house rules and school attendance. Meanwhile, Christine continued to be concerned about freedom to see her friends and respect for them. An exchange was established in which Christine could earn time with her friends in the home and noninterference with them if she would increase her school attendance to three times in the next week.

Some problems relate primarily to one individual. However, these individual concerns may have a major impact on the concerns of the family and the system as a whole. For example, Bob, a stepparent, did not feel respected by his stepson who had returned home recently from foster care. Aggravating the problem was the fact that Bob had lost his job and hence was around the house more. Bob now felt more called upon to take a disciplinary role that had previously been played by the mother. Instead of dismissing the problem of employment, session time could be taken to assist Bob in making plans to seek employment and supporting his efforts.[94]

This chapter has suggested that nonvoluntary work with families occurs more frequently than is usually thought to be the case. While family therapy perspectives and treatment methods can be useful in work with involuntary clients, I have suggested that greater attention to the role of pressures impelling family members into contact is needed to enhance effectiveness and ethical contact. Many families are approached with family therapy concerns that do not fit their request and they are not persuaded that their concerns will be met through reframing. Problems can occur if alternative choices are not emphasized at the beginning of contact and when theories of underlying family dynamics lead the practitioner to focus on issues that have not been agreed upon with family members.

Evaluation of family outcomes becomes a critical issue when the practitioner is attempting to achieve goals other than those agreed upon. Some suggest that the practitioner has an ethical responsibility to place high priority on the assessment of desired change as seen by family members.[95] There is a range of opinion about the importance of such change. Some see resolution of the family-defined problem as the sole criterion for assessing outcome, others see it as the most important, while others consider such resolution as one criterion among many.[96] Work on hidden agendas may lead to confusion in outcome should the family receive a negative evaluation if they did not stay on the boat when the practitioner changed course. While practitioners and families engaged in voluntary family treatment can perhaps afford less specificity in goals, vague goals in involuntary contact are likely to be costly to the families.

This chapter has made beginning steps in constructing an involuntary perspective for work with families by expanding the systems perspective to include those pressures that impel family members into contact and those practitioner or setting pressures that occur after contact is initiated. Practice guidelines have been suggested that are designed to assist in more informed choices in continuing family contact and enhancing voluntarism. Guidelines have not been provided for contact after the engagement phase, since many voluntary approaches can be useful at this point with originally nonvoluntary families. The guidelines do not resolve continuing issues in the potential conflict between attention to second order change goals such as assisting a family in becoming less enmeshed or more individualized and commitment to the goals that the family explicitly agrees to. Should such commitment to second-order goals conflict with agreed-upon goals, family opposition may be an expected byproduct. At worst, families may be illegally and unethically forced to work on problems that are neither their concern nor legally mandated. Practitioner insistence on goals that are neither legally required, setting requirements, nor family concerns is unethical and likely to be ineffective. There is unlikely to be motivational congruence in such situations and insistence on practitioner-defined goals that exceed appropriate limits to self-determination and restricted use of paternalism is unethical (see chapters 4 and 5). While practitioners working with voluntary families can be somewhat sure that those families will raise objections or withdraw from contact if their own identified goals are not addressed, practitioners working with nonvoluntary and mandated families have no such assurance.

While specific examples have been provided for settings such as family-based service, more specific adaptations are needed for other potentially nonvoluntary settings such as discharge planning. Chapter 13 will continue adaptations of the involuntary perspective for work with groups.

# Work with Involuntary Clients in Groups

A dozen women offenders file into the meeting room of the half-way house where they live. The program director has contracted with group leaders from an outside agency to lead a group. The group leaders describe the purpose of the group as helping the women deal with issues of abuse and violence in their lives and emphasize that this is to be *their* group.

As the leaders have led many such groups with women who were eager to attend, they are dismayed to discover the women sitting in baleful silence. After awhile, the women interrupt the presentation to say, "This is a bunch of bull. Why do we have to be here? Can we smoke? What I care about is getting a job, going back to school, not talking about this violence bull."

Finally, after several attempts to get the group away from these "distractions" and back to the purpose of the group, the women sink back into a bored, detached silence, gazing out the window, checking their watches, commenting that this had better be over soon because they have appointments to make.

These women are participating in an *involuntary group* in which members feel external pressure to participate. Involuntary groups are often led with persons with problems such as abuse and neglect,[1] domestic violence,[2] chemical dependency,[3] sexual offenses,[4] delinquency,[5] and with youth gangs.[6]

There are two kinds of involuntary groups. *Mandated groups* include legal external pressure such as occurs with imprisoned sex offenders. The second type of involuntary group is a *nonvoluntary group* that is distinguished by nonlegal external pressure from family, friends, agencies, and referral sources. These pressures often create a feeling of coerced or constrained choice such that many choose attendance as a lesser of evils. For example, Berliner notes when introducing groups for drivers convicted of driving while intoxicated (DWI), "You are here because you would rather try this than go to jail."[7] Similarly, Finn comments in a survey of domestic violence groups that "participation in the treatment program was voluntary in all cases. It was, however, understood that charges would be dropped upon completion of the program and upon recommendation of the court exam."[8] Similar nonvoluntary group transactions can occur between students and instructors in required courses and between agency staff and trainers brought in as "hired guns" to modify practitioner attitudes, beliefs, and behaviors.

Degrees of voluntarism also vary *within* groups. For example, the women offenders group described above may include some women who consider talking about abuse to be beneficial while others react to the group discussion as an unnecessary imposition. On the other hand, some ostensibly voluntary groups for teaching parenting skills often include both highly voluntary clients and others who attend "because my child welfare worker said it would be a good idea." Such groups often include so-called hard-to-reach members who attend irregularly or participate minimally. Breton suggests that "hard to reach" members may not agree with the purpose of the group, doubt its effectiveness, and attend as a lesser of evils.[9]

This chapter describes specific guidelines aimed at legal, ethical, and effective practice with involuntary groups. Application of these guidelines is designed to enhance commitment to both non-negotiable goals and voluntary group concerns. Guidelines are provided for *pregroup planning* and *beginning involuntary groups*. While specific guidelines are not provided for post-contracting intervention with involuntary groups, four frequent phases of such work are identified.

## Introduction to Involuntary Groups

There are few theoretical models for practice with involuntary groups in the social group work literature. For example, Papell and Rothman describe social group work purposes that include use of the group as an end in itself, as an instrument for social action, as a means of providing psychotherapy, and as providing structure to achieve specific purposes.[10]

Involuntary groups are not included in their list other than to note that remedial groups have been a group focus in the past. They describe the mainstream model of social group work practice as one in which the leader facilitates the group "free of remote authoritarianism."[11] This mainstream model apparently has little place for groups in which all or part of the group agenda is set by persons outside the group. Garvin, however, suggests that while resources for voluntary group work are increasingly limited, "those services that may escape destruction may be those that most fulfill social control functions."[12] Despite lack of involuntary group practice models, involuntary groups frequently occur in settings ranging from open to closed, and public to private.

Garvin defines *social control groups* as characterized by a lack of consensus on goals between members and the agency such that participation is often resisted for a long time or a common purpose is never reached.[13] Mandated groups, as defined above, are social control groups. Despite the lack of legal mandates, nonvoluntary groups too often begin and end as social control groups. Konopka suggests that preformed groups of all sorts often begin with hostility toward the practitioner. She describes the challenge of such groups as providing constructive use of limitations that value individual integrity and accept people while not accepting some of their behaviors.[14]

Participants often react to the purpose of involuntary groups as *mala prohibita* or wrongs due to law or statute rather than wrongs in themselves.[15] For example, men with domestic violence problems rarely enter groups thinking that violence is unjustified but rather acknowledging that it is illegal. They are rarely motivated to stop the abuse itself but rather to placate the court or their partners.[16] These men are characterized as tending to externalize and blame others, to believe little can be done to change them, to doubt the severity of the problem, and to doubt the efficacy of services.[17] Similarly, members of DWI groups often begin by expressing open or passive hostility, by externalizing their alcohol and drug use, and by feeling that they can handle problems on their own.[18]

Hence, a challenge of involuntary groups is to assist members in coming to recognize problems such as violent behavior or alcohol and drug abuse as *mala in se* or bad in itself.[19] Many involuntary groups never advance beyond a mala prohibita motivation and persist in a power and control phase marked by continual vying for control. A coercive symmetry often occurs with members whose behavior is described as resistant, exchanging punishing responses with harassed leaders who alternately resort to threats, cajoling, shaming, and preaching in efforts to encourage participation. The challenge for involuntary group

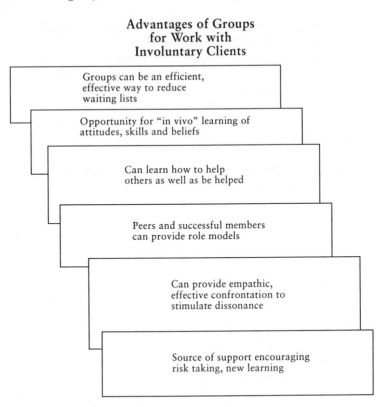

Advantages of Groups
for Work with
Involuntary Clients

Groups can be an efficient,
effective way to reduce
waiting lists

Opportunity for "in vivo" learning of
attitudes, skills and beliefs

Can learn how to help
others as well as be helped

Peers and successful members
can provide role models

Can provide empathic,
effective confrontation to
stimulate dissonance

Source of support encouraging
risk taking, new learning

*Figure  13.1*

leaders is to both meet the societal and institutional purpose of the group and also assist participants in addressing their own concerns in socially acceptable ways. Involuntary groups have both advantages for work with involuntary clients and also potential disadvantages and dangers.

*Potential advantages of involuntary groups.* Seven potential advantages of the group modality for ethical and effective work with involuntary clients are described below (see figure 13.1).

1. *The group can be a source of support.* Involuntary clients pressured to join involuntary groups frequently feel isolated, ashamed, and embarrassed by that pressure. The group setting can be less threatening than individual contact for many and support can be experienced by meeting others in a similar situation. For example, many DWI clients share multiple crises such as loss of a driver's license, pressures to enter

alcoholism treatment, legal involvement, attorney and treatment fees, increased insurance premiums, as well as family and social problems. The common mandated condition can create a useful crisis that can be reframed as a challenge in place of the original perception that it is a threat or loss.[20]

2. *The group can provide an opportunity for "in vivo" learning.* New skills, knowledge, and attitudes can be learned through instruction and practice and vicariously through observing the problem solving of others. A learning atmosphere can be stimulated that promotes both acceptance and risk taking. As members consider plans for change, they can be helped to reality test those plans in the group before trying them outside.

3. *In addition to being helped, members can learn to be helpers.* Involuntary group members can move into a helping role in which they provide support, challenge, and modeling for other members. They can become more aware of their strengths and growth as well as pursue improvement in their individual problems.

4. *Peers and successful former members can provide role models.* Since attitudes and beliefs are more likely to be changed when the person attempting influence is considered likable, trustworthy, and expert, peers can often exert a more powerful influence than professional leaders (see chapter 6). For this reason, many involuntary groups are "seeded" with successful former members or ones further along in the change process.[21]

5. *Involuntary group members who have harmed others can meet with victims.* Since involuntary group members who have acted to harm others are often unable to relate to harm caused, live presentations by victims can create empathy and acceptance of responsibility for harm. For example, presentations by the family of drunk driving victims can make denial of harm more difficult.

6. *Group members can provide empathic, effective confrontation to stimulate dissonance.* Groups can provide empathic confrontation when behaviors and attitudes persist that conflict with laws, policies, or client goals.[22] For example, when men with domestic violence problems continue to encounter circumstances in which they are tempted to use violence, peers can help them explore alternative ways for dealing with such situations.

7. *Groups can be an efficient, cost-effective way to reduce waiting lists.* The larger staff-participant ratio in groups allows settings to serve a larger population and hence reduce waiting lists. Indeed, orientation groups are sometimes helpful for those involuntary clients with domestic violence problems who are waiting to be served.[23]

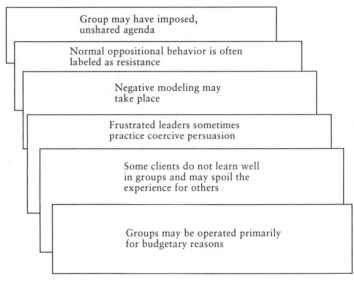

Figure 13.2

## Potential Disadvantages of Involuntary Groups

Many involuntary groups never reach the goal of providing ethical, effective help that meets both societal and individual needs. In fact, groups can be noxious as well as beneficial.[24] Most of the above advantages can be reversed to describe six dangers of involuntary groups (see figure 13.2).

1. *Involuntary groups often proceed with a completely imposed, unshared agenda.* Too often, involuntary groups proceed with an externally imposed agenda in which compliance is maintained by fear of punishment rather than by positive attraction to benefits of the group. Common goals and group process are often ignored in pursuit of individual change. Mixed messages are communicated through suggestions that "this is *your group*," as in the women offenders group at the beginning of the chapter, while in fact the agenda is not open for negotiation. Shields, writing about groups for drug-abusing adolescents in public schools suggests that "the raison d'etre for the workers' very presence in the schools is drug problems. . . . Yet if the work is defined

by the goal, the trap of focus on individual behavior change, neglecting the system, moralizing and attempts to convince or manipulate the adolescent away from drug use will almost unavoidably and inevitably heightens resistance."[25] Hence, when group purpose, methods, and rules are entirely predetermined by the agency and the leaders, many varieties of overt and covert oppositional behavior are a predictable result.

2. *Oppositional behavior is often labeled resistance.* Evasive behaviors and challenging leaders' direction often occur in involuntary groups. Oppositional behavior is often interpreted as pathological resistance without examining such behavior in the context of group interaction. Hurley suggests that so-called resistant clients may be informal group leaders who are trying to help make the group worthwhile by focusing it on personally meaningful goals.[26]

3. *Peer modeling is often negative.* While group members often learn from peers, such learning may be contrary to the goals of the group leaders. Group cohesiveness may develop the form "us against the leaders" in which the very kinds of antisocial behavior that the group is designed to reduce may be reinforced. Members may *learn* from peers how to cope with involuntary groups in manipulative, deceptive ways.

4. *Frustrated group leaders sometimes practice coercive persuasion.* Faced with so-called resistive behavior, preaching and shaming may be used more frequently than focusing on positive attractions of the group. In their eagerness to help, group leaders can violate the dignity of individual members, demand participation, and resort to a form of coercive persuasion or brainwashing.[27] Involuntary group methods that assault individual identity, provoke shame, demand pure and rigid adherence to an absolute standard, and include endless public confessions are brainwashing.

Lifton uses the term thought reform for coercive persuasion and identifies eight characteristics: a) the person is placed in a disorienting situation; b) a clear simple answer or goal is provided; c) guilt about past transgressions is induced; d) new beliefs and behaviors are modeled and rewarded; e) the individual is exposed to others who have accepted new beliefs; f) the individual has little opportunity for private thoughts and sharing of doubts with other group members at the same point; g) the individual learns first to behave in an approved way (when he or she is rewarded for this, then the behaviors become ritualized); and h) it is believed that the separation between private beliefs and public beliefs breaks down through repeated confessions.[28] The conditions that best prepare one for thought reform have been called dependency, debilitation, and dread.[29] Hence, if involuntary group members are highly dependent on the leaders and institution, deprived of adequate exercise and food, and maintained in a highly punitive environment, this is thought control.

Thoughts, attitudes, and beliefs that are neither illegal nor related to a client-defined goal are sometimes assaulted by group members or leaders. For example, an overweight member of an incarcerated sexual abusers group was verbally assaulted for not taking enough care of himself to reduce his weight. While behaviors and attitudes related to sexual abuse are appropriate for such groups, weight problems are not an appropriate subject for coercive intervention if they do not endanger self or others, or are not a voluntary concern of the individual. Attack on attitudes, beliefs, and thoughts may be illegal under laws to protect mentation, or the right to one's own thoughts.[30] Hence, a major legal and ethical issue in involuntary groups is determining the boundary between what is "fair game" for the group and what issues are matters of privacy and personal choice.

5. *Some clients do not learn well in groups and may spoil it for others.* Group composition is often a key variable in the success of groups.[31] Yet many clients are sent to groups "for their own good," whether they learn well in groups or not. As a result, those persons may not learn and also make the experience more difficult for others.

6. *Groups may be operated primarily for budgetary reasons.* Staff in institutions may be unable to consider appropriate group composition because staffing limitations require that residents be in groups for most of their time. Hence, while groups can be an efficient, effective means for service delivery, they are often required even when not effective because they keep staffing costs down. At worst, group methods become used as a form of "cheap warehousing."

## Pre-Group Planning

Six steps in pre-group planning for work with involuntary groups will be presented. These steps are designed to pursue the goal of legal, ethical, and effective practice that meets both societal needs and individual member concerns. As such planning assumes the value of structure for involuntary groups, a discussion about the use of structure is presented first.

### Value of Structure with Involuntary Groups

Empey and Ericson suggest that while involuntary group members in residential settings often seek formulas for how to get through the group, providing such structure is unproductive since the tension created by lack of structure causes useful defenses to be expressed.[32] Other writers suggest that members of unstructured groups are often blamed for the tension and lack of progress experienced in such groups.[33] In addition, when chemicals or violence have been used in the past by members to reduce tension, lack of progress in the group can inadvertently reinforce usage.[34] Shields suggests that lack of structure and ambiguity of purpose lead to prolonged dickering in the engagement phase. She notes that members want to know: "Why am I here? Are others here for the same purpose? What can I expect of the leaders and the group? What is expected of me?"[35] She comments further that

the more specific the offer of service, the more the group members have to hold onto and the clearer the boundaries, the less the energy has to go into figuring out the worker, testing the boundaries and searching out hidden agendas. Ambiguity creates anxiety which in turn intensifies defensive behavior.[36]

Similarly, Breton suggests that so-called hard-to-reach clients are motivated to maintain control, minimize risk, and avoid failing.[37] She notes that the rule of least contest can be used to address these motivations. Specifically, the practitioner can permit groups to start on their own turf, work with an intermediary person already trusted by group members, respect the values of the group, and give members an opportunity to state their own goals.[38]

The challenge with involuntary groups is to provide both clear structure about non-negotiable conditions of service *and* clear opportunities for sharing in developing the processes of the group in negotiable areas. It was suggested in chapter 7 that opposition to threats to valued freedoms can be usefully reframed as expectable reactance. Providing structure can reduce reactance by a) clarifying boundaries by describing specific non-negotiable requirements; b) clarifying available freedoms and choices, even though constrained; and c) clarifying areas open for negotiation. Prospective group members are entitled to information about the goals of the group, basic rules, the qualifications of the leaders, the techniques to be employed, and their rights.[39] Such information can be disseminated through preparation of written descriptions of the group, meeting with prospective members individually, or through informational group sessions.[40] For example, if the women offenders described at the beginning of the chapter could have received a flyer describing the group and had been invited to an informational session in which required purposes and negotiable possibilities for the group would be discussed, the initial level of opposition expressed might have been reduced (see figure 13.3).

## Pre-Group Preparation

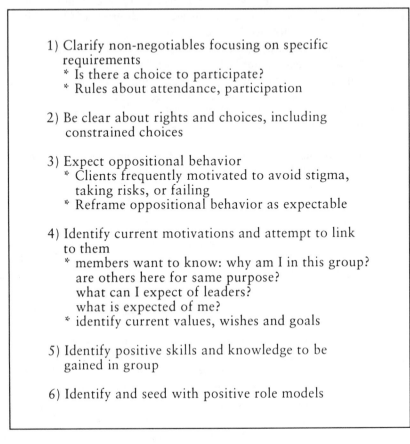

1) Clarify non-negotiables focusing on specific
   requirements
   * Is there a choice to participate?
   * Rules about attendance, participation

2) Be clear about rights and choices, including
   constrained choices

3) Expect oppositional behavior
   * Clients frequently motivated to avoid stigma,
     taking risks, or failing
   * Reframe oppositional behavior as expectable

4) Identify current motivations and attempt to link
   to them
   * members want to know: why am I in this group?
     are others here for same purpose?
     what can I expect of leaders?
     what is expected of me?
   * identify current values, wishes and goals

5) Identify positive skills and knowledge to be
   gained in group

6) Identify and seed with positive role models

*Figure 13.3*

1. *Clarify non-negotiables focusing on specific requirements.* Reactance is likely to be high if members perceive that they will be powerless in the group. Unnecessary reactance can be reduced by specifying basic ground rules of group participation and consequences for failure to follow those rules. When clients may be in a mandated status, their requirements, choices, and alternatives regarding participation in this group need to be clarified. If membership is required, basic member expectations regarding attendance and participation need to be clear. In addition, requirements of leaders that they report attendance and assess participation should also be clear.

Prospective members of nonvoluntary groups always have the right to choose *not* to participate in the group. If they choose to participate, they will need to be aware of the ground rules for group membership. For example, prospective members of a parenting group may need to agree to discuss at least one problem in parenting with which they are concerned.

2. *Clarify rights and choices.* Reactance is likely to be reduced if members are clear about their rights and can make at least constrained choices. The most basic right or choice is whether the prospective member can choose to be in this group or not. For example, unnecessary reactance among many of the woman offenders might have been reduced if they could have *chosen* to participate in the abuse group or a group devoted to another issue. If membership in the group is not a choice, then members need to know their rights and choices within the group. For example, in some mandated groups, members are permitted a limited number of excused absences. They can make a constrained choice for how and when they take those absences. Members also need to know their rights and choices about participation in group activities. Can group members participate in the selection of agenda items? Can they participate in the selection of the order for presentation of any required items? Can they pick a problem or goal they want to work on?

3. *Expect oppositional behavior.* Membership in an involuntary group often represents a stigmatized status that members respond to with denial, shame, guilt, anger and embarrassment.[41] If motivations to avoid stigma and risks of failing in order to maintain a sense of personal control are to be expected, then opposition to external direction can be reframed as reactance to threatened freedoms. Group leaders can empathize with this feeling of pressure and reinforce available choices, opportunities for learning skills, and knowledge consistent with at least some of the group members' current motivations.

4. *Identify current motivations and attempt to link to them.* For involuntary group members to move from a "mala prohibita" (bad

because illegal) to a "mala in se" (bad in itself) motivation, they will need opportunities to identify their own goals. Too often, those individually expressed goals are rejected by group leaders as inappropriate. For example, when clients in residential settings say that they want to "get out of here," this motivation is often rejected as inadequate. While group leaders might wish that members begin with male in se motivations, beginning with current mala prohibita motivation is better than none. Linkage with current values and goals can enhance the possibility of at least semi-voluntary motivation. For example, recognizing that men about to enter domestic violence groups are unlikely to want to be there and wish to get out of the court system is one way of acknowledging mala prohibita motivation.

5. *Identify positive skills and knowledge that can be learned as an alternative to illegal or disapproved behavior.* The involuntary group is likely to be more successful if members can expect to have some of their own concerns met. Such skills and knowledge are more likely to be accepted if they will probably be rewarded such that members can see progress in a time-limited period.[42] Leaders can prepare by "tuning in" to the concerns of the population.[43] For example, Shields suggests that awareness of adolescent desires to be autonomous and avoid stigma can assist in linking with expectable motivations.[44] Similarly, leaders of domestic violence groups can be aware of motivations to avoid loss of control.[45] The group can be described as a place where men can choose to learn manly ways to deal with disputes without resorting to violence. In fact, the positive focus for the group can be reinforced with a name such as "alternatives to aggression."[46]

6. *Identify possible role models to "seed" in the group.* As involuntary group members are more likely to be influenced by peers than group leaders, finding role models is recommended. Former members who have completed the group successfully or are further along in the intervention process might assist in recruitment for and operation of the group. For example, I found that group enrollment and attendance for groups of potential high school drop-outs increased when "junior leaders" were recruited to assist in running groups.[47]

## Beginning Involuntary Groups

Involuntary groups often start, end, or persist indefinitely in power struggles between leaders and participants. Such participant efforts to regain control are to be expected in involuntary groups. While leaders of voluntary groups can share agenda setting on most issues with the group, many issues in involuntary groups may not be subject to negotiation. Yet even mandated groups often include at least constrained choices such that activities to pursue in the group can be selected from limited alternatives. Too often, involuntary groups struggle over non-negotiable requirements and never explore the negotiable.

The goal for the beginning session is to establish a basis for collaborative work that is at least semi-voluntary, and includes both a framework of non-negotiable expectations and choices that individuals and the group as a whole may make.[48] This goal is pursued through negotiation of a contract that is the convergence of agency-mandated purposes and rules and goals expressed by participants.[49] Six steps in the initial session will be suggested: 1) arrange the meeting room; 2) make an introductory statement that clarifies non-negotiable issues and rights and negotiable issues; 3) solicit member goals and attempt to link to group goals; 4) negotiate some group process rules; 5) use tactful, experiential confrontation; and 6) clarify expectations for the next session.

1. *Arrange the meeting room.* Involuntary group members want to know what to expect from the group and what is expected of them. They gather answers to some of these questions through pre-group individual sessions and handouts. They probe for further answers both from what is said in the group and through nonverbal messages conveyed by leaders and physical arrangements of the group setting. If member participation is to be reinforced and status hierarchies diminished, then leaders should consider arranging chairs in a circle and not separating themselves from the group. Refreshments might also be made available. Posters welcoming participants and handouts with the agenda can also clarify structure and choices.

2. *Make an introductory statement that begins to establish realistic expectations.* Leaders can begin to establish realistic expectations by: a) welcoming the group, b) searching for common concerns, c) clarifying circumstances of the referral, d) clarifying non-negotiable expectations of leaders and members, e) clarifying rights, freedoms, choices, and areas for negotiation, and f) empathizing with pressure experienced. Leaders can suggest common concerns in in a matter-of-fact, nonjudgmental tone and empathize with feelings of pressure experienced by some without supporting the behavior that may have led to the referral. For example, many members may be expected to be ambivalent about group membership. They may have conflicted wants that include both attraction to the group and desires to avoid it. To address such conflicted wants, Berliner begins DWI groups with a statement such as:

INITIAL
SESSION OF
INVOLUNTARY
GROUP

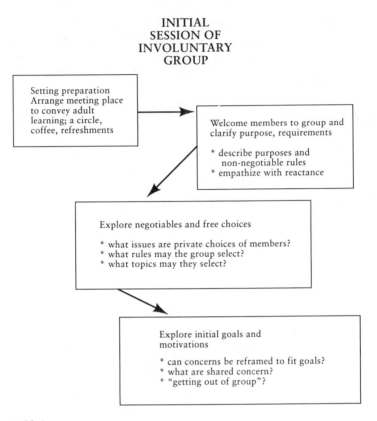

Setting preparation
Arrange meeting place
to convey adult
learning; a circle,
coffee, refreshments

Welcome members to group and
clarify purpose, requirements

* describe purposes and
  non-negotiable rules
* empathize with reactance

Explore negotiables and free choices

* what issues are private choices of members?
* what rules may the group select?
* what topics may they select?

Explore initial goals and
motivations

* can concerns be reframed to fit goals?
* what are shared concern?
* "getting out of group"?

*Figure 13.4*

No one wishes to be here (*commonality*). We all would like to stay out of
trouble, but we may not wish to stop drinking (*conflicted wants*). You are here
because you decided you would rather try this than go to jail (*choices*).[50]

Berliner notes that he hopes that clients will infer from this statement
that people are responsible for what happens to them, that they can
make choices even though those choices may be between undesirable
alternatives. He identifies "no one wants to be here" as an area of
commonality and identifies wishing to stay out of trouble but not wishing to stop drinking as a commonality without judging it.[51] While Berliner suggests beginning the group with such a statement, I recommend
that members have the opportunity to express how *they* feel about
coming to the group before making statements about shared concerns.

In addition to identifying common concerns and emphasizing choices, leaders can describe circumstances of the referral and expectations of the group and the leaders. Shields reports an introduction made by the leader of a group with drug-dependent adolescents in high schools as follows. The group leader identifies drug use leading to hassles with parents and teachers as common concerns, that members will not be judged and will have to make their own choices about drug use, and begins to identify expectations of the leader and of members.

This is what I know: all of you are in trouble here in school because of drugs. The principal has spoken to all of your parents and has told them that you are all one step from being expelled (the students all agree) (*commonality*). Now the principal asked me to meet you (*circumstances of referral*). I've been thinking about what I can do to help. I think your drug use, whether a little or a lot, has gotten you into trouble with your families and here in school (*nonjudgmental description of commonality*). Now, I know I can't stop you from getting high, and I'm not going to preach about drugs (*emphasizes choices and nonjudgmental attitude*). You've heard all that. I know you make your own decisions about getting high (*emphasizes choices*), since all of you are facing similar hassles—like probation here in school, feeling everybody is watching you, hassles with your parents, decisions about drugs (*areas of commonality*)—I think you can help each other work these things out, and I can help you do that (*what leader can do*). You've all told me you want to stay in school (*commonality*), and I'd like to help you do that, but it will mean work—looking hard at how you make decisions about getting high in school, how you handle the restrictions of probation and problems that arise with teachers here at school (*what members can do*). Now, I think we can work these things out together—I can help you work together on these issues here in group. I can help you talk to teachers and maybe parents or I can even talk to them with you (*what leader can do*), but you have to be willing to really share and work together here on the hassles you're facing if group is going to help (*what members can do*). How about it? Can we do it? (*emphasizes choices*).[52]

The introduction is also a time to describe beliefs and philosophies of the program. For example, many domestic abuse programs believe that the abuser is responsible for his or her own violence, is not provoked to use violence, chooses violence as a way of coping, that abuse rarely stops spontaneously, and that abuse is learned behavior.[53] While involuntary group members cannot realistically be expected to accept these beliefs as their own at the beginning of the group, they must be aware of the program's rationale.

Some mandated groups contain many non-negotiable rules. Even in such groups, constrained choices can be emphasized. For example, in an "alternatives to prostitution" group, Joanne, a co-leader, begins with the following introduction.

Welcome, everybody. I expect that a lot of you are feeling as if you don't want to be here today, and that's okay. It's a hard choice, but I also think you've made a positive choice for yourself by being here today (*supports choices*). The purpose of this group is to explore alternatives to prostitution (*describes purpose*). The group will also be a place for getting support from the other women. You can look at some of the choices that you've made and how you can change some of those choices that might have gotten you into this program (*supports choice*). You can look at how you can stay out of the system so that you no longer have someone always controlling your life (*area of commonality*).

The introduction for mandated groups includes the non-negotiable rules and expectations of members and leaders. Requirements in this particular group included: 1) attendance to at least sixteen of nineteen sessions (two instances of being five minutes late were counted as an absence); 2) selection of a personal goal for work from a list including employment, education, and driver's education; 3) confidentiality of group work, except in the case where leaders would be expected to provide notes on general progress to probation officers; and 4) no use of drugs or alcohol on the day of the group. These requirements also include constrained choices and rights. As members could miss 3 of 19 sessions and still complete the group, they could choose which sessions to miss. While required to work on a personal goal, they could select that goal from an approved list or suggest another goal as an alternative. As the rules are described, members interject comments and questions about the rules. When the lateness rule is presented, a member responds:

WENDY: That's pretty harsh.
SARA (CO-LEADER): Yes, the rule is clear.
KAREN: And how many misses do we get?
SARA: You're allowed three misses. So it's real important not to use those misses up with being late.
JOANNE (CO-LEADER): If you are going to be late or you're not coming, we would appreciate it if you'd give us a call and let us know what's going on with you.
SARA: We recommend that you not use up your misses at the beginning of the group, because nineteen weeks is a long time. It's real important that you save your misses so if an emergency arises, you have that leeway to miss.
KAREN: What happens if you're dismissed from the group? I mean, like we were kind of told we had to come here, so why does it matter if we're dismissed? (*Raises issue about consequences.*)
JOANNE: That is a good question. If you don't follow the conditions of your probation, and you don't make it through the group, you will

have to go back to court. Any of you who have jail time suspended might have to spend that time in jail.

Groups often become entangled in clarifying and arguing about the fairness of the non-negotiable rules. It is important to keep these rules to the minimum necessary and be prepared to offer a rationale for them. Leaders can reduce the arguing and clarification by sharing a written list of non-negotiable expectations with prospective members *prior* to the first session.

Leaders should move as soon as possible to identifying rights, free choices, constrained choices, and areas for negotiation. For example, in the above group, members could choose to participate in programs for getting their GED, getting their driver's license, or completing a job readiness program. If none of these programs met an expressed need of the participant, other goals, such as financial management or housing, could be explored.

Nonvoluntary groups include more emphasis on choices to participate than mandated groups. Empathy with feelings of pressure experienced by nonvoluntary members in otherwise voluntary groups can be expressed. For example, in a parenting skills group, including some who joined the group voluntarily and others who came through pressure from their child welfare worker, the leader assures any members feeling pressure to attend that such pressure is external to the group. A reframing to identify what the prospective member would like to receive from the group rather than a focus on the referral source's agenda is suggested.

Some of you have come to this group because you think that it can help you with some parenting issues you are concerned about. Others may be here because someone suggested that you come and you felt as if you had to take their advice (*identifies areas of commonality*). It can be difficult when you feel as if you don't have a choice (*empathizes with feelings of pressure*). I want to make it clear to any of you who feel as if you don't have a choice that we are not requiring that you be here. You can decide not to come to the group and go back and talk it over with the person who referred you. You can also decide to remain and see if the group meets some of your own concerns. If you are unsure, I would suggest that you avoid making a decision until today's session ends. You might want to think about what you could get out of this group *for yourself*, not for the person who sent you (*emphasizes choices*).

3. *Solicit member goals and attempt to link to group goals.* It was suggested in chapter 5 that self-attributed changes in behaviors and attitudes tend to last longer than changes produced primarily by reward or punishment. For members to self-attribute change and become at least semi-voluntary, their own goals need to be explored. It should be

expected that many of these goals will be of the "mala prohibita" sort at this point. Leaders can accept some of these motivations while beginning to encourage members to explore additional goals of their own. For example, Smith reports that members of an adolescent drug use group originally expressed motivations such as wanting to end involvement with the criminal justice system, to be released from the facility, or fear that further drug use would lead to incarceration.[54] Other members suggested, probably quite candidly, that they wanted to continue to use drugs and avoid getting caught!

The leaders can attempt to link individually expressed goals of the former kind with the mandated goals of the group. They can also identify common themes as group goals. For example, the leaders of the drug alternatives group could suggest that by learning about the dangers of illegal drug use and alternatives to it, members could also learn ways to avoid further involvement with the criminal justice system. Additional goals may be shared by members but be unrelated to the group mandate. For example, Shields reports that one such common goal in drug abuse groups for adolescents was dealing with feeling stigmatized by others (see figure 13.5).[55]

As members express goals, leaders can support those goals or parts of them and, in some cases, reach for goals slightly beyond the "mala prohibita" level. Leaders asked members of the "alternatives to prostitution" group to talk about why they had come to the group and what they hoped to receive from the group.

KAREN: Well, I'll go first. I'm here because my probation officer told me that I had to come here. I don't really know much else why I'm here, because I don't know that I really need to be here. I mean I'm not working the streets anymore. I don't want to. I'm going to go to school. I'm making changes in my life.

JOANNE (CO-LEADER): I'm glad that you are making some personal goals. Even though pressured by your probation officer, you decided to come to the group. Besides dealing with your p.o., what else do you plan to get out of the group? (*Emphasizes choice and reaches for additional goals.*)

KAREN: I don't really even know why I'm here, except for that my probation officer said that she thought it would be a good idea for me to come to these groups. And I guess I had to come here, or I had to go to jail.

SARA (CO-LEADER): Well I'm real glad you're here, though. Welcome. (*Reinforces choice.*)

## Linkage of "Mala In Se" and "Mala Prohibita" Goals

---

**Mala Prohibita Motivation**

* end involvement with criminal justice system
* get out of institution

---

**Linkage of Mala Prohibita
and Mala In Se Motivations**

* learn about consequences of dangerous
  drug use
* learn how to get needs met without using
  dangerous drugs
* learn how to deal with others who
  reject you
* learn how to stay out of the system

---

**Mala In Se Motivation**

* adolescent drug users feel stigmatized
  by school officials, peers

---

*Figure 13.5*

JOANNE: Thanks for going first.

SARA: Would you like to go next?

LIZ: I'm here for prostitution. I guess I came because I didn't want to
go to jail.

SARA: Glad you chose to come here, Liz. (*Emphasizes choice.*)

LIZ: It wasn't much of a choice.

SARA: Yeah, but it was a choice.

WENDY: I'm here for the same reason that they're here. And I have other places I'd rather be, that's for sure.

JOANNE: How did you get involved in this group?

WENDY: This group? Well, because of prostitution. And because I was court-ordered.

JOANNE: Okay. Do you have any goals for yourself while you're involved in the program?

WENDY: I have a lot of goals, but it definitely has nothing to do with this group. Except to get out of the group.

SARA: So one of your goals while you're here in the program is to finish. (*Reach for a goal.*)

WENDY: Yeah, that is.

JOANNE: Wendy, I think you made a good point in mentioning that you have other goals. I hope that you will share them with the other group members, because others may also have goals they wish to work on.

PAT: I'm Pat, and I'm here for the same reason, and I want to get out, too. I just want to get through it.

SARA: Could you be more specific about why you're here today. How did you get here?

PAT: The bus. (group laughter)

SARA: Could you be more specific about what you want to get out of the group?

PAT: I just want to get through it and do whatever I'm supposed to do and be done. Maybe learn something along the way, we'll see.

JOANNE: Well, that's good you're leaving the door open to learn some other things. I think that's real positive. (*Reinforces suspending judgement.*)

PAT: I've already started some volunteer work. I'm going to be maybe working there. I mean, they want me to have my GED, which I'll have soon. And they also want me to be a law-abiding citizen for a certain length of time before they'll hire me. I'm doing the volunteer stuff, and it's really great. I'm working with the little kids at the battered women shelter. My shirt . . .

WENDY: What does it say?

PAT: It says, "Women, you can't beat them."

SARA: That's great.

PAT: You know, it's clean work, and it feels really exciting, and I like being with the little kids. And someday have some of my own, so.

SARA: So it sounds like you're getting some good stuff for yourself. (*Supports development of a personal goal.*)

While beginning this group must have felt like pulling teeth for the leaders, they emphasize choices and support existing motivations for participating in the group. Since several participants mentioned "I didn't want to go to jail" as the reason for coming, the leaders might have explored whether avoiding jail was a goal that other women in the group would agree with. If so, this goal might have been established as a common goal of the members. Later efforts to influence attitudes and beliefs are more likely to succeed if they are connected to a shared goal such as staying out of jail.

The leaders also begin to reach for goals beyond the "mala prohibita" level of avoiding jail by asking for additional goals. These additional goals do not emerge immediately, but we begin to see Pat reporting some positive results from involvement with her volunteer work.

Group leaders also avoid unnecessary confrontations. When Pat interjects humor by saying that she came to the group by bus rather than by prostitution, the leaders do not confront her for not being serious or deliberately misunderstanding. They recognize the humor as an effort to reduce group tension.[56]

4. *Negotiate some process rules of the group.* If some rules for the group are non-negotiable, as in the attendance policy stated for this group, it is important to state these first before the floor is open to discuss other group-generated rules. Involuntary groups often have unexplored possibilities to share power in the process of the group. For example, within an overall non-negotiable framework of exploring issues in drug education, Smith reports that members were able to carry out a nominal group process to develop specific agenda topics for the group.[57] Using this process, common themes were identified from member suggestions and an agenda was developed to address these member-identified themes in the sessions ahead. Agreements can be negotiated about expectations for member participation and group decision making.[58] For example, rules about times for breaks, when and where members might smoke, and rules about food in the group might be negotiated in the group.

5. *Use tactful experiential confrontation.* Guidelines were suggested in chapter 11 about the use of confrontation with individuals that are also relevant for work with groups.[59] Confrontation is appropriate when behavior or attitudes are expressed that are illegal, dangerous, violate group rules, or are inconsistent with the person's own goals. Inconsistency with a member's own expressed goal is most likely to be effective, since dissonance may not be stimulated if the person does not consider the behavior or attitude in question to be "mala in se." Since clients are more likely to be persuaded by persons they like, trust, and feel to be

expert, leaders are unlikely to be sources of powerful influence in early group sessions if they are not yet seen by members as possessing these attributes.

Confrontation in groups is often initiated by group members and may lack the characteristics of specificity and empathy identified in chapter 11. On the other hand, other members may be more likely to be seen as similar and hence more powerful sources of influence. Therefore, confrontation in groups can be a powerful source of influence. It can also be a source of abuse when the member cannot choose not to receive it, when empathy is not expressed, and when choices are not available. Group leaders can shape, take the edge off of confrontation, or in fact sharpen it to make the point clear. They can also model how to confront nonjudgmentally. In the following section, Wendy expresses a goal that signals problems for other members and the leaders:

WENDY: I have in mind a service where if people want to have a date for the evening, I can set them up with a date, and that's all it necessarily has to be. So businessmen that come in town that may need to have an escort someplace, whether it be a convention or just dinner out or something like that. I would have on staff women who would want to do that. And it's legitimate.

JOANNE: Liz, you're laughing.

LIZ: That's just what my pimp does.

WENDY: What does he do?

LIZ: Same thing.

WENDY: So were you an escort?

LIZ: Were you?

WENDY: Not an escort. Although . . .

SARA: What do other people think about the line of business that Wendy's talking about going into? (*Involves group in providing feedback without judging.*)

KAREN: I think it, I don't know, I think it sounds, sounds a lot like still working the streets, Wendy.

WENDY: I'm not working the streets. I'm done with it. I have no desire to work the streets. I'm totally out of that. I just want to have my own business, and I know this escort service business. It has nothing to do in my mind with prostitution. What they want to do in the evening is up to them. As far as I'm concerned, it's going to be clean.

SARA: Wendy, I hear that you are trying to develop a legitimate business that uses skills which you now have. You will have to make up your own mind about whether this is a good way to go for you. Do you hear the concern that other people have that the escort service sounds a lot like the type of behavior that created troubles in the past? It may not be the same, but there are some similarities. (*Supports goal and choices; restates feedback in nonjudgmental way.*)

JOANNE: Wendy, I appreciate your taking a risk in bringing up an idea that others might not agree with. This group will be one where others of you can try out ideas and get feedback on them before you try them. I hope that you can give each other feedback on different things that we're doing. (*Rewards leadership act shown by taking a risk; provides support after confrontation.*)

The leaders acted to see Wendy's behavior as possible leadership rather than resistance to group rules. They involve other members in providing feedback without judging Wendy's contribution. They might, however, have asked her if she were open to hearing other people's reactions to her plan. The danger of providing unsolicited negative feedback when a member takes a risk for the first time is that other members may conclude that risk taking is dangerous and will confine their offerings to safe subjects.

One of the frequent difficulties in involuntary groups occurs when leaders set all rules and become enforcers for violations. In addition, leaders often discover a need for a rule after it has been violated. By punishing the behavior rather than pointing to a need for a rule, leaders can give mixed messages that "this is your group" when in reality the leaders enforce unwritten rules beyond the verbally agreed-upon rules. For example, at one point in the session, Wendy was whispering to another member when the co-leader Joanne, was speaking.

JOANNE: Wendy, excuse me, when I'm talking, I'd appreciate if you'd listen. Thank you. I think it is important that we share with each other some of our experiences so that we can get some insight into ourselves and help each other with the whole process of learning how to become more independent.

Again, later in the group session:

JOANNE: Before we move on, Wendy, I'd appreciate it if you could take your file and put it away. That can be distracting when people are talking. I know when I'm talking, it kind of distracts me as you're filing. I feel as if you're not listening to what I'm saying. So could you please put it away? Thank you.

PAT: It doesn't bother me that she's filing her nails.

WENDY: It's fine. I know what you're saying.

While Joanne provides specific feedback and a rationale for it, she is enforcing rules that have not yet been set in the group. In addition, she may be inadvertently reinforcing Wendy as a negative leader in the group, as Pat immediately responds to support Wendy. Hence, choices have to be made about the enforcement of rules and their importance. In the first instance, Joanne might have avoided the confrontation by helping the group to consider a rule that members will listen to and attend to one another. In the second, she might either have ignored the filing or asked others if they were bothered by it. By choosing to exercise power in these instances, Joanne runs the risk that members will conclude that the group is hers and not join in that ownership.

6. *Clarify expectations for the next session.* Expectations of any tasks to be completed outside of the session should be reviewed before the session ends. Where possible, such tasks should be selected by members from several possibilities, or members should be encouraged to generate their own tasks. For example, the members of the prostitution group might have been asked to think of topics they would like to have discussed in the group. They might also examine the alternative programs for individual goals such as pursuing further education, acquiring job skills, getting a driver's license, or bring in their own alternative ideas for an individual plan. In chemical dependency groups, members may be asked to read specified chapters of a text and bring in questions. As suggested in chapter 9, such initial tasks should be specific and highly likely to succeed such that a positive momentum might be generated.

## Post-Contracting Work with Involuntary Groups

Once a working contract is established that meets both non-negotiable purposes and individual goals, many forms of continued work are possible. Too often, involuntary groups never reach this stage. Activities after the contracting phase become much more specific to the type of group and problems addressed.

However, some general differences occur between open-ended and closed groups. For example, open-ended groups continue to add members and are ongoing, while other groups have closed membership and may last for a specific time-limited period. Open-ended groups offer members the opportunity to move through stages in the group from initiate to role model and are easier to staff, since the same group is used for persons at different stages. However, open-ended groups often have difficulty in maintaining a sense of forward progress, since attention must continually be given to orienting new members. Longer-term members, however, can often assist in this orientation process by describing their experience in the group and sharing group norms.

Closed, topic-oriented groups have the advantage of grouping persons according to where they are in a predictable sequence of change processes. For example, some writers propose that different group purposes are needed for the changing needs of alcoholics at early, middle, and ongoing support stages of the recovery process.[60]

Whether a single group or a sequence of groups is planned, a series of four phases is often found. Involuntary groups begin with an *orientation phase* in which information about the problem area is shared, followed by a *skill-learning phase* in which alternative behavioral skills are learned and practiced. Groups then often move to an *examination of attitudes and beliefs,* followed by attention to *preparation for experiences after the group ends.* These phases are described in more detail below (see figure 13.6).

1. *Orientation phase.* After the initial meeting described above, many involuntary groups continue with an orientation phase that is aimed at providing information and assisting members in making decisions about how they will use the group experience. The orientation phase works best when members are presented with information in a factual, non-blaming fashion, assisted in self-assessment of problem behaviors, and encouraged to make proactive choices. Cognitive dissonance may be stimulated by the provision of information that indicates dangers to meeting the member's own goals.

a. *Presentation of problem behavior in factual, nonblaming ways.* As involuntary groups usually begin with greater concern for the "mala prohibita" goals, the orientation phase often includes a presentation of problem behavior in matter-of-fact, nonjudgmental ways. Hence, in DWI and alcoholism treatment groups, tapes and films examining the consequences of drunken driving or physical consequences of drug abuse are often shared at this point. Experts are also used to provide information. For example, Smith reports using credible, outside experts to describe effects of chemical use with chemically dependent adolescents. The experts discussed problem drug use in two-sided arguments (see chapter 6) and did not pressure the adolescents to change beliefs or behavior.[61] At this point, members are not pressed to take personal responsibility for having "a problem," but rather are asked to be open to hearing information about the consequences of such behaviors.

b. *Facilitate decisions about dealing with problem behavior.* A frequent goal of the orientation phase is for members to make a decision about whether or not to deal with the problem behavior. For example, van Wormer describes orientation groups for problem drinkers in which

## Phases of Involuntary Groups

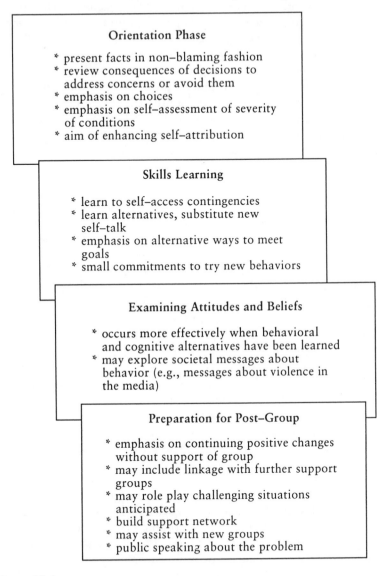

**Orientation Phase**

* present facts in non–blaming fashion
* review consequences of decisions to address concerns or avoid them
* emphasis on choices
* emphasis on self–assessment of severity of conditions
* aim of enhancing self–attribution

**Skills Learning**

* learn to self–access contingencies
* learn alternatives, substitute new self–talk
* emphasis on alternative ways to meet goals
* small commitments to try new behaviors

**Examining Attitudes and Beliefs**

* occurs more effectively when behavioral and cognitive alternatives have been learned
* may explore societal messages about behavior (e.g., messages about violence in the media)

**Preparation for Post–Group**

* emphasis on continuing positive changes without support of group
* may include linkage with further support groups
* may role play challenging situations anticipated
* build support network
* may assist with new groups
* public speaking about the problem

*Figure 13.6*

### Format for Self–Confrontation

| No | Yes |
|---|---|
| Are you powerless over alcohol? Has your life become unmanageable? | Did you ever have a blackout? Do you make promises to yourself about cutting down on drinking that you are unable to keep? Do you find it easier to confront someone who has done something to bother you after you have been drinking? Are there times when you drink or use drugs and can not predict the outcome? Is drinking interfering with your ability to solve problems and achieve your goals? |

*Figure 13.7*

members are encouraged to make a decision about whether or not to confront alcohol issues.[62] Contact with persons who have successfully completed the group often assists in this decision making process.[63]

Decision making is often facilitated by asking members to complete a self-assessment of their own problem behavior. For example, Smith reports that adolescent drug users were helped to construct a behavioral definition of dangerous drug usage followed by completing an individual assessment of their own danger using the group-constructed definition.[64] To facilitate such self-assessment, members of alcoholism treatment groups are often asked to complete a written self-assessment of dangerous drug usage. Citron recommends that these questions be asked in a matter-of-fact, nonjudgmental fashion, avoiding value-laden questions such as "Are you powerless over alcohol?" (see figure 13.7).[65]

Involuntary clients might be expected to respond more to factual questions about behavior and consequences than to take on self-blame for the problem, especially when they are unaware of other alternatives in getting needs met.

*2. Instruction in behavioral alternatives.* Change in orientation from "mala prohita" to "mala in se" is more likely to occur if members become aware of alternative ways to meet their own goals. Hence, instruction in developing alternative behavioral, affective, and cognitive responses to problem situations often follows the orientation phase. For example, skills groups for domestic violence often include instruction in relaxation methods, substitution of positive self-messages for negative self-talk, and practice of alternative behavioral responses such as taking time outs and making assertive requests.[66] Teaching men to observe their own cues that indicate a potentially violent or anger-provoking situation is particularly important. When such situations occur, men are taught to record both positive and negative self-talk and to generate behavioral alternatives.[67]

Similarly, in alcoholism treatment, assertiveness training groups can focus on alternative ways of dealing with situations that have led to drinking in the past.[68] In the S.O.B.E.R. program, members are taught to slow down, relax, analyze the behavioral exchange, and recognize the methods they use to deal with situations that in the past have led to alcohol use.[69]

Smith suggests that exploration of behavioral alternatives is more likely to be successful if there is emphasis on trying a new behavior with little external reward, with some emphasis on the difficulty of the task, and with anticipation of obstacles.[70]

3. *Examination of attitudes and beliefs.* It is often the hope in involuntary groups that members will not only change behaviors but also beliefs and attitudes supporting those behaviors. Members of involuntary groups may be more likely to consider change in attitudes and beliefs if completion of the two previous phases has stimulated dissonance and alternative means of reaching goals have been learned. Domestic violence groups often address attitudes and beliefs at this stage by presenting violence as learned behavior frequently reinforced by society.[71] Men who batter are seen as partly victims themselves of domestic violence through their lack of skills, fear of intimacy, and dependency on women.[72] They are seen as the products of a society that often teaches men to be unaware of their feelings, to have an action orientation, and to see less than perfect performance as failure.[73]

Such normalizing and nonblaming attention to attitudes and beliefs may assist in the modification of values. However, the process is not smooth and many members continue to express values or carry out behavior that is contrary to group purposes. Some members leave the group during this phase. Group leaders eager to change a person's attitudes and behavior at this point are susceptible to use of abusive confrontation (see chapter 11) that violates individual dignity, the right not to participate and to withdraw within him or herself.[74] Bratter suggests that unless the individual retains the right to self-determination in choosing whether and how to change behavior and attitudes, group leaders can become tyrants.[75]

When denial persists, Purdy and Nickle suggest asking direct factual questions about time and information gaps in reports of violence and asking about discrepancies in reports.[76] Emphasis on choices and consequences of behavior and attitudes that are obstacles to member's *own goals,* followed by empathy, are more likely to be successful forms of confrontation than assaults on attitudes and behavior.[77] In particular, confrontation around values and attitudes that the member does not have are unlikely to be successful. Without such self-attribution, members are likely to change overt behavior and attitudes only under the pressure of threatened punishment or tangible rewards. Evidence that such self-attribution is difficult to attain is suggested in domestic violence treatment research reports that men completing the program were more likely to reduce physical violence while maintaining or increasing psychological violence.[78] This finding suggests that while physical violence remained "mala prohibita," psychological violence did not become "mala in se."

4. *Preparation for experiences after the group ends.* If involuntary groups are to assist members in maintaining changes after the group ends, generalization to other settings and linkage with other resources must be facilitated. For example, role plays of situations in which peers attempt to influence a member to engage in renewed problem behavior can be helpful in preparing for difficulties. Planning for possible setbacks and regression can be beneficial in which a crisis plan, including means of maintaining an ongoing support plan, is developed. In addition, some members may move on to join ongoing support groups or assist in running new groups. Support for choices should be especially encouraged since self-attributed change is more likely to persist in the absence of the kinds of rewards and punishments that were available in the group.

This chapter has suggested that involuntary groups can be ethical and effective sources of influence that both meet societal needs and individual goals. Dangers of abuse of group leader power have also been described. Hence, a major issue is the determination of whether the specific purposes of a mandated or nonvoluntary group are legal and ethical. Questions to ask when an involuntary group's purpose are to be supported include: What role can individuals play in meeting their own goals? How can they participate in structuring the group? If structure is so rigid that neither leaders nor members can modify it, member efforts to regain some control can be expected, or, if they are unsuccessful, mute, passive acceptance. Are members required to participate who do not benefit and inhibit the benefit that others might obtain?

The chapter has also suggested that attitudes and beliefs may be more subject to change in groups through the influence of peers than is normally possible in work with individuals. While that influence can be ethical and effective, the danger of abusive confrontation in the group was also described. Remembering that confrontation is more appropriate as a persuasion method than as a method of punishment, questions should be asked about its use in the group. What choice does a member have in receiving confrontation? Corey suggests that members should be free to decline participation,[79] that groups are "not appropriate for endless interrogation . . . beating into submission."[80] How is confrontation related to the members' own goals? To what extent is confrontation used as a means of venting frustration over progress perceived to be too slow by the leaders?[81]

Practice methods for work in groups are greatly influenced by agency and institutional setting policies. Chapter 14 returns to the concept of the involuntary practitioner, introduced in chapter 1, and considers ways the practitioner can manage his or her stress and work to modify inappropriate setting policies.

# The Involuntary Practitioner
# and the System

The previous six chapters have provided guidelines to assist practitioners in providing legal, ethical, effective service to involuntary clients. Too often, the practitioners providing services to involuntary clients feel involuntary as well. They describe agency and societal pressures that cause many of them to feel almost as powerless as the involuntary clients they serve. Such pressures include ever-increasing paperwork demands, rising caseloads, and reduced discretion needed to carry out a skilled practice. Practitioner responses to such pressures have often been considered nothing more than incipient burnout, implying that it is simply an individual problem with an individual solution, while ignoring organizational and structural causes and solutions.

This chapter will explore the dilemmas of involuntary practitioners and suggest guidelines for reducing work-related stress and advocating to improve service conditions in agencies. In addition, a research and practice agenda for further development of strategies for work with involuntary clients and agencies will be suggested. Finally, the chapter will close with reflections about a societal context of ambivalence toward legal, ethical, effective service with involuntary clients.

I will begin with a few excerpted case study interviews conducted with practitioners trained in the methods for working with involuntary clients described in this book. The practitioners were asked to describe how these methods have been more and less helpful.

James, 35, a child protection worker: "The contracting strategies have helped me engage with involuntary clients much better than I could before I knew how to use them. However, carrying out abuse and neglect investigations takes so much time that I don't have a lot of time and energy left for contracting. If only working with involuntary clients was my biggest problem. I am overwhelmed by paperwork. I spend so much time filing case plans and reports that sometimes it seems that the priority is to file the report correctly rather than do a good job with the client."

Marge, 28, a case manager with a private agency providing services to clients with serious and persistent mental illness, replied, "Knowing about reactance and self-presentation strategies has helped me better understand the involuntary situations our so-called voluntary clients experience. While few of our clients are legally mandated to receive services, they have to jump through a lot of hoops to get what they want. Our agency also jumps through hoops set by the public agency for our purchase of service contracts, since workers have to be laid off if the contracts reduce. Our caseloads have increased and we are forced to focus on billable services to prioritize our work rather than think more broadly about what a client wants and needs. The time pressures mean that I know how to do a lot more with my clients than I have time to do. I feel guilty that I can't keep up with what needs to be done. I just struggle to keep my head above water. In taking care of myself, it becomes easier to do it the short way, to make do, not make waves. On the other hand, as a single parent, there are advantages here because I can set my schedule and make it fit with child care."

Bart, 35, is a psychotherapist for a hospital outpatient clinic, working with members of a health maintenance organization. Bart said, "When I took this job, I thought I would be able to provide 'real' therapy with voluntary clients. While many of my clients are voluntary, many others come in under pressure. Parents frequently bring adolescents in to be 'fixed.' Employees come in because their supervisor 'suggested' that they needed to 'get help.' Understanding that they come to the clinic under pressure has helped me to use contracting skills to increase their voluntarism. But working with involuntary clients is easier than working with the organization. As a private business, the priority of this organization is to get the bills paid and make money, not provide service to the client. If a client can't pay or needs a special service, we can't do anything. We sometimes fudge diagnoses in order to get a client or family seen. Our caseloads have gotten so high that as a group the therapists here have stopped replacing people in our schedule who cancel appointments. We take this as recovery time. I am looking at other jobs. But there are trade-offs: I can get a smaller caseload somewhere else, but I would also have to take lower pay."

James, Marge, and Bart could be considered *involuntary practitioners* if they consider themselves disadvantaged because desirable alternatives are believed to be available elsewhere and if they feel forced to remain in the situation because they consider the cost of leaving too high. Just as the involuntary state can create dissonance and reactance in clients, similar responses are reported by involuntary practititioners.

Involuntary practitioners often feel that they make *constrained choices* to continue such work. While practitioners such as Bart might prefer to leave the organization, they feel constrained to remain in it by the threatened loss of other benefits such as income, pension plans, and convenience. For Marge, keeping a job compatible with child care needs was a major factor in staying. Some public agency practitioners speak of well-paid work with involuntary clients as "golden handcuffs" since they might prefer working elsewhere but could not receive equal pay. Hence, their motivation to remain in their jobs may be more influenced by rewards available rather than an intrinsic valuing of the work.

Involuntary practitioners often feel a *lack of motivational congruence with the system.* Many of the intervention guidelines suggested in this book are not currently compatible with the policies of organizations employing involuntary practitioners. Hence, reading this book may in fact stimulate cognitive dissonance. Practitioners may come to doubt the legality, ethics, or effectiveness of the services provided in their settings. They may believe that an overemphasis on punitive options and a lack of choices and inducements might act to maintain behavior that comes to be labeled as reluctant, disgruntled, hard-to-reach, and resistant in involuntary clients. They may experience dissonance when their settings have beliefs that focus on client pathology and ignore situational explanations for client responses to involuntary circumstances. Cognitive dissonance theory suggests that if practitioners cannot change their behavior to fit their values, they may reduce dissonance by changing those values.

Practitioners may respond to nonvoluntary situations in ways that are similar to those patterns described for clients in nonvoluntary situations. For example, practitioners experiencing nonvoluntary pressure from persons perceived to have more power may find themselves using *self-presentation strategies* such as self-promotion, exemplification, and ingratiation when that higher-power person controls access to needed resources. Similarly, practitioners may experience *reactance* when valued freedoms are threatened. In such circumstances, practitioners often report procrastinating or "finding the loophole" in an unwelcome task by carrying out the required task in a narrow way while undercutting the purpose of the task. Of particular concern is the pattern suggested in reactance theory that repeated failed attempts to reassert valued freedoms may result in learned helplessness.[1] Hence, practitioners who may be resourceful and empowering in work with their clients, may also conclude that nothing will work to change their own work setting.

Sherman and Wenocur describe a sequence of disempowerment that often occurs in public welfare agencies.[2] Probationary staff often start with a *skill and routine mastery* stage in which they become oriented to the job in the context of limited caseloads and access to frequent supervision. This "honeymoon" period is followed by *social integration* in which the protections are removed: caseloads increase and access to supervision decreases. Practitioners come to realize that no matter how hard and skillfully they work, the agency lacks sufficient resources for them to carry out their jobs as described. This realization leads to a *moral outrage* stage in which workers become angry and confront their supervisors with the incongruity of resources and demands. Too often, this complaint meets with a double-bind response: you are right, but do the job and meet all needs anyhow. Sherman and Wenocur suggest that this outrage is followed by feelings of guilt, frustration, repressed anger, and depression. Similarly, clients frustrated by the lack of resources dump anger on the practitioner held responsible for the lack of resources.

Sherman and Wenocur then suggest six ways of coping with this conflict between job descriptions and lack of resources. The *capitulator* resolves the conflict by identifying with the organization: do what is possible without guilt, stop advocating, shut down empathy, and shuffle papers. In contrast, the *noncapitulator* continues to fight by rejecting the values of the organization. Such practitioners identify with client anger rather than powerlessness. According to the authors, they also often become isolated, identified as mavericks and house radicals, such that they come to resign, are counseled out, or are fired. A third response is *niche finding* in which the practitioner finds a special position such as training director in which they can use their skills outside of the line of fire of high client contact and low resources. This solution can last as long as the person holds the position. A fourth response is *withdrawal* in which practitioners leave the job in hopes of finding a less constrained environment. Sherman and Wenocur suggest that frustrations may recur within similarly constrained positions unless conflict management skills are learned. *Self-victimization/martyrdom* occurs when the practitioner identifies with the powerless client and tries to overcome the guilt over ineffectiveness by overworking.

While each of these five responses are understandable styles of coping with the dissonance over conflicting job descriptions and limited resources, Sherman and Wenocur describe a *functional noncapitulator* response as more functional. In this response, conflict is managed by acting responsibly to influence the organization. Functional noncapitulators pick their battles, deciding when to capitulate and when to take calculated risks in negotiating the conditions of work. This response also models a form of empowerment that enables them to negotiate with their clients within boundaries.

Sherman and Wenocur recommend voluntary mutual support groups to enable practitioners to assess their responses to working conditions and to support experimentation with the functional noncapitulator role. Agencies can assist this process by allowing time and space for such meetings to occur.

Powerless, involuntary practitioners can provide little benefit to involuntary clients or to themselves. We will now explore ways in which the involuntary practitioner can act toward empowerment and carrying out the functional noncapitulator role in order to become at least semi-voluntary. Four major steps are suggested.

1. *Involuntary practitioners can assess the pressures they experience and locate their source.* Do those pressures emanate from work with involuntary clients? Do they come from the organization? Do they come from larger community and societal sources? Which of these pressures appear modifiable and, if so, at what cost?

2. *Involuntary practitioners can identify their own responses to job conflicts and stresses.* They can review the typology of responses suggested by Sherman and Wenocur to see if any appear descriptive of their style of coping.

3. *Involuntary practitioners can remind themselves of their choices, however constrained.* Unlike mandated clients, they are not mandated or court-ordered to remain in their positions. They can choose to leave if circumstances become intolerable. To assess this, they need to figure out their own "bottom line".[3] At what point do they choose to leave and take the consequences of losing other benefits of the job, pay, looking for other work, as costs of the choice?

4. *If involuntary practitioners choose to remain in their situation, they can do so proactively by making choices, however constrained, to*

The Involuntary Practitioner

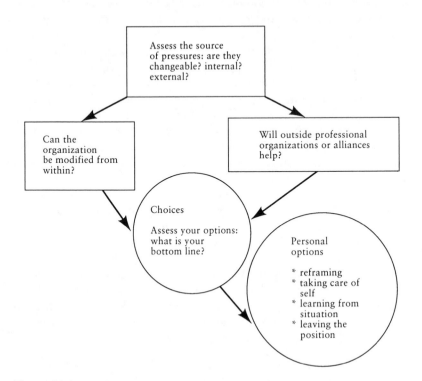

Assess the source
of pressures: are they
changeable? internal?
external?

Can the
organization
be modified from
within?

Will outside professional
organizations or alliances
help?

Choices

Assess your options:
what is your
bottom line?

Personal
options

* reframing
* taking care of
  self
* learning from
  situation
* leaving the
  position

*Figure 14.1*

*reduce reactance and feelings of impotence and become semi-voluntary.*
They can use stress reduction strategies to conserve their own energy
and resources. They can reframe the situation as an opportunity to learn.
They can make alliances within the organization and attempt to influence policies and beliefs.[4] They can ally with outside professional organizations and advocacy groups to promote needed changes (see figure
14.1). We will explore each of these responses in more detail below.

## Burnout and Job Stress

Burnout has been used widely to describe stresses experienced by
human service professionals. The term has come to have a life of its own
with some describing it as an excuse for ineffective coping and others
feeling labeled as deviant for responding to pressures largely out of their

control. Burnout has been defined in terms of emotional exhaustion, depersonalization, and feelings of reduced work accomplishment.[5] While there are over a thousand articles and studies of burnout in fields as varied as police work, child care, law, and health care, most articles are impressionistic; a review of the literature prior to 1981 found that only 15 percent involved systematic data collection and burnout was measured in inconsistent ways.[6] Despite these limitations, there have been consistent findings that higher levels of burnout are associated with negative ratings of aspects of the work environment, such as level of autonomy, comfort, challenge, client contact, and coworker support. Burnout has also been associated with lower levels of job satisfaction and greater intention to quit the job, lower levels of self-esteem, lower use of coping mechanisms, more hassles in daily life, and lower scores on type A personality tests.[7]

Both negative environment and negative personal factors have been linked to burnout, though the causal linkages are not clear.[8] Similarly, both client and organizational characteristics associated with involuntary clients and settings appear to be related to high stress levels and burnout (see figure 14.2). The type and severity of client problems, prognosis for change, and client reactions to staff are associated with greater job stress.[9] Hence, work with involuntary clients is a predictable source of job stress if it entails hostile, unappreciative reactions from involuntary clients and little noticeable change resulting from practitioner efforts.[10]

Settings in which involuntary clients are frequently encountered are also associated with greater job stress and turnover. For example, much has been written about the stress, burnout, and turnover in child protective services in which practitioners and clients frequently begin as adversaries.[11] Settings that provide little comfort, challenge, support, and practitioner autonomy are associated with greater stress.[12]

## Strategies for Coping with Job Stress

A literature has grown about methods that combat or reduce job stress and burnout and an extrapolation from that literature to work with involuntary clients follows.[13] Pines, Aronson, and Kafry suggest that coping with or managing stress is often a more reasonable goal than eliminating it completely.[14]

When the source of the stress can be modified, efforts to change that source of the stress by confronting or reframing it are described as *direct-active coping*.[15] In the excerpt above, James spoke of being buried under paperwork in the form of never-ending case plans and case notes. Devel-

STRESS AND
BURNOUT

> **Recipient of Care**
>
> * complex problems
> * chronic conditions in
>   which little progress
>   is expected
> * acute conditions in which
>   must act on little information
> * hostile client reaction
> * client problems relevant
>   to provider

> **Personal Factors**
>
> * overdedicated
> * impatient
> * intolerant of
>   obstacles
> * lack of
>   self-confidence
> * seeks too much
>   gratification from
>   work
> * neglect outside life

> **Organizational Factors**
>
> * role ambiguity and conflict
> * amount of support
> * discretionary resources
> * amount and type of direct
>   contact

*Figure 14.2*

oping client contracting formats that were useful to clients and practitioners such as James, as well as for external accountability purposes, would be an example of direct-active coping. Similarly, when Marge spoke of doubled caseloads and punitive options for clients, reducing caseload sizes, increasing client options, and eliminating unnecessarily punitive conditions would also be examples of direct-active coping. Clearly, many such changes involve collaboration with and initiative from supervisors and managers and resource support from funding bodies as well as individual practitioner efforts (see figure 14.3).

Practitioners can also engage in direct-active coping by reframing

## Coping Grid

| | Active | Inactive |
|---|---|---|
| **Direct** | * change the source of the stress<br>* confront the source<br>* reframe the source | * ignore source<br>* avoid source<br>* leave |
| **Indirect** | * talk about source<br>* change self<br>* become involved in other activities | * use alcohol and drugs<br>* get sick<br>* collapse |

*Figure 14.3*

perceived client hostility. Reframing occurs when oppositional behavior is understood as expectable responses to involuntary conditions mediated by interaction with the practitioner and agency rather than emerging solely from internal client characteristics. When oppositional responses are understood as reactance and as self-presentation strategies designed to cope with low power and the deviant labeling process, practitioners can personalize the responses less and be more empathic to them (see chapter 7). Second, by developing semi-voluntary contracts with limited, feasible goals, involuntary clients can be empowered and experience less frustration. Third, by confronting carefully and appropriately, rather than in a scattershot fashion, unnecessary hostility may be avoided.

Practitioners have to weigh risks, costs in time and energy, and need to involve others in choosing direct-active coping. Hence, a major issue in the selection of coping strategies is determining whether the source of the stress can be modified. Direct-active coping is the preferred coping mode when the source of stress is changeable, since continued coping responses may not be required.[16] Practitioners often assume that the source cannot be modified, and therefore confine coping efforts to attempting to escape from the stress or changing themselves to adapt to the stress. If practitioners cannot change the source of the stress or deem it too costly, then they may have to resort to *direct-inactive or indirect-active coping.*[17]

Direct-inactive coping refers to removing oneself emotionally or physically from the stress. Emotional distancing is often referred to as detached concern or a form of caring that is compartmentalized rather than pervasive. Among the helpful attitudes for detached concern are acknowledging that success in human services is often not clear-cut, letting go of goals beyond the practitioner's control or influence such as ultimate responsibility for changing clients, and focusing on goals within the practitioner's control such as facilitating client empowerment, and celebrating smaller successes.[18]

> For example, Maureen, 31, worked in the same child welfare setting as James. She used both direct-inactive coping and direct-active coping frequently in dealing with her own job stress and relieving involuntary client stress. She reported: "I avoid feeling burned out by having limited goals with each case. I can usually find someone who is willing to work together on something. I find opportunities to link people with resources in almost every case. I try to get people bus passes, cab fare, or child care whenever it is available and would help them reach goals. I don't hold myself responsible for everything working, everyone changing and liking me. I think that clients are generally doing the best they can." Such detached concern can be reinforced in the work setting by supervisors and managers who do not hold the practitioner responsible for "curing" everyone, but rather for making a good effort with what is known and with recognizing that some clients may not be helped with current methods and resources.

Direct-inactive coping also refers to limiting contact with stressful conditions.[19] For example, efforts to separate one's home life from work can be a form of direct-inactive coping. Obviously, such separation is difficult on those days when the practitioner carries a beeper at home. Many practitioners report that having a break or "decompression time" between the end of work and the beginning of home activities can facilitate coping. Similarly, travel time to and from appointments can be a time for decompression. Agencies can affect direct-inactive coping by using team approaches, providing time-outs, and rotating high-stress job responsibilities such as carrying a beeper and responding to emergency calls.[20]

Should high stress be unchangeable and reach an unbearable level, then a decision to seek a transfer or leave the job can be a constructive strategy. James ultimately decided both that the stresses were unchangeable and that his coping methods were not working and left the child welfare agency.

Use of any coping mechanism to the extreme and excluding others can be nonproductive. For example, extreme emotional distancing can be the emotional insulation and depersonalization associated with burnout. Adjusting to intolerable working conditions and unethically repressive circumstances for involuntary clients without efforts to change them can resemble the capitulator response described by Sherman and Wenocur. Too often, this response can relieve anxiety by focusing on the details of policies and procedures while ignoring their effects on live people. Such a response can be the functional equivalent of swabbing the decks of a sinking ship.

Indirect-active coping refers to to talking about the source of the stress, changing oneself in response to the stress, and getting involved in other activities.[21] Practitioners using indirect-active coping recognize their own stamina as a valuable resource through means such as attention to diet, exercise, and hobbies. Similarly, practitioners who are supported by their peers, supervisors, and work groups report being able to cope with unchangeable stress better than those who do not have access to this kind of help. However, venting without focusing on proactive means for coping often provides short-lived relief. Hence, practitioners who find themselves part of a perpetually complaining group may have to consider distancing themselves from such groups to enhance their own coping.

Finally, *indirect-inactive coping* is not a conscious strategy to cope with stress but a temporary escape through medication, smoking, alcohol, drugs, overeating, overworking to the point of illness, and collapse.[22] The absence of a proactive coping style such as one of the three above often results in indirect-inactive coping.

Practitioners can attempt to avoid falling into indirect-inactive coping by a) monitoring their own stress levels such that they are sensitive to their own signs of high stress; b) assessing the nature of the stress; c) examining the coping mechanisms they are using and experimenting with new ones if the familiar ones are not working; and d) implementing a coping mechanism and monitoring its success. If one is exercising or engaging in hobbies and the stress remains unmanageable, it may be time to experiment with other strategies (see figure 14.4).[23]

All of the coping styles, with the exception of indirect-inactive coping, can be useful stress responses. Personal style plays a role, as practitioners often find that they use one coping style more than others. Flexibility and adapting to the needs of the situation are more important than learning a new style. The styles vary in the degree to which they attempt to *change* the source of stress as opposed to *adapting* to it. If efforts to change the source are successful, then continued stress reduction efforts are not necessary. On the other hand, efforts that change the self and not the source may have to be maintained indefinitely for stress to be reduced.[24]

## Involuntary Practice in Agencies

Patti suggests that organizations that are responsive to client need are characterized by six dynamics: 1) tasks are assigned based on assessment of practitioner knowledge, skills, and experience, and used flexibly; 2) there is a shallow hierarchy such that supervisors have authority to coordinate service and staff judgment and discretion is often relied upon to make case decisions; 3) staff with knowledge and skills relevant to particular decisions participate in those decisions; 4) rules and procedures both provide guidance and sufficient latitude to respond to client needs; 5) communication proceeds both up and down the hierarchy; and 6) higher value is placed on staff commitment than on blind compliance.[25]

James, Marge, and Bart, the involuntary practitioners introduced earlier might respond:

But our work settings do not fit this model. Tasks are assigned to get the job done and the crisis handled rather than according to staff abilities. Communication comes from the top down and discretion is very limited. Compliance is expected rather than commitment. A lot of people become burned out and stay on to become supervisors or senior workers. I am tired. I don't have the time and it is not my job to change the agency. You said above that I should learn how to let go and not take on too much.

This book emphasizes transactions between involuntary clients and practitioners in individual, family, and group settings. While beyond the scope of the book to provide extensive guidelines for agency change, those transactions are greatly influenced by the setting context, the laws and policies governing it, and broader societal attitudes. The domain and jurisdiction of the setting set policies governing practitioner discretion and goals of practice that may facilitate or inhibit legal, ethical, effective practice. As described in chapter 3, public agencies are often characterized by a reactive style guided primarily by legal procedures in order to avoid lawsuits. Such procedures often limit practitioner discretion and flexibility. Similarly, when agency policies or court orders specify a uniform set of expectations, practitioners may be expected to carry out rigid, compliance-oriented practice. Such rigidity may predictably result in high client reactance and often be interpreted as client resistance and pathology. Internal advocacy to change policies, proce-

## Steps in Personal Coping

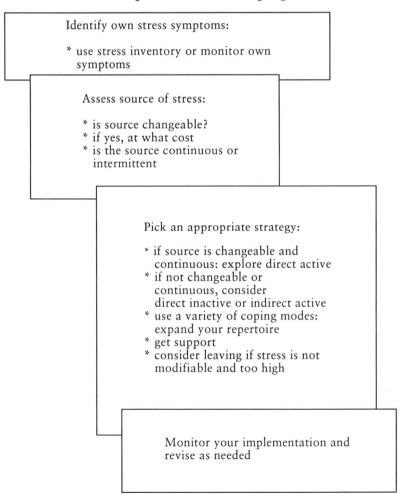

Identify own stress symptoms:

* use stress inventory or monitor own
  symptoms

Assess source of stress:

* is source changeable?
* if yes, at what cost
* is the source continuous or
  intermittent

Pick an appropriate strategy:

* if source is changeable and
  continuous: explore direct active
* if not changeable or
  continuous, consider
  direct inactive or indirect active
* use a variety of coping modes:
  expand your repertoire
* get support
* consider leaving if stress is not
  modifiable and too high

Monitor your implementation and
revise as needed

*Figure 14.4*

dures, and programs to become more effective or remove deleterious conditions is called for.

The initiatives provided here for direct practice with individuals, families, and groups in involuntary situations need parallel developments in relevant nonvoluntary relationships such as supervisor-supervisee, supervisor-manager, manager-funding body or board of directors.

While practitioners are tempted to locate the cause of their difficulties in uncooperative clients and rigid supervisors and policies, supervisors caught in the sandwich between administrative requirements and practitioner needs often find themselves overwhelmed and powerless. Similarly, managers face ever-increasing requirements for mandated services without parallel increase in resources. The triage strategy selected often forces them to target resources to the highest-risk populations, to promise quick, accountable solutions to social problems at low cost. Methods that empower supervisors and managers to advocate for changes, to make persuasive cases for needed resources are needed.

When practitioners and supervisors attempt to change their organizations, several guidelines suggested by Resnick and Patti can be useful. First, agency opposition to change can be predicted according to the generality and depth of changes suggested. Hence, changes that might occur on an individual or program level rather than at the level of the whole organization are less likely to provoke opposition. Consequently, an innovation in the way a particular practitioner approaches his or her work or the way a unit organizes its client contact is less likely to be opposed than an immediate appeal to restructure the entire organization. Similarly, innovations that affect program and procedures rather than extend to the basic mission of services are less likely to be opposed.[26] In addition, Patti and Resnick suggest that efforts to influence decision makers and others who control key resources should consider values that are likely to be influential with them. For example, appeals to improved client service are but one consideration in decisions about change. Furthermore, implications for power, money and other resources, prestige, security, convenience, ideological commitment, and professional competence might be considered. Hence, appeals that emphasized increased achievement of already existing mission statements and efficient use of resources might be received more positively than attacks on the basic mission (see figure 14.5).

As practitioners, supervisors, and managers consider changes in organizational policy and climate to support legal, ethical, effective practice with involuntary clients, the following questions are suggested to guide an internal audit.

1. *To what extent do involuntary clients have significant input into the development of semi-voluntary contracts as opposed to passive involvement in involuntary case plans or "notices of agency intent"?* Much service planning lacks the motivational congruence required to be considered contracting. As noted at many earlier points, "notices of agency intent" and involuntary case plans are developed that describe what the

# Value Orientations of
# Decision Makers

**Power**
* authority and control over organizational behavior

**Money**
* increased income or income substitutes

**Professional Competence**

**Client Service**

**Prestige**
* respect and approval of funders, those with power to
  promote, hire, and fire

**Ideological Commitment**
* individual and organizational values

**Security**
* protect against loss of personal power, prestige

**Convenience**
* avoiding conditions requiring extra effort

*Figure 14.5*

practitioner and setting hope will happen without reference to motivational congruence.

Practitioners, supervisors, and administrators might assess service agreement forms to determine the degree to which they facilitate motivational congruence by a) making non-negotiable policies and procedures specific and limited; b) clarifying negotiable items, those subject to practitioner and client discretion; and c) free choices and rights of clients.

They might then also assess the degree to which those service agreements reflect large numbers of non-negotiable requirements and limited attention to client concerns. If the number of non-negotiable requirements is high, then high reactance should be expected. Choices among negotiable requirements should be assessed to determine the degree to which clients have options in completing programs.

2. *To what extent are goals legal, ethical, clear, specific, and feasible?* Goals are often cast at such an abstract level that it is difficult for the client, practitioner, or outside parties to know if they have been accomplished. Paternalistic pressures often influence practitioners to include as client goals topics that involuntary clients neither wish nor are legally required to pursue.

First steps include examining legal limits and requirements for goal setting and restricting goals that pursue paternalistic aims beyond legal requirements and client wishes. Agency guidelines that support client self-determination and delineate appropriate use of paternalism should be specified. Focusing goals on these more limited legal requirements and expressed client priorities should assist in achieving greater success.

3. *To what extent is pejorative labeling of client behavior avoided?* Categorization of client behavior in terms of legal and diagnostic categories is often unavoidable. However, such required categorization should be monitored when it includes pejorative labeling of involuntary clients as hostile, resistant, or unmotivated and results in a self-fulfilling prophecy of failure. Case records might be assessed to determine the extent to which client behavior is described in a normalizing, nonblaming fashion that includes the impact of other factors such as agency methods and procedures.

4. *How is power used and understood?* Chapter 6 suggested that compliance strategies such as coercion and inducement and persuasion strategies are appropriate in different circumstances and have both expectable effects and byproducts. Chapter 7 emphasized that the availability of coercive means often restricts the use of persuasion methods. Particular confusion occurs around the use of confrontation that is meant to be a persuasive means of influence but often becomes coercive. Influence methods are too often carried out by habit or policy without examining either their effectiveness or legal and ethical appropriateness.

Assessment of practice might then include the extent to which influence methods are used consciously, mindful of predictable effects and appropriate usage. Examination of the degree to which confrontation is used as an ethical, effective means of persuasion rather than an as unethical, ineffective form of coercion is particularly suggested.

5. *To what extent is there parallel process in the use of power in the*

**Parallel Process**

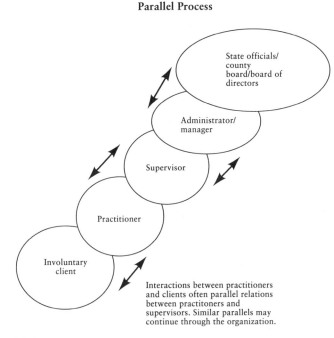

Interactions between practitioners and clients often parallel relations between practitoners and supervisors. Similar parallels may continue through the organization.

*Figure 14.6*

*setting?* Parallel process has been described as a process in which similar interactional dynamics are repeated across several hierarchical levels of an organization.[27] For example, organizational styles that emphasize compliance methods and distrust of staff may be reproduced in similar practitioner-client interactions. On the other hand, managers and supervisors who treat staff with respect, separate negotiables from non-negotiables, respect free choices in other areas, may find that practitioners are more likely to use empowering strategies with clients (see figure 14.6).

## The Societal Context of Practice with Involuntary Clients

Practice with involuntary clients occurs in a larger context of national moods and trends. A rehabilitation philosophy in juvenile justice has lost ground to a justice model that gives priority to providing fair punishment that protects society from threat.[28] Wattenberg suggests that a war on poverty that was at least partly addressed to correcting structural conditions contributing to poverty has been replaced by a war on the poor.[29] Barbara Ehrenreich suggests that the negative effects of affluence on the middle class have been projected onto the poor: passivity, lack of saving, lack of discipline, and a focus on consumption.[30] The Low Income Opportunity Board submits recommendations for fighting poverty, has them dismissed by the current administration because they are unlikely to show immediate rewards while billions are allocated for bailing out the savings and loan industry.[31] A costly war with Iraq was undertaken at a time when domestic programs were stalled and the federal deficit skyrocketed.[32] Programs to help the poor "pick themselves up by their bootstraps" were replaced by programs that charge the poor for those bootstraps.

Hence, practice technologies for work with involuntary clients such as those described in this book exist within the context of larger social beliefs about the nature of deviance. As described in chapter 7, individual pathology and structural views remain competing perspectives for explaining the cause and solution of the "involuntary problem." The Reagan era marked a return to a residual view that considered persons requiring the federal assistance of a "safety net" to be a small number of worthy poor since society and the economy were considered basically sound. The structural or institutional perspective that assumed that the state needs to act to meet many unmet needs not resolved by the family and the market economy came into disfavor. Liberalism became the "L" word: a deviant label designating misguided compassion destructive of the work ethic, a permissiveness destructive of basic values, and judged to be motivated by desires to create jobs for liberals rather than for reducing poverty.[33]

Some suggest that the Reagan era marked a return to a more realistic view of the role of government in ameliorating problematic social conditions.[34] In this view, government should be expected to be fair, efficient, and dependable but not benevolent. Goals of redistribution of income to assist the lower income groups should be abandoned in favor of accepting measures to support a strong economy that would ultimately benefit the poor through a "trickle down".[35] These policies seem to assume different motivations for different classes. The more affluent were expected to assert themselves to the public good by reinvesting and creating jobs, while working people were considered to respond only to punishment.[36] Yet Kevin Phillips reports that the results of a major income redistribution increased the concentration of wealth among the richest and further impoverished the middle class and poor. The societal investment in rewards for the wealthy resulted in irresponsible speculation as in the savings and loans crisis for which the taxpayer must spend.[37]

The resurgence of the residual view has influenced practice with involuntary clients on at least two levels: focus on tertiary prevention and the prominence of individual pathology views. Limits on social service expenditures have led to resource targeting for those populations considered to be at greatest risk.[38] By focusing on tertiary prevention or amelioration of depleted conditions of those most at risk, prevention of the conditions that led to those depleted states are ignored. Focus on tertiary prevention to the exclusion or providing resources and supports to prevent the problem from occurring may result in achieving measurable gains on short-term, realistic goals while in the long term creating ever larger numbers of involuntary clients. Focus on tertiary prevention may create more involuntary clients than it eliminates.

The popularity of family-centered home-based services (FCHBS) can be considered an example of this tertiary prevention phenomenon. FCHBS is typically targeted at those families for which out-of-home placement would occur in the absence of outside intervention.[39] The program is appealing since there are reports of successful prevention of unnecessary out-of-home care for 75 percent and above of families served, in reports of savings accrued through avoidance of placement costs, and in the emphasis on empowering families to deal with their own problems.[40] Brenda McGowan cautions, however, that the targeting of services on limited feasible goals creates the illusion that problems not amenable to short-term services are the fault of families rather than of a shortage of resources such as longer-term supports.[41] By restricting usage of such services to those most in danger of removal from the home, expressed concerns by families that fall short of imminent danger may be interpreted paradoxically that clients seeking services really don't "need" services. Such a view is analogous to calling the fire department when you find that fire from a skillet has ignited the kitchen and being advised by the fire department to call again when the whole house is on fire or make way for the fire trucks when a neighbor notices an out of control conflagration. In short, as described in chapter 2, mandated and nonvoluntary FCHBS clients may be created by the lack of access to voluntary services.

This targeting of resources is also experienced in work with clients with serious and persistent mental illness. As a triage strategy is implemented in the face of increased mandates and decreased funds, the amount of discomfort required to access public funds increases. There is increased use of case managers as brokers and coordinators of services aimed at avoiding duplication. In the face of often unavailable services, case managers often find themselves managing paper and coordinating inadequate services. They find themselves trying to "beat the system" by plotting to get the "right" psychologist to provide the "right" diagnosis in order to get the client served.

The residual view is also served by the increasing prominence of individual pathology explanations for deviance. The French social philosopher Michel Foucault suggested that society uses separation procedures to create and control subgroup populations in order to "normalize" or create people who behave in an orderly fashion and are not dangerous.[42] These separation procedures increasingly operate under the aura of scientific control and use therapy rather than penal solutions to organize and control the poor and the deviant.[43] Foucault suggests that the separation procedures create ever-larger numbers of persons labeled deviant without effectively eradicating the deviance, yet increasing the numbers of persons involved in carrying out the therapeutic eradication procedures. Similarly, Epstein suggests that "medicine, psychiatry, and social science have become the linchpins of systematic normalization technologies that create, classify and control 'anomalies' in the social body. The therapeutic technologies and their offshoots isolate anomalies . . . identify and define problems . . . and . . . normalize anomalies through corrective or therapeutic procedures."[44]

Influenced by the individual pathology view, the therapeutic community may be inclined to welcome an increase of coercive outreach methods as providing the necessary leverage to bring disturbed people in for the help they need. Hence, court orders and coerced choices for persons who have violated the rights of others, such as domestic batterers, sexual perpetrators, and pregnant women addicted to crack, are welcomed. Concerns are raised, however, by extension of coercive methods when others are not harmed or laws violated. For example, mandated drug testing and proposals to extend civil commitment to coerce chemical dependency treatment, whether or not laws have been violated or others have been harmed, raise questions about illegal violations of civil liberties and unethical paternalism.[45] Drug problems are attacked by punishing users and seeking to eliminate the source and ignoring social conditions that lead to drug use.

Programs for the poor have tended to locate the source of poverty in character flaws such as abuse of alcohol, laziness, and promiscuity, rather than in external conditions.[46] Attraction to coercive measures is now seen in income support programs as benefits are increasingly attached to behavioral requirements with penalties for lack of compliance. According to Atherton, the view that some goods are so basic that all should have them regardless of contribution makes no sense to the average person since it removes all moral responsibility from individuals for their actions and considers them merely as victims of the welfare state.[47] An example of this extension of coercive measures is the Learnfare program that has been implemented in Wisconsin in which single-parent Aid to Families with Dependent Children (AFDC) mothers have their payments reduced or are removed from welfare rolls if they are unable to keep their children in school.[48] Such coercive actions have been defended on the paternalistic assumption that Learnfare acts as a partial substitute for an absent parent who would presumably have provided the authority figure needed to keep children in school.

The principle of individual responsibility for socially appropriate behavior in return for economic benefits appears, once again, focused on one subgroup of beneficiaries, the poor, rather than extended to other groups. If this principle were applied fairly across groups benefiting from government resources, then it would follow that those wealthy persons who benefited from income redistribution upward should be penalized financially if they did not act to reinvest that benefit and create more jobs.

From the structural viewpoint, practitioners working with the expanding pools of involuntary clients created by increased coercion and targeting of "high risk" populations to the exclusion of others might be likened to "sanitary engineers of society, sweeping up the human refuse off the street."[49] Hence, practitioners using the engagement strategies proposed in this book might be considered providing social control with a smiling face, talking of empowerment while actually aiming for greater compliance. At worst, such methods might be likened to greasing the skids under involuntary clients, by making an increasingly heartless, repressive system seem more palatable by making small, insignificant choices available, by disguising the stark social message that you deserve your situation, by softening rather than diverting the blow.

How might practitioners carry out unethical means without experiencing dissonance? Robert Jay Lifton described psychological processes that he suggests allowed Nazi doctors to participate in the separating out, experimentation on, and killing of Jews. He posits a doubling process that permits doctors to proceed without feeling cognitive dissonance for violating the Hippocratic oath. Dissonance could be avoided by considering Jews a lower form of life, not human, such that respect for human life did not apply. Second, if the experiments carried out with Jews were considered a noble, patriotic task for the betterment of the *real* human race, then inhuman means to nonhuman people was an unfortunate but necessary cost.[50] While the actions are not so extreme, the doubling process might give practitioners pause when they consider whether unethically intrusive means are used to coercively change those labeled deviant.

Some suggest that the flight from public social services to private practice is influenced by such coercive trends and tiring of work with low-income groups.[51] John Ehrenreich suggests that the social work flight contributes to a loss of professional identity: "Social work seems rudderless, insecure, suffering from a loss of unity and a clear sense of self-identity . . . more like a collection of disparate occupations. . . . If what makes social work unique is its recognition of social forces as determinants of life experience, then what are we to make of the rush of social workers to private practice with middle class clients, clients who presumably are less the helpless pawns of social forces than are the poor or less powerful people?"[52]

Walz concludes in a review of studies of social work student values that current cohorts are less committed to the concerns of the poor, to social action and advocacy approaches, and more supportive of the social class system than student cohorts of the 1960s.[53] He suggests that students aspire to positions serving middle-class clients with middle-class problems by wishing to become school social workers, medical social workers, family therapists, and psychiatric social workers.[54] While suggesting that selective cutbacks in public funding and expansion of the private market contribute to these trends, Walz joins Ehrenreich in recommending that social work concentrate scarce resources on the needs of the most politically oppressed in society rather than serving more economically secure clients who have many other options.

The movement away from public services in social work has also been influenced by a drive to enhance professional status through licensing. Ehrenreich suggests that if the drive for professionalism is a search for status that abandons social justice goals and defends professional concerns as greater than client concerns, then enhanced professional status is hardly a worthwhile goal:

Professionals must accept the judgment of their own high standards to the extent that professionalism represents a real effort to maintain competence and high ethical standards . . . a commitment to client needs even when they conflict with agency rules . . . a commitment to openness and collegiality . . . a commitment to the goal and actuality of social justice . . . needs no defense.[55]

Whether or not the professional flight from public social services continues, work with involuntary clients will go on in both public and private agencies. Paraprofessionals and nonprofessionals will be hired for positions that professionals leave. In addition, mandated clients follow professionals to private agencies under purchase-of-service agreements and the "invisible involuntary" clients pressured by formal and informal sources abound.

## Future Development and Study of Work with Involuntary Clients

This book has proposed a framework for guiding involuntary practice based on available empirical research, theory, and practice literature. Many areas of model development remain incomplete and evaluation of the effectiveness of proposed guidelines is needed before widespread adoption is advisable. On the other hand, it is hoped that the empirically derived practice guidelines presented here are an improvement over practice guided by untested theory.[56]

Intervention models have often been implemented without either adequate model development or testing of effectiveness. Hence, Thomas suggests that the history of social services is littered with the wreckage of expensive failures.[57] Intervention research, also known as developmental research, can be a useful guide in the design, testing, evaluation, and dissemination of innovative solutions to practice problems.[58] The primary product of intervention research is empirically based service approaches in the form of service manuals and program designs with knowledge development about practice as a byproduct.[59]

Intervention research has influenced the model development in this book by suggesting content areas that should be consulted to inform model development. For example, law, basic and applied research, practice theory, and ethics were explored to inform model development in chapters 1 through 7.[60] Second, basic and applied research results were summarized into generalizations to guide model development in chapters 5 and 6 following intervention research procedures.[61] Finally, implementation guidelines presented in chapters 8–13 were constructed according to intervention research recommendations.[62]

Pilot testing of the implementation guidelines is now under way with practitioners working in child welfare settings. Evaluation of training effects focuses on assessment of the degree to which practitioners learn skills and knowledge imparted in the training and how that content is implemented in actual work with clients.[63] Questions guiding the current research and suggested for future evaluation include the following.

1. *Can practitioners be trained to implement the involuntary practice guidelines as they have been described?* Intervention research can be used to test whether the model guidelines proposed here can be appro-

priately implemented in practice settings. Rather than prematurely focus on the effectiveness of the model as a whole, Rothman suggests that pilot testing in intervention research is guided by questions such as: Does the guideline work in action? How does it work in action? How effectively and efficiently does it work? Can it be easily replicated? How well do instruments work designed to monitor its implementation?[64] Reid suggests additional questions such as how often is the innovation used? How successful is it in obtaining immediate objectives? What factors distinguish successful from unsuccessful applications? To what extent does the innovation contribute to case outcome? What does the innovation look like when used? What are obstacles to its implementation?[65]

Such questions are guiding the pilot testing of the model guidelines suggested here. Rather than focus on the model as a whole, such beginning efforts will focus on the engagement phase with individual clients. Such pilot testing should reveal ways the approach can be implemented as designed, gaps in development, and adaptations needed for particular settings.

2. *Does the intervention model enhance effectiveness in reaching both interim and longer-term goals?* Pilot testing in intervention research is followed by main field testing that attempts to perfect the innovation.[66] Effectiveness becomes a more central concern as attention is devoted to the connection between the innovation and the achievement of both interim and longer-term goals. For example, it would be hypothesized that use of the socialization and contracting procedures would result in reduction of client opposition and an increase in collaboration as an interim goal. Operational measures of opposition could include a list of observable behaviors such as anger at the practitioner or the agency, silent withdrawal, and lack of compliance with agreed-upon goals and tasks. Collaboration, on the other hand, might be measured by task completion and attendance. In addition, implementation of socialization and contracting guidelines by practitioners could be monitored by examining case records or securing audiotaped samples of practice.

Longer-term goals include enhanced compliance with mandated and non-negotiable goals as well as client satisfaction with progress on problems of their own concern. Intervening variables that may affect goal completion need to be explored. For example, task complexity, number of required tasks and environmental supports may have a major effect on goal completion. Further, specific contracting strategies may have particular effects on outcome. For example, it might be hypothesized that problems approached with agreeable mandate strategies would have

### Research Agenda

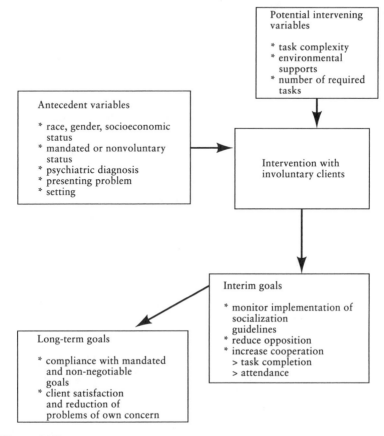

*Figure 14.7*

longer-lasting effects because of enhanced self-attribution than quid pro quo and "get rid of the pressure" strategies (see figure 14.7).

3. *How are the guidelines modified for involuntary clients with different types of problems and different sorts of settings?* Client variables such as race, gender, socioeconomic status, and psychiatric diagnosis should be studied. The amount of client prior contact with the setting or agency may be an important variable in effectiveness.

The challenge to evaluate involuntary practice by legal, ethical, and effective criteria is recommended for all work with involuntary clients, whether by the means suggested in this book or not. Since the practice guidelines suggested here may conflict with current practice with some problems such as treatment of chemical dependency, comparative effectiveness of the contracting and confrontation procedures described here might be examined with more aggressive confrontational methods. Hence, alternative intervention methods might be assessed on the basis of how effectively they meet their goals, the extent to which clients are legally protected, and the extent to which unethical paternalism is avoided.

Social welfare has always been characterized by dual commitments to compassion to alleviate suffering and protection of society.[67] Whether causes are perceived as structural or psychological, growing concern is raised by what has been referred to as the expanding underclass.[68] Prospects for the implementation of legal, ethical, effective approaches for work with involuntary clients depend in part on societal attitudes to the underclass, who make up an ever-larger proportion of persons who become involuntary. For example, the specter of high school drop-outs having children and maintaining a cycle of poverty haunts the country. Lizbeth Schorr urges an attitude of compassion *and* public self-interest rather than blaming:

High rates of violent juvenile crime, school failure, and adolescent childbearing add up to an enormous public burden, as well as widespread private pain. Our common stake in preventing these damaging outcomes of adolescence is immense. We all pay to support the unproductive and incarcerate the violent. We are all economically weakened by lost productivity. We all live in fear of crime in our homes and on the streets. We are all diminished when large numbers of parents are incapable of nurturing their dependent young, and when pervasive alienation erodes the national sense of community.[69]

Emphasis on protection of society driven by fears of violence has recently had the upper hand. This book presents the challenge of pursuing legal, ethical, and effective practice that both protects society and deals with involuntary clients as people rather than targets. Efforts to protect society by the increased used of coercive means run the risk of teaching avoidance rather than integrating changes through self-attributed change and motivational congruence.

Involuntary practitioners can avoid greasing the skids under involuntary clients by maintaining awareness of structural causes, by raising their sights beyond the interview room through advocacy of organizational and societal reform. Walz recommends a clinical activist role that would not only treat individuals and families but also identify and understand social causal factors and move to redress causes.[70] James,

Marge, and Bart, the involuntary practitioners introduced at the beginning of the chapter, might respond that such work is difficult and often not rewarded by society. That difficulty is not to be underestimated. Such work, however, offers self-respect and empowers the involuntary practitioner to become semi-voluntary.

# Training Videotapes on Strategies for Work with Involuntary Clients

Selections from several videotapes were used to illustrate the use of intervention methods in chapters 8–12.

Seven tapes are available from the University of Minnesota. For information write to: University of Minnesota, School of Social Work, Involuntary Client Training Videotapes, 400 Ford Hall, 224 Church Street SE, Minneapolis, Minnesota 55455.

1. "Nonvoluntary Client Contracting." Walter Mirk. 25 minutes. This tape depicts an actual initial session between a county mental health worker and a nonvoluntary client pressured by her public agency social worker to seek help (see chapters 8 and 9).

2. "Reconstructing with Mike: Task-Centered Case Management." Jane Macy-Lewis. 22 minutes. This tape depicts a recontracting session between a case manager for an adult, disabled, and mentally ill caseload in a small rural county, and Mike, her actual client, who is unhappy in his current group home placement. Macy-Lewis specifies the problem, reviews options and helps Mike make plans about future living arrangements in a clear model of commitment to client self-determination and normalization inherent in the task-centered approach (see chapters 9 and 10).

3. "Socialization with Probation Client." Bill Linden. 26 minutes. Contracting with a mandated client about to enter prison presents a

challenge for any practitioner. Linden demonstrates ways in which choice and respect for the client can be introduced into an otherwise highly coercive situation. Linden also demonstrates well-timed, respectful confrontation with this actual client (see chapters 8 and 9).

4. "Contracting for Home-Based Services." Ron Rooney and Betty Woodland. 52 minutes. Family-centered, home-based services are a form of in-home assistance to families usually aimed at preventing out-of-home placement. This tape depicts contracting with a mother and daughter to reduce the problems that caused the mother to seek out-of-home placement. The tape models involuntary contracting strategies, persuasion, work with a highly oppositional client (the mother), and ways of bringing the situation to a productive focus (see chapter 12).

5. "Work with Involuntary Client in Middle Phase." Cheri Brady. 22 minutes. This tape depicts a middle-phase session with a nonvoluntary client. The methods used draw heavily on the task-centered approach. The tape models methods for dealing with tasks that have not been completed, examination of obstacles, role plays, developing new tasks, appropriate middle-phase confrontation, and summarization (see chapters 10 and 11).

6. "Socialization at Chemical Dependency Intake." Dick Leonard. 40 minutes. Chemical dependency settings have been associated with strongly confrontive methods designed to challenge and crack the defenses and denial of chemically dependent clients. Leonard models two different methods to approach intake situations in chemical dependency inpatient settings. The same intake interview is hence presented twice, using different methods in each. The tape was developed with an actual client (see chapters 8 and 10).

7. "Case Management: Linking Clients with Resources." Paula Childers. 31 minutes. This tape demonstrates middle-phase skills in the task-centered approach with special emphasis on effective linkage with resources. Of special interest is sensitive modeling of empathic, effective confrontation (see chapter 11).

There are three training tapes available from the University of Wisconsin, School of Social Work, Video Resources Department, 425 Henry Mall, Madison, Wisconsin 53706:

1. "Permanency Planning: Use of the Task-Centered Model with an Adolescent toward Independent Living. The Contracting Phase." Nancy Taylor. 474-I-C. This tape demonstrates the contracting process with an actual adolescent client (see chapters 8, 9, and 10).

2. "Permanency Planning: Use of the Task-Centered Model with an

Adolescent toward Independent Living. The Middle Phase." Nancy Taylor. 475-I-C. This tape demonstrates the six-week review session in which obstacles to original contracted goals are identified and new tasks are developed with an actual adolescent client. The tape includes a model of effective, middle-phase confrontation. It also includes a follow-up interview conducted by Ron Rooney (see chapter 11).

3. "Permanency Planning: Work with the Family of an Adolescent." Vicky Arenson. 465-I-C. This tape demonstrates the transformation of a contract focused on changing the behavior of an adolescent to work on broader family concerns. The practitioner uses the task-centered method to skillfully construct a contract to which adolescent, mother, and stepfather can agree.

A training videotape is available from the University of Chicago, School of Social Service Administration, 959 E. 60th Street, Chicago, Illinois 60637.

1. "Return from Foster Care." Ron Rooney. This tape demonstrates an actual session with a client in the middle phase. Mrs. Carter wishes to regain custody of her children in foster care and is assisted through the development of in-session tasks to plan for ways she can work toward this goal.

# Notes

## 1. Introduction to Involuntary Practice

1. Charles C. Garvin and Brett A. Seabury, *Interpersonal Practice in Social Work: Processes and Procedures* (Englewood Cliffs, N.J.: Prentice-Hall, 1984), p. 83.

2. John W. Thibaut and Harold H. Kelley, *The Social Psychology of Groups* (New York: Wiley, 1959), p. 169.

3. Ibid., p. 186.

4. Judith Cingolani, "Social Conflict Perspective on Work with Involuntary Clients," *Social Work* 29 (September-October 1984):442–446.

5. Carol M. Anderson and Susan Stewart, *Mastering Resistance: A Practical Guide to Family Therapy* (New York: Guilford, 1985).

6. Martin H. Ritchie, "Counseling the Involuntary Client," *Journal of Counseling and Development* 64 (April 1986):516–518.

7. Isabel Wilkerson, "Schools of Social Work Swamped by Applicants," *New York Times*, November 9, 1987, p. A-18.

8. See, for example, Hayes A. Hatcher, *Correctional Casework and Counseling* (Englewood Cliffs, N.J.: Prentice-Hall, 1978); Clemens Bartollas, *Correctional Treatment: Theory and Practice* (Englewood Cliffs, N.J.: Prentice-Hall, 1985); George A. Harris and David Watkins, *Counseling the Involuntary and Resistant Client* (College Park, Md.: American Correctional Association, 1987).

9. Useful resources include Lloyd E. Ohlin, Herman Piven, and Donnel Pappenfort, "Major Dilemmas of the Social Worker in Probation and Parole," *National Probation and Parole Association Journal* 2 (July 1956):211–225; Eliot Studt, "Casework in the Correctional Field," *Federal Probation* 18 (Sep-

tember 1954):19–26; Peter R. Day, *Social Work and Social Control* (New York: Tavistock, 1981); Peter Raynor, *Social Work, Justice and Control* (New York: Blackwell, 1985); Ritchie, "Counseling the Involuntary Client."

10. R. J. Riordan, K. B. Matheny, and C. Harris, "Helping Counselors Minimize Counselor Reluctance," *Counselor Education and Supervision* 18 (1978):6; J. Vriend and W. Dyer, "Counseling the Reluctant Client," *Journal of Counseling Psychology* 20 (1973):240; J. B. Enright and R. Estep, "Metered Counseling for the Reluctant Client," *Psychotherapy: Theory, Research and Practice* 10 (1973):305–307; M. J. Larrabee, "Working with Reluctant Clients Through Affirmation Techniques," *Personnel and Guidance Journal* 61 (1982):105–109.

11. L. E. Patterson and S. Eisenberg, *The Counseling Process*, 3d ed. (Boston: Houghton Mifflin), p. 153; Vriend and Dyer, "Counseling the Reluctant Client," p. 240.

12. Ritchie, "Counseling the Involuntary Client"; Patterson and Eisenberg, *The Counseling Process*, p. 153; Scott Briar and Henry Miller, *Problems and Issues in Social Casework* (New York: Columbia University Press, 1971); Helen Harris Perlman, *Relationship: The Heart of Helping People* (Chicago: University of Chicago Press, 1979); Alan Pincus and Anne Minahan, *Social Work Practice: Model and Method* (Itasca, Ill.: F. E. Peacock, 1973); Abraham Alcabes and James A. Jones, "Structural Determinants of Clienthood," *Social Work* 30 (January 1985):49–55; Eileen Gambrill, *Casework: A Competency-Based Approach* (Englewood Cliffs, N.J.: Prentice-Hall, 1983).

13. Marvin R. Goldfried, "Resistance and Clinical Behavioral Therapy," in Paul Wachtel, ed., *Resistance: Psychodynamic and Behavioral Approaches* (New York: Plenum Press, 1982) pp. 108–109; Arnold A. Lazarus and Allen Fay, "Resistance or Rationalization: A Cognitive Behavioral Perspective," in Wachtel, *Resistance*, p. 123.

14. Jay Haley, *Strategies of Psychotherapy* (New York: Grune and Stratton, 1963), p. 183.

15. David Heller, *Power in Psychotherapeutic Practice* (New York: Human Sciences Press, 1985).

16. Carl Rogers, *Counseling and Psychotherapy* (Boston: Houghton Mifflin, 1942) pp. 108–114.

17. Anderson and Stewart, *Mastering Resistance*, p. 223.

18. Thomas S. Szasz, "Justifying Coercion Through Theology and Therapy," in Jeffrey K. Zeig, ed., *The Evolution of Psychotherapy* (New York: Brunner-Mazel, 1987), p. 421.

19. Neil Gilbert and Harry Specht, eds., *Handbook of the Social Services* (Englewood Cliffs, N.J.: Prentice-Hall, 1981).

20. Studt, "Casework in the Correctional Field," p. 19.

21. Bertha Capen Reynolds, *Between Client and Community* (Silver Springs, Md.: NASW Classic Series, 1982; first published in 1934).

22. Eliot Studt, "An Outline for Study of Social Authority Factors in Casework," in Shankar A. Yelaja, ed., *Authority and Social Work: Concept and Use* (Toronto: University of Toronto Press, 1971).

23. Ohlin, Piven, and Pappenfort, "Major Dilemmas," p. 216.

24. Martin Rein and Sheldon White, "Knowledge for Practice," in Gilbert and Specht, *Handbook of the Social Services,* p. 624.

25. Ibid., p. 625.

26. Yeheskel Hasenfeld, "Power in Social Work Practice," *Social Service Review* 61(3) (September 1987):469–483.

27. Rein and White, "Knowledge for Practice," p. 626.

28. Henry Miller, "Value Dilemmas in Social Casework," *Social Work* 13 (January 1968):33.

29. Ibid., pp. 31–32.

30. Irving Piliavin, "Restructuring the Provision of Social Services," *Social Work* 13 (January 1968):34–41.

31. C. D. Cowger and C. R. Atherton, "Social Control: A Rationale for Social Welfare," *Social Work* 19 (1974):456–462.

32. Ibid., p. 461.

33. Apparently others may not agree that the debate is over. The theme for the 1988 Annual Program Meeting of the Council on Social Work Education in Atlanta was "Social Control and Social Enhancement: Do They Conflict?"

34. Day, *Social Work and Social Control,* pp. 212–215.

35. Briar and Miller, *Problems and Issues;* Perlman, *Relationship;* Pincus and Minahan, *Social Work Practice;* Gambrill, *Casework,* p. 13.

36. William J. Reid, *The Task-Centered System* (New York: Columbia University Press, 1978).

37. Ronald L. Simons and Stephen M. Aigner, *Practice Principles: A Problem-Solving Approach to Social Work* (New York: Macmillan, 1985), p. 11.

38. Allison D. Murdach, "Bargaining and Persuasion with Non- Voluntary Clients," *Social Work* 25(6) (November 1980):458.

39. Cingolani, "Social Conflict Perspective," p. 442.

40. Ibid.

41. See Carl Hartman, *Sexual Expression: A Manual for Trainers* (New York: Human Sciences Press, 1981), p. 4.

42. Tom Walz, "The Mission of Social Work Revisited: An Agenda for the 1990's," William R. Hodson Lecture, School of Social Work, University of Minnesota, May 4, 1989.

43. Gisela Konopka, "The Social Group Work Method: Its Use in the Correctional Field," *Federal Probation* 14 (1950):25–30; Kenneth L. Pray, "The Place of Social Casework in the Treatment of Delinquency," *Social Service Review* 19(2) (June 1945):235–248.

44. Haley, *Strategies of Psychotherapy.*

45. Carel Germain and Alex Gitterman, *The Life Model of Social Work Practice* (New York: Columbia University Press, 1980); Pincus and Minahan, *Social Work Practice;* Perlman, *Relationship;* F. J. Turner, *Social Work Treatment* (New York: Free Press, 1974); Mary E. Woods and Florence Hollis, *Casework: A Psychosocial Therapy,* 4th ed. (New York: McGraw-Hill, 1990).

46. William Schwartz, "Between Client and System," in R. W. Roberts and

H. Northen, eds., *Theories of Social Work with Groups* (New York: Columbia University Press, 1976); Ruth E. Smalley, "The Functional Approach to Casework Practice," in R. E. Roberts and R. H. Nee, eds., *Theories of Social Casework* (Chicago: University of Chicago Press, 1970); Germain and Gitterman, *The Life Model of Social Work Practice.*

47. Elizabeth D. Hutchison, "Use of Authority in Direct Social Work Practice with Mandated Clients," *Social Service Review* 61 (December 1987):581–598.

48. Elizabeth Howe, "Public Professions and the Private Model of Professionalism," *Social Work* 25(3) (1980):182; John P. Flynn, "Social Control Components in Public Welfare and Social Work Systems," *Public Welfare* 32 (Summer 1973):34–38; Reynolds, *Between Client and Community.*

49. Frederic G. Reamer, "Conflicts of Professional Duty in Social Work," *Social Casework* 63 (1982):579–585.

50. Charles H. Shireman and Frederic G. Reamer, *Rehabilitating Juvenile Justice* (New York: Columbia University Press, 1986); Phyllida Parsloe, "Social Work and the Justice Model," *British Journal of Social Work* 6(1) (1976):71–90; Brooke E. Spiro, "The Future Course of Corrections," *Social Work* 23 (July 1978):315–320; Thomas P. Brennan, Amy E. Gedrich, Susan E. Jacoby, Michael J. Tardy, and Katherine B. Tyson, "Forensic Social Work: Practice and Vision," *Social Work* 67(6) (June 1986):340–350.

51. Cingolani, "Social Conflict Perspective," p. 43.

52. See reference to *Kaimowitz v. Michigan Department of Mental Health,* 42 U.S.L., week 263 (Michigan Cir. Ct., Wayne Cty., July 10, 1973) quoted in Reed Martin, "Legal Issues in Preserving Client Rights," in Gerald T. Hannah, Walter P. Christian, and Hewitt B. Clark, eds., *Preservation of Client Rights: A Handbook for Practitioners Providing Therapeutic, Educational and Rehabilitative Services* (New York: Free Press, 1981), pp. 3–13.

53. Rollo May, *Power and Innocence* (New York: W. W. Norton, 1972).

54. *Rouse v. Cameron,* 373 F.2d. 451 (D.C. Cir. 1966); *Wyatt v. Stickney,* 324 F. Supp. 781 (M.D. Ala. 1971); *O'Connor v. Donaldson,* 422 U.S. 563, 45 L.Ed.2d. 396, 1975).

## 2. The Involuntary Transaction

1. Brett A. Seabury, "The Contract: Uses, Abuses and Limitations," *Social Work* 21 (January 1976):16–21.

2. See Cingolani, "Social Conflict Perspective," pp. 442–446. See also Murdach, "Bargaining and Persuasion," pp. 458–461 and Hutchison, "Use of Authority," pp. 581–598.

3. Germain and Gitterman, *Life Model of Social Work Practice,* pp. 10–12.

4. Hasenfeld, "Power in Social Work Practice," pp. 472–473.

5. Ibid.

6. Laura Epstein, *Helping People: The Task-Centered Approach* (Columbus, Oh.: Charles Merrill, 1988). See also Donald Brieland and John Lemmon, *Social Work and the Law* (St. Paul, Minn.: West Publishing, 1977).

7. Graeme Newman, *Comparative Deviance: Perception and Law in Six Cultures* (New York: Elsevier, 1976).

8. Craig B. Little, *Understanding Deviance and Control: Theory, Research and Social Policy* (Itasca, Ill.: F. E. Peacock, 1983).

9. Jeffrey Edleson, "Working with Men Who Batter," *Social Work* 29(3) (May-June 1984):237–242.

10. Raymond M. Berger, "Homosexuality: Gay Men," in *The Encyclopedia of Social Work*, 18th ed. (Silver Springs, Maryland: National Association of Social Workers, 1987), p. 801. See also R. Bayer, *Homosexuality and American Psychiatry: The Politics of Diagnosis* (New York: Basic Books, 1981).

11. Aaron T. Beck, *Cognitive Therapy and the Emotional Disorders* (New York: International University Press, 1976). See also Aaron T. Beck, *Cognitive Therapy of Depression* (New York: Guilford Press, 1979).

12. Hasenfeld, "Power in Social Work Practice."

13. Barbara Bryant Solomon, "Value Issues in Working with Minority Clients," in Aaron Rosenblatt and Diana Waldfogel, eds., *Handbook of Clinical Social Work* (San Francisco: Jossey-Bass, 1983), pp. 866–887. See also Jerald Shapiro, "Commitment to Disenfranchised Clients," in Rosenblatt and Waldfogel, *Handbook of Clinical Social Work*, pp. 888–903..

14. D. C. McGuire, *A New American Justice* (Garden City, N.Y.: Doubleday, 1980).

15. See, for example, Mimi Abramovitz, *Regulating the Lives of Women: Social Welfare Policy from Colonial Times to the Present* (Boston: South End Press, 1988); June Gary Hopps, "Oppression Based on Color," *Social Work* 27(1) (1982):3–5; Edwin M. Schur, *Labelling Women Deviant* (New York: Random House, 1984); Walter P. Christian, Hewitt B. Clark, and David E. Luke, "Client Rights in Clinical Counseling Services for Children," in Gerald T. Hannah, Walter P. Christian, and Hewitt B. Clark, eds., *Preservation of Client Rights: A Handbook for Practitioners Providing Therapeutic, Educational and Rehabilitative Services* (New York: Free Press, 1981), pp. 19–41; Berger, "Homosexuality"; Natalie Jane Woodman, "Homosexuality: Lesbian Women," in *Encyclopedia of Socal Work*, pp. 805–812; William J. Wilson, "The Underclass: Issues, Perspectives and Public Policy. *Annals of the American Academy of Political and Social Sciences* 501 (January 1989):182–192.

16. June Gary-Hopps, "Minorities of Color," in *Encyclopedia of Social Work*, pp. 161–171.

17. M. M. Gordon, *Assimilation in American Life*. (New York: Oxford University Press, 1964).

18. Abramovitz, *Regulating the Lives of Women*, p. 1.

19. Linda E. Jones, "Women," in *Encyclopedia of Social Work*, p. 877.

20. See Abramovitz, *Regulating the Lives of Women*, and Wilson, "The Underclass."

21. See Gary-Hopps, "Minorities of Color," and T. B. Edsall, *The New Politics of Inequality*. (New York: W. W. Norton, 1984).

22. John F. Longres, *Human Behavior in the Social Environment*. (Itasca, Ill.: F. E. Peacock, 1990), p. 157.

23. Ibid., p. 169, and C. Wright Mills, *The Sociological Imagination.* (New York: Penguin, 1971). See also William Ryan, *Blaming the Victim.* (New York: Vintage, 1971).

24. Wynetta Devore and Elfriede G. Schlesinger, "Ethnic-Sensitive Practice," in *Encyclopedia of Social Work,* p. 515; Wynetta Devore and Elfriede G. Schlesinger, *Ethnic-Sensitive Practice,* 2d ed. (Columbus, Oh.: Charles Merrill, 1987).

25. R. Weatherly and M. Lipsky, "Street Level Bureaucrats and Institutionalized Innovations: Implementing Special Education Reform," *Harvard Educational Review* 47(2) (1977):171–197.

26. Samuel O. Miller, "Practice in Cross-Cultural Settings," in Rosenblatt and Waldfogel, *Handbook of Clinical Social Work,* p. 497.

27. Hasenfeld, "Power in Social Work Practice," p. 477.

28. See Margaret Cooke and David Kipnis, "Influence Tactics in Psychotherapy," *Journal of Consulting and Clinical Psychology* 54(1) (1986):22–26.

29. Richard L. Emerson, "Power-Dependency Relations," *American Sociological Review* 27 (1962):31–41.

30. See Abramovitz, *Regulating the Lives of Women,* and Hasenfeld, "Power in Social Work Practice."

31. Adapted from Thibaut and Kelley, *The Social Psychology of Groups,* pp. 173–186.

32. Ibid.

33. Laura Epstein, *Talking and Listening: A Guide to Interviewing* (Columbus, Oh.: Charles Merrill, 1985), p. 248.

34. Studt, "An Outline for Study of Social Authority Factors in Casework," p. 233.

35. Arlene D. Jackson and Michael J. Dunne, "Permanency Planning in Foster Care with the Ambivalent Parent," in Anthony N. Maluccio and Paula A. Sinanoglu, eds., *The Challenge of Partnership: Working with Parents of Children in Foster Care* (New York: Child Welfare League of America, 1980).

36. Eliot Studt, "Worker-Client Authority Relationships in Social Work," in Shankar A. Yelaja, ed., *Authority and Social Work: Concept and Use* (Toronto: University of Toronto Press, 1971).

37. Thibaut and Kelley, *The Social Psychology of Groups.*

38. Ibid.

39. According to *Webster's New Collegiate Dictionary* (Springfield, Mass.: Merriam Company, 1979).

40. Hasenfeld, "Power in Social Work Practice"; David Kipnis, "Does Power Corrupt?" *Journal of Personality and Social Psychology* 24(1) (1972):33–41.

41. Hutchison, "Use of Authority"; Garvin and Seabury, *Interpersonal Practice in Social Work.*

42. Epstein, *Helping People.*

43. Hutchison, "Use of Authority," p. 583.

44. Ibid.

45. Frederic G. Reamer, *Ethical Dilemmas in Social Services* (New York: Columbia University Press, 1982).

46. Garvin and Seabury, *Interpersonal Practice in Social Work,* p. 84.

47. Hasenfeld, "Power in Social Work Practice," p. 471.

48. Beulah R. Compton and Burt Galaway, *Social Work Processes*, 4th ed. (Belmont, Cal.: Wadsworth, 1989), pp. 177–188.

49. Hasenfeld, "Power in Social Work Practice," p. 475.

50. Compton and Galaway, *Social Work Processes*, pp. 605–606.

51. William J. Reid, *Family Problem Solving* (New York: Columbia University Press, 1985), p. 34.

52. Ibid.

53. See Abramovitz, *Regulating the Lives of Women.* See also Judith M. Davidoff, "Learnfare: What's to be Learned? Is it Fair? *Isthmus* 15(2) (June 22–28, 1990):1, 8, 9; and Ellen Goodman, "Punishing Parents for Kids' Sins," *Minneapolis Star-Tribune*, May 22, 1990, p. 14a.

54. Compton and Galaway, *Social Work Processes*, p. 76; Thibaut and Kelley, *The Social Psychology of Groups*, p. 169.

55. See Sandra M. Stehno, "Family-Centered Child Welfare Services: New Life for a Historic Idea," *Child Welfare* 65 (May/June 1986):231–240; Kristine E. Nelson, Miriam J. Landsman, and Wendy Deutelbaum, "Three Models of Family-Centered Placement Prevention Services," *Child Welfare* 69 (January-February 1990):3–21.

56. Reid, *The Task-Centered System.*

57. Alan Keith-Lucas, *Giving and Taking Help* (Chapel Hill: University of North Carolina Press, 1972), p. 20.

58. Hasenfeld, "Power in Social Work Practice."

59. John E. Mayer and Noel Timms, "Clash in Perspective between Worker and Client," *Social Casework* 50 (1969):32–40; Anthony N. Maluccio, *Learning from Clients* (New York: Free Press, 1979).

60. David Showalter and Charlotte Williams Jones, "Marital and Family Counseling in Prisons," *Social Work* 25 (May 1980):224–228.

61. Sol L. Garfield, "Research on Client Variables in Psychotherapy," in Sol L. Garfield and Allen E. Bergin, eds., *Handbook of Psychotherapy and Behavior Change*, 3d ed. (New York: John Wiley, 1986), pp. 213–256; Lynn Videka-Sherman, *Harriett M. Bartlett Practice Effectiveness Project: Report to NASW Board of Directors* (Washington, D.C.: NASW, 1985): Videka-Sherman found that 27 percent of the studies she reviewed had no identifying client information. See also Lynn Videka-Sherman, "Meta-Analysis of Research on Social Work Practice in Mental Health," *Social Work* 33(4) (July-August 1988):325–337.

62. Videka-Sherman, *Bartlett Practice Effectiveness Project*, pp. 27–28, 39.

## 3. The Legal Foundation for Work with Involuntary Clients

1. Donald Brieland and Samuel Goldfarb, "Legal Issues and Legal Services," in *Encyclopedia of Social Work*, pp. 30–32.

2. Selected from a series of seven articles in the *New York Times* by Josh Barbanel, "Woman Battles Koch's Program for Mentally Ill," November 2, 1987; "Hospitalization of Homeless Challenged," November 3, 1987; "Forcibly

Hospitalized Woman Identified," November 5, 1987; "In Hospital Courtroom, Plea for Freedom," November 6, 1987; "Four Women Reach Out to Their Homeless Sister," November 7, 1987; "Koch's Plan Faces a Test," November 11, 1987; "Homeless Woman Sent to Hospital under Koch Plan is Ordered Freed," November 13, 1987.

3. Judge Lippman noted in his decision that the standards of city homeless shelters were so poor that the decision *not* to live in them might be more an indication of her sanity than insanity.

4. P. S. Appelbaum and T. G. Gotheil, "Rotting with Their Rights On: Constitutional Theory and Clinical Reality in Due Process by Psychiatric Patients," *Bulletin of the American Academy of Psychiatry and Law* 7 (1977):306–315.

5. Barbanel, "Four Women."

6. Joseph E. Hasazi, Richard C. Surles, and Gerald T. Hannah, "Client Rights in Psychiatric Facilities," in Gerald T. Hannah, Walter P. Christian, and Hewitt B. Clark, eds., *Preservation of Client Rights: A Handbook for Practitioners Providing Therapeutic, Educational and Rehabilitative Services* (New York: Free Press, 1981), pp. 365–381; Kenneth Culp Davis, *Discretionary Justice: A Preliminary Inquiry* (Urbana: University of Illinois Press, 1971).

7. Robert L. Sadoff, *Legal Issues in the Care of Psychiatric Patients: A Guide for the Mental Health Professional* (New York: Springer, 1982), p. 109.

8. Donald T. Dickson, "Law in Social Work: Impact of Due Process," *Social Work* 21 (July 1976):276.

9. Z. M. Lebensohn, "Defensive Psychiatry or How to Treat the Mentally Ill without Being a Lawyer," in W. E. Barton and C. J. Sanborn, eds., *Law and the Mental Health Professions* (New York: International Universities Press, 1978), p. 29.

10. Gary G. Melton, John Petrala, Norman G. Poythress, and Christopher Slobogin, *Psychological Evaluations for the Courts* (New York: Guilford, 1987), pp. 4–5.

11. Reed Martin, "Legal Issues in Preserving Client Rights," in Hannah, Christian, and Clark, *Preservation of Client Rights*, p. 4.

12. *NASW Code of Ethics* (Silver Springs, Md.: National Association of Social Workers, 1980).

13. Frederic G. Reamer, "Conflicts of Professional Duty in Social Work," *Social Casework* 63 (1982):579–585.

14. Chapter 1 suggested that many practitioners resolve these dilemmas by placing the interests of the agency and the profession ahead of client wishes. See Andrew Billingsley, "Bureaucratic and Professional Orientation Patterns in Social Casework," *Social Service Review* 38 (December 1964):400–407.

15. Martin, "Legal Issues in Preserving Client Rights," p .9.

16. Joseph J. Senna, "Changes in Due Process of Law," *Social Work* 19 (May 1974):319–324.

17. Sadoff, *Legal Issues in the Care of Psychiatric Patients*, p. 27; Dickson, "Law in Social Work," p. 274.

18. Andrea Saltzman and Kathleen Proch, *Law in Social Work Practice* (Chicago: Nelson-Hall, 1990), pp. 317–318.

19. Frederic G. Reamer, "Informed Consent in Social Work," *Social Work* 32 (September-October 1987):425.

20. Fay A. Rozovsky, *Consent to Treatment: A Practical Guide* (Boston: Little, Brown, 1987), pp. xxxv, 3.

21. Reamer, "Informed Consent in Social Work," p. 426.

22. Ibid., p. 425.

23. Melton et al., *Psychological Evaluations for the Courts*, p. 255.

24. Saltzman and Proch, *Law in Social Work Practice*, p. 312.

25. See *Kaimowitz v. Michigan Department of Mental Health*, 42 U.S.L. Week 2063 (Mich. Cir. Ct., Wayne Cty., July 10, 1973); Hasazi, Surles, and Hannah, "Client Rights in Psychiatric Facilities," p. 375; Saltzman and Proch, *Law in Social Work Practice*, p. 364; Melton et al., *Psychological Evaluations for the Courts*, pp. 245–269.

26. *Ref V. Weinberger*, 372 F. Supp., 1196, DDC 1974.

27. Reamer, "Informed Consent in Social Work," p. 427.

28. Ibid.

29. See Charles W. Lidz, Alan Meisel, Eviatar Zerubavel, Mary Carter, Regina M. Sestak, and Loren H. Roth, *Informed Consent: A Study of Decision Making in Psychiatry* (New York: Guilford, 1984), pp. 11–12.

30. Melton et al., *Psychological Evaluations for the Courts*, p. 256.

31. Saltzman and Proch, *Law in Social Work Practice*, p. 392.

32. Sadoff, *Legal Issues in the Care of Psychiatric Patients*, p. 6; Saltzman and Proch, *Law in Social Work Practice*, p. 392.

33. Sadoff, *Legal Issues in the Care of Psychiatric Patients*, p. 19.

34. *Tarasoff v. the Regents of the University of California*, 17 Cal. 3d 425, 131 Cal. Rptr. 14, 551 P. 2nd 334 (1976).

35. Melton, et al., *Psychological Evaluations for the Courts*, pp. 51–52.

36. Ibid., 50.

37. Saltzman and Proch, *Law in Social Work Practice*, p. 415.

38. Ibid., p. 422.

39. Ibid., pp. 411–412; Brieland and Goldfarb, "Legal Issues and Legal Services"; Sadoff, *Legal Issues in the Care of Psychiatric Patients*, p. 62.

40. Saltzman and Proch, *Law in Social Work Practice*, p. 416.

41. Ibid., p. 423. See also Douglas Besharov, *The Vulnerable Social Worker* (Silver Springs, Md.: National Association of Social Workers, 1985).

42. Saltzman and Proch, *Law in Social Work Practice*, pp. 423–430.

43. Three major secondary sources form the basis of most of the following review: Saltzman and Proch, *Law in Social Work Practice*; Melton et al., *Psychological Evaluations for the Courts*; Hannah, Christian, and Clark, *Preservation of Client Rights*.

44. Saltzman and Proch, *Law in Social Work Practice*, p. 312; Melton et al., *Psychological Evaluations for the Courts*, pp. 211–212.

45. *O'Connor v. Donaldson*, 422 U.S. 563 (1971).

46. Saltzman and Proch, *Law in Social Work Practice,* p. 314.

47. *Addington v. Texas,* 441 U.S. 418 (1979).

48. Melton et al., *Psychological Evaluations for the Courts.*

49. Barbanel, "Woman Battles Koch's Program for Mentally Ill."

50. Saltzman and Proch, *Law in Social Work Practice,* p. 314.

51. John S. Wodarski, "Legal Requisites for Social Work Practice," *Clinical Social Work Journal* 8(2) (1980):94–97.

52. See *Lake v. Cameron,* 362 F.2d 657 (D.C. Cir. 1966); see also *Lessard v. Schmidt,* 349 F. Supp. 1078 (E.D. Wisc. 1972).

53. *Rouse v. Cameron,* 373 F. 2d 451 (D.C. Cir. 1966).

54. *Johnson v. Solomon,* 484 F. Supp. 278 (1979).

55. See *Wyatt v. Stickney,* 344 F. Supp. 373 (M.D. Ala. 1972). See also Charles S. Prigmore and Paul R. Davis, "*Wyatt v. Stickney:* Rights of the Committed," *Social Work* (July 1973):10–18; Frank R. Johnson, "Court Decisions in the Social Services," *Social Work* 20 (September 1975):343–347; Wodarski, "Legal Requisites for Social Work Practice," p. 93.

56. Johnson, "Court Decisions in the Social Services"; Dickson, "Law in Social Work"; Wodarski, "Legal Requisites for Social Work Practice," p. 92.

57. Saltzman and Proch, *Law in Social Work Practice,* p. 361.

58. Melton et al., *Psychological Evaluations for the Courts,* p. 253.

59. *Jarvis v. Levine,* Minnesota Supreme Court, C2-86-1633.

60. Glen Warchol, "A Disturbed System," *Twin Cities Reader* (November 30-December 6, 1988), p. 9.

61. Saltzman and Proch, *Law in Social Work Practice,* p. 362.

62. Ibid., p. 342.

63. Ibid., p. 394.

64. Ibid., pp. 346–347.

65. K. Anthony Edwards and Jan Sheldon-Wildgen, "Providing Nursing Home Residents' Rights," in Hannah, Christian, and Clark, *Preservation of Client Rights,* p. 320.

66. Ibid., p. 321.

67. Omnibus Budget Reconciliation Act of 1987, pp. 100–203.

68. Edward J. Callahan and Richard A. Rowsom, "Extending Client Rights to Narcotics Addicts," in Hannah, Christian, and Clark, *Preservation of Client Rights,* p. 190.

69. Ibid., p. 195. See also J. T. Ziegenfuss and G. Gaughan-Fisher, "Alternatives to Present Programs and Client Civil Rights: A Question," *Contemporary Drug Problems* (1976):207–217.

70. Melton et al., *Psychological Evaluations for the Courts,* p. 54.

71. Steve Goldberg, "Should We Force Drug Abusers into Treatment?" *Lawrence (Mass.) Eagle Tribune,* August 22, 1989, p. 44.

72. Senna, "Changes in Due Process of Law," p. 320; Dickson, "Law in Social Work," p. 275.

73. Brieland and Goldfarb, "Legal Issues and Legal Services," p. 31; Theodore J. Stein, "The Vulnerability of Child Welfare Agencies to Class-Action Suits," *Social Service Review* 61 (December 1987):636–654.

74. J. Goldstein, A. Freud, and A. D. Solnit, *Beyond the Best Interests of the Child* (New York: Free Press, 1973).

75. Barbara S. Kuehn and Edward R. Christopherson, "Preserving the Rights of Clients in Child Abuse and Neglect," in Hannah, Christian, and Clark, *Preservation of Client Rights,* p. 54.

76. Indian Child Welfare Act 25 U.S.C. §1901 et seq.

77. Richard T. Crow, "The Rights and Treatment of Prisoners," in Hannah, Christian, and Clark, *Preservation of Client Rights,* pp. 383–384.

78. Ibid., p. 385.

79. See the decision of Judge Bazelon in *Rouse v. Cameron,* 373 F.2 451 (D.C. Cir. 1966); Rudolph Alexander, Jr., "The Right to Treatment in Mental and Correctional Institutions," *Social Work* 34(2) (1989): 109–114.

80. *Holt v. Sarver,* 309 F. Supp. 36c (E.P. 1980), 380.

81. *Hudson v. Palmer,* 468 U.S. 517 (1984).

82. Senna, "Changes in Due Process of Law," p. 320.

83. Brieland and Goldfarb, "Legal Issues and Legal Serivces."

84. Saltzman and Proch, *Law in Social Work Practice,* p. 162.

85. *In re. Gault,* 387 U.S. 1 (1967).

86. Walter P. Christian, Hewitt B. Clark, and David E. Luke, "Client Rights in Clinical Counseling Services for Children," in Hannah, Christian, and Clark, *Preservation of Client Rights,* pp. 19–41.

87. *Parham v. J. R.,* 442 US 584 (1979).

88. Saltzman and Proch, *Law in Social Work Practice,* p. 321.

89. G. P. Koocher, *Childrens' Rights and the Mental Health Professions* (New York: Wiley, 1976).

90. Judith V. Becker and Gene G. Abel, "The Rights and Treatment of the Sexually Abused Client," in Hannah, Christian, and Clark, *Preservation of Client Rights,* pp. 136–156.

91. Christian, Clark, and Luke, "Client Rights in Clinical Counseling Services for Children," p. 23.

92. Ibid., p. 22.

93. Ibid., p. 24.

94. Saltzman and Proch, *Law in Social Work Practice,* pp. 312, 359, 362, 390, 394.

95. Martin, "Legal Issues in Preserving Client Rights," p. 6.

96. See *Kaimowitz v. Michigan Department of Mental Health,* 42 U.S.L. Week 2063 (Mich. Cir. Ct., Wayne Cty., July 10, 1973).

97. See *Shelton,* 364, U.S. 479 (1960), and *Wyatt v. Stickney,* 344 F. Supp. 373 (M.D. Ala. 1972).

98. Sadoff, *Legal Issues in the Care of Psychiatric Patients,* p. 109; Wodarski, "Legal Requisites for Social Work Practice."

99. Dickson, "Law in Social Work."

100. Walter E. Barton and Gail M. Barton, *Ethics and Law in Mental Health Administration* (Morris Falk Foundation, 1984).

101. Sadoff, *Legal Issues in the Care of Psychiatric Patients.*

102. Barton and Barton, *Ethics and Law in Mental Health Administration.*
103. Martin, "Legal Issues in Preserving Client Rights," p. 9.

## 4. *The Ethical Foundation for Work with Involuntary Clients*

1. Frederic G. Reamer, *Ethical Dilemmas in Social Services* (New York: Columbia University Press, 1982).

2. Alan Keith-Lucas, "Ethics in Social Work," in *Encyclopedia of Social Work,* pp. 350–355.

3. Frederic G. Reamer, "The Concept of Paternalism in Social Work," *Social Service Review* 57 (June 1983):255; Marcia Abramson, "The Autonomy-Paternalism Dilemma in Social Work Practice," *Social Casework* 66 (1985):388; Ann Wieck and Loren Pope, "Knowing What's Best: A New Look at Self-Determination," *Social Casework* 69(1) (1988):10–16.

4. Saul Bernstein, "Self-Determination: King or Citizen of the Realm of Values," *Social Work* 5(1) (1960):3–8.

5. Frederic G. Reamer, "Conflicts of Professional Duty in Social Work," *Social Casework* 63 (1982):579–585; Keith-Lucas, "Ethics in Social Work," p. 350. Howe suggests that this problem of conflicting loyalties is particularly characteristic of public professions such as social work which have a private model of responsibility to individual clients yet often receive public monies and are employed by the public. Elizabeth Howe, "Public Professions and the Private Model of Professionalism," *Social Work* 25(3) (1980):179–191.

6. John Stuart Mill, "On Liberty," in Samuel Gorovitz, ed., *Mill: Utilitarianism* (Indianapolis: Bobbs-Merrill, 1971).

7. F. E. McDermott, ed., *Self-Determination in Social Work* (London: Routledge and Kegan Paul, 1975).

8. Mill, "On Liberty"; Delores B. Reid, "Child Protective Services. What Happens When Our Values Conflict with Those of Our Clients?" *Practice Digest* 6(4) (1984)15–16.

9. Reamer, "Paternalism in Social Work"; Frank Loewenberg and Ralph Dolgoff, *Ethical Decisions for Social Work Practice* (Itasca, Ill.: F. E. Peacock, 1982).

10. Felix P. Biestek, "The Principle of Client Self-Determination," *Social Casework* 32 (November 1951):369–375; Bernstein, "Self-Determination," pp. 3–8.

11. McDermott, *Self-Determination in Social Work,* p. 118.

12. Ibid., p. 131.

13. Bernstein, "Self-Determination," pp. 3–8.

14. Reamer, "Paternalism in Social Work," pp. 254–256.

15. Ibid., pp. 257–259.

16. Abramson, "Autonomy-Paternalism Dilemma," p. 390.

17. Reamer, "Paternalism in Social Work," p. 261.

18. Reamer, *Ethical Dilemmas in Social Services*, p. 262; Reamer, "Paternalism in Social Work," pp. 261–263.

19. Ibid., p. 263.

20. Ibid., p. 265.

21. Ibid., pp. 265–267.

22. Ibid., p. 268; Abramson, "Autonomy-Paternalism Dilemma," p. 391.

23. Ibid.

24. Reamer, "Paternalism in Social Work," p. 268.

25. Frederic G. Reamer, "Ethics Committees in Social Work," *Social Work* 32 (May-June 1987):188–192.

26. Reamer, *Ethical Dilemmas in Social Services*, p. 78; Reamer, "Paternalism in Social Work," p. 266.

27. Ibid., p. 265; Reamer, *Ethical Dilemmas in Social Services*, p. 96.

28. Reamer, "Paternalism in Social Work," p. 268.

29. Gerald Corey, Marianne Schneider Corey, and Patrick Callanan, *Professional and Ethical Issues in Counseling and Psychotherapy* (Monterey, Calif.: Brooks-Cole, 1979); Dean H. Hepworth and Jo Ann Larsen, *Direct Social Work Practice: Theory and Skills*, 3d ed. (Belmont, Calif.: Wadsworth, 1990).

30. Keith-Lucas, "Ethics in Social Work," pp. 350–355.

31. Ronald L. Simons and Stephen M. Aigner, *Practice Principles: A Problem-Solving Approach to Social Work* (New York: Macmillan, 1985).

32. Brett A. Seabury, "Negotiating Sound Contracts with Clients," *Public Welfare* 38 (Spring 1979):33–38.

33. Keith-Lucas, "Ethics in Social Work," p. 351; Peter Raynor, *Social Work, Justice and Control* (New York: Basil Blackwell, 1985); Harold Lewis, "Morality and the Politics of Practice," *Social Casework* 53 (July 1972):407; Gambrill, *Casework*, p. 381.

34. Alan Keith-Lucas, "Philosophies of Public Service," *Public Welfare* 31 (Spring 1973):23.

35. Wodarski, "Legal Requisites for Social Work Practice," pp. 94–97.

36. Keith-Lucas, "Ethics in Social Work," p. 350.

37. Corey, Corey and Callanan, *Professional and Ethical Issues*, p. 140.

38. Keith-Lucas, "Ethics in Social Work," p. 334.

39. Arnold P. Goldstein, Kenneth Heller, and Lee B. Sechrest, *Psychotherapy and the Psychology of Behavior Change* (New York: John Wiley, 1966); Jay Haley, *Strategies of Psychotherapy* (New York: Grune and Stratton, 1963).

40. Colin Whittington, "Self-Determination Re-Examined," *British Journal of Social Work* 1 (Autumn 1971):293–303.

41. George A. Harris and David Watkins, *Counseling the Involuntary and Resistant Client* (College Park, Md.: American Corectional Association, 1987).

42. Sharon S. Brehm and Timothy W. Smith, "Social Psychological Approaches to Psychotherapy and Behavior Change," in Garfield and Bergin, *Handbook of Psychotherapy and Behavior Change*, pp. 69–115; Corey, Corey, and Callanan, *Professional and Ethical Issues*, p. 142.

43. Keith-Lucas, "Ethics in Social Work," p. 354; Lewis, "Morality and the

Politics of Practice," p. 411; Howe, "Public Professions and the Private Model of Professionalism," p. 190; Willard C. Richan, *Social Work: The Unloved Profession* (New York: Franklin Watts, 1973); Hasenfeld, "Power in Social Work Practice," pp. 469–483.

44. Margaret L. Rhodes, *Ethical Dilemmas in Social Work Practice* (Boston: Routledge and Kegan Paul, 1986); Arnold Panitch, "Advocacy in Practice," *Social Work* 19 (1979):326–332.

45. Stuart Rees and Fred Edwards, "Power and Influence in Social Work," *Social Work Today* 3 (January 1973):17–20.

46. Keith-Lucas, "Ethics in Social Work," p. 353.

47. Gambrill, *Casework*, p. 381. See also R. Martin, *Legal Challenges to Behavior Modification: Trends in Schools Corrections and Mental Health* (Champaign, Ill.: Research Press, 1975). Criteria such as those by Theodore J. Stein and Tina L. Rzepnicki, *Decision Making at Child Welfare Intake: A Handbook for Practitioners* (New York: Child Welfare League of America, 1983), can be useful here in providing clear criteria for intrusion and nonintrusion.

48. Loewenberg and Dolgoff, *Ethical Decisions for Social Work Practice*, p. 17; Simons and Aigner, *Practice Principles*, p. 23.

49. Reamer, "Paternalism in Social Work"; Loewenberg and Dolgoff, *Ethical Decisions for Social Work Practice*.

50. Minnesota Statute 626.55.

51. "Risk Criteria Indicators," Hennepin County Child Protection Program, 1973.

52. Stein and Rzepnicki, *Decision Making at Child Welfare Intake*.

53. Minnesota Statute 626.55.

54. Seymour L. Halleck, "The Impact of Professional Dishonesty on Behavior of Disturbed Adolescents. *Social Work* 8 (April 1963):49–57; Studt, "Worker-Client Authority Relationships in Social Work."

55. Lewis, "Morality and the Politics of Practice," p. 407.

56. Gambrill, *Casework*, p. 381.

57. Ronald H. Rooney, "Socialization Strategies for Involuntary Clients," *Social Casework* 69 (March 1988):131–140.

58. Keith-Lucas, "Philosophies of Public Service"; Studt, "Worker-Client Authority Relationships in Social Work"; Loewenberg and Dolgoff, *Ethical Decisions for Social Work Practice*.

59. Simons and Aigner, *Practice Principles*, p. 23.

60. Studt, "Worker-Client Authority Relationships in Social Work."

61. Frederic Reamer, personal communication, 1986.

62. Reamer, *Ethical Dilemmas in Social Services*, p. 110.

63. Gary Heymann, "Mandated Child Abuse Reporting and the Confidentiality Privilege," in Louis Everstine and Diana Sullivan Everstine, eds., *Psychotherapy and the Law* (New York: Grune and Stratton, 1986), p. 145.

64. Reamer, *Ethical Dilemmas in Social Services*, pp. 78–79.

65. Hutchison, "Use of Authority"; Reamer, "Paternalism in Social Work."

66. Kay Harris, "On Corrections," *Practice Digest* 6(4) (Spring 1984):13.

67. Sally Gadow, "Advocacy: An Ethical Model for Assisting Patients with Treatment Decisions," in Cynthia Wong and Judith Swazley, eds., *Dilemmas of Dying* (Boston: G. K. Hall, 1981), pp. 135–142.

68. David Soyer, "The Right to Fail," *Social Work* 8(3) (July 1963):72.

69. This case study is adapted from Reamer, *Ethical Dilemmas in Social Services*, pp. 114–123.

70. Carleton Pilseker, "Values: A Problem for Everyone," *Social Work* 23 (1978):54–57; Dale G. Hardman, "Not with My Daughter, You Don't!" *Social Work* 20(4) (July 1975):278—285; Reamer, "Paternalism in Social Work."

71. Stanley Benn, "Freedom and Persuasion," in McDermott, *Self-Determination in Social Work*, pp. 224–239.

72. Ronald Paul Salzberger, "Casework and a Client's Right to Self-Determination," *Social Work* 24 (1979):398–400.

73. Ronald L. Simons, "Inducement as an Approach to Exercising Influence," *Social Work* 30(1) (January 1985):56–62.

74. Mona Wasow, "Deinstitutionalization," *Practice Digest* 6(4) (Spring 1984):10–12.

75. Ibid.; Reamer, "Conflicts of Professional Duty in Social Work."

76. Reamer, "Paternalism in Social Work," pp. 255, 268.

## 5. Research on Effectiveness with Involuntary Clients

1. Miriam Kelty, "Protection of Persons Who Participate in Applied Research," Hannah, Christian, and Clark, *Preservation of Client Rights*, p. 403.

2. Ibid. See also Jay Katz, *Experimentation with Human Beings* (New York: Russell Sage, 1972); George F. Annas, Leonard H. Glantz, and Barbara F. Katz, *Informed Consent to Human Experimentation: The Subject's Dilemma* (Boston: Ballinger, 1977), pp. 6–7.

3. Seth A. Bloomberg and Leslie T. Wilkens, "Ethics of Research Involving Human Subjects in Criminal Justice," *Crime and Delinquency* 23 (1977):437; Paul Davidson Reynolds, *Ethics and Social Science Research* (Englewood Cliffs, N.J.: Prentice-Hall, 1982), p. 115; Stephanie B. Stolz, Louis A. Wienckowski, and Bertram S. Brown, "Behavior Modification: A Perspective on Critical Issues," *American Psychologist* 29 (November 1975):1043.

4. Gerald C. Davison and Richard B. Stuart, "Behavioral Therapy and Civil Liberties," *American Psychologist* 29 (July 1975):760.

5. Kelty, "Protection of Persons Who Participate in Applied Research," p. 405.

6. Davison and Stuart, "Behavioral Therapy and Civil Liberties."

7. Bloomberg and Wilkens, "Ethics of Research," pp. 436–437; David F. Gillespie, "Ethical Issues in Research," in *Encyclopedia of Social Work*, p. 503.

8. Reynolds, *Ethics and Social Science Research*, p. 33.

9. Kelty, "Protection of Persons Who Participate in Applied Research," pp. 407–410.

10. Reynolds, *Ethics and Social Science Research;* Kelty, "Protection of Persons Who Participate in Applied Research," p. 411; Bloomberg and Wilkins, "Ethics of Research," p. 436–437.

11. Videka-Sherman, *Bartlett Practice Effectiveness Project,* p. 40. See also Videka-Sherman, "Meta-Analysis of Research on Social Work Practice in Mental Health," pp. 325–338.

12. Joel Fischer, "Is Casework Effective? A Review," *Social Work* 19(1) (1973):19.

13. See, for example, Edwin Powers and Helen Witmer, *An Experiment in the Prevention of Delinquency: The Cambridge-Somerville Youth Study* (New York: Columbia University Press, 1951); Walter B. Miller, "The Impact of a Total Community Delinquency Control Project," *Social Problems* 9 (Fall 1962):168–191; William C. Berleman and Thomas W. Steiner, "The Execution and Evaluation of a Delinquency Prevention Program," *Social Problems* 14 (Spring 1967):413–423; Maude M. Craig and Phillip W. Furst, "What Happens after Treatment? A Study of Potentially Delinquent Boys," *Social Service Review* 39 (June 1965):165–171.

14. Henry J. Meyer, Edgar Borgatta, and Wyatt Jones, *Girls at Vocational High: An Experiment in Social Work Intervention* (New York: Russell Sage, 1965).

15. Katherine M. Wood, "Casework Effectiveness: A New Look at the Research Evidence." *Social Work* 23 (November 1978):438.

16. Ibid., p. 440.

17. Robert Martinson, "What Works? Questions and Answers about Prison Reform," *The Public Interest* 35 (1974):22–54; D. Lipton, R. Martinson, and J. Weeks, *The Effectiveness of Correctional Treatment* (New York: Praeger, 1974).

18. Charles H. Shireman and Frederic G. Reamer, *Rehabilitating Juvenile Justice* (New York: Columbia Univesity Press, 1986). See also Dennis A. Romig, *Justice for Children* (Lexington, Mass.: D.C. Heath, 1978).

19. Daniel Glaser, "A Review of Crime Causation Theory and Its Applications in Crime and Justice," in Norval Morris and Michael Tonry, eds., *Crime and Justice: An Annual Review of Research* (Chicago: University of Chicago Press, 1979).

20. Stuart Adams, *Evaluation: A Way Out of Rhetoric in Rehabilitation, Recidivisim and Research* Hackensack, N.J.: National Council on Crime and Delinquency, 1976).

21. Shireman and Reamer, *Rehabilitating Juvenile Justice,* p. 88.

22. The literature review strategy employed here to develop summary generalizations is influenced by principles from intervention and developmental research as developed by Thomas and Rothman. See Jack Rothman, *Social R and D: Research and Development in the Human Services* (Englewood Cliffs, N.J.: Prentice-Hall, 1980), and Edwin J. Thomas, *Designing Interventions for the Helping Professions* (Beverly Hills, Calif.: Sage, 1984).

23. Videka-Sherman, *Bartlett Effectiveness Project,* p. 40.

24. Brehm and Smith, "Social Psychological Approaches to Psychotherapy and Behavior Change," p. 88. She cites studies by Bastien and Adelman (1984),

Goldenberg, Smith, and Townes (1980), Gove and Fain (1977), and Spensley, Edwards, and White (1980) in reaching this conclusion.

25. Walter R. Gove and Terry Fain, "A Comparison of Voluntary and Committed Psychiatric Patients," *Archives of General Psychiatry* 34 (June 1977):669–676.

26. James Spensley, Daniel W. Edwards, and Edward White, "Patient Satisfaction and Involuntary Treatment," *American Journal of Orthopsychiatry* 50(4) (1980):725–727.

27. E. E. Goldenberg, T. E. Smith, and B. D. Townes, "Comparing Treatment Patterns of Involuntary and Voluntary Patients," *Psychiatric Forum* 6 (1980):34.

28. R. T. Bastien and H. S. Adelman, "Noncompulsory Versus Legally Mandated Placement, Perceived Choice and Response to Treatment among Adolescents," *Journal of Consulting and Clinical Psychology* 52 (1984):171–179.

29. Ibid., p. 175.

30. William R. Miller, "Increasing Motivation for Change," in Reid K. Hester and William R. Miller, eds., *Handbook of Alcoholism Treatment Approaches* (New York: Pergamon, 1989), p. 72. Miller cites studies by R. G. Smart, "Employed Alcoholics Treated Voluntarily and under Constructive Coercion: A Follow-Up Study," *Quarterly Journal of Studies on Alcohol* 35 (1974):169–209; E. J. Freedberg and W. E. Johnston, "Effects of Various Sources of Coercion on Outcome of Treatment of Alcoholism," *Psychological Reports* 43 (1978):1271–1278; E. J. Freedberg and W. E. Johnston, "Outcome with Alcoholics Seeking Treatment Voluntarily or after Confrontation by Their Employer," *Journal of Occupational Medicine* 22 (1980):83–86; D. M. Gallant, M. P. Bishop, B. Stoy, M. A. Faulkner, and L. Paternostro, "The Value of a 'First Contact' Group Intake Session in an Alcoholism Outpatient Clinic: Statistical Confirmation," *Psychosomatics* 7 (1966):349–352; W. R. Miller, "Behavioral Treatment of Problem Drinkers: A Comparative Outcome Study of Three Controlled Drinking Therapies," *Journal of Consulting and Clinical Psychology* 46 (1978):74–86; C. Rosenberg and J. Liftik, "Use of Coercion in the Outpatient Treatment of Alcoholism," *Journal of Studies on Alcohol* 37 (1976):58–62.

31. Miller, "Increasing Motivation for Change," p. 70.

32. P. Flores, "The Efficacy of the Use of Coercion in Getting DWI Offenders into Treatment," *Journal of Alcohol and Drug Education* 28 (1983):18–27; Rosenberg and Liftik, "Use of Coercion."

33. Ibid.; O. Ben-Arie, L. Swartz, and G. C. George, "The Compulsory Treatment of Alcoholic Drunk Drivers Referred by the Courts: A 7 to 9 Year Outcome Study," *International Journal of Law and Psychiatry* 8 (1986):229–235. See also Denis Foley, "The Coerced Alcoholic: On Felons, Throwaways and Others. in Aaron Rosenblatt, ed., *For Their Own Good: Essays on Coercive Kindness* (Albany: Nelson A. Rockefeller Institute of Government, State University of New York, 1988), pp. 115–148.

34. Freedberg and Johnston, "Effects of Various Sources of Coercion."

35. Ibid., p. 1277.

36. Patricia Yancy Martin and Kathy L. Pilkerton, "Mandatory Treatment in the Welfare State: Research Issues," in Rosenblatt, *For Their Own Good*, pp. 31–52.

37. Ana M. Irueste-Montes and Francisco Montes, "Court-Ordered vs. Voluntary Treatment of Abusive and Neglectful Parents," *Child Abuse and Neglect* 12(1) (1988):33–39.

38. B. Star, *Helping the Abuser: Interviewing Effectively in Family Violence* (New York: Family Service Association, 1983); D. Wolfe, J. Aragona, K. Kaufman, and J. Sandler, "The Importance of Adjudication in the Treatment of Child Abusers: Some Preliminary Findings," *Child Abuse and Neglect* 4 (1980):127–135.

39. William J. Reid and Patricia Hanrahan, "Recent Evaluations of Social Work: Grounds for Optimism," *Social Work* 27 (July 1982):331.

40. Garfield, "Research on Client Variables in Psychotherapy," pp. 213–256.

41. Raymond P. Lorion and Robert D. Felner, "Research on Psychotherapy with the Disadvantaged," in Garfield and Bergin, *Handbook of Psychotherapy and Behavior Change*, pp. 739–776.

42. Reid and Hanrahan, "Recent Evaluations of Social Work."

43. Videka-Sherman, *Bartlett Effectiveness Project.*

44. Flores, "Efficacy of the Use of Coercion."

45. Mark Peyrot, "Coerced Voluntarism: The Micropolitics of Drug Treatment," *Urban Life* 13(4) (January 1985):345. See also D. Waldorf, "Social Control in Therapeutic Communities for the Treatment of Drug Addicts," *International Journal of Addictions* 6 (1971):29–43.

46. Irueste-Montes and Montes, "Court-Ordered vs. Voluntary Treatment," p. 38.

47. Jeffrey L. Edleson, David M. Miller, Gene W. Stone, and Dennis G. Chapman, "Group Treatment for Men Who Batter," *Social Work Research and Abstracts* 21 (1985):18–21.

48. Richard M. Tolman and Gauri Bhosley, "A Comparison of Two Types of Pre-Group Preparation for Men Who Batter." Paper presented at Third Symposium on the Empirical Foundations of Group Work, Chicago, May 15–18.

49. Reid and Hanrahan, "Recent Evaluations of Social Work," pp. 328–340.

50. Anthony N. Maluccio, *Learning from Clients* (New York: Free Press, 1979); John E. Mayer and Noel Timms, "Clash in Perspective between Worker and Client," *Social Casework* 50 (1969):32–40; Garfield, "Research on Client Variables in Psychotherapy," pp. 213–256.

51. Videka-Sherman, *Bartlett Effectiveness Project*, p. 40.

52. Brehm and Smith, "Social Psychological Approaches to Psychotherapy and Behavior Change," p. 88.

53. J. Cooper, "Reducing Fears and Increasing Assertiveness: The Role of Dissonance Reduction," *Journal of Experimental Social Psychology* 16 (1980):199–213; D. Axsom and J. Cooper, "Reducing Weight by Reducing

Dissonance: The Role of Effort Justification in Inducing Weight Loss," in E. Aronson, ed., *Readings about the Social Animal* (San Francisco: Freeman, 1981); D. A. Devine and P. S. Fernald, "Outcome Effects of Receiving a Preferred, Randomly Assigned, or Nonpreferred Therapy," *Journal of Consulting and Clinical Psychology* 41 (1973):104–107; R. M. Gordon, "Effects of Volunteering and Responsibility on Perceived Value and Effectiveness of a Clinical Treatment," *Journal of Consulting and Clinical Psychology* 44 (1976):799–801; G. R. Liem, "Performance and Satisfaction as Affected by Personal Control over Salient Decisions," *Journal of Personality and Social Psychology* 31 (1975):232–240; S. M. Champlin and P. Karoly, "Role of Contract Negotiation in Self-Management of Study Time," *Psychological Reports* 37 (1975):724–726.

54. Pamela J. Mendonca and Sharon S. Brehm, "Effects of Choice on Behavioral Treatment of Overweight Children," *Journal of Social and Clinical Psychology* 1(4) (1983):343–358.

55. Brehm and Smith, "Social Psychological Approaches to Psychotherapy and Behavior Change," p. 90.

56. E. J. Langer, "The Illusion of Control," *Journal of Personality and Social Psychology* 32 (1975):311.

57. Ibid., p. 325.

58. E. J. Langer and J. Rodin, "The Effects of Choice and Enhanced Personal Responsibility for the Aged: A Field Experiment in an Institutional Setting," *Journal of Personality and Social Psychology* 32 (1976):951–955. See also J. Rodin and E. J. Langer, "Long-Term Effects of a Control-Relevant Intervention with the Institutionalized Aged," *Journal of Personality and Social Psychology* 33 (1977):897–902.

59. Miller, "Increasing Motivation for Change," p. 71.

60. M. W. Parker, D. K. Winstead, and F. J. P. Willi, "Patient Autonomy in Alcohol Rehabilitation. I: Literature Review," *International Journal of the Addictions* 14 (1979):1015–1022; B. Kissen, A. Platz, and W. H. Su, "Selective Factors in Treatment Choice Outcome in Alcoholism," in N. K. Mello and J. H. Mendelson, eds., *Recent Advances in Studies of Alcoholism,* (Washington, D.C.: U.S. Government Printing Office, 1971), pp. 781–812; R. M. Costello, Alcoholism Treatment and Evaluation: In Search of methods," *International Journal of Addictions* 10 (1975):251–271.

61. Selmer Wathney and Bill Baldridge, "Strategic Interventions with Involuntary Patients," *Hospital and Community Psychiatry* 31(10) (October 1980):696–701; Perry London, *Behavior Control* (New York: Harper and Row, 1969).

62. Mendonca and Brehm, "Effects of Choice on Behavioral Treatment of Overweight Children," p. 355.

63. Miller, "Increasing Motivation for Change," p. 72.

64. Brehm and Smith, "Social Psychological Approaches to Psychotherapy and Behavior Change," p. 91.

65. E. J. Phares, "Defensiveness and Perceived Control," in L. C. Perlmeuter and R. A. Monty, eds., *Choice and Perceived Control* (Hillsdale, N.J.: Erlbaum, 1979). See also C. R. Snyder and R. E. Ingram, "'Company Motivates the Miserable': The Impact of Consensus Information on Help Seeking for Psycho-

logical Problems," *Journal of Personality and Social Psychology* 45 (1983):1118–1127.

66. K. A. Matthews, M. F. Scheier, B. I. Brunson, and B. Carducci, "Attention, Unpredictability and Reports of Physical Symptoms: Eliminating the Benefits of Predictability," *Journal of Personality and Social Psychology* 38 (1980):525–537. See also S. M. Miller, "Predictability and Human Stress: Toward a Clarification of Evidence and Theory," in L. Berkowitz, ed., *Advances in Experimental Social Psychology,* vol. 14 (New York: Academic Press, 1981).

67. Gordon, "Effects of Volunteering and Responsibility," pp. 799–801.

68. Garfield, "Research on Client Variables in Psychotherapy"; J. B. Heitler, "Preparation of Lower-Class Patients for Expressive Group Psychotherapy," *Journal of Consulting and Clinical Psychology* 41 (1973):251–260; J. B. Heitler, "Preparatory Techniques in Initiating Expressive Psychotherapy with Lower-Class, Unsophisticated Clients," *Psychological Bulletin* 83 (1976):339–352; M. T. Orne and P. H. Wender, "Anticipatory Socialization for Psychotherapy: Method and Rationale," *American Journal of Psychiatry* 124 (1968):1202–1212.

69. Videka-Sherman, *Bartlett Effectiveness Project,* p. 52; Videka-Sherman, "Meta-Analysis of Research on Social Work Practice in Mental Health," p. 328.

70. John S. Brekke, "The Use of Orientation Groups to Engage Hard to Reach Clients: Model, Method and Evaluation," *Social Work with Groups* 12(2) (1989):75–88.

71. Tolman and Bhosley, "A Comparison of Two Types of Pre-Group Preparation for Men Who Batter," p. 9.

72. Diane Kravetz and Sheldon Rose, *Contracts in Groups: A Workbook* (Dubuque, Ia.: Kendall-Hunt, 1973), p. viii.

73. Mayer and Timms, "Clash in Perspective between Worker and Client."

74. Reid and Hanrahan, "Recent Evaluations of Social Work," p. 338.

75. Allen Rubin, "Practice Effectiveness: More Grounds for Optimism," *Social Work* 30 (6) (1975):474.

76. T. J. Stein, E. A. Gambrill, and K. T. Wiltse, *Children in Foster Homes: Achieving Continuity of Care* (New York: Prager, 1978). See also Theodore Stein, Eileen Gambrill, and Kermit Wiltse, "Foster Care: The Use of Contracts," *Public Welfare* 32(4) (Fall 1979):20–25.

77. Brett A. Seabury, "The Contract: Uses, Abuses and Limitations," *Social Work* 21 (January 1976):16–21.

78. Dorothea Hosch, *Use of the Contract Approach in Public Social Services* (Los Angeles: Regional Research Institute in Child Welfare, University of Southern California, 1973).

79. Seabury, "The Contract," p. 19.

80. Brett A. Seabury, "Negotiating Sound Contracts with Clients," *Public Welfare* 38 (Spring 1979):33–38.

81. Ibid., p. 36.

82. Ibid.

83. Donald Meichenbaum and Dennis C. Turk, *Facilitating Treatment Adherence: A Practitioner's Guidebook* (New York: Plenum Press, 1987), p. 20.

84. B. J. Masek, "Compliance and Medicine," in D. M. Doleys, R. L. Meredith, and A. R. Ciminero, eds., *Behavioral Medicine: Assessment and Treatment Strategies* (New York: Plenum Press, 1982); D. L. Sackett and J. C. Snow, "The Magnitude of Compliance and Noncompliance," in R. B. Haynes, D. W. Taylor, and D. L. Sackett, eds., *Compliance in Health Care* (Baltimore: Johns Hopkins University Press, 1979).

85. Meichenbaum and Turk, *Facilitating Treatment Adherence*, p. 25.

86. E. J. Larkin, *The Treatment of Alcoholism: Theory, Practice and Evaluation* (Toronto: Addiction Research Foundation, 1974); W. A. Hunt and D. A. Bespalec, "An Evaluation of Current Methods of Modifying Smoking Behavior," *Journal of Clinical Psychology* 30 (1974):431–438.

87. P. Vincent, "Factors Influencing Patient Noncompliance: A Theoretical Approach," *Nursing Research* 20 (1971):509–516.

88. Rona L. Levy and Robert D. Carter, "Compliance with Practitioner Instigations," *Social Work* 21 (May 1976):188–193.

89. Martin and Pilkerton, "Mandatory Treatment in the Welfare State."

90. Ibid.

## 6. Influencing Behaviors and Attitudes

1. Alfred Kadushin, *The Social Work Interview* (New York: Columbia University Press, 1972), p. 67.

2. L. Krasner, "Studies of the Conditioning of Verbal Behavior," *Pscyhological Bulletin* 55 (1958):148–170.

3. W. A. Gamson, *Power and Discontent* (Homewood, Ill.: Dorsey Press, 1968). See also Simons and Aigner, *Practice Principles*, p. 116.

4. D. L. Fixsen, E. L. Phillips, and M. M. Wolf, "Achievement Place: Experiment in Self-Government with Pre-Delinquents," *Journal of Applied Behavior Analysis* 6 (1973):31–47.

5. H. C. Kelman, "Compliance, Identification and Internalization: Three Processes of Attitude Change," in H. Proshansky and B. Sendenberg, eds., *Studies in Social Psychology* (New York: Holt, Rinehart, Winston, 1965), pp. 140–148. See also Shiela Feld and Norma Radin, *Social Psychology for Social Work and the Mental Health Professions* (New York: Columbia University Press, 1982), p. 188.

6. Harold Lewis, "Morality and the Politics of Practice," *Social Casework* 53 (July 1972):404–417.

7. Stephanie Stolz, Louis A. Wienckowski, and Bertram S. Brown, "Behavior Modification: A Perspective on Critical Issues," *American Psychologist* 29 (November 1975):1028.

8. Arthur Schwartz, "Behavioral Principles and Approaches," in Rosenblatt and Waldfogel, *Handbook of Clinical Social Work*, pp. 202–228.

9. Simons and Aigner, *Practice Principles*, p. 247.

10. Zvi C. Eisikovitz and Jeffry D. Edleson, "Intervening with Men Who Batter: A Critical Review of the Literature," *Social Service Review* 63(3) (September 1989):384–414.

11. Simons and Aigner, *Practice Principles*. See also Martin Sundel and Sandra Stone Sundel, *Behavior Modification in the Human Services* (Englewood Cliffs, N.J.: Prentice-Hall, 1982).

12. Simons and Aigner, *Practice Principles*, p. 254.

13. Burt Galaway, "Crime Victim Offender Mediation as a Social Work Strategy," *Social Service Review* 62(4) (1988); Burt Galaway, "Social Services and Criminal Justice," in Gilbert and Specht, *Handbook of the Social Services*, pp. 205–280.

14. William B. Janzen and William Love, "Involving Adolescents as Active Participants in Their own Treatment Plans," *Psychological Reports* 41 (1977):931–934.

15. Stolz, Wienckowski, and Brown, "Behavior Modification."

16. Simons and Aigner, *Practice Principles*, p. 254; Stoltz, Wienckowski, and Brown, "Behavior Modification," p. 1039.

17. Ibid., p. 1038.

18. Ibid., p. 1036.

19. Simons and Aigner, *Practice Principles*.

20. Freedberg and Johnston, "Effect of Various Sources of Coercion on Outcome of Treatment of Alcoholism," pp. 1271–1278.

21. M. Bruner-Orne, F. T. Iddings, and J. Rodrigues, "A Court Clinic for Alcoholics," *Quarterly Journal of Studies on Alcohol* 12 (1951):592–600.

22. Simons and Aigner, *Practice Principles*, p. 122.

23. R. M. Tolman, S. Beeman, and C. Mendoza, "The Effectiveness of a Shelter-Sponsored Program for Men Who Batter: Preliminary Results," Paper presented at the Third National Family Violence Research Conference, Durham N.H.

24. Simons and Aigner, *Practice Principles*, pp. 122–123, 253.

25. Stoltz, Wienckowski, and Brown, "Behavior Modification," p. 1038; David Kipnis, "Does Power Corrupt?" *Journal of Personality and Social Psychology* 24(1) (1972):33–41.

26. Milgram's studies of obedience indicate that persons can be induced to inflict pain when it is described as their duty to do so. S. Milgram, "Behavioral Study of Obedience," *Journal of Abnormal and Social Psychology* 67 (1963):371–378; S. Milgram, "Issues in the Study of Obedience: A Reply to Baumrind," *American Psychologist* 19 (1964):848–852; S. Milgram, "Some Conditions of Obedience and Disobedience to Authority," *Human Relations* 18(1) (1965):57–76.

27. Kelman, "Compliance, Identification and Internalization."

28. Simons and Aigner, *Practice Principles*, p. 56.

29. Fixsen, Phillips, and Wolf, "Achievement Place." See also T. Ayllon and N. H. Azrin, *The Token Economy* (New York: Appleton, Century, Crofts, 1968).

30. Rudolph Alexander, Jr., "The Right to Treatment in Mental and Correctional Institutions," *Social Work* 34(2) (1989):109–114.

31. See Ronald L. Simons, "Inducement as an Approach to Exercising Influence," *Social Work* 30(1) (January 1985):56–62.

32. R. A. Winett and R. C. Winkler, "Current Behavior Modification in the Classroom. Be Still, Be Quiet, Be Docile," *Journal of Applied Behavioral Analysis* 5 (1972):499–504. See also K. D. O'Leary, "Behavior Modification in the Classroom: A Rejoinder to Winnett and Winkler," *Journal of Applied Behavior Analysis* 5 (1972):505–511.

33. K. S. Cook and R. M. Emerson, "Power, Equity, Commitment in Exchange Networks," *American Sociological Review* 43 (1978):721–739. See also Simons and Aigner, *Practice Principles,* p. 150.

34. Ibid.

35. Janzen and Love, "Involving Adolescents as Active Participants in Their own Treatment Plans."

36. Simons and Aigner, *Practice Principles.*

37. C. A. Kiesler, *The Psychology of Commitment* (New York: Academic Press, 1971).

38. Simons, "Inducement as an Approach to Exercising Influence."

39. Ronald L. Simons, "Strategies for Exercising Influence," *Social Work* 27(3) (May 1982):268. Also Gamson, *Power and Discontent,* and C. Y. Larson, *Persuasion: Reception and Responsibility,* 3d ed. (Belmont, Calif.: Wadsworth, 1983), p. 281.

40. Feld and Radin, *Social Psychology for Social Work,* p. 164; Simons, "Strategies for Exercising Influence," p. 269.

41. Feld and Radin, *Social Psychology for Social Work,* p. 104.

42. Ibid., p. 157.

43. Ibid., p. 186.

44. F. Heider, *The Psychology of Interpersonal Relations* (New York: John Wiley, 1958); C. E. Osgood and P. H. Tannenbaum, "The Principle of Consistency in the Prediction of Attitude Change," *Psychological Review* 62 (1955):42–55.

45. Simons, "Strategies for Exercising Influence," p. 268.

46. Heider, *Psychology of Interpersonal Relations;* Osgood and Tannenbaum, "Principle of Consistency in the Prediction of Attitude Change."

47. Simons and Aigner, *Practice Principles,* p. 138.

48. Ibid., pp. 137–138.

49. Simons, "Strategies for Exercising Influence," pp. 138, 273.

50. Michael E. Roloff and Gerald E. Miller, *Persuasion: New Directions in Theory and Research* (London: Sage, 1968).

51. Bill Moyers, Public television programs on "The Public Mind" entitled "Consuming Images" and "Leading Questions," September 1990.

52. Peter Raynor, "Compulsory Persuasion: A Problem for Correctional Social Work," *British Journal of Social Work* 8(4) (1978):411–424.

53. Simons, "Strategies for Exercising Influence," p. 269.

54. J. G. Good Tracks, "Native-American Non-Interference," *Social Work* 23 (November 1973):30–35.

55. Jack W. Brehm, *A Theory of Psychological Reactance* (New York: Academic Press, 1966); Robert A. Wicklund, *Freedom and Reactance* (Potomac, Md.: Lawrence Erlbaum Associates, 1974).

56. Ronald L. Simons, "Generic Social Work Skills in Social Administration: The Example of Persuasion. *Administration in Social Work* 11 (1987):241–254.

57. P. F. Secord and C. W. Backman, *Social Psychology* (New York: McGraw-Hill, 1974).

58. J. S. Coleman, E. Katz, and H. Mengel, *Medical Innovation: Diffusion Study* (New York: Bobbs-Merrill, 1966).

59. William Glasser, *Reality Therapy* (New York: Harper and Row, 1965).

60. Simons and Aigner, *Practice Principles,* p. 134.

61. Ibid., p. 135.

62. Simons, "Strategies for Exercising Influence," p. 272. See also D. W. Johnson and R. D. Matross, "Attitude Modification Methods," in F. H. Kanfer and A. P. Goldstein, eds., *Helping People Change* (New York: Pergamon, 1985), p. 75.

63. Simons, "Strategies for Exercising Influence," pp. 268–274.

64. Feld and Radin, *Social Psychology for Social Work,* p. 177; D. G. Saunders, "Counseling the Violent Husband," in D. A. Keller and L. G. Ritt, eds., *Innovations in Clinical Practice,* vol. 1 (Sarasota, Fla.: Professional Resource Exchange, 1982).

65. L. Festinger, *A Theory of Cognitive Dissonance* (Stanford, Calif.: Stanford University Press, 1957); L. Festinger and J. M. Carlsmith, "Cognitive Consequences of Forced Compliance," *Journal of Abnormal and Social Psychology* 58 (1959):203–310; Michael F. Hoyt, Marc D. Henley, and Barry E. Collins, "Studies in Forced Compliance: Confluence of Choice and Consequence on Attitude Change," *Journal of Personality and Social Psychology* 23 (1972):205–210.

66. Feld and Radin, *Social Psychology for Social Work,* p. 175; J. L. Freeman and S. C.Fraser, "Compliance without Pressure: The Foot-in-the-Door Technique," *Journal of Personality and Social Psychology* 4(2) (1966):195–202.

67. Feld and Radin, *Social Psychology for Social Work,* p. 179; Simons, "Strategies for Exercising Influence," p. 270.

68. Feld and Radin, *Social Psychology for Social Work,* p. 170.

69. Simons, "Strategies for Exercising Influence," p. 268.

70. C. I. Hovland, A. A. Lumsdaine, and F. D. Sheffield, *Experiments in Mass Communication* (Princeton, N.J.: Princeton University Press, 1949).

71. Simons, "Strategies for Exercising Influence," p. 269.

72. David W. Johnson and Ronald P. Mattross, "Attitude Modification Methods," in Frederick Kamfer and Arnold P. Goldstein, eds., *Helping People Change* (New York: Pergamon, 1975), pp. 51–88.

73. Edleson, "Working with Men Who Batter," pp. 237–242.

74. Feld and Radin, *Social Psychology for Social Work,* p. 195.

75. Simons and Aigner, *Practice Principles,* p. 121.

76. Feld and Radin, *Social Psychology for Social Work,* p. 196; H. C. Triandos, *Attitudes and Attitude Change* (New York: John Wiley, 1971).

77. Feld and Radin, *Social Psychology for Social Work,* p. 183.

78. Raynor, "Compulsory Persuasion," p. 402.

79. Marguerite Q. Warren, "Correctional Treatment and Coercion: The Differential Effectiveness Perspective," *Criminal Justice and Behavior* 4(4) (December 1977):355–375.

80. Miller, "Increasing Motivation for Change," p. 78.

## 7. Assessing Initial Contacts in Involuntary Transactions

1. Epstein, *Helping People*, p. 135; Gambrill, *Casework*, p. 31; Garvin and Seabury, *Interpersonal Practice in Social Work*, p. 125.

2. Simons and Aigner, *Practice Principles*, p. 85.

3. Garvin and Seabury, *Interpersonal Practice in Social Work*, p. 126.

4. Dean H. Hepworth and Jo Ann Larsen, *Direct Social Work Practice: Theory and Skills*, 3d ed. (Belmont, Calif.: Wadsworth, 1990).

5. Stuart A. Kirk and Herb Kutchins, "Deliberate Misdiagnosis in Mental Health Practice," *Social Service Review* 62(2) (June 1988):225–237; Herb Kutchins and Stuart A. Kirk, "DSM-III and Social Work Malpractice," *Social Work* 32(2) (May-June 1987):205–212; Herb Kutchins and Stuart A. Kirk, "The Reliability of DSM-III: A Critical Review," *Social Work Research and Abstracts* 22(4) (Winter 1986):3–12; Herb Kutchins and Stuart A. Kirk, "The Business of Diagnosis: DSM-III and Clinical Social Work," *Social Work* 33 (May-June 1988):215–220; Gambrill, *Casework*, p. 34.

6. Garvin and Seabury, *Interpersonal Practice in Social Work*, p. 126; Simons and Aigner, *Practice Principles*, p. 42; Gambrill, *Casework*, p. 59.

7. Germain and Gitterman, *Life Model of Social Work Practice*, p. 19; Garvin and Seabury, *Interpersonal Practice in Social Work*, p. 125.

8. Hepworth and Larsen, *Direct Social Work Practice*, p. 158.

9. Ibid., p. 161; Garvin and Seabury, *Interpersonal Practice in Social Work*, p. 136.

10. Harry Specht and Riva Specht, "Social Work Assessment: Paths to Clienthood-Part I," *Social Casework* 67 (November 1986):525–533; Harry Specht and Riva Specht, "Social Work Assessment: Routes to Clienthood-Part II," *Social Casework* 67 (December 1986):587–592.

11. Cingolani, "Social Conflict Perspective," pp. 442–446.

12. Germain and Gitterman, *Life Model of Social Work Practice*, p. 19.

13. Hepworth and Larsen, *Direct Social Work Practice*, p. 31; Epstein, *Helping People*, p. 36.

14. Sharon S. Brehm and David A. McAllister, "A Social Psychological Perspective on the Maintenance of Therapeutic Change," in P. Karoly and J. J. Steffen, eds., *Improving the Long-Term Effects of Psychotherapy* (New York: Gardner Press, 1980), pp. 381–406.

15. Alfred Kadushin, *Child Welfare Services*, 2d ed. (New York: Macmillan, 1974), pp. 240–241.

16. Kai T. Erikson, "Notes on the Sociology of Deviance," in Howard S. Becker, ed., *The Other Side: Perspectives on Deviance* (Glencoe, Ill.: Free Press, 1964), pp. 4–21.

17. Cingolani, "Social Conflict Perspective," p. 442.

18. Stuart A. Kirk, "Clients as Outsiders: Theoretical Approaches to Deviance," *Social Work* 17 (March 1972):24–32.

19. *Social Casework: Generic and Specific* (New York: American Association of Social Work, 1929), p. 16. Also quoted by Max Siporin, "Deviant Behavior Theory in Social Work: Diagnosis and Treatment," *Social Work* 10 (July 1965):59–67.

20. Kirk, "Clients as Outsiders," pp. 24–25.

21. Roger M. Nooe, "A Model for Integrating Theoretical Approaches to Deviance," *Social Work* 25(5) (1980):366; Nicholas Kittrie, *The Right to Be Different: Deviance and Enforced Therapy* (Baltimore: Penguin, 1974).

22. Kirk, "Clients as Outsiders."

23. Ibid., p. 32.

24. Joel F. Handler, *The Coercive Social Worker: British Lessons for American Social Services* (Chicago: Rand-McNally, 1973), p. 42.

25. Robert K. Merton, "Social Structure and Anomie," in Stuart H. Traub and Craig B. Little, eds., *Theories of Deviance*, 2d ed. (Itasca, Ill.: F. E. Peacock, 1980), pp. 105–138. Similarly, Liazos points out that sociologists have replaced the study of social problems with the study of deviance, with disproportionate concentration on lower class deviants, nuts, sluts, and preverts with less attention on white collar crime. See Alexander Liazos, "The Poverty of the Sociology of Deviance: Nuts, Sluts and Preverts," in Traub and Little, *Theories of Deviance*, pp. 330–351.

26. Robert F. Meier, "The New Criminology: Continuity in Criminological Theory," *Journal of Criminal Law andCriminology* 67 (1977):4.

27. Thio addresses this problem in his adaptation of the structural view. In his power perspective on deviance, he argues that persons from all segments of society may at times be attracted to deviant acts as a way of reaching their goals and, further, that higher-power persons may be more able to escape detection and benefit from societal focus on low income deviants; see Alex Thio, *Deviant Behavior* (Boston: Houghton Mifflin, 1978).

28. Nooe, "Model for Integrating Theoretical Approaches to Deviance," p. 366; Mitchell W. Robin and Regina Spires, "Drawing the Line: Deviance in a Cross-Cultural Perspective," *International Journal of Group Tensions* 13 (1983):1–4, 106–131.

29. Howard S. Becker, *Outsiders: Studies in the Sociology of Deviance* (London: Free Press, 1963).

30. Kirk, "Clients as Outsiders," p. 26.

31. It has been argued that in the case of ascribed deviance or that deviance which occurs because of physically identifiable traits such as blindness or skin color, that social reaction may be sufficient to explain deviant careers. In other cases, when one must first *act*, it might be better explained as *achieved* deviance. See Milton Mankoff, "Social Reaction and Career Deviance: A Critical Analysis, in Traub and Little, *Theories of Deviance*, pp. 277–296.

32. Nooe, "Model for Integrating Theoretical Approaches to Deviance," p. 366.

33. Ibid., p. 367.

34. Ibid.

35. Kadushin, *Child Welfare Services,* p. 229.

36. Kadushin, *Social Work Interview,* p. 161.

37. Kirk, "Clients as Outsiders," p. 30; Nooe, "Model for Integrating Theoretical Approaches to Deviance," p. 366; Aaron Cicourel, *The Social Organization of Juvenile Justice* (New York: John Wiley, 1968); Irving Piliavin and Scott Briar, "Police Encounters with Juveniles," *American Journal of Sociology* 9 (September 1964):206–214.

38. Hasenfeld, "Power in Social Work Practice," pp. 469–483; David Fanshel and Eugene B. Shinn, *Children in Foster Care: A Longitudinal Investigation* (New York: Columbia University Press, 1978); Shireman and Reamer, *Rehabilitating Juvenile Justice,* pp. 47–53.

39. Edward Sagarin, *Deviants and Deviance* (New York: Praeger, 1975); Nooe, "Model for Integrating Theoretical Approaches to Deviance"; John P. Clark, "Acceptance of Blame and Alienation among Prisoners," *American Journal of Orthopsychiatry* 33(3) (1963):557–561; Erving Goffman, "The Moral Career of the Mental Patient," *Psychiatry* 22(2) (1959):123–142.

40. Sagarin, *Deviants and Deviance.*

41. Edwin M. Lemert, *Social Pathology* (New York: McGraw- Hill, 1951), p. 76; Nooe, "Model for Integrating Theoretical Approaches to Deviance," p. 369.

42. Shireman and Reamer, *Rehabilitating Juvenile Justice,* p. 127.

43. Nooe, "Model for Integrating Theoretical Approaches to Deviance," p. 369.

44. Ibid., p. 370.

45. Judith C. Nelsen, "Dealing with Resistance in Social Work Practice," *Social Casework* 56 (December 1975):587; Judith E. Gourse and Martha W. Chescheir, "Authority Issues in Treating Resistant Families," *Social Casework* 62 (February 1981):67–73.

46. Nelsen, "Dealing with Resistance," 588; Alex Gitterman, "Uses of Resistance: A Transactional View," *Social Work* 28(2) (March-April 1983):127.

47. Ira D. Turkat and Victor Meyer, "The Behavior Analytic Approach," in Paul Wachtel, ed., *Resistance: Psychodynamic and Behavioral Approaches* (New York: Plenum Press, 1982), pp. 157–184, and Herbert J. Schlesinger, "Resistance as Process," in ibid., pp. 25–44.

48. According to Fenichel, resistance is everything that prevents the patient from providing material from the unconscious. Otto Fenichel, *The Psychoanalytic Theory of Neuroses* (New York: W. W. Norton, 1945), p. 27; see Gitterman, "Uses of Resistance," 127–131.

49. Nelsen, "Dealing with Resistance," p. 587.

50. Patricia Ewalt, "Understanding Resistance: Seven Social Workers Debate," *Practice Digest* 5(1) (June 1982):6; Arnold A. Lazarus and Allen Fay, "Resistance or Rationalization? A Cognitive-Behavioral Perspective, in Wachtel, *Resistance,* pp. 133–156.

51. Ewalt, "Understanding Resistance."

52. Nelsen, "Dealing with Resistance," p. 587.

53. Murdach, "Bargaining and Persuasion," p. 458.

54. Ewalt, "Understanding Resistance"; Murdach, "Bargaining and Persuasion," p. 458; Renata Frankenstein, "Agency and Client Resistance," *Social Casework* 63 (January 1982):24–28.

55. William J. Reid, "Understanding Resistance: Seven Social Workers Debate," *Practice Digest* 5(1) (June 1982):10–11; Janet Moore-Kirkland, "Mobilizing Motivation: From Theory to Practice," in Anthony N. Maluccio, ed., *Promoting Competence in Clients: A New/Old Approach to Social Work Practice* (New York: Macmillan, 1981), pp. 27–54.

56. Martin Sundel, "Understanding Resistance: Seven Social Workers Debate," *Practice Digest* 5(1) (June 1982):5–24.

57. George Ruppel and Theodore J. Kaul, "Investigation of Social Influence Theory's Conception of Client Resistance," *Journal of Counseling Psychology* 29(3) (1982):232–239.

58. Carel Germain, "Understanding Resistance: Seven Social Workers Debate," *Practice Digest* 5(1) (June 1982):5–24.

59. Gitterman, "Uses of Resistance," p. 128; Reid, "Understanding Resistance," p. 10.

60. Carol M. Anderson and Susan Stewart, *Mastering Resistance: A Practical Guide to Family Therapy* (New York: Guilford, 1985), p. 33.

61. Brehm, *Theory of Psychological Reactance*, p. 3.

62. Ibid., p. 4; Sharon S. Brehm, *The Application of Social Psychology to Clinical Practice* (New York: John Wiley, 1976), p. 19; Robert A. Wicklund, *Freedom and Reactance* (Potomac, Md.: Lawrence Erlbaum Associates, 1974), p. ix.

63. Brehm, *Theory of Psychological Resistance*, p. 10.

64. Brehm, *Application of Social Psychology to Clinical Practice*, p. 19.

65. S. Worchel, "The Effect of Three Types of Arbitrary Thwarting on the Instigation to Aggression," *Journal of Personality* 42 (1974):300–318.

66. Sharon S. Brehm and Jack W. Brehm, *Psychological Reactance: A Theory of Freedom and Control* (New York: Academic Press, 1981), pp. 213–227.

67. Brehm, *Application of Social Psychology to Clinical Practice*, pp. 15–16.

68. B. Wortman and J. W. Brehm, "Responses to Uncontrollable Outcomes: An Integration of Reactance Theory and the Learned Helplessness Model," in L. Berkowitz, ed., *Advances in Experimental Social Psychology*, vol. 8 (New York: Academic Press, 1975).

69. Brehm, *Application of Social Psychology to Clinical Practice*, p. 17.

70. J. W. Brehm, L. K. Stires, J. Sensening, and J. Shaban, "The Attractiveness of an Eliminated Choice Alternative," *Journal of Experimental Social Psychology* 2 (1966):301–311.

71. Brehm, *Application of Social Psychology to Clinical Practice*, p. 17.

72. Thomas Dowd, Christopher R. Milne, and Steven L. Wise, "The Therapeutic Reactance Scale: A Measure of Psychological Reactance," paper presented at American Psychological Association convention, Toronto, Ontario, (August 1984).

73. R. D. Morgan, "Individual Differences in the Occurrence of Psychological Reactance and Therapeutic Outcome," Ph.D. dissertation, University of Nebraska, 1986.

74. Brehm and Brehm, *Psychological Reactance*, pp. 213–227; Joel Brockman and Melissa Elkind, "Self-Esteem and Reactance: Further Evidence of Attitudinal and Motivational Consequences," *Journal of Experimental Social Psychology* 21 (1985):346–361.

75. Brehm and Brehm, *Psychological Reactance*, pp. 281–294.

76. Gisla Grabitz-Gniech, "Some Restrictive Conditions for the Occurrence of Psychological Reactance," *Journal of Personality and Social Psychology* 19(2) (1971):188–196.

77. Brehm, *Application of Social Psychology to Clinical Practice*, p. 58.

78. Wortman and Brehm, "Responses to Uncontrollable Outcomes"; Brehm and McAllister, "Social Psychological Perspective on the Maintenance of Therapeutic Change."

79. Brehm and Smith, "Social Psychological Approaches to Psychotherapy and Behavior Change," p. 94.

80. Michael Rohrbaugh, Howard Tennen, Samuel Press, and Larry White, "Compliance, Defiance and Therapeutic Paradox: Guidelines for Strategic Use of Paradoxical Interventions," *Americal Journal of Orthopsychiatry* 51(3) (July 1981):454–467.

81. E. Thomas Dowd, Shari L. Hughes, Linda Brockbank, and Dale Halpain, "Compliance-Based and Defiance-Based Intervention Strategies and Psychological Reactance in the Treatment of Free and Unfree Behavior," *Journal of Counseling Psychology* 35(4) (1988):370–376; Brehm and Brehm, *Psychological Reactance*, p. 324.

82. Ibid.

83. Brehm and Smith, "Social Psychological Approaches to Psychotherapy and Behavior Change."

84. Brehm, *Application of Social Psychology to Clinical Practice*, p. 21.

85. Perhaps the closest to such a study is the finding that when a threat to competence is perceived, a person is unlikely to give up control over a task to another. Michael J. Strube and Carol Warner, "Psychological Reactance and the Relinquishment of Control," *Personality and Social Psychology Bulletin* 10(2) (June 1984):225–234.

86. Brehm, *Application of Social Psychology to Clinical Practice*, p. 16; Wicklund, *Freedom and Reactance*.

87. Brehm, *Application of Social Psychology to Clinical Practice*, p. 19.

88. Brehm and Smith, "Social Psychological Approaches to Psychotherapy and Behavior Change." See also David Kipnis and Richard Vanderveer, "Ingratiation and the Use of Power," *Journal of Personality and Social Pscyhology* 17(3) (1971):281; and David Kipnis, *The Powerholders* (Chicago: University of Chicago Press, 1976), p. 3.

89. Peter M. Blau, *Exchange and Power in Social Life* (New Brunswick, N.J.: Transaction Books, 1986), p. 117.

90. Kipnis, "Does Power Corrupt?" p. 36.

91. Ibid.

92. Margaret Cooke and David Kipnis, "Influence Tactics in Psychotherapy," *Journal of Consulting and Clinical Psychology* 54(1) (1976):22–26.

93. Ibid., p. 26.

94. Ibid., pp. 25–26.

95. Martin and Pilkerton suggest that this is a kind of circumstance in which clients have choices, but the available alternatives threaten their goal or intent, to get a divorce in this case. See Patricia Y. Martin and Kathy L. Pilkenton, "Mandated Treatment in the Welfare State: Research Issues," in Aaron Beckerman, ed., *For their Own Good: Essays on Coercive Kindness* (Albany, N.Y.: Nelson A.Rockefeller Institute of Government, 1988), p. 33.

96. Edward E. Jones and Thane S. Pittman, "Toward a General Theory of Strategic Self-Presentation," in J. Suls, ed., *Psychological Perspectives on the Self* (Hillsdale, N.J.: Erlbaum, 1982), p. 233; see also Myrna L. Friedlander and Gary S. Schwartz, "Toward a Theory of Strategic Self-Presentation in Counseling and Psychotherapy," *Journal of Counseling Psychology* 32 (1985):485.

97. Feld and Radin, *Social Psychology for Social Work*, p. 199.

98. Ibid.; Edward E. Jones, *Ingratiation: A Social Psychological Analysis* (New York: Appleton-Century-Crofts, 1964), p. 194.

99. Jones and Pittman, "Toward a General Theory of Strategic Self-Presentation," pp. 237–238.

100. Kipnis and Vanderveer, "Ingratiation and the Use of Power," 281.

101. E. E. Jones and K. E. Davis, "From Acts to Dispositions," in L. Berkowitz, *Advances in Experimental Social Psychology*, 2:219–266.

102. Jones and Pittman, "Toward a General Theory of Strategic Self-Presentation," p. 238.

103. Ibid., p. 241.

104. Ibid., p. 247.

105. Friedlander and Schwartz, "Toward a Theory of Strategic Self-Presentation," p. 489.

106. Jones and Pittman, "Toward a General Theory of Strategic Self-Presentation," p. 241.

107. Ibid., p. 245.

108. Feld and Radin, *Social Psychology for Social Work*, pp. 199–202.

109. Friedlander and Schwartz, "Toward a Theory of Strategic Self-Presentation," p. 495.

110. Epstein, *Helping People*.

## 8. Socialization Strategies for Individual Involuntary Clients

1. Reid, *Task-Centered System*.

2. Cingolani, "Social Conflict Perspective on Work with Involuntary Clients," pp. 442–446.

3. Ibid.

4. Ibid.

5. Brehm, *Application of Social Psychology to Clinical Practice*, p. 58.

6. Sally E. Palmer, "Authority: An Essential Part of Practice," *Social Work* 28 (March-April 1983):120–125.

7. Brehm, *Application of Social Psychology to Clinical Practice*, p. 24.

8. Ibid., p. 61; Simons, "Strategies for Exercising Influence," pp. 268–269.

9. Epstein, *Helping People*.

10. Brehm, *Application of Social Psychology to Clinical Practice;* Raynor, "Compulsory Persuasion," pp. 411–424.

11. Theodore J. Stein, "The Vulnerability of Child Welfare Agencies to Class-Action Suits," *Social Service Review* 61 (December 1987):636–654.

12. Lawrence Shulman, *The Skills of Helping Individuals and Groups* (Itasca, Ill.: F. E. Peacock, 1979).

13. This selection of dialogue is abstracted from a training videotape entitled *Socialization and Contracting with a Chemical Dependency Client* by Dick Leonard. This videotape is available from the author. See appendix for list of training tapes available and ordering informationn.

14. This tape, entitled *Nonvoluntary Client Contracting*, by Walter Mirk, is available from the author. See appendix.

15. Murdach, "Bargaining and Persuasion," p. 459. See also Frankenstein, "Agency and Client Resistance," p. 25.

16. Videka-Sherman, *Bartlett Practice Effectiveness Project;* Abraham Alcabes and James A. Jones, "Structural Determinants of Clienthood," *Social Work* 30 (January 1985):52.

17. Galaway, "Social Services and Criminal Justice."

18. Gambrill, *Casework;* Epstein, *Helping People*.

19. Theodore J. Stein and Tina L. Rzepnicki, *Decision Making at Child Welfare Intake: A Handbook for Practitioners* (New York: Child Welfare League of America, 1983).

20. Sagarin, *Deviants and Deviance;* Robert E. Saltmarsh, "Client Resistance in Talk Therapies," *Psychotherapy: Theory, Research and Practice* 13 (Spring 1976):34–39.

21. Nooe, "Model for Integrating Theoretical Approaches to Deviance," pp. 366–370; Kirk, "Clients as Outsiders," pp. 24–32; Palmer, "Authority."

22. Rooney, "Socialization Strategies for Involuntry Clients," p. 136.

23. Hepworth and Larsen, *Direct Social Work Practice*, pp. 550–557.

24. See Ronald H. Rooney, "Confrontation with Involuntary Clients," unpublished paper.

25. Thomas E. Smith, "Group Work with Adolescent Drug Abusers," *Social Work with Groups* 8(1) (Spring 1985):55–63.

26. See examples of self-assessment in Judy Kopp, "Self-Observation: An Empowerment Strategy in Assessment," *Social Casework* 70 (1989):276–284; Judy Kopp, "Self-Monitoring: A Literature Review of Research and Practice," *Social Work Research and Abstracts* 24 (Winter 1988):8–20.

27. D. Hammond, D. Hepworth, and V. Smith, *Improving Therapeutic Communication* (San Fransisco: Jossey-Bass, 1977), pp. 286–318.

28. Hepworth and Larsen, *Direct Social Work Practice*, p. 551.

29. Ibid., p. 552.

30. D. G. Saunders, "Counseling the Violent Husband," in D. A. Keller and L. G. Ritt, eds., *Innovations in Clinical Practice*, vol. 1 (Sarasota, Fla.: Professional Resource Exchange, 1982), p. 20.

31. Wynetta Devore and Elfriede Schlesinger, *Ethnic-Sensitive Social Work Practice* (St. Louis: C. V. Mosby, 1981).

32. John Longres, "A Status Model of Ethnic-Sensitive Practice," presentation at Council on Social Work Education, Reno, Nevada, March 1990.

## 9. Negotiation and Contracting with Involuntary Clients

1. Cingolani, "Social Conflict Perspective," pp. 442–446.

2. See Palmer, "Authority," pp. 120–126.

3. See John R.P. French and Bertram Raven, "The Bases of Social Power," in Dorwin Cartwright and Alvin Zander, eds., *Group Dynamics, Research and Theory* 9New York: Harper and Row, 1968), pp. 259–269.

4. Cingolani, "Social Conflict Perspective."

5. Murdach, "Bargaining and Persuasion," pp. 458–461.

6. Seabury, "The Contract," p. 16.

7. Chris Rojek and Stewart A. Collins, "Contract or Con Trick?" *British Journal of Social Work* 17 (1987):199–211.

8. Seabury, "Negotiating Sound Contracts with Clients," pp. 33–38; see also Emanuel Berman and Ruth Segal, "The Captive Client: Dilemmas of Psychotherapy in the Psychiatric Hospital," *Psychotherapy: Theory, Research and Practice* 19(1) (1982):31–42; David Wineman, "Captors, Captives and Social Workers in a Civil Society," position statement by faculty and students, School of Social Work, Wayne State University, Detroit, Michigan, 1968.

9. Seabury, "Negotiating Sound Contracts with Clients."

10. Murdach, "Bargaining and Persuasion"; Cingolani, "Social Conflict Perspective."

11. Murdach, "Bargaining and Persuasion," p. 459.

12. Rooney, "Socialization Strategies for Involuntary Clients," pp. 131–140.

13. This interview segment comes from a training videotape entitled *Permanency Planning: Use of the Task-Centered Model with an Adolescent toward Independent Living. The Contracting Phase.* See the appendix for information on where the tape can be ordered.

14. Frankenstein, "Agency and Client Resistance," pp. 24–28; Judith E. Gourse and Martha W. Chescheir, "Authority Issues in Treating Resistant Families," *Social Casework* 62 (February 1981):67–73.

15. Carol M. Anderson and Susan Stewart, *Mastering Resistance: A Practical Guide to Family Therapy* (New York: Guilford, 1985).

16. This dialogue is edited from a training videotape entitled *Socialization with Probation Client*, with Bill Linden as practititioner. See the appendix for further information.

17. Ronald H. Rooney, "A Task-Centered Reunification Model for Foster

Care," in Anthony N. Maluccio and Paula A. Sinanoglu, eds., *The Challenge of Partnership: Working with the Parents of Children in Foster Care* (New York: Child Welfare League of America, 1981), pp. 101–116.

18. Gourse and Chescheir, "Authority Issues in Treating Resistant Families," p. 73.

19. Such deadlocks are frequent in health care. See Marcia Abramson, "Ethical Dilemmas for Social Workers in Discharge Planning," *Social Work in Health Care* 6(4) (Summer 1981):33–42.

20. Jones and Pittman, "Toward a General Theory of Strategic Self-Presentation," p. 233; see also Friedlander and Schwartz, "Toward a Theory of Strategic Self-Presentation," p. 485.

21. Simons and Aigner, *Practice Principles;* Feld and Radin, *Social Psychology for Social Work;* Charles A. Kiesler, *The Psychology of Commitment* (New York: Academic Press, 1971).

22. Epstein, *Helping People.*

23. Indian Child Welfare Act. 25 U.S.C. <<SS>>1901 et seq. See Marc Mannes, ed., *Family Preservation and Indian Child Welfare* (Albuquerque, N.M.: American Indian Law Center, 1990).

24. Ronald L. Simons, "Inducement as an Approach to Exercising Influence," *Social Work* 30(1) (January 1985):56–62.

25. Janet Moore-Kirkland, "Mobilizing Motivation: From Theory to Practice," in Anthony N. Maluccio, ed., *Promoting Competence in Clients: A New/ Old Approach to Social Work Practice* (New York: Macmillan, 1981), pp. 27–54.

26. Compton and Galaway, *Social Work Processes.*

27. Epstein, *Helping People.*

28. Michael Rohrbaugh, Howard Tennen, Samuel Press, and Larry White, "Compliance, Defiance and Therapeutic Paradox: Guidelines for Strategic Use of Paradoxical Interventions," *Americal Journal of Orthopsychiatry* 51(3) (July 1981):454–467.

29. Brehm and Smith, "Social Psychological Approaches to Psychotherapy and Behavior Change," pp. 69-115.

30. Ronald H. Rooney and Marsha Wanless, "A Model for Caseload Management Based on Task-Centered Practice," in Anne Fortune, ed., *Task-Centered Practice with Families and Groups* (New York: Springer, 1985), pp. 187–199.

31. James K. Whittaker, Jill Kinney, Elizabeth Tracy, and Charlotte Booth, eds., *Improving Practice Technology for Work with High-Risk Families: Lessons from the "Homebuilders" Social Work Education Project* (Seattle: Center for Social Welfare Research, School of Social Work, University of Washington, 1989).

32. Roger Fisher and William Ury, *Getting to Yes: Negotiating Agreement without Giving In* (Boston: Houghton Mifflin, 1981).

33. Seabury, "The Contract," pp. 16–21.

34. A. Rosen, E. K. Procter, and S. Livne, "Planning and Direct Practice," *Social Service Review* 59 (1985):161–177.

35. Haley, *Strategies of Psychotherapy;* Arnold P. Goldstein, Kenneth Heller, and Lee B. Sechrest, *Psychotherapy and the Psychology of Behavior Change* (New York: Wiley, 1966).

36. Janet R. Hutchinson and Kristine E. Nelson, "How Public Agencies Can Provide Family-Centered Services," *Social Casework* 75 (June 1985):367–371.

37. Seymour L. Halleck, "The Impact of Professional Dishonesty on Behavior of Disturbed Adolescents," *Social Work* 8 (April 1963):48–56.

38. Raynor, "Compulsory Persuasion," pp. 411–424.

39. Cingolani, "Social Conflict Perspective."

## 10. Formalizing the Contract and Initial Task Development with Involuntary Clients

1. Edleson, "Working with Men Who Batter," pp. 237–242; D. G. Saunders, "A Model for the Structured Group Treatment of Male-to-Female Violence," *Behavior Therapy* 2(3) (1980):2–9; E. M. Blum and R. H. Blum, *Alcoholism: Modern Psychological Approaches to Treatment* (San Fransisco: Jossey-Bass, 1967); F. Marlatt and Peter E. Nathan, *Behavioral Approaches to Alcoholism* (New Brunswick, N.J.: Rutgers Center of Alcohol Studies, 1978).

2. Reid, *Task-Centered System;* Epstein, *Helping People.*

3. William J. Reid and Ann W. Shyne, *Brief and Extended Casework* (New York: Columbia University Press, 1969).

4. Richard A. Wells and Phillip A. Phelps, "The Brief Psychotherapies: A Selective Overview," in Richard A. Wells and Vincent Gianetti, eds., *Handbook of the Brief Psychotherapies* (New York: Plenum Press, 1990), pp. 3–26. See also S. L. Garfield, "Research on Client Variables in Psychotherapy," in Garfield and Bergin, *Handbook of Psychotherapy and Behavior Change,* pp. 213–256; M. P. Koss and J. M. Butcher, "Research on Brief Psychotherapy," in Garfield and Bergin, *Handbook of Psychotherapy and Behavior Change,* pp. 627–670; M. J. Lambert, D. A. Shapiro, and A. E. Bergin, "The Effectiveness of Psychotherapy, in Garfield and Bergin, *Handbook of Psychotherapy and Behavior Change,* pp. 157–211.

5. Epstein, *Helping People,* pp. 8–9.

6. Ibid., p. 64.

7. Reid, *Task-Centered System,* p. 5.

8. Ibid.

9. Epstein, *Helping People,* p. 11.

10. Reid, *Task-Centered System,* p. 20.

11. Epstein, *Helping People,* p. 24.

12. Ibid., pp. 131–132.

13. Ibid., p. 112.

14. Ibid.

15. Ibid., p. 120; Reid, *Task-Centered System,* p. 3.

16. Epstein, *Helping People,* p. 37.

17. Reid, *Task-Centered System,* p. 25.

18. Epstein, *Helping People*, pp. 223–232.

19. Reid, *Task-Centered System*, p. 85.

20. Ibid., p. 86.

21. E. Matilda Goldberg, Jane Gibbons, and Ian Sinclair, *Problems, Tasks and Outcomes: The Evaluation of Task-Centered Casework in Three Settings* (London: George Allen and Unwin, 1985); Michael H. Phillips, Neal DeChillo, Daniel Kronenfeld, and Verona Middleton-Jeter, "Homeless Families: Services Make a Difference," *Social Casework* 169 (January 1988):48–53; Elin Cormican, "Task-Centered Model for Work with the Aged," *Social Casework* 58 (October 1977):490–494; Barbara Dierking, Margo Brown, and Anne E. Fortune, "Task-Centered Treatment in a Residential Facility for the Elderly: A Clinical Trial," *Journal of Gerontological Casework* 21 (Spring 1980):225–240; Michael P. Nofz, "Alcohol Abuse and Culturally Marginal Indians," *Social Casework* 69 (February 1988):67–73; Lester B.Brown and Ronald G. Lewis, "An Adaptation of the Task-Centered Model for Work with American Indians in a Mental Health Setting," paper presented at National Conference on Social Welfare Authors Forum, Philadelphia, 1979; Kent Newcome, "Task-Centered Group Work with the Chronically Mentally Ill in Day Treatment," in Fortune, *Task-Centered Practice*, pp. 78–91; Rooney, "Task-Centered Reunification Model for Foster Care"; Rooney and Wanless, "Model for Caseload Management," pp. 187–199; William J. Reid, "A Test of a Task-Centered Approach," *Social Work* 20(1) (January 1975):3–9; J. S. Gibbons, J. Butler, P. Urwin, and J. L. Gibbons, "Evaluation of a Social Work Service for Self-Poisoning Patients," *British Journal of Psychiatry* 133 (1978):111–118; J. S. Gibbons, I. J. Bow, J. Butler, and J. Powell, "Client Reactions to Task-Centered Casework: A Follow-Up Study," *British Journal of Social Work* 9(2) (1978):203–214.

22. E. M. Goldberg, D. Walker, and J. Robinson, "Exploring Task-Centered Casework," *Social Work Today* 9(2) (1977):9–14.

23. E. M. Goldberg and James Robinson, "An Area Office of an English Social Service Department," in William J. Reid and Laura Epstein, eds., *Task-Centered Practice* (New York: Columbia University Press, 1977), pp. 242–269; M. O. Hofstad, "Treatment in a Juvenile Court Setting," in Reid and Epstein, *Task-Centered Practice*, pp. 195–201; W. Salmon, "Service Program in a State Public Welfare Agency," in Reid and Epstein, *Task-Centered Practice*, pp. 113–122.

24. L. B. Brown, "Treating Problems of Psychiatric Out-Patients," in Reid and Epstein, *Task-Centered Practice*, p. 227; K. Newcome, "Task-Centered Group Work with the Chronically Mentally Ill in Day Treatment," in Fortune, *Task-Centered Practice*, pp. 78–91.

25. Salmon, "Service Program in a State Public Welfare Agency," p. 113.

26. Goldberg and Robinson, "Area Office of an English Social Service Department," p. 266; M. Bass, "Toward a Model of Treatment for Runaway Girls in Detention," in Reid and Epstein, *Task-Centered Practice*, p. 183; Gibbons et al., "Client Reactions to Task-Centered Casework," p. 204; Salmon, "Service Program in a State Public Welfare Agency," p. 122.

27. Bass, "Runaway Girls in Detention," p. 191. See also Gloria Cunningham, "Crisis Intervention in a Probation Setting," *Federal Probation* 36(4) (1977):16–25.

28. Goldberg and Robinson, "Area Office of an English Social Service Department," p. 247.

29. Epstein, *Helping People,* pp. 223–233.

30. Goldberg and Robinson, "Area Office of an English Social Service Department," p. 10; Rooney and Wanless, "Model for Caseload Management."

31. Salmon, "Service Program in a State Public Welfare Agency," p. 117.

32. Epstein, *Helping People,* p. 11.

33. Rooney, "Task-Centered Reunification Model."

34. T. L. Rzepnicki, "Task-Centered Intervention in Foster Care Services: Working with Families Who Have Children in Placement," in Fortune, *Task-Centered Practice,* pp. 172–184.

35. Rooney, "Task-Centered Reunification Model."

36. Brown, "Treating Problems of Psychiatric Outpatients," p. 225; Epstein, *Helping People.*

37. Ibid., p. 230.

38. Rooney, "Task-Centered Reunification Model"; Rzepnicki, "Task-Centered Intervention"; David Fanshel and Eugene B. Shinn, *Children in Foster Care* (New York: Columbia University Press, 1978).

39. John L. Levitt and William J. Reid, "Rapid Assessment Instruments for Practice," *Social Work Research and Abstracts* 17 (1981):13–19; Martin Bloom and Joel Fischer, *Evaluating Practice Guidelines for the Accountable Professional* (Englewood Cliffs, N.J.: Prentice-Hall, 1982), pp. 166–198.

40. This dialogue segment is selected from a training tape entitled "Task-Centered Work with an Adolescent toward Independent Living." The tape was developed in conjunction with the Children's Bureau. Further information is available in the appendix.

41. This dialogue segment comes from a training videotape entitled "Task-Centered Case Management with Handicapped Client" with Jane Macy-Lewis as the practitioner. See the appendix for ordering information.

42. Epstein, *Helping People.*

43. Lydia Rapoport, "Crisis Intervention as a Mode of Brief Treatment," in Robert W. Roberts and Robert H. Nee, eds., *Theories of Social Casework* (Chicago: University of Chicago Press, 1970).

44. Richard A. Wells, *Planned Short-Term Treatment* (New York: Free Press, 1982), p. 18.

45. Arnold P. Goldstein, Kenneth Heller, and Lee B. Sechrest, *Psychotherapy and the Psychology of Behavior Change* (New York: Wiley, 1966).

46. A videotape of actual work done in this case is available from the School of Social Service Administration, University of Chicago under the title "Return from Foster Care."

47. Reid, *Task-Centered System,* pp. 138–178.

48. Ibid.

49. Epstein, *Helping People.*

50. Aaron T. Beck, A. J. Rush, B. I. Shaw, and G. Emery, "Cognitive Therapy of Depression: A Treatment Manual," unpublished paper, Center for Cognitive Therapy, University of Pennsylvania.

51. "Return from Foster Care."

52. Brehm and McAllister, "Social Psychological Perspective on the Maintenance of Therapeutic Change," pp. 395–397.

53. This selection comes from a training videotape entitled "Socialization at Chemical Dependency Intake," with Dick Leonard as the practitioner. See appendix for ordering information.

54. Rooney, "Task-Centered Reunification Model."

55. Reid, *Task-Centered System*, p. 167.

56. This selection comes from a training videotape entitled "Work with Involuntary Client In Middle Phase," with Cheri Brady as the practitioner. See appendix for ordering information.

57. Rooney, "Socialization Strategies for Involuntary Clients."

58. Martin Sundel and Sandra Stone Sundel, *Behavior Modification in the Human Services* (Englewood Cliffs, N.J.: Prentice-Hall, 1982.)

59. Simons, "Strategies for Exercising Influence," pp. 268–274.

60. This selection comes from a training videotape entitled, "Task Development with Depressed Client," with Hoan Nguyen as the practitioner. See appendix for ordering information.

61. See Albert Bandura, *Psychological Modelling: Conflicting Theories* (Chicago: Aldine-Atherton, 1971).

62. Reid, *Task-Centered System*, pp. 159–162.

63. Ibid., p. 159.

64. Rooney, "Task-Centered Reunification Model."

65. Epstein, *Helping People.*

## 11. Middle-Phase Intervention and Termination with Involuntary Clients

1. Brehm and McAllister, "Social Psychological Perspective on the Maintenance of Therapeutic Change," p. 389; C. A. Kiesler, R. Nisbett, and M. Zanna, "On Inferring One's Beliefs from One's Behavior," *Journal of Personality and Social Psychology* 11 (1969):321–327; see also D. Bem, "Self-Perception Theory," *Advances in Experimental Social Psychology* 6 (1972):1–62.

2. Simons, "Strategies for Exercising Influence," pp. 268–274.

3. Brehm, *Application of Social Psychology to Clinical Practice.*

4. A. E. Kazdin, "Recent Advances in Token Economy Research," in M. Herzen, R. M. Eisler, and P. M. Miller, eds., *Progress in Behavior Modification*, vol. 1 (New York: Academic Press, 1975), p. 252.

5. Feld and Radin, *Social Psychology for Social Work and the Mental Health Professions.*

6. Ibid.

7. Brehm and McAllister, "Social Psychological Perspective on the Maintenance of Therapeutic Change," p. 393.

8. Simons, "Strategies for Exercising Influence."

9. Peter Johnson and Allen Rubin, "Case Management in Mental Health: A Social Work Domain?" *Social Work* 28(1) (January-February 1983):49–54. See also Gerald O'Connor, "Case Management: System and Practice," *Social Casework* (February 1988):97–106; J. Franklin, B. Solovitz, M. Mason, J. Clemons, and G. Miller, "An Evaluation of Case Management," *American Journal of Public Health* 77 (1987):674–678; see also David Austin and Penelope Caragonne, *A Comparative Analysis of 22 Settings Using Case Management Components. The Case Management Research Project* (Austin: School of Social Work, University of Texas, 1980).

10. Ibid.

11. Franklin et al. "Evaluation of Case Management"; L. Levine and M. Fleming, *Human Resource Development: Issues in Case Management* (University of Maryland: Center for Rehabilitative and Manpower Services, 1989).

12. O'Connor, "Case Management," p. 98.

13. Ibid.

14. Johnson and Rubin, "Case Management in Mental Health," p. 49.

15. H. Richard Lamb, "Rehabilitation in Mental Health," *American Mental Health Review* 2(3) (1977); H. Richard Lamb, "Therapist Case Managers: More than Brokers of Services," *Hospital and Community Psychiatry* 31 (November 1980):763.

16. Johnson and Rubin, "Case Management in Mental Health," 52–53; D. Salem, E. Seidman, and J. Rappaport, "Community Treatment of the Mentally Ill: The Promise of Mutual Help Organizations," *Social Work* 33 (1988):403–408.

17. Stephen M. Rose and Bruce L. Black, *Advocacy and Empowerment: Mental Health Care in the Community* (Boston: Routledge and Kegan Paul, 1985).

18. Ruth Wilk, "Involuntary Outpatient Commitment of the Mentally Ill," *Social Work* 33 (1988):133–137.

19. Stuart A. Kirk and James R. Greenley, "Denying or Delivering Services?" *Social Work* 19 (1974):439–447.

20. Epstein, *Helping People*, pp. 192–194.

21. Ibid., p. 193. See also Andrew Weissman, "Industrial Social Services: Linkage Technology," *Social Casework* 57(1) (1976):50–54.

22. Ibid.

23. Brehm, *Application of Social Psychology to Clinical Practice.*

24. Epstein, *Helping People*, pp. 196–197.

25. Ibid., p. 123.

26. Rooney, "Task-Centered Reunification Model."

27. Vernon E. Johnson, *Intervention: How to Help Someone Who Doesn't Want Help* (Minneapolis, Minn.: Johnson Institute, 1976), p. 61.

28. Vernon E. Johnson, *I'll Quit Tomorrow* (San Fransisco: Harper and Row, 1980).

29. Edwin J. Thomas, Cathleen Santa, Denise Bronson, and Daphna Oyser-

man, "Unilateral Family Therapy with the Spouses of Alcoholics," *Journal of Social Service Research* 10 (Spring 1987):156.

30. Edwin J. Thomas and Marianne R. Yoshioka, "Spouse Interventive Confrontation in Unilateral Family Therapy for Alcohol Abuse," *Social Casework* 70 (June 1989):340–347.

31. Ibid., p. 346.

32. Brehm, *Application of Social Psychology to Clinical Practice.*

33. Samuel Yochelson and Stanton E. Samenow, *The Criminal Personality: The Change Process,* vol. 2, 2d ed. (New York: Jason Aronson, 1985), p. ix.

34. Kenneth B. Reid, "The Use of Confrontation in Group Treatment: Attack or Challenge," *Clinical Social Work Journal* 14(3) (Fall 1986):224–237.

35. Robert R. Carkhuff and Bernard G. Berenson, *Beyond Counseling and Therapy* (New York: Holt, Rinehart, Winston, 1987), pp. 208–212; Gary G. Forrest, *Confrontation in Psychotherapy with the Alcoholic* (Holmes Park, Fla.: Learning Publications, 1982), p. 8; Leonard Blank, "Confrontation Techniques: A Two-Sided Coin," in Leonard Blank, Gloria B. Gottsegen, and Monroe G. Gottsegen, eds., *Confrontation: Encounters in Self and Interpersonal Awareness* (New York: Macmillan, 1971), p. 500; Frederick H. Stoller, "Marathon and Encounter Approaches in Therapeutic and Rehabilitative programs, in Blank, Gottsegen, and Gottsegen, *Confrontation,* pp. 303–326.

36. Morton A. Lieberman, Irvin D. Yalom, and Matthew A. Miles, *Encounter Groups: First Facts* (New York: Basic Books, 1973).

37. Reid, "Use of Confrontation in Group Treatment," p. 227; D. Corydon Hammond, Dean H. Hepworth, and Veon G. Smith, *Improving Therapeutic Communication: A Guide for Developing Effective Techniques* (San Francisco: Jossey-Bass, 1977), p. 282.

38. Carl Hartman and Diane Reynolds, "Resistant Clients: Confrontation, Interpretation and Alliance," *Social Casework* 68 (April 1987):205–213. See also J. Douds, B. Berenson, R. Carkhuff, and R. Pierce, "In Search of an Honest Experience: Confrontation in Counseling and Life," in R. Carkhuff and B. Berenson, *Beyond Counseling and Therapy.*

39. Forrest, *Confrontation in Psychotherapy with the Alcoholic,* p. 111.

40. Reid, "Use of Confrontation in Group Treatment," p. 226.

41. Epstein, *Helping People.*

42. The discussion of termination is adapted from ibid.

## 12. Working with Involuntary Families

1. Whittaker et al. *Improving Practice Technology for Work with High-Risk Families;* Kristine E. Nelson, Miriam J. Landsman, and Wendy Deutelbaum, "Three Models of Family-Centered Placement Prevention Services," *Child Welfare* 69 (January-February 1990):3-21; Janet R. Hutchinson and Kristine E. Nelson, "How Public Agencies Can Provide Family-Centered Services," *Social Casework* 75 (June 1985):367–371.

2. Gayla Margolin, "Ethical and Legal Considerations in Marital and Family Therapy," *American Psychologist* 37(7) (1982):794–795.

3. Reid, *Family Problem Solving,* p. 37.

4. Ibid.

5. Jack Weitzman, "Engaging the Severely Dysfunctional Family in Treatment: Basic Considerations," *Family Process* 24 (December 1985):473–485.

6. Geraldine McKinney, "Adapting Family Therapy to Multi-Deficit Families," *Social Casework* 51 (June 1970):327–333.

7. Shirley B. Schlosberg and Richard M. Kagan, "Practice Strategies for Engaging Chronic Multi-Problem Families," *Social Casework* 69 (January 1988):3–9.

8. Ibid., 3; Lisa Kaplan, *Working with Multi-Problem Families* (Lexington, Mass.: D. C. Heath, 1986).

9. M. E. Bryce, "Home-Based Care: Development and Rationale," in S. Maybanks and M. Bryce, eds., *Home-Based Services for Children and Families* (Springfield, Ill.: Charles Thomas, 1979); Ludwig L. Geismar and Katherine Wood, *Family and Delinquency: Resocializing the Young Offender* (New York: Human Services Press, 1976); D. H. Sprenkle and C. L. Storm, "Divorce Therapy Outcome Research: A Substantive and Methodological Review," *Journal of Marital and Family Therapy* 9 (1983):239–259; Arthur Weidman, "Family Therapy with Violent Couples," *Social Casework* 67 (April 1986):211–218; Thomas N. Tavantzis, Martha Tavantzis, Larry G. Brown, and Michael Rohrbaugh "Home-Based Structural Family Therapy for Delinquents at Risk of Placement," in M. P. Mirkin and S. L. Koman, eds., *Handbook of Adolescent and Family Treatment* (New York: Gardner, 1985), pp. 69–88; David Showalter and Charlotte Williams, "Marital and Family Counseling in Prisons," *Social Work* 25 (May 1980):224–228.

10. M. Duncan Stanton, "Family Treatment Approaches to Drug Abuse Problems: A Review," *Family Process* 18 (1980):251–280.

11. Ibid., p. 254.

12. Curtis Janzen, "Families in the Treatment of Alcoholism," *Journal of Studies on Alcohol* 38(1) (1977):114–130.

13. Ibid., p. 125.

14. J. Alexander, C. Barton, R. S. Schiavo, and B. V. Parsons, "Systems Behavioral Intervention with Families of Delinquents. Therapist Characteristics, Family Behavior and Outcome," *Journal of Consulting and Clinical Psychology* 49 (1976):656–669.

15. Sprenkle and Storm, "Divorce Therapy Outcome Research."

16. M. D. Stanton, T. C. Todd, and associates, *The Family Therapy of Drug Abuse and Addiction* (New York: Guilford Press, 1981).

17. Schlosberg and Kagan, "Practice Strategies for Engaging Chronic Multi-Problem Families."

18. C. Barton and J. F. Alexander, "Functional Family Therapy," in A. Gurman and D. Kniskern, eds., *Handbook of Family Therapy* (New York: Brunner-Mazel, 1981).

19. See Willam J. Reid, Richard M. Kagan, and Shirley B. Schlosberg, "Prevention of Placement," *Child Welfare* 67 (1981):25–36.

20. Carol M. Anderson and Susan Stewart, *Mastering Resistance: A Practical Guide to Family Therapy* (New York: Guilford, 1983), p. 31.

21. Margolin, "Ethical and Legal Considerations in Marital and Family Therapy," p. 795.

22. Ana M. Irueste-Montes and Francisca Montes, "Court-Ordered Involuntary Treatment of Abusive and Neglectful Families," *Child Abuse and Neglect* 12(1) (1988):33–39.

23. Reid, *Family Problem Solving*, p. 37.

24. Rooney, "Task-Centered Reunification Model"; Rzepnicki, "Task-Centered Intervention."

25. Eleanor R. Tolson, "Conclusions: Toward a Metamodel for Eclectic Family Practice," in E. R. Tolson and W. J. Reid, eds., *Models of Family Treatment* (New York: Columbia University Press, 1981), p. 350.

26. Ibid., p. 6.

27. Ibid., p. 7.

28. Ibid.

29. Ibid., pp. 348–349.

30. Ibid., p. 6.

31. Ibid., p. 7.

32. Haley, *Strategies of Psychotherapy*.

33. Pam Luckhurst, "Resistance and the 'New' Epistemology," *Journal of Strategic and Systemic Therapies* 4(1) (1985):3–12.

34. William Pinsof, "Integrative Problem-Solving Therapy: Toward the Synthesis of Family and Individual Psychotherapies," *Journal of Marital and Family Therapy* 9 (1983):20.

35. Harriette C. Johnson, "Emerging Concerns in Family Therapy," *Social Work* 31 (July/August 1986):300.

36. Ibid.

37. Reid, *Family Problem Solving*, p. 4.

38. Kenlie Sturkie, "Frameworks for Comparing Approaches to Family Therapy," *Social Casework* 67 (December 1986):613–621.

39. Ibid., p. 614.

40. Duncan Stanton, "Strategic Approaches to Family Therapy," pp 361-402 in Gurman and Kniskern, *Handbook of Family Therapy*, pp. 361–402.

41. Paul Watzlawick, J. H. Weakland, and Richard Fisch, *Change: Principles of Problem Formation and Resolution* (New York: W. W. Norton, 1974).

42. Sturkie, "Frameworks for Comparing Approaches to Family Therapy," p. 620.

43. Joan Laird and JoAnn Allen, "Family Theory and Practice," in Rosenblatt and Waldfogel, *Handbook of Clinical Social Work*, p. 176.

44. Anderson and Stewart, *Mastering Resistance*, p. 64.

45. Tolson, "Toward a Metamodel for Eclectic Family Practice," p. 340.

46. Harvy Frankel, "Family-Centered, Home-Based Services in Child Protection: A Review of the Research," *Social Service Review* 62 (March 1988):137–157.

47. M. D. Stanton and T. C. Todd, "Principles and Techniques for Engaging Resistant Families into Treatment," in Stanton et al., *The Family Therapy of Drug Abuse and Addiction*, pp. 71–102.

48. Steve de Shazer, *Patterns of Brief Family Therapy: An Ecosystemic Approach* (New York: Guilford, 1982), p. 9.

49. Ibid., p. 13.

50. Ibid., pp. 9–10.

51. Ibid., p. 13.

52. Steve de Shazer, "Post-Mortem. Mark Twain Did Die in 1910," *Family Process* 23 (March 1984):20–21.

53. Susan Stewart and Carol M. Anderson, "Resistance Revisited: Tales of My Death Have Been Greatly Exaggerated (Mark Twain)," *Family Process* 23 (March 1984):17–20.

54. Ibid., p. 19.

55. Ibid.

56. Tolson, "Toward a Metamodel for Eclectic Family Practice," p. 335.

57. Anderson and Stewart, "Resistance Revisited," pp. 223–224.

58. Schlosberg and Kagan, "Practice Strategies for Engaging Chronic Multi-Problem Families," p. 4.

59. Reid, *Family Problem Solving*, p. 98.

60. Daniel B. Wile, *Couples Therapy: A Nontraditional Approach* (New York: Wiley, 1981), p. 28.

61. Reid, *Family Problem Solving*, p. 101.

62. Anderson and Stewart, "Resistance Revisited."

63. Margolin, "Ethical and Legal Considerations in Marital and Family Therapy," p. 790.

64. Ibid., p. 795.

65. Ibid., p. 794.

66. Ibid., p. 795; Stanton, "Strategic Approaches to Family Therapy,"; see also J. Wendorf and R. J. Wendorf, "A Systemic View of Family Therapy Ethics," *Family Process* 24 (December 1985):443–453; and Johnson, "Emerging Concerns in Family Therapy," p. 303.

67. Reid, *Family Problem Solving*, p. 7.

68. Ibid., p. 71.

69. Alexander et al., "Systems Behavioral Intervention with Families of Delinquents," p. 657.

70. Anderson and Stewart, "Resistance Revisited"; Timothy Weber, James E. McKeever, and Susan H. McDaniel, "A Beginner's Guide to the Problem-Oriented First Family Interview," *Family Process* 24 (1985):357–364.

71. Schlosberg and Kagan, "Practice Strategies for Engaging Chronic Multi-Problem Families," p. 5.

72. A videotape of the interview in which this dialogue took place, entitled "Contracting for Home-Based Services," is available from the University of Minnesota. See the appendix for details.

73. Reid, *Family Problem Solving*, p. 37.

74. Gourse and Chescheir, "Authority Issues in Treating Resistant Families," pp. 67–73.

75. Weidman, "Family Therapy with Violent Couples," p. 215.

76. Margolin, "Ethical and Legal Considerations in Marital and Family Therapy," pp. 794–795.

77. Tavantzis et al., "Home-Based Structural Family Therapy," p. 75.

78. Weidman, "Family Therapy with Violent Couples," pp. 216–217.

79. Bryce, "Home-Based Care," p. 20.

80. Schlosberg and Kagan, "Practice Strategies for Engaging Chronic Multi-Problem Families," p. 6.

81. Tavantzis et al., "Home-Based Structural Family Therapy," p. 77.

82. T. J. Stein, E. D. Gambrill, and Kermit T. Wiltse, *Children in Out of Home Placement: Achieving Continuity of Care* (New York: Praeger, 1978).

83. Weidman, "Family Therapy with Violent Couples," p. 214.

84. Ibid., pp. 215–216.

85. Tavantzis et al., "Home-Based Structural Family Therapy," p. 78; Stanton and Todd, "Principles and Techniques for Engaging Resistant Families into Treatment."

86. Richard Kagan, William J. Reid, Stephen E. Roberts, and Jan Silverman-Pillow, "Engaging Families of Court Mandated Youth in an Alternative to Institutional Placement," *Child Welfare* 66(4) (1987):370.

87. Ibid., p. 368.

88. Reid, *Family Problem Solving*, p. 36; de Shazer, *Patterns of Brief Family Therapy*.

89. Watzlawick, Weakland, and Fisch, *Change*.

90. Tavantzis et al., "Home-Based Structural Family Therapy," p. 77.

91. Kagan et al., "Engaging Families," p. 368.

92. Tavantzis et al., "Home-Based Structural Family Therapy," p. 80.

93. Reid, Kagan, and Schlossberg, "Prevention of Placement."

94. The videotape in which this problem occurred is entitled "Permanency Planning: Work with the Family of an Adolescent," and is available from the University of Wisconsin, Madison. See appendix for details.

95. L. C. Wynne, "Definable Problems in Family Therapy Efficacy Research," paper presented at the NIMH Conference on the State of the Art in Family Therapy Research, Rockville, Md., 1984.

96. Alan S. Gurman, David P. Kniskern, and William M. Pinsof, "Research on the Process and Outcome of Marital and Family Therapy," in Garfield and Bergin, *Handbook of Psychotherapy and Behavior Change*, p. 609.

## 13. Work with Involuntary Clients in Groups

1. Ann Tuszynski, "Group Treatment that Helps Abusive or Neglectful Parents," *Social Casework* 66 (1985):556–562.

2. Saunders, "Model for the Structured Group Treatment of Male-to-Female Violence," pp. 2–9; Edleson, "Working with Men Who Batter," pp. 237–242.

3. Thomas E. Smith, "Group Work with Adolescent Drug Abusers," *Social Work with Groups* 8(1) (Spring 1985):55–63; see also Sally Ann Shields, "Busted and Branded: Group Work with Substance Abusing Adolescents in Schools," *Social Work with Groups* 9 (1986):61–81; William C. Panepinto, James A. Garrett, William R. Williford, and John A. Prieke, "A Short Term Group Treatment Model for Problem Drinking Drivers," *Social Work with Groups* 5 (1982):33–40; Arthur K. Berliner, "Group Counseling with Alcoholic Offenders: An Analysis and Typology of DWI Probationers," *Social Work with Groups* 10(1) (1987):17–31.

4. Lawrence V. Annis, "A Residential Treatment Program for Male Sex Offenders," *International Journal of Offender Therapy and Comparative Criminology* 26(3) (1982):223–234.

5. G. A. Fashimpar and L. T. Harris, "Social Work at 30 MPH: Mini-Bike Rehabilitation Groups for Juvenile Delinquents," *Social Work with Groups* 10 (1987):33–60; Janice M. Delange, Judy A. Barton, and Susan Lanham, "The Wiser Way. A Cognitive Behavioral Model for Group Social Skills Training with Juvenile Delinquents," *Social Work with Groups* 4(3/4) (1981):37–48.

6. Jerry R. Fox, "Mission Impossible: Social Work Practice with Black Urban Youth Gangs," *Social Work* 30 (January-February 1985):25–31.

7. Berliner, "Group Counseling with Alcoholic Offenders," pp. 20–21.

8. Jerry Finn, "Men's Domestic Violence Treatment Groups: A Statewide Survey," *Social Work with Groups* 8(3) (Fall 1985):84.

9. Margot Breton, "Reaching and Engaging People: Issues and Practice Principles," *Social Work with Groups* 8(3) (Fall 1985):7–21.

10. Catherine Papell and Beulah Rothman, "Relating the Mainstream Model of Social Work with Groups to Group Psychotherapy and the Structured Group Approach," *Social Work with Groups* 3(2) (Summer 1980):5–23.

11. Ibid., pp. 5–11.

12. Charles D. Garvin, "The Changing Contexts of Social Group Work Practice," *Social Work with Groups* 7(1) (Spring 1984):3–19.

13. Charles D. Garvin, *Contemporary Group Work* (Englewood Cliffs, N.J.: Prentice-Hall, 1981).

14. Gisela Konopka, *Social Group Work: A Helping Process,* 2d ed. (Englewood Cliffs, N.J: Prentice-Hall, 1972), p. 168.

15. Smith, "Group Work with Adolescent Drug Abusers," p. 57.

16. Tolman and Bhosley, "A Comparison of Two Types of Pre-Group Preparation for Men Who Batter," p. 1.

17. John S. Brekke, "The Use of Orientation Groups to Engage Hard to Reach Clients: Model, Method and Evaluation," *Social Work with Groups* 12(2):75–88.

18. Berliner, "Group Counseling with Alcoholic Offenders," p. 20.

19. Smith, "Group Work with Adolescent Drug Abusers," p. 57.

20. Panepinto et al., "A Short Term Group Treatment Model for Problem Drinking Drivers," pp. 34–35.

21. Garvin, *Contemporary Group Work;* Panepinto et al., "A Short Term Group Treatment Model for Problem Drinking Drivers."

22. Reid, "The Use of Confrontation in Group Treatment," pp. 224–237.

23. Brekke, "Use of Orientation Groups."

24. Janice H. Schopler and Maeda Galinsky, "When Groups Go Wrong," *Social Work* 26 (1981):424–429; Helen Levinson, "Uses and Misuses of Groups," *Social Work* 18(1) (January 1973):66–73.

25. Shields, "Busted and Branded," p. 67.

26. Dermot J. Hurley, "Resistance and Work in Adolescent Groups," *Social Work with Groups* 1 (1984):71–81.

27. Phillip Cushman, "The Self Besieged: Recruitment, Indoctrination Processes in Restrictive Groups," *Journal for the Theory of Social Behavior* 16(1) (March 1986):1–32; Thomas E. Bratter, Edward P. Bratter, and Jessica F. Helmsberg, "Uses and Abuses of Power and Authority in American Self-Help Residential Communities: A Perversion or a Necessity?" in George DeLeon and Jancie T. Ziegenfus, Jr., eds., *Therapeutic Communities for Addiction: Readings in Theory, Research and Practice* (Springfield, Ill.: Charles C. Thomas, 1986), p. 207.

28. Robert T. Lifton, *Thought Reform and the Psychology of Totalism: A Study of Brainwashing in China* (New York: W. W. Norton, 1961).

29. Edgar H. Schein, Inge Schneier, and Curtis H. Barker, *Coercive Persuasion: A Socio-Psychological Analysis of American Civilian Prisoners by the Chinese Communists* (New York: W. W. Norton, 1961).

30. See Rudolph Alexander, Jr., "The Right to Treatment in Mental and Correctional Institutions," *Social Work* 34(2) (1989):109–114.

31. Theodore J. Kaul and Richard L. Bednar, "Research on Group and Related Therapies," in Garfield and Bergin, *Handbook of Psychotherapy and Behavior Change*, pp. 671–714.

32. LaMar T. Empey and Maynard L. Ericson, *The Provo Experiment* (Lexington, Mass.: Lexington Books, 1972).

33. Edith M. Freeman, "Consultation for Improving Group Services to Alcoholic Clients," *Social Work with Groups* 10(3) (Fall 1987):99–115.

34. Katherine van Wormer, "Group Work with Alcoholics in Recovery: A Phase Approach," *Social Work with Groups* 10(3) (Fall 1987):86.

35. Shields, "Busted and Branded," p. 9.

36. Ibid., p. 70.

37. Breton, "Reaching and Engaging People."

38. Ibid., p. 16.

39. Gerald Corey, Marianne Schneider Corey, and Patrick Callanan, "Ethical Considerations in Using Group Techniques," *Journal for Specialists in Group Work* 7 (September 1982):140–148.

40. Garvin, *Contemporary Group Work*; Brekke, "Use of Orientation Groups."

41. Shields, "Busted and Branded."

42. Delange, Barton, and Lanham, "The Wiser Way"; Sharon B. Orosz, "Assertiveness in Recovery," *Social Work with Groups* 5 (1982):25–31; see also Alan Brody, "S.O.B.E.R. A Stress Management Program for Recovering Alcoholics," *Social Work with Groups* 5 (1982):15–23.

43. Shulman, *The Skills of Helping Individuals and Groups.*

44. Shields, "Busted and Branded."

45. Edleson, "Working with Men Who Batter," pp. 237–242.

46. Groups with this name are operated by the Family Service of Madison, Wisconsin.

47. R. H. Rooney, "Adolescent Groups in Public School," in Reid and Epstein, *Task-Centered Practice,* pp. 168–182.

48. Richard D. Casey and Leon Cantor, "Group Work with Hard to Reach Adolescents," *Social Work with Groups* 6 (1983):9–22; JoAnn Larsen and Craig T. Mitchell, "Task-Centered Strength Oriented Group Work with Delinquents," *Social Casework* 61 (1980):154–163.

49. Shields, "Busted and Branded," p. 68.

50. Berliner, "Group Counseling with Alcoholic Offenders," p. 21.

51. Ibid., pp. 20–21.

52. Shields, "Busted and Branded," p. 69.

53. Patrick Reilly and Roger Grusznky, "A Structured Didactic Model for Men for Controlling Family Violence," *International Journal of Offender Therapy and Comparative Criminology* 28(3) (1984):222–235; see also Frances Purdy and Norm Nickle, "Practice Principles for Working with Groups of Men Who Batter," *Social Work with Groups* 4(3/4) (Fall/Winter 1981):111–122.

54. Smith, "Group Work with Adolescent Drug Abusers," p. 60.

55. Shields, "Busted and Branded," p. 77.

56. Hurley, "Resistance and Work in Adolescent Groups."

57. Smith, "Group Work with Adolescent Drug Abusers," p. 58.

58. Larsen and Mitchell, "Task-Centered Strength Oriented Group Work with Delinquents," p. 54.

59. Reid, "Use of Confrontation in Group Treatment."

60. Mark Cohen and Allyne Sinner, "A Group Curriculum for Outpatient Alcoholism Treatment," *Social Work with Groups* 5 (1982):5–13; van Wormer, "Group Work with Alcoholics in Recovery."

61. Smith, "Group Work with Adolescent Drug Abusers," p. 57.

62. Van Wormer, "Group Work with Alcoholics in Recovery," p. 84.

63. Panepinto et al., "A Short Term Group Treatment Model for Problem Drinking Drivers"; Peggy Citron, "Group Work with Alcoholic Poly-Drug Involved Adolescents with Deviant Behavior Syndrome," *Social Work with Groups* 1(1) (1978):48.

64. Smith, "Group Work with Adolescent Drug Abusers," p. 59.

65. Citron, "Group WOrk with Alcoholic Poly-Drug Involved Adolescents."

66. Daniel Saunders, "Husbands Who Batter," *Social Casework* 65 (June 1984):347–353; Saunders, "Model for the Structured Group Treatment of Male-to-Female Violence," pp. 2–9.

67. Edleson, "Working with Men Who Batter," p. 238.

68. Orosz "Assertiveness in Recovery"; Brody, "S.O.B.E.R."

69. Ibid., p. 21.

70. Smith, "Group Work with Adolescent Drug Abusers."

71. Finn, "Men's Domestic Violence Treatment Groups."

72. Edleson, "Working with Men Who Batter"; Purdy and Nickle, "Practice Principles for Working with Groups of Men Who Batter."

73. Ibid., p. 111.

74. Bratter, Bratter, and Helmsberg, "Uses and Abuses of Power."

75. Ibid., p. 207.

76. Purdy and Nickle, "Practice Principles for Working with Groups of Men Who Batter," p. 114.

77. Tony Roffers and Michael Waldo, "Empathy and Confrontation Related to Group Counseling Outcomes," *Journal for Specialists in Group Work* 8(3) (1983):106–113.

78. Tolman and Bhosley, "A Comparison of Two Types of Pre-Group Preparation for Men Who Batter."

79. Corey, Corey, and Callanan, "Ethical Considerations in Using Group Techniques," p. 144.

80. Ibid., p. 145.

81. Lieberman, Yalom, and Miles, *Encounter Groups.*

## 14. The Involuntary Practitioner and the System

1. Wortman and Brehm, "Responses to Uncontrollable Outcomes"; see also J. G. Barber, "The Promise and Pitfalls of Learned Helplessness Theory for Social Work Practice," *British Journal of Social Work* 16(5) (1986):557–570.

2. Wendy R. Sherman and Stanley Wenocur, "Empowering Public Welfare Workers through Mutual Support," *Social Work* 28(5) (1983):375–379.

3. Fisher and Ury, *Getting to Yes.*

4. George Brager and Stephen Holloway, "A Process Model for Changing Organizations from Within," *Administration in Social Work* 1(4) (1977):349–358.

5. Christina Maslach, *Burnout-The Cost of Caring* (Englewood Cliffs, N.J.: Prentice-Hall, 1982), p. 3.

6. Christina Maslach, "Burnout Research in the Social Services: A Critique," in David F. Gillespie, ed., *Burnout among Social Workers* (New York: Haworth, 1987), pp. 95–105; T. F. Rigger, ed., *Stress Burnout: An Annotated Bibliography* (Carbondale: Southern Illinois University Press, 1985).

7. See Maslach, "Burnout Research in the Social Services," pp. 97–98.

8. Ibid.

9. Myrna M. Courage and David W. Williams, "An Approach to the Study of Burnout in Professional Care Providers in Human Service Organizations," in Gillespie, *Burnout among Social Workers*, pp. 7–22; C. Maslach, "The Client Role in Staff Burnout," *Journal of Social Issues* 34(4) (1978):111–124.

10. Srinika Jayaratne, Wayne A. Chess, and Dale A. Kunkel, "Burnout: Its Impact on Child Welfare Workers and Their Spouses," *Social Work* 31(1) (1986):53–59.

11. Michael R. Daley, "Burnout: Smoldering Problem in Protective Services," *Social Work* 24 (September 1979):375–379; Marjie C. Barrett and Jane Mc-Kelvey, "Stresses and Strains of the Child Welfare Worker," *Child Welfare* 59

(May 1980):277–285; W. David Harrison, "Role Strain and Burnout in Child Protective Services," *Social Service Review* 54 (March 1980):31–34; Pauline C. Zischka, "The Effect of Burnout on Permanency Planning and the Middle Management Supervisor in Child Welfare Agencies," *Child Welfare* 60(9) (1981):611–616; Srinika Jayaratne and Wayne A. Chess, "Job Satisfaction, Burnout and Turnover: A National Study," *Social Work* 29(5) (1984):448–453.

   12. Jayaratne, Chess, and Kunkel, "Burnout"; see also V. Savicki and E. Cooley, "The Relationship of Work Environment and Client Contact to Burnout in Mental Health Professionals," *Journal of Counseling and Development* 65(5) (1987):249–252; A. McCullock and L. O'Brien, "The Organizational Determinants of Worker Burnout," *Children and Youth Services Review* 8 (1986):175–190.

   13. Gambrill, *Casework*, pp. 395–405; Maslach, *Burnout;* Donald Meichenbaum and Matt E. Jarenko, eds., *Stress Reduction and Prevention* (New York: Plenum Press, 1983); Ayala M. Pines and Elliot Aronson with Ditsa Kafry, *Burnout: From Tedium to Personal Growth* (New York: Free Press, 1981); Marybeth Shinn, Margaret Rosario, Hanne Morch, and Dennis E. Chestnut, "Coping with Job Stress and Burnout in Human Services," *Journal of Personality and Social Psychology* 46 (1984):864–876.

   14. Pines, Aronson, and Kafry, *Burnout*, p. 158.

   15. Ibid., p. 157.

   16. Ibid., p. 160.

   17. Ibid., p. 159.

   18. Gambrill, *Casework*, pp. 395–405.

   19. Pines, Aronson, and Kafry, *Burnout*, p. 159.

   20. Ibid., pp. 103–119.

   21. Ibid., p. 157.

   22. Ibid.

   23. Ibid., pp. 161–167.

   24. Ibid., pp. 157–161.

   25. Rino J. Patti, "Social Work Practice: Organizational Environment," in Herman Resnick and Rino J. Patti, *Change from Within: Humanizing Social Welfare Organizations* (Philadelphia: Temple University Press, 1984), p. 53.

   26. Rino J. Patti, "Organizational Resistance and Change," in ibid., pp. 114–131. See also Rino J. Patti, "Managing for Service Effectiveness in Social Welfare Organizations," *Social Work* 32 (1987):377–381; Yeheskel Hasenfeld, *Human Service Organizations* (Englewood Cliffs, N.J.: Prentice-Hall, 1987), p. 27; Eva M. Kahn, "Parallel Process in Social Work Treatment and Supervision," *Social Casework* 60(9) (1979):520–528.

   28. Shireman and Reamer, *Rehabilitating Juvenile Justice.*

   29. Esther Wattenberg, "War on Povery Becomes a War against the Poor," *Minneapolis Star & Tribune,* May 7, 1990:11A; Frances Fox Piven and Richard A. Cloward, *The New Class War: Reagan's Attack on the Welfare State and Its Consequences* (New York: Pantheon Books, 1982).

   30. Barbara Ehrenreich, *Fear of Falling: The Inner Life of the Middle Class* (New York: Pantheon Books, 1989), p. 52.

   31. Notes and Comment, *The New Yorker,* July 23, 1990:21–22.

32. Notes and Comment, *The New Yorker*, January 7, 1991:19–20.

33. See Ehrenreich, *Fear of Falling*. See also Harold L. Wilensky and Charles N. Lebeaux, *Industrial Society and Social Welfare* (New York: Russell Sage, 1958), p. 211, and John H. Ehrenreich, *The Altruistic Imagination: A History of Social Work and Social Policy in the United States* (Ithaca, N.Y.: Cornell University Press, 1985).

34. Charles R. Atherton, "Liberalism's Decline and the Threat to the Welfare State," *Social Work* 35(2) (March 1990):163–168. See also Peter F. Drucker, *The New Realities: In Government and Politics/ In Economics and Business/ In Society and World View* (New York: Harper and Row, 1989).

35. Atherton, "Liberalism's Decline," p. 166.

36. Piven and Cloward, *The New Class War*, p. 39.

37. Kevin Phillips, *The Politics of Rich and Poor* (New York: Random House, 1990).

38. Sheila B. Kamerman and Alfred J. Kahn, *Social Services for Children, Youth and Families in the United States* (New York: Annie E. Casey Foundation, 1989).

39. See Sandra M. Stehno, "Family-Centered Child Welfare Services: New Life for a Historic Idea," *Child Welfare* 65 (May/June 1986):231–240, and Kristine E. Nelson, Miriam J. Landsman, and Wendy Deutelbaum, "Three Models of Family-Centered Placement Prevention Services," *Child Welfare* 69 (January–February 1989):3–21.

40. Frankel, however, suggests that most studies lack the kinds of controls necessary to demonstrate that FCHBS caused the difference in placement rates. See Harvey Frankel, "Family-Centered, Home-Based Services in Child Protection: A Review of the Research," *Social Service Review* 62 (March 1980):137–157.

41. See Brenda G. McGowan, "Family-Based Services and Public Policy: Context and Implications," in Whittaker et al., *Improving Practice Technology for work with High-Risk Families*, p. 79.

42. Michel Foucault, *Madness and Civilization* (New York: Random House, 1965); Michel Foucault, "The Birth of the Asylum," in *The Foucault Reader*, edited by Paul Rabinow (New York: Pantheon Books, 1984), pp. 273–289. See also Laura Epstein, "The Therapeutic Idea in Contemporary Society," Kenneth L. Pray Lecture, University of Pennsylvania School of Social Work, April 6, 1989, p. 18.

43. Michel Foucault, "The Politics of Health in the Eighteenth Century," in Colin Gordon, ed., *Power/Knowledge: Selected Interviews and Other Writings, 1972–1977* (New York: Pantheon, 1980).

44. Epstein, "Therapeutic Idea in Contemporary Society," p. 18.

45. Steve Goldberg, "Should We Force Drug Abusers into Treatment?" *Lawrence Eagle Tribune* Tuesday, August 22, 1989, p. 44.

46. Michael B. Katz, "Historical Obstacles to Welfare Reform," 7–32 in Clarke A. Chambers and Esther Wattenberg, eds., *To Promote the General Welfare* (Minneapolis: Center for Urban and Regional Affairs, University of Minnesota, 1987).

47. Atherton, "Liberalism's Decline," pp. 165–168.

48. Judith M. Davidoff, "Learnfare: What's to be Learned? Is it Fair?" *Isthmus* 15(2) (June 22–28, 1990):1, 8, 9. See also Ellen Goodman, "Punishing Parents for Kids' Sins," *Minneapolis Star-Tribune,* Tuesday, May 22, 1990, p. 14a.

49. David Gill quoted at Council on Social Work Education Annual Program Meeting, March 1988.

50. Robert Jay Lifton, *The Nazi Doctors: Medical Killing and the Psychology of Genocide* (New York: Basic Books, 1986).

51. Thomas Walz, "The Mission of Social Work Revisited: An Agenda for the 1990s," Hodson Memorial Lecture, University of Minnesota School of Social Work, May 4, 1989.

52. J. Ehrenreich, *The Altruistic Imagination,* p. 210.

53. G. F. Koeske and M. A. Crouse, "Liberalism-Conservatism in Samples of Social Work Students and Professionals," *Social Service Review* 55 (June 1981):193–205; J. D. Orten, "Influencing Attitudes: A Study of Social Work Students," *Social Work Research and Abstracts* 17(3) (1981):11–17; L. G. Reeser and I. Epstein, "Social Workers' Attitudes Toward Poverty and Social Action: 1968–1984," *Social Service Review* 61 (December 1987):610–666; Harry Specht, "Social Work and the Popular Psychotherapies," *Social Service Review* 64 (September 1990):345–357; Howard J. Karger, "Private Practice: The Fast Track to the Shingle?" *Social Work* 34 (November 1989):366–367.

54. Walz, "The Mission of Social Work Revisited," p. 6.

55. J. Ehrenreich, *The Altruistic Imagination,* p. 230.

56. William J. Reid, "Social Work for Social Problems," *Social Work* 22 (1977):374–382.

57. Edwin J. Thomas, "Advances in Developmental Research," *Social Service Review* 63 (1989):578–595.

58. I will use the term "intervention research" to refer to both the developmental approach suggested by Thomas and the developmental research and utilization approach described by Rothman. See Jack Rothman, "Intervention Research: Application to Runaway and Homeless Youth," *Social Work Research and Abstracts* 25 (March 1989):13–18; Rothman, *Social R & D;* Edwin J. Thomas, *Designing Interventions for the Helping Professions* (Beverly Hills, Cal.: Sage, 1984).

59. William J. Reid, "Research in Social Work," in *Encyclopedia of Social Work,* p. 480.

60. Thomas, *Designing Interventions,* pp. 96–214. See also Ronald H. Rooney, "Promoting Utilization and Gaining Support for Intervention Research in the University Setting," in Jack Rothman and Edwin J. Thomas, eds., *Intervention Research* (New York: Haworth Press, in press).

61. Thomas, *Designing Interventions,* pp. 42–95; Rothman, *Social R & D,* pp. 59–85, 86–106. See also Edward J. Mullen, "The Construction of Personal Models for Effective Practice. A Method for Utilizing Research Findings to Guide Social Interventions," *Journal of Social Service Research* 2(1) (1978):45–63.

62. Thomas, *Designing Interventions,* pp. 96–214.

63. Ronald H. Rooney, Grant entitled "Child Welfare Training in Work with Involuntary Clients," Office of Human Development Services, OHDS/ 05CT22001, 1991.

64. Rothman, *Social R & D*, pp. 114–123.

65. William J. Reid, "Evaluating an Intervention in Developmental Research," *Journal of Social Service Research* 11(1) (1987):4.

66. Rothman, *Social R & D*, p. 128.

67. Ralph E. Pumphrey, "Compassion and Protection: Dual Motivations in Social Welfare," in Frank R. Breul and Steven J. Diner, eds., *Compassion and Responsibility: Readings in the History of Social Welfare Policy in the United States* (Chicago: University of Chicago Press, 1980), pp. 5–13.

68. William J. Wilson, "The Underclass: Issues, Perspectives and Public Policy," *Annals of the American Academy of Political and Social Science*, 501 (January 1989):182–192.

69. Lisbeth B. Schorr with Daniel Schorr, *Within our Reach: Breaking the Cyle of Disadvantage* (New York: Anchor Press, 1988), pp. xix, xx.

70. Walz, "The Mission of Social Work Revisited," p. 12.

# Subject Index

# Author Index*